DIVORCE AND REMARRIAGE AMONG MUSLIMS IN INDIA

Divorce and Remarriage among Muslims in India

Edited by

IMTIAZ AHMAD

MANOHAR
2003

First published 2003

ISBN 81-7304-493-7

Published by
Ajay Kumar Jain for
Manohar Publishers & Distributors
4753/23 Ansari Road, Daryaganj
New Delhi 110002

Typeset by
A J Software Publishing Co. Pvt. Ltd.
New Delhi 110005

Printed at
Print Perfect
New Delhi 110064

To my sisters

Contents

Preface

This book is concerned with divorce and remarriage among Muslim communities in India. There are two distinct perspectives that can be applied to the study of divorce in any society. One can focus on the corpus of legal rules defining the rights of the husband and wife in the event a divorce is contemplated, the rights the spouses enjoy with respect to children and property, and the procedure laid down for giving the seal of final authority to a divorce. Or, one can focus on divorce as a sociological phenomenon and explore the processes that are set in motion once the stability of a marriage is threatened and divorce is contemplated. In the latter case the emphasis is on the factors that contribute to the breakdown of marriages, the role that kinsmen and social relations play in trying to work towards a possible reconciliation between the estranged spouses, the procedure that is followed to give effect to a divorce and the consequences that follow for the spouses, and particularly women, as a result of the divorce. This perspective does not treat divorce in isolation but tries to look at it in the wider context of social structure.

This book deals with divorce and remarriage among Muslims in terms of the second perspective. It examines, in the light of empirical evidence, the incidence of divorce and separation, the manner in which divorce takes place, social and other causes due to which the practice of divorce and separation persists, and the position of divorced and separated women in society as well as their prospects of remarriage. As Muslims claim to follow the Qur'an and are bound by Muslim Personal Law, Qur'anic and legal injunctions relating to divorce and the extent to which they are actually adhered to in practice are also dealt with. Quite often, the adherence of Muslims to their religious prescriptions and formal legal codes is taken for granted. It is assumed that their practices are shaped by what religion and law formally lay down. It is hardly ever contemplated that their social practices may be a reflection of more immediate existential pressures and conditions rather than of the formal codes laid down by Qur'anic or Muslim Personal Law. This book seeks to examine the degree of congruity between Qur'anic injunctions and legal codes and actual social practices prevalent in Muslim communities as this has the potential to show how there is often a wide gap between religious theory and social practice.

The book has an immediate practical aim as well. For some years the Muslim law of divorce, particularly the provision of triple divorce which vests a unilateral right in the husband to pronounce a summary divorce upon his wife by simply stating three times at one sitting that he is divorcing her, has been the subject of considerable controversy. On one side, those opposed to the practice of triple divorce—and this includes chauvinist and liberal Hindus as well as liberal Muslims—argue that the legal provision allowing a Muslim husband to pronounce divorce upon his wife at one go renders the position of a Muslim woman extremely weak and vulnerable and should be changed. On the other, those opposed to any change in the existing social practice of triple divorce reason that divorce rates are extremely low among Muslims in India and suggest that the assertion that Muslim divorce practices render the position of Muslim women particularly weak and vulnerable is foolhardy. Both positions have been pressed into the controversy without any effort to ascertain the empirical situation.

This book should make an academic intervention in this controversy. Since the essays brought together in this book are sociological analyses of divorce and remarriage among Muslims in India, the data thrown up as part of these analyses would clear some of the points in the controversy. Essentially, the papers included here represent attempts to work towards an understanding of the wide variety of social dimensions that determine the stability of a marriage and the social factors that come into play when marriages break down. One would not be far wrong in assuming that the general ethos of Muslims in India and the Islamic legal framework would have a bearing on what factors determine the stability of a marriage and what social factors come into play in the breakdown of a Muslim marriage. Even so, this cannot be assumed from a study of either Islamic precepts or the provisions of Muslim Personal Law. This would have to be systematically established through the empirical study of Muslims in specific social contexts. This is precisely the task that this book seeks to accomplish.

There has been a general paucity of sociological research on

Muslims in India and for anyone to attempt a comprehensive monograph on divorce and remarriage among Muslims in India would have been difficult. Under the circumstances, the second best alternative that seemed to suggest itself was to ask those who had carried out research among Muslims in India to write for this book. Even this seemed to pose difficulties as divorce and remarriage are not mainline areas of sociological research and most of those who had carried out sociological research among Muslim communities had not collected data that would enable them to write for this book. This has restricted both the areas and the range of dimensions that could be covered. It is hoped that this book will prompt more substantial and thoroughgoing research on this important aspect.

Academic credit for this book to have come out at all belongs to the contributors who so warmly responded to my suggestion that they cull out from their sociological research data on divorce and remarriage among Muslims in India and write it up for this book. I need to place on record my gratitude to them for putting up with constant nagging that they do so quickly. I hope they will be satisfied and happy with the shape their patience and effort has taken. Also, I should like to acknowledge the kindness of the editors of *Contribution to Indian Sociology*, Asghar Ali Engineer and Gyan Publishing House, New Delhi, in permitting me to reproduce the articles by Patricia Jeffery and Geetanjali Gangoli. I am alone to blame for any deficiencies the book still suffers from.

New Delhi IMTIAZ AHMAD

Introduction: Theology, Law and the Sociology of Muslim Divorce Practices in India

Imtiaz Ahmad

This book is concerned with a sociological exploration of divorce in Muslim communities in India. When divorce in Muslim communities is discussed, the tendency quite often is to place theology and law at the centre. From them inferences are often drawn about the actual behaviour of people. Thus, it is commonplace in discussions of divorce in Muslim communities to presume that the theologically or legally permitted simplicity of procedure[1] would lead to frequency of divorce, rendering a Muslim wife particularly weak and vulnerable. Rarely, if ever, is an attempt made to examine whether the simplicity of divorce procedure actually results in frequency of divorce in Muslim communities.[2] This book recognizes that divorce in Muslim communities entails substantial theological and legal dimensions, but takes as its point of departure the view that it is only by placing divorce in the social and cultural context that meaningful conclusions can be arrived at. This is what it set out to demonstrate, and this Introduction seeks to summarize the principal results of this exercise.

Even though theology and law are not directly relevant to the understanding of divorce as a social phenomenon, there is need to deal with both dimensions for two reasons. One, theological and legal dimensions crop up and are raised in local communities whenever a divorce takes place. Personnel supposed to be familiar with Muslim theology and law are consulted to ascertain the formal theological or legal position. Two, many of the contributors to this volume refer to the theological and legal dimensions and couch their subsequent analysis in terms of positions they feel best represents the correct theological or legal position. For these reasons, I propose to deal with the theological and legal issues relevant to a consideration of divorce in Muslim communities in India before turning to the picture that emerges from the empirical evidence that the different contributions have succeeded in producing. It is also worthwhile taking the theological and legal issues up for discussion because a great deal of the controversy and rhetoric surrounding divorce in Muslim communities in India revolves around those issues and ways of settling them through reinterpretation and reform processes.

On the theological side the issue of central concern in the study of divorce is whether the simplicity of divorce procedure which vests an almost unilateral right in the husband to dismiss his wife at will without assigning a reason can be said to enjoy religious sanction. In other words, can it appropriately be considered a part of the *shar'iat* which Muslims believe to be of divine origin and therefore immutable. Upon this issue opinion has been clearly divided, both historically and in contemporary times. A great deal of energy has been vested in debating this ticklish question with the traditionalists and the reformist sections taking clearly opposed positions. The traditionalists argue that the simplicity of divorce procedure constitutes an integral part of the Islamic *shar'ia* and is therefore impervious to interference or change. On the other hand, the reformists argue that the *shar'ia* comprises both divine and man-made prescriptions and the simplicity of divorce procedure, which is contemporaneously recognized as part of Muslim law on divorce, came to be incorporated in the corpus of the *shar'iat* at a later date, some two hundred years after the death of Prophet Muhammad. The central argument of the reformists is that if the divorce procedure were to be changed or rendered more difficult both the frequency of divorce and arbitrariness in the pronouncement of divorce would be curtailed. Therefore, they press for a re-interpretation of the *shar'ia* to what they contend are the ill-effects of divorce upon Muslim communities in India, namely, that the frequency of divorce is high and it tends quite often to be arbitrary.

Settling this tangled theological issue one way or the other has proved intractable so far, but any attempt to understand its precise nature requires us to go back into the historical development of Islamic theology. It is only by placing this issue in historical depth that the validity or otherwise of those who argue that the simplicity of divorce procedure constitutes a part of the *shar'ia* and is therefore immutable and those who want the divorce procedure to be changed or rendered more difficult can be assessed and a projection on the relative possibilities of social reforms gauged. For, without such serious analysis, the issue is bound to remain entangled with the traditionalists and the reformists engaging in constant rhetoric which is neither new to Muslim societies nor has even been settled to the satisfaction of either line of opinion. I wish to discuss this issue not because this can contribute to a reconciliation of their positions. I do so to bring out and pin-point the complexities involved and to ask whether the positions of the traditionalists and the reformists can actually be reconciled in the face of the theological premises upon which both raise their rhetoric.

Crucial to a consideration of the theological dimension of divorce with which we are concerned here is a tension that has characterized Islam from fairly early times. This is the tension between the pragmatic and ethical perceptions, both forming a part of Islam and susceptible of being simultaneously invoked.[3] Leila Ahmed notes:

> There appear . . . two distinct voices within Islam, and two competing understandings of gender, one expressed in the pragmatic regulations for society . . . , the other in the articulation of an ethical vision. Even as Islam instituted marriage as a sexual hierarchy in its ethical voice—a voice virtually unheard by rulers and lawmakers—it instantly stressed the importance of the spiritual and ethical dimensions of being and the equality of all individuals. While the first voice has been extensively elaborated into a body of political and legal thought, which constitutes the technical understanding of Islam, the second—the voice to which ordinary believing Muslims, who are essentially ignorant of the details of Islam's technical legacy, give their assent—has left little trace on the political and legal heritage of Islam. The unmistakable presence of an ethical egalitarianism explains why Muslim women frequently insist, often inexplicably to non-Muslims, that Islam is not sexist. They hear and read in its sacred text, justly and legitimately, a different message from that heard by the makers and enforcers of orthodox, androcentric Islam.
>
> The debate as to which voice to hear and what kind of faith and what kind of society Muhammad meant to institute has gone on throughout history. . . . From the beginning there were those who emphasized the ethical and spiritual message as the fundamental message of Islam and

argued that the regulations Muhammad put into effect, even his own practices, were merely the ephemeral aspects of the religion, relating only to that particular society at that historical moment. Thus, they were never intended to be normative or permanently binding for the Muslim community (1992: 65-6).

Even though these conflicting discourses existed from early times, the theological legacy which defined Islam after the death of Prophet Muhammad was decided by the establishment Islam.[4] Of course, the decision to regard the androcentric position as being binding for all times and in all places where Muslims lived was an interpretative action conditioned by the crisis of authority which arose within Islam after the death of Prophet Muhammad[5] and the expansion of Islam beyond the confines of its historical origin. On both points Leila Ahmed's articulation, endorsed by a long line of Islamic scholars, is remarkably instructive. As to the first factor, Ahmed writes:

The problem of interpretation and of the biases and assumptions that a particular age brought to its readings and renderings of a text is pertinent to all the central texts of Islam. . . . With respect to the central texts at the core of the entire edifice of orthodox Islam interpretation played a vital but more hidden role. Interpretation is of necessity part of every act of reading or inscribing a text. According to Islamic orthodoxy, the text of the Qur'an represents the exact words of the Qur'anic revelation as recited by Muhammad. Orthodoxy holds that the Qur'an was perfectly preserved in oral form from the beginning and that it was written down during Muhammad's lifetime or shortly thereafter when it was collected and arranged for the first time by his Companions. . . .

The physical transcription of a text in this place and period was also attended by difficulties, lending an element of uncertainty to readings. Not only were rough materials such as animal shoulder blades used to write down Qur'anic verses during Muhammad's lifetime but the Arabic letters used at this point were incomplete. The dots necessary to distinguish between the consonants were lacking. . . . Similarly, deciding which vocalization and which meaning were to be the canonical ones with respect to a text in which only consonants were written was also an act of interpretation and could decisively affect meaning (1992: 93-4).[6]

About the consequences of Islam's expansion outside the area of its birth, Leila Ahmed writes:

Within ten years of Muhammad's death Arab conquest had carried Islam to lands far beyond, and fundamentally different from Arabia—to societies that were urban and that already had elaborate scriptural and legal traditions and established social mores. These societies were more restrictive toward women and more misogynist; at least their misogyny and their modes of controlling women by law and by custom were more fully articulated administratively and as inscribed code. The differences between the fundamental assumptions about women in Arabia at the time of the rise of Islam and elsewhere in the Middle East are suggested by the contrast between the Quranic verses *addressing* women and unambiguously declaring the spiritual equality of men and women and in certain remarks of the supreme theologian of the Abbasid age al-Ghazali. . . .

Noticeably, al-Ghazali's sentiments about women were far closer to those of Tertullian or Augustine than to those that found expression in the Quran. Thus the attitudes to women expressed in the urban centres of the Mediterranean Middle East appear to have formed part of a cultural continuum extending over the territories that had formed part of the Byzantine and Sasanian empires. Through its conquests Islam was to inherit not only the Iraq-Iran region, which was to bring forth an al-Ghazali, but also the Mediterranean Middle East, which had nurtured such figures as Augustine and Origen. It was in these societies that major Muslim institutions and the edifices of Muslim . . . scripture were to be given shape over the next centuries (1992: 67-8).

Clearly, the tension between these interpretations—those that lay emphasis upon the pragmatic interpretations of Islam as enshrined subsequently by the Islamic establishment and those that emphasize the ethical-spiritual legacy of Islam—have remained a permanent feature of the theological discourse within Islam. Each rests on entirely different theological premises and tries to displace the other, but the interpretation which continues to hold solid ground is that we have here called the pragmatic voice of Islam. It continues to enjoy a powerful sway over those who control the resources of religious knowledge and are heard by the large majority of the faithful within Muslim communities. As such, those who assert that alternate interpretation of Islam's credo in terms of its ethical-spiritual voice is possible continue to beat their wings in the void without making their particular interpretation of Islam acceptable to the large body of Muslims.

This brings us to the question of law. On the face of it, the Islamic law of divorce would appear to be remarkably modern. Three elements make it easily comparable to the laws considered modern. On a comparative view of divorce laws across the different societies, it appears that in order to qualify as modern a divorce law should have at least three characterstics. First, it should allow for divorce, though there are significant differences across the world in the degrees of ease with which divorce in the different societies is allowed.[7] Traditionally, divorce laws in different religious traditions disallowed divorce altogether. Under Hindu law, at least the part of the law that governed marriage practices of higher castes, divorce was not permissable at all. Virtually the same was the case with the Christian law before the rise of Protestantism. Catholic law laid down that a validly contracted marriage could not be dissolved and divorce was therefore disallowed. This doctrine underlay the ideology and law of marriage in Europe for centuries and the history of divorce since the sixteenth century has been, for the most part, a rejection of the Catholic position. On the contrary, Islamic position on divorce was from the beginning more reasonable. While divorce was openly condemned as the most despised by God, provision for divorce was made. Conditions under which divorces could be allowed as well as the procedure to give legal effect to a divorce were clearly laid down.

Second, a modern divorce law is supposed to vest the initiative to decide whether the marriage should be sustained or whether it would be better in the interest of the spouses to divolve it on the spouses rather than an external authority. If we trace the development of divorce laws in different countries in Europe and America, it would be clear that the change has been in two significant directions. On the one hand, the trend has been to shift the responsibility for defining marriage breakdown. Historically, a divorce was defined as a legal solution only in those unions where one of the partners had been the victim of a matrimonial offence and sought to free himself from the contract on these grounds. The guilty party could not sue for divorce on a unilateral basis and hence was kept in marital bondage at other legal partners' discretion. The great difficulties faced in legally disengaging oneself from marriage impressed upon the individual the seriousness of the marriage vows. Even if it was normally easy for individuals to embark upon the contract, these obstacles acted as a disincentive to their harbouring ideas of easily breaking it. This position has changed.

Moreover, the church and the state established the criteria for acceptable behaviour in marriage by limiting the grounds on which a separation or divorce might be obtained. On the other hand, the trend has been in a direction away from the imperative of apportioning or attributing blame to either spouse. Modern divorce legislation simply recognizes that a marriage can break down in such a way that it is 'irremediable', 'irreconcilable', or 'irretrievable'. The law does not require information on the reasons for the breakdown of the marriage but simply evidence of it. The evidence required by most of these laws is that the couple has lived apart for a certain number of years. Legislations passed in recent years in most European countries enable couples to terminate unions on the ground that their marriages have broken down and are quite beyond repair. Therefore, no-fault divorce without the necessity of the divorce court having to go into the reasons for the breakdown of marriage is the second significant characteristic of a modern divorce law.

Judged against these criterion, Islamic law is again remarkably modern. For one thing, it allows no-fault divorce: a marriage can be ended on the ground that it does not work; and there is no necessity to allocate blame and retribution between the two partners. Second, it places the power to pass judgement on the viability of a conjugal relationship within the control of the individual husbands and wives. It does not vest this power into any outside agency and the role assigned in traditional Muslim practice to the Qazi is merely that of seeing that divorce has followed the procedure laid down in law and not to adjudicate on or pass judgement on the viability of a conjugal relationship. This in itself may help to make the process of marital breakdown a more dignified and less punitive experience, although there are many dimensions to this experience only some of which are directly attributable to wider social institutions such as the law and the sanctions that it exerts on the individual. Finally, Islamic law allows for reconciliation between the spouses even after the process of divorce has been initiated. The Qur'an repeatedly exhorts reconciliation between estranged spouses.

The third characteristic of a modern law of divorce is that it should be fair and just towards both partners. The Muslim practice of triple divorce, which vests a unilateral right upon the husband to pronounce a summary divorce on his wife by simply stating three times at one sitting that he is divorcing her, would appear on the face of it to be weighted against the wife. Judged against modern conceptions of gender justice, this provision of Muslim law would be found deficient on several counts: (1) both procedure and conditions are not placed equally on the two partners, (2) a woman dces not have the right to pronounce a divorce by uttering the formula, (3) the procedure for seeking divorce is cumbersome in the case of the wife, (4) the husband has the right to have four wives but a similar right is not given to a woman, and (5) where the wife asks for *khula*, the husband is exonerated of his obligation to pay *mehr*. It is on this count that the courts in India have held this law to be repugnant to the principle of equity, justice and good conscience. Modern conception of gender justice is alien to the framework of thought of most traditions and Islam is no exception.[8]

Whether the Islamic law of divorce is fair to both partners has to be assessed in terms of a distinction that is central to the study of law. This is the distinction between jurisprudence and the application of law in specific contexts. As a rule, Islamic law of divorce recognized three distinct modes of dissolution of a marriage. *Talaq* is dissolution of marriage at the initiative of the husband and takes place the moment he utters the formula of divorce three times. *Fask* is a mode of dissolution of marriage by mutual consent. Under this form, both partners have to approach the duly constituted judicial-legal authority with the prayer that they are no longer interested in sustaining their marriage and it should be legally dissolved. *Khula* is dissolution of marriage at the initiative of the wife without the intervention of the husband. All she needed to do was to invoke the duly constituted legal authority to dissolve the marriage whether or not the husband agreed to it. This form of dissolution of marriage has undergone a substantial change in the process of application. It has assumed a form where the woman appeals to her husband to pronounce divorce on the condition that she would forgo her claim to *mehr* and shall not ask for return of dowry. It can be appropriately characterized as *khula* by *talaq*.

Many people are prone to seeing the absence of codification as a serious problem and demand that the contemporary difficulties would be greatly mitigated only if the law were to be properly codified. As far as *khula* as a mode of dissolution of marriage is concerned, an attempt was made in India through the enactment of the Dissolution of Muslim Marriages Act, 1939, to codify the law. One of the consequences of this enactment was that the right of the wife was greatly restricted by limiting the exercise of *khula* to a limited set of reasons many of which are virtually difficult to prove in a court of law. Consequently, *khula* by *talaq* whereby a wife can only appeal to her husband to pronounce a divorce came in vogue. This has had the effect of reinforcing the patriarchal bias in the application of law and rendering it unfair to the wife. Those advocating codification should take instruction from this and recognize that codification is not always, not necessarily at least, progressive and can result in greater distortions.

There is a powerful line of reasoning among Muslims that does not fight shy of asserting with uncanny aggressiveness that Islam offers a complete blueprint for life for all times and cannot be changed. If the revealed text was quite as explicit as average Muslims commonly believe is truly the case, there would indeed have been no basis for this kind of variation to prevail. Yet, the fact of the situation is that such variation currently exists, leading to a curious situation that one can talk in the same breadth, as it were, of a Qur'anic law and a Muslim Personal Law. The two are not necessarily consonant, not at least on many points in respect of divorce practices. Formal Muslim scholarship has not been successful in dealing and coming to terms with this dichotomy, which continues to prevail even today, and is to a considerable extent unresolvable because the revealed injunctions are either self-contradictory (one revealed injunction cancels out another) or are not sufficiently precise so as to rule out conflicting interpretations. This has resulted in an unhappy and uncomfortable situation where, despite claiming to derive its authority from the Qur'an, each school of Islamic law interprets it differently in a way that a diversity of forms and formal procedures is allowed to prevail in respect of divorce practices among different Muslim communities.[9]

One must in order to understand this contradictory picture retrace the historical development of Islamic law and examine the processes whereby that law eventually came to be articulated. Law in classical Islamic theory, as Coulson has cogently argued, 'is the revealed will of God, a divinely ordained system preceding and not preceded by the Muslim state, controlling and not controlled by Muslim society'

(1964: 1). Even so, Islamic law did evolve gradually over time through a complicated process of historical evolution divided by traditional doctrine into several stages.[10] As Coulson has graphically outlined: 'Master-architects were followed by builders who implemented the plans; successive generations of craftsmen made their own particular contribution to the fixtures, fittings, and interior décor until, the task completed, future jurists were simply passive caretakers of the eternal edifice' (1964: 2).

What substantially contributed to this process of historical evolution of Islamic law were two elements. One was that the authorities did not have a settled policy which would guide the judicial decision-making and were content to leave adjudication of legal disputes to the qazi whose primary function was to apply local law.[11] Local law varied considerably throughout the territories of Islam. For example, the society in Medina was wedded to the traditional concepts of Arab tribal law under which arranging of a marriage alliance was the prerogative of the male members of the family. As such, a woman in Medina could not contract marriage on her own and had to be given away in marriage by her guardian. On the other hand, in the society of Kufa, which started out as a military encampment and had a more cosmopolitan milieu because of the admixture of diverse ethnic groups, women had the right to conclude their own marriage contracts without the intervention of male members of the family (Coulson, 1964: 30; also see Ahmed, 1992: 81-7). The other element was that the latitude allowed to the individual judge to decide cases according to his own personal opinion was considerable.[12]

Coulson illustrates this diversity by citing two cases relating to maintenance to a divorced wife. The first case, which Coulson himself points out arose from the uncertainty in the text of the Qur'an itself, concerned the rights of an irrevocably divorced wife during *iddat* or 'waiting period'. The official text of the Qur'an addressed to husbands reads: 'Lodge them where you lodge according to your circumstances'. However, the text transmitted by Ibn-Masud, a companion of Prophet Muhammad who hailed from Kufa, contained the additional words: 'Lodge them where you lodge *and bear their expenses. . . .*' Accordingly, the practice in Kufa was to allow a divorced wife full maintenance during the *iddat* period, but elsewhere she was given the bare right of shelter in the husband's house (Coulson, 1964: 31).

The second case relates to the precise legal implications of the moral injunction of the Qur'an urging husbands to make 'a fair provision' in favour of a divorced wife. Coulson writes:

Ibn-Hujayra, *qadi* of Egypt . . . , considered such provision, which came to be called *mut'a*, to be obligatory. He fixed the amount at three *dinars* and arranged for its recovery by ordering the pay-roll official to make the necessary deduction from the husband's stipend. On the other hand, a later *qadi*, Tauba ibn-Namir opined that the Qur'anic injunction was directed only to the husband's conscience. When a husband refused his request to provide a *mut'a* for his repudiated wife, Tauba 'fell silent, for he did not consider that it was legally binding upon the husband'; although in a later case where the same husband appeared as a witness, Tauba refused to accept his testimony, on the ground that he was not to be numbered 'among the virtuous and the pious'. Under Tauba's successor, Khayr ibn-Nu'aym, *mut'a* once became a strict legal obligation (1964: 31-2).

By the end of the ninth century, which was the period of Abbasid efflorescence, this openness had clearly died down and in its place Islamic law as a divinely ordained system was instituted. Reputed Islamic schools, having successfully established their doctrinal positions, were content to declare Islamic law to be a rigid and immutable system embodying eternally valid and absolute norms which could not be susceptible to modification by any legislative authority (see Coulson, 1964: 5, 72). The legal fiction employed to achieve this closure was the argument that, access to revelation of the divine will having ceased upon Prophet Muhammad's death, the *shar'ia* had achieved its perfect expression and had to be static and immutable. 'Floating above Muslim society as a disembodied soul, freed from the currents and vicissitudes of time, it [Islamic law] represented the eternally valid ideal towards which society must aspire', concludes Coulson (1964: 2). This development determined the future course of Islamic law. Coulson adds:

'With the spread of the area of law covered by divine revelation came an increasing rigidity of doctrine; the scope for independent activity was progressively restricted as the particular terms of the law, through the Traditons, were identified with the command of God. The spring of juristic speculation, which had supplied the rapidly moving stream of Islamic jurisprudence in its early stages, gradually ceased to flow; the current slowed, until eventually and inevitably, it reached a point of stagnation (1964: 73).

This development brought about in the domain of Muslim law the same situation that had come to exist in the field of Muslim theology. As we demonstrated, a clear dichotomy developed between the pragmatic and ethical-spiritual perspectives in theology. In law a dichotomy came to exist between those who subscribed to the view that Muslim law constituted a static and immutable system as an embodiment of the divine will and command and those who argued that law is shaped by the needs of society and could not be rendered completely closed and unchanging as classical Muslim jurisprudence made it. Central to this dichotomy is a clash over the dictates of the traditional law and the demands of society. The principle according to the classical Muslim jurists and their contemporary followers is that the law can operate only within limits set by divine commands. According to those who see law as evolving in response to contemporary needs, the will of God was never expressed in terms as rigid as classical legal doctrine maintains, but admits of 'varying interpretations and varying applications' (Coulson, 1964: 7) according to demands of time.

This difference over principle continues to remain a bone of contention in Muslim law and jurisprudence. Establishment Islam continues to hold that changes in law cannot be justified only on the ground of necessity even though it can truly be demonstrated that Islamic law developed as the implementation of the precepts of divine revelation within the framework of contemporary social conditions. A juristic basis must be found to support the principle that the contemplated changes in law are expressly or impliedly endorsed by the divine will. Unless this is done, the law cannot retain its form as an expression of the divine will and command. Since finding a bridge between these differing positions has proved difficult, if not impossible, each perspective vies with the state for triumph and ultimate supremacy. Schacht summarizes this succinctly when he writes:

> Modernist legislation does not, generally speaking, arise out of genuine public demand. There exist the two well-defined groups of the '*ulema*', who are for the greater part traditionalists, and of the modernists, many of whom are modern lawyers. Modernist legislation is imposed by a government whenever the modernists have succeeded in gaining its support and the government feels strong enough to overcome resistance of the traditionalists.

Modernist Islamic legislation therefore often appears somewhat haphazard and arbitrary (1964: 105).

Until colonial powers penetrated the Muslim world the theological and legal debates were confined within the framework of the Islamic tradition. Islam was the reference point of those who took what we have here characterized as the pragmatic view of Islam or subscribed to the ideological position that Muslim law was founded on divine command and was immutable, as well as those who argued in terms of ethical-spiritual vision of Islam and maintained that Muslim law could be changed according to social conditions. With the penetration of Western influences both Muslim law and the terms of the theological and legal debates have been altered. This has further complicated matters. One area where transformation came about was the administration of Islamic law. After British rule was established in India, for example, Islamic law came to be administered through the ordinary civil court from which a final appeal lay, prior to independence and partition, to the Judicial Committee of the Privy Council' (Coulson, 1964: 163). The British did not fully appreciate or accept the doctrine of strict adherence to established authorities. Wherever it seemed necessary on general grounds of equity, justice and good conscience, the courts unhesitatingly formulated novel principles by way of supplement to the traditional Islamic law.[13] Sometimes judicial decisions were based on an imperfect and partial appreciation of the terms of the traditional Islamic law, and the principles and institutions of the *shar'ia* were interpreted in the light of English legal concepts.

Anglo-Muhammadan law, thus, grew as an expression of Islamic law 'unique not only in form—for it to be genuinely applied as a case-law system through a hierarchy of courts which observes the doctrine of binding precedent—but also in substance, inasmuch as it has absorbed English influences, particularly those of Equity, in as generally facile a manner as nascent Islamic law had absorbed Roman influences in the earliest historical period' (Coulson, 1964: 171). One consequence of this development is that in dealing with divorce we are required to contend with three different sets of corpus of rules: (1) the original message to which the word *shar'ia* was originally applied, (2) the corpus of rules articulated centuries after the death of Prophet Muhammad by establishment Islam in the light of dominant patriarchal ethos of the emerging society which is also characterized by the ulema as *shar'ia* though it was entirely the creation of a human agency and should not have been vested with the sanctity of either being revealed or divine, and (3) Anglo-Muhammedan law evolved by the colonial courts in their effort to apply the laws of the Qur'an in cases where the parties happened to be Muslims. This is also construed as the *shar'ia* even though it was the handiwork of those who were not even nominally Muslims. This is justified through the legal fiction that the courts were not interpreting the *shar'ia* but merely applying it.

Colonial penetration, backed and supported by its distinctive cultural and ideological package, also introduced new frameworks for debates which had traditionally existed within Muslim societies and were being fought on typically Islamic terrain. Contemporaneously, a great deal of confusion prevails over the rationale for reform in the contemporary discourse in Muslim societies. Those who argue in favour of reform couch their position in terms of the concept of gender justice as articulated in modern democratic and liberal theory. According to this theory, men and women should have equal rights. This presumes that any religious or cultural tradition that does not believe in absolute equality of men and women, and does not accord them absolutely equal rights in every sphere of life, lacks a concept of gender justice. This has proved to be highly problematic.

Within all traditions and religious or cultural communities, opinions are divided between those who want to adhere to relatively conservative interpretations and those who would want to explore the possibilities for more broad-based interpretations to advance the general good. The arguments of both sections of opinion are within the tradition and the disputation is really over matters of interpretation. On the other hand, when the case for reform is anchored to a framework which lies outside the tradition, the terms of the discourse are immediately transformed. The question then is transposition of the values of one tradition by the value premises of another. When this happens, the basis for dialogue easily breaks down and a hardening of attitude takes place. The liberal and democratic framework recognizes no space for a tradition that is not in consonance with its values. The other tradition sees no reasons to interact and respond where autonomy of its own values is not even conceded. It becomes a question of the tradition either surviving through open resistance or being vanquished by another tradition.

Many would be inclined to argue that this mode of posing the interaction between the liberal-democratic and religious-cultural traditions is somewhat exaggerated. They would contend that what one is anticipating is not a complete displacement of one tradition or its value premises by another, but rather for a degree of cultural acculturation where one tradition takes from the liberal-democratic tradition what it lacks without jeopardizing its own viability. This line of reasoning ignores two significant dimensions. First, acculturation is a process that is definitely shaped and governed by a relationship of power. Under the circumstances, any anticipation that a transposition of values can take place through a process of acculturation misses the point that all traditions, whether religious and cultural or liberal-democratic, carry a conception of their own worth on which they can compromise only under duress and that too not without putting up stiff resistance. Acculturation or adoption of liberal-democratic values by traditions whose value premises are different is inherently problematic. Second, where this acculturation is imposed, whether by the pressures generated by liberal-democratic values from outside or by advocates of reform from within, the response is either defensive or apologetic such as we have often seen when countries have struggled against colonial domination where the pressure for acculturation was probably the heaviest.

Faced with a hard choice, the antagonists of reforms tend to argue that a conception of gender justice is not unique to the liberal-democratic tradition. Other traditions too have conceptions of gender justice, except that their conceptions may not be quite in consonance with the conception of gender justice in the liberal-democratic tradition. Consider, for example, the case of Islam, though much of what one might say about Islam would hold equally for other religious traditions, whether Eastern or Western. The antogonists of reforms question the proposition implicit in the position of the reformists that Islam does not have a concept of gender justice. They ask that when it is said that Islam lacks a conception of gender justice what is the criterion on which one is basing one's judgement? Is one basing it on an evaluation of the Islamic tradition in terms of the value-premises of the liberal-democratic tradition? Or, is one basing it on the evaluation of Islam on its own value premises? They assert that when one asserts that Islam lacks a concept of gender justice what one is really saying is that judged against the yardsticks provided by liberal-democratic values Islam cannot be said to contain a concept of gender justice. This is not the same thing as saying that Islam does not have a concept of gender justice.

The antogonists of reform contend that Islam too has a conception of gender justice which differs significantly from the liberal-democratic conception of gender justice. Under the Islamic concept of gender justice, men and women are not seen as equal nor are they acutally conceded absolutely equal rights and privileges (as in the liberal-democratic tradition), but a woman is recognized as a jural person with clearly recognized rights. A great deal of emphasis is also placed upon treating women with consideration and ensuring justice to them. This concept may not entirely accord with the liberal-democratic concept of gender justice, but then insisting that the concepts of gender justice in other traditions must necessarily subscribe to the liberal-democratic concept is tantamount to denying autonomy to other traditions and their conceptions of the good life. This is a predicament that feminists and liberals eager to promote reforms in personal laws fail to come to terms with.[14]

What needs to be appreciated is that those who argue that the system of divorce laid down in Muslim theology and law constitutes a part of the divine will and those who believe that it can be changed in response to social exigencies are both correct depending on how the Qur'anic text is interpreted and applied to everyday life. If one takes the view that the Qur'an is just a set of moral principles or guidelines which were offered to the believers to order their lives, then it would appear that the system of divorce can be changed in response to historical exigencies or contemporary social conditions. Thus, for example, if it can be demonstrated that the simplicity of divorce procedure allowed in Islam leads to a higher frequency of divorce or that the divorce process itself is arbitrary, then there should be no bar in changing it. On the other hand, if one takes the view that the Qur'an did not merely lay down moral guidelines but contained a blueprint for life, it would be difficult to concede that that law, itself conceived as the expression of divine will and command, can be easily susceptible to change.[15] The power to determine how the text should be interpreted or what the law is unfortunately lies with the establishment Islam. This makes the discussion on divorce in Muslim communities in theological and legal terms remarkably tangled. The divergence of opinions with respect to modes of interpretation is not susceptible to easy resolution.

One way out of this virtual impasse is to turn to the ground realities and to try to explore how the theological and legal prescriptions translate themselves in social practice. Of course, to say so the intention is not to suggest that the theological and legal perspectives on divorce in Muslim communities in India are not in themselves important or relevant. Divorce is fundamentally a legal process. A marriage can be terminated by desertion or even dissolved informally, but a couple is not considered divorced unless the dissolution of their marriage has been sanctioned by law (Phillips, 1991: 93). However, law is only one of the variables that comes into interplay and contributes to the incidence of divorce. Other more potent factors include prevalent social attitudes towards marriage, the personal commitment of the spouses to sustaining their marriage, the presence of social support necessary for a marriage to continue and the factors that affect possibilities of conflict resolution that lead to marital breakdown. Phillips rightly comments:

> Divorce is not an isolated legal event that is unrelated to other personal, familial, and social actions and circumstances, but is the final stage of a marital process. In crude and schematic terms the main stages of the process are marriage, marriage breakdown, the decision by one or both spouses to terminate the marriage, and finally its legal dissolution by divorce. Needless to say, far from all marriages experience this process; only a minority do so, as the divorce statistics attest. Some, however, might go the point of breakdown without any manifestation of it in social or legal terms. Yet other broken marriages are terminated socially, the spouses living apart independently without the intervention or imprimatur of the law. At each stage of the process, then, proportion of the total population of marriages goes no further. Many marriages never breakdown. . . . Others breakdown but show no outward sign of it, others breakdown and terminate informally. Finally, other couples—those that contribute to the divorce rate—experience breakdown, decide to terminate the marriage, and can, and eventually do, divorce (1991: 93-4).

A common presumption often made in the context of divorce in

Muslim communities is that the frequency of divorce is high because of the simplicity of divorce procedure which Islam allows for termination of marriage and, since a Muslim husband has superior rights under this procedure, women tend quite frequently to be divorced arbitrarily. Some contributors to this volume premise their analysis in terms of such a proposition. Ignoring the evidence that the explanations offered by the spouses for their marital breakdown and eventual divorce are reducible to definite sociological variables, they go on to presume that what is commonly believed has certain validity. Consequently, they engage in an elaborate discussion of theology and law and argue in favour of a change of divorce procedure so that women are not short-charged or cast arbitrarily by their unscrupulous husbands who are seen in this kind of a construction to be ever prone to divorcing their wives. What has prompted some of them to this academic orientation is difficult to gauge, but it would appear that this is partly a function of the methodology they have adopted for analysing divorce processes.

Community study is the ideal method for the study of divorce as it allows for collection of all the cases of divorce and marital breakdown so that firm estimates of frequency of divorce can be arrived at.[16] Patricia Jeffery's contribution illustrates the merits of such a methodological approach and should be emulated by those who take up the study of divorce in Muslim communities in the future. Most contributors have instead relied upon case studies as a method.[17] One consequence of this methodological approach is that one obtains one's data from the divorced wife and the conclusions are drawn from the testimony offered by her. Since divorce itself is an acrimonious and painful experience, one presumption that we can safely make is that the women whose case studies were explored chose deliberately to emphasize that their divorce was not so much the result of a prolonged conflict but rather an act of arbitrariness on the part of the husband. Even in these case studies, there is considerable evidence, which some of the contributors have chosen to ignore, that suggests that the divorce or separation was not a sudden development. The couples were leading an uneasy or conflict-ridden existence and something precipitated the last straw so that the husband either pronounced divorce on the wife or she herself took the decision to return to her natal home.

As to the contention that divorce in Muslim communities in India tends to be quite often arbitrary, the evidence brought together by the contributions in this book clearly suggests that divorce is not an individual act on the part of the husband. Everywhere there is some kind of a social mechanism in place for the regulation of divorce. For one thing, the relatives or neighbours, unless they are themselves interested in a divorce coming about, which is also eloquently brought out by a number of case studies, mediate in the divorce process. Second, when a divorce is contemplated, the pronouncement of divorce itself takes place in the presence of relatives, village elders or some formal authority.[18] This is not to suggest that despite this there are no cases where divorce takes place without the intervention or supervision of relatives or religious functionaries of one kind or another. Where the husband lives in a social setting outside the zone of influence of kinsmen and community members, there is a strong possibility that the decision to pronounce and convey divorce is arrived at independently without the intervention of close relatives or members of the local community. What needs to be recognized is that even in these cases, as indeed in all cases where the divorce is pronounced or the decision for separation is taken without the immediate intervention of close relatives or community leaders, the decision to pronounce divorce may not be sudden or ad hoc. There may be a background of marital discord or alienation and the divorce is the final culmination point. If this does not come through the case studies, there is a strong possibility that this aspect was not sufficiently deeply investigated.

This appears to be the case on two significant counts. First, conflict is endemic to marriage, and divorce or separation comes about only when the couple or the other members of the immediate family fail to resolve that conflict. As such, unless one is predisposed to dismissing a divorce as arbitrary or an act of caprice on the part of the husband for reasons other than those intrinsic to the marital union, summary judgement on the nature of divorce or separation cannot be passed without going deep into the background which led one or both spouses to come to a decision to terminate their marriage. Second, since the importance of being married is not merely a matter of individual predilection but is socially and culturally reinforced[19] in no uncertain manner, a divorce would not come about unless there are powerful reasons in favour of that decision. It is only when there are powerful pressures on either spouse to take the precipitate step of terminating a marital union and for the members of his or her immediate family to endorse or support that action that divorce comes about. On both counts, it would appear that we must recognize the existence of conflict in marriage, conflict which is then resolved through marital dissolution, and ask why marriages break down and why many marriages remain intact and survive.[20]

In the sociological literature on marriage and the family in India little attention has been paid to the management of conflict between husbands and wives though other kinds of conflicts within the family, particularly those arising between the mother-in-law and sisters-in-law on the one hand and the daughter-in-law on the other, have been elaborated extensively. As a consequence marital discord is not seen as a problem. Family sociology, thus, offers no clues as to the level of friction which is found among married couples, nor about the means commonly employed to deal with conflict. Evidence brought together by the contributors consists of two kinds. One relates to the bickerings between the wife and her mother-in-law and sisters-in-law. Such bickerings may relate to dowry brought by her. Or, they may relate to division of household chores between them. Or, they may relate to the background of the wife and her natal family. What emerges quite clearly from the evidence adduced in the contributions is that usually a wife is subjected to taunts on any or all of these counts and the husband is often called upon to mediate their conflicts. Often enough, such bickerings stop after some time, particularly after the couple has had a child. Where such bickerings have the propensity to persist and the husband is not able to deal with the conflict which they produce, he eventually gives up. He then resorts to divorce as a way out of the predicament of having to take a mediatory position between his wife and his mother and sisters.[21]

The second kind of evidence that comes through these contributions consists of the reasons offered by the divorced women as to why their divorces came about. Several features about this evidence are noteworthy. First, even though some of the women alleged that their husbands had arbitrarily left or divorced them, they offered one reason or another for their separation or divorce. This would seem to imply that these women were aware that something was amiss in their relationship with their husbands. It is another matter that they may not have quite apprehended that their spouse would eventually go so far as to pronounce a divorce on them. Therefore, while representing their case to the investigator they may have argued that their husbands had acted arbitrarily in divorcing them, they were already in the know of the factor which led their husbands into deciding to divorce them. There is a strong plausibility of this for the simple reason that divorce is by its very nature an acrimonious event and each spouse uses every opportunity to malign the other partner, telling avid stories of how shabbily they had been dealt with. Unless we draw this inference from the evidence made available by several of the case studies, it would make no sense that women should allege that they had been divorced arbitrarily and yet be able to provide an explanation why their divorce had come about.

Second, the explanations given by the divorced women are as a rule reducible to a limited set of reasons. These include wife's barrenness, incurable illness of the spouse, dowry demands which the spouse or her family members were unable to meet, wife's or husband's bad looks, differences in the cultural background of the husband and wife, quarrelsome nature of the spouse, and husband either having a clandestine relationship with another woman or bringing her home after getting married to her. These reasons are not quite specific to Muslim communities. Indeed, they operate as factors leading to separation or divorce more generally in all social communities and groups. As analysts we may not find some of these explanations quite satisfactory or adequate—they may not appear deep enough—but we should recognize that, unless there is an alternative arrangement on hand, or some opportunity to break out of the relationship, marriage would have most likely survived. Marriages usually survive because the institutional parameters of social structure generate a high level of commitment to marriage. At the same time, as pointed out earlier, conflict is endemic to most marriages and can end up in divorce. Constraints of normative pressures in time reduce the options spouses have to make alternative choices. Casual explanations of marital breakdown must therefore aim to find out those factors which act to reduce the level of commitment to marriage, exacerbate conflict between the spouses or limit their capacity to manage tension, and increase the opportunities for one of the spouses to walk out of marriage.

If we analysed the kinds of explanations that the divorced women whose case histories the contributors report, we find that in some cases there are definite social values which would seem to endorse divorce as a way out of a marital relationship. Consider childlessness or barrenness of the wife. There is a great deal of normative pressure in Indian society for a couple to have children.[22] Moreover, given the great emphasis placed on having children, particularly sons, as a social security in old age, the couple is always under pressure to have the first child soon after marriage. If a woman is not able to bear children,[23] the husband would in normal circumstances be under great mental and social pressure to have a full family. He can do so either through taking a second wife or divorcing his first wife and contracting a second marriage. Ultimately which course he adopts is likely to depend upon his material conditions, that is, whether or not he can afford to maintain a second wife and the social attitude towards polygamy prevalent in the community within which he lives.

The same would hold true for other explanations too. Each explanation can be found to be backed by a counter value. Critical to a marital breakdown is not the fact that there is a value that justifies separation or divorce but rather whether there exist cultural or social mechanisms which can neutralize those values. If such mechanisms are in place, then a couple may not break up even if those reasons exist. On the contrary, if those mechanisms are absent, then a marriage is most likely to end up in divorce. Given that the majority of women whose case histories are reported were living in close kin networks, the only mechanism available in their case would have been their immediate relatives. If the attitudes of the relatives in whose midst the couples usually lived were positive, they would have intervened to make sure that the marriage did not end up in divorce. If the attitudes were negative, then there would also be a strong predisposition on their part to play upon the sentiments and feelings of the husband or the wife to bring about the dissolution of marriage. Many case studies show that close family members of the husband were negatively predisposed towards the wife right from the beginning—they would harp on the wife's look, her lack of culture and mannerisms, her failure to bring a large dowry, her quarrelsomeness, etc. Small wonder, then, that the marriages ended in divorce.

It is not only values likely to offer a justification for divorce and negative attitudes of close kin, in-laws in particular, that play a key role in divorce. Location in the social and economic ladder is also a powerful factor. There is overwhelming evidence in the case studies that the frequency of divorce is far higher among the members of lower castes and poor households than among those belonging to higher castes and enjoying a relatively better socio-economic status.[24] What is it about their socio-economic situation that seems to accentuate their propensity for divorce has to be carefully investigated in the Indian context. One can, however, hazard a few plausible explanations in the light of existing research on divorce. It can be that their deprived background makes for greater marital instability; poverty of their material circumstances gives rise to marital discord which results in a higher frequency of divorce. It can be that the husband and wife living at a near bare subsistence level have less to lose if they separate. Their material life does not depend so critically on conjugal exchange relationship and this removes one of the most important forces for stability in marriage. It is equally possible that the nature of the economy in which most poor participate does not create strong incentives for marital stability.

Marital breakdown is a long-drawn process and divorce constitutes the end of that process. Divorce, thus, leaves the spouses in a state of shock, depression and social and material deprivation: routinized behaviours lose their meaning, the pattern of life is undermined, and the problem of coping with the unknown and the unexpected assume overwhelming proportions.[25] The divorcee is made to feel marginal and stigmatized. This personal disorganization and trauma varies by individual personality traits as well as the degree of mental preparedness.[26] It can be safely predicted that the spouse who takes the decision in favour of divorce is the one who is likely to experience far less personal disorganization and trauma. In that partner's case the decision to go in for divorce must be the outcome of a great deal of premeditation and he or she may already have worked out some alternative pattern of life. On the other hand, the partner who might have been hoping against hope that the marriage might still be salvaged would experience personal disorganization and trauma the most. Even so, given their strong socialization for the conjugal role and their dependent status, women are definitely at a greater disadvantage in a divorce.[27] However, as the case studies clearly demonstrate, the difficulties of the divorced woman are substantially mitigated by the role support provided by her natal family. Almost, as a rule she is able to revert back to her natal family where her parents or brothers take financial responsibility for her.

Remarriage is one way out of the hardships that a divorced woman is forced into. While there is no bar on a divorced Muslim woman to remarry, the ground realities are quite complicated.[28] There are significant variations in attitudes to remarriage across classes. Among the lower classes, where the incidence of divorce is also quite common, attitudes towards remarriage are quite relaxed. Among the higher and middle classes, remarriage is often looked down upon. Unless the divorcee is too young and a suitable match is available, remarriage hardly takes place. Since remarriage is not universal, the question of sustenance of the divorced wife remains. Her only option is to revert back to her parents or brothers. This is less of a problem in economically well-off families as they have the means to shoulder the burden of maintaining their divorced daughter and her children, if they have accompanied her after divorce, though even in such cases she has to make compromises and adjust to the taunts and curses of her family members, especially their sisters-in-law who look upon her as an intruder and a burden on the family resources. However, in the case of women from lower class families this poses serious problems. Lower class families are already leading a hand to mouth existence and reversion of a divorced daughter and her children puts severe strain on their meagre resources. In such families the divorced woman has to face considerable humiliation and is often blamed for adding to the already difficult situation of the family. Sooner or later, she engages in some work that can provide her additional resources to contribute to the family economy.

In practice then, as distinct from legal prescription, divorce results in hardships on many women and their children. Women do not have access to the skilled workforce, and social welfare systems do not exist to provide assistance in particularly deserving cases. Thus, divorced women, especially those with children to care for, constitute a distinct economically disadvantaged group within most communities in India. Even if they work, their wages are too meagre as the case studies have shown. Muslim divorced women might have the promise of *mehr*, but the evidence in the case studies shows that it is hardly ever paid. Moreover, since most divorced women are from the lower socio-economic strata, the amount of *mehr* is too small. The courts are prepared to order former husbands to pay maintenance and child support, but compliance is seen in only a minority of the court orders.[29] In effect, then, divorce has the effect of producing a new class of poor; divorced women and their children. To point to some of these negative consequences is merely to raise a question about the desirability and usefulness of efforts at reforming divorce procedures.[30] Changes in legislations and the procedures for divorce can certainly make divorce less capricious and arbitrary, but that does not guarantee that such reformed legislations, even if such legislation were possible, would be necessarily progressive and positive.[31] Law and policies have to be responsive to the implications of divorce for the lives of women and children after divorce.[32]

NOTES

1. There is a long-standing tradition in Muslim legal history which recognizes the husband's right to summarilly dismiss his wife without giving a reason. He has only to say, 'I divorce you', three times. Most accounts say that the words must be spoken before witnesses, and in many cases this formal requirement is adhered to, but this does not always seem to be the case because the requirement to register the repudiation is held to be equivalent. Once he has said 'I divorce you' three times—and he may do this in one breadth—the divorce is irrevocable. Or rather, it cannot be cancelled unless in the meantime the woman has married another man and this man is willing to divorce her. Some people arrange for this purpose a formal marriage to be instantly dissolved, but Islam requires that any marriage which is duly solemnized should be consummated. J.N.D. Anderson summarizes this tradition succinctly: '. . . the Islamic law of divorce . . . is the major cause of suffering to Muslim woman. The Muslim wife indeed has always lived, so far as the law is concerned, under the ever-present shadow of divorce, a shadow mitigated only in comparatively rare cases by certain precautionary devices' (1959: 51-2).
2. Cross-cultural evidence strongly suggests that, while divorce rates tend almost always to rise when divorce procedures are simplified, simplicity or otherwise of procedure cannot explain the frequency of divorce (see Mair, 1971). When the liberal divorce law of 1792 in France was replaced by the restrictive Napoleonic divorce code in 1902, the number of divorces fell appreciably (Phillips, 1991: 93). Contrariwise, when from being difficult to

obtain and effectively reserved for the better-off social groups divorce became widely available to all social strata in England, divorce rate underwent a steady increase (Phillips, 1991: 185). Even so, most analysts of divorce in Western societies recognize that divorce procedure is a poor guide to an understanding of the divorce process (see Bott, 1957; Phillips, 1991; Hart, 1976). Evidence from Muslim societies reaffirms this broad formulation. Mair writes: 'The ease of divorce in Muslim countries . . . is substantiated by recorded cases from a number of them. For example, Cunincon calculated from a small sample that about 55 per cent of marriages contracted among a tribe of Baggara Arabs in the Sudan end in divorce; and Judith Djamour, using official records, found that divorce rates (the proportion of divorces to marriages in a given year) ranged from 41 to 61 per cent in Java, while the Malay state of Perli in 1952 had a rate of 92.7 per cent and most of Malaya over 50 per cent, that for Malays in Singapore being 55.7 per cent in 1949' (Mair, 1971: 191). Yet there are many Muslim societies in which men do not avail themselves of the opportunities that Islam gives them. 'For some, to be placed in a situation where one has to divorce a wife is an occasion of great shame. Among the Pathans in Swat it would be assumed that the wife had been unfaithful with a man whom the husband did not dare to challenge. To divorce a wife over whom one is supposed to have absolute authority is . . . to admit defeat' (Mair, 1971: 195). Of the Bakhtiari of Iran an instance is recorded in which homicide was preferred to divorce. A woman whose husband persistently ill-treated her begged her father to let her divorce him. The father preferred to kill the husband.

3. Leila Ahmed elaborates on this dimension in detail: '. . . some Qur'anic verses regarding marriage and women appear to qualify and undercut others that seemingly establish marriage as a hierarchical institution unequivocally privileging men. Among the former are the verses that read: "Wives have rights corresponding to those which husbands have, inequitable reciprocity"' (Surat: 229). Similarly, verses such as those that admonish men, if polygamous, to treat their wives equally and that go on to declare that husbands would not be able to do so—using a form of Arabic negative permanent impossibility—are open to being read to mean that men should not be polygamous. In the same way, verses sanctioning divorce go on to condemn it as 'abhorrent to God' (1992: 63).
4. cf. Leila Ahmed: '. . . throughout history it has not been those who have emphasized the ethical and spiritual dimensions of the religion who have held power. The political, religious, and legal authorities in the Abbasid period in particular whose interpretative and legal legacy defined Islam ever since heard only the androcentric verses of Islam, and they interpreted the religion as intending to institute . . . androcentric vision in all Muslim societies throughout the time' (1992: 67). Elaborating on the same theme,

she goes on to add: 'Some dissenting sects understood Islam's ethical teachings to be the fundamentals of its message and regarded Muhammad's practices and regulations he put into effect as relevant primarily to their immediate social context and thus as not necessarily binding (as orthodoxy considered them to be) on Muslim societies at all times in all places. Orthodox Islam, on the contrary, gave paramountcy . . . to the practices and regulations Islam had enunciated, paying little heed . . . regarding women to the religion's ethical teachings, particularly its emphasis on the spiritual equality of women and men and its injunctions to treat women fairly. As a result, the religion's emphasis on equality and the equal justice to which women were entitled has left little trace . . .' (1992: 88).

5. Until Prophet Muhammad was alive, he could be readily consulted and the issues of interpretation settled. 'But after his death, that living authority was no longer available and had to be transformed into a doctrine of Infallibility. This means that whatever decisions or pronouncements of the Prophet were authoritative during his life time became infallible after his death' (Rahman, 1979: 125-6). Thus, the *sunna* (the doings and sayings of the Prophet) became the second source of the *shar'ia.* Thus arose the need to determine what practices and precepts of the Prophet were truly authoritative. To further complicate matters, the *sunna* later came to include the precedents of the first four Caliphs (Rahman, 1979: 70). When followers of the faith began reporting doings and sayings of the Prophet, there arose another problem, that of sorting out the genuine hadiths from the false ones. If any hadith went contrary to the Qur'an, it could easily be rejected. In case where this principle could not be applied, the genuineness of the said hadith was established on the basis of *ijma,* consensus of the ulema, the learned and the accepted teachers among the believers.
6. The role of interpretation in the preservation and inscription of the Qur'an is, however, suppressed in orthodox doctrine and the belief that the text is precisely as Muhammad recited it is itself a tenet of orthodox faith (see Ahmed, 1992: 94).
7. Civilized opinion has been veering around to the point that a system of divorce should not be such as to make marriage itself into an oppressive bond. Nor should it make divorce so easy that one can get out of the marriage bond with ease. It should make it possible for marriage stability to subsist, but at the same time it should provide for dissolution of a marriage where spouses legitimately feel that they cannot live together for whatever reasons. In other words, the system of divorce should not be such as to allow for a free interplay of caprice and flimsiness. For instance, the jurisprudence that the Supreme Court in India has been evolving is that legitimate divorce should be easily allowed, but capricious and flimsy divorce should be discouraged. It is against this kind of evolving jurisprudence that the conception of Muslim divorce should be formulated.

Unless this is done, there is danger that the system of divorce may render a divorce extremely difficult and complicated so much so that it may turn out to be oppressive for even those genuine cases where dissolution of marriage may seem to be the only way out for the spouses to exist in mutual social and mental health and harmony.

8. I am grateful to Zarina Bhatty for suggesting this point. I should also like to thank Irfan Ahmad, Syed Zainuddin and Shahjahan Madampat for useful comments.
9. Contrary to popular perceptions, reinforced by the common belief that Muslim law is derived from the Qur'an and must be the same for all Muslims, there is a great deal of legal pluralism among Muslims on this count. For instance, the different schools of law and theology take highly divergent views of the validity of this procedure. Those following the Hanafi and Shafei legal schools and some sub-sects among the Shias uphold this procedure to be divinely sanctioned and therefore a part and parcel of the *shar'iat* (the canonical law of Islam). They would, therefore, brood no change in it. On the other hand, those following other theological and legal persuasions—such as the Shia and Ahl-e-Hadis, for example—reject this procedure altogether and deny the validity accorded to it by other theological and legal schools.
10. Joseph Schacht has argued that the classical theory of *shar'ia* law was the outcome of a complex historical process spanning a period of nearly three centuries (1964).
11. Cf. Coulson: 'for the administration of Shari'a family law classical Muslim tradition recognized one judicial organ only: the court of a single *qadi*. No hierarchy of Shari'a courts existed and no system of appeal as such, although dissatisfied litigants could always seek the intervention of the political authority through his *Mazalim* jurisdiction' (1964: 163).
12. Coulson elaborates this second element: 'No real unifying influence was exerted by the central government and there was no hierarchy of superior courts whose binding precedents might have established the uniformity of a case law system. Nor can it be said that the Qur'anic laws provided a strong unifying element. Apart from their limited scope, whether or not the Qur'anic norms were applied at all depended upon the degree of knowledge and piety possessed by the individual judge. But even for the pious *qadis* the interpretations of the Qur'anic provisions was largely a matter of personal discretion, so that, apart from the simple and basic rules, their application often added to rather than subtracted from the prevailing diversity in legal practice' (1964: 30-1).
13. Cf. Coulson: 'A widow, for example, was given a privileged position in regard to her claim for unpaid dower against her deceased husband's estate . . .' (1964: 165).
14. Two possible courses are open to those trying to bring about reforms in

traditional societies where the conceptions of good life have an intrinsic integrity of their own and are contemporaneously at variance with liberal-democratic values. One is to try to graft liberal-democratic values on to the tradition. The other is to take the tradition as an integral whole and to work towards enlarging the traditional conception of good life to subserve contemporary ends. If the first course is adopted, one is forced to take an outsider position vis-a-vis the tradition and is likely to end up fighting the battle for reform on a hostile terrain. If the second course is followed, one has the advantage of struggling for reform from within the tradition and the terrain is neither altogether hostile nor entirely foreign. The protagonists of reform must have a clear conception both of the modality for reform and the terrain over which they would like to fight.

15. Conflict over what constitutes the original message and who has the right to determine it is endemic to most religions and Islam is no exception. Through a long historical process the ulema succeeded in abrogating this right to them though the situation in this respect should have varied between Shia and Sunni `Islạm. In Shia Islam the mujtahid is the representative of God until such time that the mahdi reappears on the earth. This gives the Shia mujtahid the status of interpreter and guardian of the faith. This is not true of Sunni Islam where Allah, having revealed his faith, left the individual believer to understand and interpret it and act as its guardian. As such, the wholesale metamorphosis of the original message brought about by the Muslim establishment, which is shared widely by common Muslims, has no basis in Sunni theology.

16. Elizabeth Bott (1957) and Nicky Hart (1967) raise certain substantive questions with respect to an appropriate method for the study of divorce. Essentially, the point that needs to be noted is that rates or frequency of divorce are difficult to arrive at unless one's data are drawn from community studies. Unless such studies become available, and they are not at present with reference to any group, whether Muslim or non-Muslim, any projections about frequency of divorce in Muslim communities remain in the realm of estimates or hearsay. Therefore, when it is asserted that divorce rates tend to be high among Muslim communities in India because divorce procedure is easy and simple, such assertions need to be seriously examined. Evidence adduced in the contributions suggests that frequency of divorce is not particularly high in the communities on which we have data. Khan finds only 20 cases of divorce and separation in a sample of 200. Equally, others (notably Rafat, Moinuddin and Waheed) estimate far lower frequency of divorce in the communities they have studied than popular assertions on this count will suggest. It is rather curious that those who have relied upon case study method for the collection of information do implicitly suggest that women are prone to be divorced but make no projections as to the frequency of divorce in the

communities studied. One is led to wonder if it is not actually the case that, since they focused on specific divorced women, they allowed themselves to be persuaded into believing that divorces are frequent and that these divorces are quite often arbitrary.

17. My point here is not that the case study method is in itself deficient for the exploration of divorce. Given the highly personal nature of the divorce experience, case study can be an extremely useful instrument for the exploration of that experience and how spouses view it. My point is about the manner in which the case study method is used and what kinds of issues or dimensions are sought to be explored in the course of the interviews. If the interviews are not in-depth and if they do not call into question some of the facile or damaging statements that the spouses may chose to make about one another, the usefulness of this method is considerably reduced. Except for Mistry, Dasgupta, and Saheb, most contributors who used the case study method fail to give evidence that they explored the cases far enough to dig up sufficiently rich information.
18. Hussain documents the existence of Imarat-e-Shar'ia which settles matrimonial matters. Saheb shows that the marital disputes of members of Muslim castes organized into caste jamats are settled through the functionaries of the caste jamat or the prayer leaders of the mosques established by the caste jamat. Moinuddin shows that the qazi or the moulvi is not called upon to preside over the pronouncement of divorce, but divorce takes place in the presence of the village elders. Again, Rasheed shows that relatives are involved wherever a case of marital breakdown takes place. Vatuk, Nishat and Saheb note that there are officially designated qazis who not only perform and record marriages but also supervise divorce proceedings. Nishat points out that this system of officially designated qazis has existed from fairly early times and, if anything, their prominence and role has weakened over the years.
19. It is obvious to anyone familiar with the Indian cultural ethos that men and women are both subject to institutionalized pressures that sanction the married state as normative for adults. These pressures are partly religious and social in origin and are reflected in the set of stereotypes with which individuals are bombarded in their everyday socialization. They also emanate from the organization of adult life around couples and from the preponderance of couples which, as Hart has argued in the context of England, 'makes conjugality a *sine qua non* of "status integration"' (1967: 42). This pressure is also economic, deriving in part from the prevalent division of labour wherein the man is perceived as the breadwinner and the wife as the homemaker and mother of children. Of course, this institutionalized pressure is far greater on women who are

economically dependent on men and do not generally develop skills that carry high material rewards. It is only within marriage that they can hope to enjoy status and a reasonable standard of living and practice the role for which they have been socialized. Unless one argues that Muslims are immune to this institutionalized pressure, which would be far-fetched, it would seem that this pressure is common to all Indian men and women.

20. Hart (1964: 57-8) identifies two opposed models of married life—one stressing the common identity of spouses and the other which sees marriage as a product of bargains between two negotiating individuals with unequal resources and opposed interests. 'It is surely preferable', writes Hart, 'to conceive of conjugal relationships as the product of a dialectic between the shared "we" and the independent "I", a dialectic that is dynamic and that may at any time be resolved, temporarily or permanently, in favour of consensus or conflict. The nature of marriage, when viewed from this perspective, becomes a matter for empirical determination rather than one of *a priori* theoretical assumption' (1964: 57).
21. Almost all the contributors (notably Rasheed, Rafat, Mistry and Bano), give detailed accounts of such bickerings. It is to be noted that conflicts arising out of such bickerings take divergent forms and are handled differently by different families. Bano notes, 'when it becomes clear that the differences and conflicts . . . are irresolvable or one of the spouses is indifferent to or unwilling to recognize and negotiate those conflicts and differences that the precipitate step of pronouncing divorce or walking out of the matrimonial home in the hope of taking divorce later on is taken by the aggrieved spouse. There are strong individual differences and some spouses reach the threshold of their patience and tolerance sooner than others. Nonetheless, divorce comes about only after that threshold has been reached' (p. 223).
22. One of the points conclusively established by social research on Muslims in India is the continuing influence of Indian cultural ethos in the life of Indian Muslims. Even though every Muslim in India (and this holds true for Muslims everywhere) claims adherence to the Qur'an (and therefore to the Islamic *shari'a*), the truth is that on many aspects his attitudes and behaviour deviate from textual religious values and norms because of the continuing hold of cultural orientations and practices that enjoy legitimacy in the Indian environment.
23. Childlessness may be a function of the physical or biological deficiency of either partner, but curiously enough in Indian society it is always the wife who is blamed for failure to produce a child. It is only after he fails to have a child even from a second or third wife that people are willing to recognize that the deficiency might actually lie with him and not with his

first wife. By that time it is in any case too late for him to make amends. There are in the reported case studies the case of a husband having gone back to his first wife when his second also failed to produce children. Mistry reports the case of Kaleemun, whom her husband married after divorcing his first wife, who failed to produce children. After Kaleemun conceived and delivered a child, he brought his first wife back and had children also from her. Such are often the vagaries of marital life.

24. Rafat and Moinuddin adduce convincing evidence of this. Moinuddin finally comes up with the plea that any talk of ameliorating the situation of divorced women is meaningless unless steps are taken to attack the grinding poverty in which the majority of respondents whom he studied eke out their daily existence. Cross-cultural evidence also shows a strong positive correlation between marital breakdown and income levels (see Phillips, 1991: 109-10 and 249-50; Hart, 1978: 144; Gibson, 1974: 86; Snell, 1985; Hufton, 1974). This finding directly challenges the argument of those who are inclined to project a higher frequency of divorce in Muslim communities in India on the basis of the ease of divorce procedure. In terms of their projection, frequency of divorce should be high across the different social and economic strata of Muslims. But that is not what the evidence adduced by the contributors suggests. What it suggests is that the family economy, in which the large majority of Muslims participate, does not pose a serious barrier to separation and divorce.
25. Several contributors (notably Rafat, Nishat, Dasgupta and Hussain) refer to the pathetic state of the divorced woman, probably in a bid to support the case for a more stringent law that would restrict easy divorce.
26. One can easily predict that those couples who experience a higher level of interdependence find the costs of marital breakdown particularly high and are not able to manage a new life for themselves. Men and women who come to rely on their marriage partner to a degree which is not reciprocated find it extremely difficult to lead an independent existence outside the framework of marriage (see Hart, 1976: 56).
27. Cf. Hart: 'The situation of divorcee is in many ways comparable with widowhood, particularly when the person concerned is a mother with young children. The immediate period after death/separation is for both a time of loneliness, emotional stress, and economic anxiety. But at least in the short term this is where the analogy ends, for the widow's access to sympathetic support . . . places her in a much more favourable position than her divorcee counterpart' (1976: 137).
28. It is commonplace in discussions on divorce in Muslim communities in India to implicitly make a comparison with Hindu women. This has the effect of setting Muslim women apart and creating the belief and

impression that the problems Muslim women face are unique and distinct. This cannot be presumed. It has to be demonstrated empirically. Religous values and laws relating to Hindu and Muslim women are divergent and contrasting. Textual Hindu values relating to women are far more gender discriminatory than textual Islamic values. Nonetheless, whether these differences of textual values and legal privileges make for actual differences in the social standing of Hindu and Muslim women within marriage and family is open to serious question. Jeffery demonstrates that there are strong similarities between them.

29. There is no study detailing the effects of these factors in the Indian context. However, a study by Lenore Weitzman in the US seems to confirm this picture (see Weitzman, 1985).

30. At present, the protagonists of reform are divided along a series of different lines. Some are likely to be satisfied if a marriage contract is designed so that a Muslim wife cannot be sumarrily dismissed. Others demand abrogation of the legal provision for easy divorce which, according to them, is a cause of real misery for Muslim women. Still others want that a system of registration of Muslim marriages is adopted or a uniform law of marriage and divorce is enacted so that all women are entitled to the same privileges and rights without any discrimination on the ground of religion and culture. These differences of opinion seem, in my view, to emanate from a lack of knowledge of the real sources of hardships for Muslim women in the event of divorce and the conception one carries of marriage stability as a value in itself. Such differences of viewpoints and strategies are likely to confuse the nature of the precise reforms that appear called for to deal with ground realities.

31. One obvious legal implication of imposing a simple ban on the practice of triple divorce would be that the power to pass judgement on the viability of a conjugal relationship would pass on to some external authority, be it the divorce court judge or an institution that might be created within the framework of the community (which I would not feel very comfortable with at any rate, because the patriarchal ethos widely prevalent in the community would then have a backdoor to enter and act to the detriment of women). Since the use of the triple divorce procedure is widespread among Muslim men of lower social strata, chances are that they would simply desert their wives to fend for themselves or bring in a case if they want the marital relationship to be formally terminated. Or, if they decide to move the authority empowered to dissolve a marriage, their wives would be obliged to spend on litigation required to contest the husband's intention where the outcome is in any case uncertain. This will bring in elements of adversarial procedure into the divorce process and will make it less dignified and more punitive.

32. This comes out clearly from the large number of cases that Muslim women are beginning to bring to the courts. They are not asking for their divorce to be annulled so that they are taken back by their husbands. Nor are they necessarily arguing that the Muslim practice of triple divorce should be abolished. At best, where that issue has been agitated at all, the argument has been that triple divorce has to adhere to a formally prescribed procedure under which the husband must pronounce divorce on three different occasions, separated each time by a month, after a representative, each of the wife and the husband, has concluded that the couple cannot live together (this is brought out forcefully by Fatima Rashid's case in Dasgupta). What they are, instead, asking is that, if their husbands choose to divorce them, they should at least have the assurance that they can subsist at the level of poverty which their married life provided. In other words, the husband should be liable to pay their dower and provide them maintenance. If the protagonists of reform in Muslim divorce law settle for a ban on the practice of triple divorce, the agenda that most of the women who are seeking rights of sheer economic survival through the courts, and many more who would like to, but are prevented from doing so by the high costs of litigation, would die a natural death.

REFERENCES

Ahmed, Leila (1992), *Women and Gender in Islam: Historical Roots of a Modern Debate*, New Haven and London, Yale University Press.

Bott, Elizabeth (1957), *Family and Networks*, London, Tavistock Publications.

Coulson, Noel J. (1964), *A History of Islamic Law*, Edinburgh, Edinburgh University Press.

______ (1969), *Conflicts and Tensions in Islamic Jurisprudence*, Chicago, Chicago University Press.

Gibson, C. (1974), 'The association between Divorce and Social Class in England and Wales', *British Journal of Sociology*, vol. 25, no. 3, pp. 79-98.

Hart, Nicky (1976), *When Marriage Ends: A Study in Status Passage*, London, Tavistock Publications.

Hufton, Olwen (1974), *The Poor of Eighteenth-Century France, 1750-1789*, Oxford, Oxford University Press.

Mair, Lucy (1971), *Marriage*, London, Pelican Books.

Phillips, Rodeerick (1991), *Untying the Knot: A Short History of Divorce*, Cambridge, Cambridge University Press.

Rahman, Fazlur (1979), *Islam*, London, Hutchinson and Nicholson.

Schacht, Joseph (1964), *An Introduction to Islamic Law*, London, Clarendon Press.

Snell, K.D.M. (1985), *Annals of the Labouring Poor*, Cambridge, Cambridge University Press.

Weitzman, Lenore (1985), *The Divorce Revolution: The Unexpected Social and Economic Consequences for Women and Children in America*, New York, John Wiley.

1

Between Two Worlds: Divorce among Asamiya Muslims of Guwahati

Anindita Dasgupta

> At the women's conference in Beijing, a delegate from one of the Middle East countries came up to me, pointed at my slightly exposed midriff and angrily asked, 'What is this you are wearing? Are you not a Muslim?'
> 'I am wearing a *mekhela-sador*, the traditional attire of my state', I replied.
> She did not look convinced. Then I tried to explain to her that I was first an Asamiya and only then a Muslim.
> I still remember her walking away in a great huff.
>
> DR. MAHFUZA RAHMAN,
> Asamiya Muslim Academician and Activist

A Muslim woman? Very simple, say the masters of simple definitions. She is a demure, purdah-clad, faceless creature with a dozen children, a likely second or third wife of a licentious man, living in a small, cluttered house in some narrow, crowded lane behind the Jama Masjid in perennial fear of divorce. The words 'Muslim woman' continue to conjure up myriad of images ranging from the stereotyped '*tawaif*-with-a-golden-heart' popularized by Hindi films like *Pakeeza*, *Muqaddar ka Sikandar* and *Umrao Jaan Ada*, to the old, frail and emaciated Shah Bano, to the sombre image of the modern and educated Niloufer, a victim of triple *talaq* in the film *Nikaah*. In part because of the way in which the sociological agenda has been constructed, and in part because the sociologist's craft has never been particularly comfortable with matters such as Muslims in general and women in particular, the popular stereotypes of Muslim women in India have been drawn up almost entirely by investigative journalists and Hindi film-makers.

When at all one chances upon a treatise on Muslim women, one finds that 'the poor reader who only wanted to learn a few things about Muslim women in India ends up knowing much more, about the Arab world, not of today but of 1400 years ago' (Haniff, 1983: 186). This calls for serious reflection on what might be the best approach to the study of Muslim women in India. But critical reflection is precisely the response that is missing when academics and writers all over the world rush to take control over her so-called destiny. Fortunately, in recent years, researchers have been trying to shake off the fixed notion of 'essence' and humbly accept 'differences' both vertical and horizontal.

If one goes beyond stereotypes, at once a barrage of questions comes to mind: Is there something religiously ordained about the condition of Muslim women in India and elsewhere? Is the condition of the Muslim woman unfavourable because she is a Muslim, or is it because she is a woman? Are the discriminations or privileges she experiences rooted in religion or the society she lives in? This paper is not about the status of women in Islam but about women living in a community the members of which happen to be Muslims. It is an attempt to examine the response of the Asamiya Muslim women to pressures of divorce and remarriage in the comparatively urban set-up of Guwahati city, the capital of the north-eastern state of Assam.

Given the general neglect of Muslims in sociology, the historiographical neglect of the frontier state of Assam and the methodological neglect of women in the social sciences as a whole, the circumstances in which Asamiya Muslim women live are virtually unknown to the academic universe. Consequently, they continue to be either 'muted' in the social sciences or tagged with popular and filmi stereotypes. But India is a country where one group of Muslims does not follow what another lot does and that is the rationale behind this study.

METHODOLOGY

Keeping in view the subject under study, the methodology followed is primarily qualitative. This is a non-mathematical analytic procedure whose findings are derived from data gathered by a variety of means that include observations and interviews, but might also include documents, books, videotapes, and even data that have been quantified for other purposes such as census data (Strauss and Corbin, 1990: 18). Rather than providing quantitative information on divorce among Asamiya Muslims, this study looks into the human dimensions of the problem using the qualitative method. Again, as ours is a historical approach, we have studied persons and events by situating them in time and space.

The instruments of data collection were interviews, structured questionnaires, dialogues and participant observation. A large part of the data was gathered from 40 divorced women with a similar economic background, in the city of Guwahati, and some key informants whose evidence is presented as case-studies. All of the respondents had been living in Guwahati for generations and were in the age-group of 25-45. Some of them lived in the so-called 'old Muslim localities' of the city like Lakhtokia, Kumarpara, Tokobari, Hidayatpur and Gharigaon while others in the newly settled posh residential areas like Kharguli Hillside and Zoo Road.

Because of the small number of respondents, it was possible to use a variety of methods to get information. In some cases where the women were not very cooperative, only interviews were taken. In other cases, structured questionnaires were given to them in addition. Floppy discs were supplied to the computer-friendly. The more cooperative respondents were interviewed over 4 to 5 days at a stretch. In the case of Zeenat Fatema Rashid, a large number of newspaper-clippings were also used as sources. Interviews were also conducted with at least one family member of the respondents, wherever possible.

A random survey was also conducted among 40 other Asamiya Muslim men and women belonging to the same background, on attitudes towards divorce and re-marriage within their own community.

While this study cannot be used for warranted generalizations, it can serve to deal with certain questions that do arise in the context of discussion of divorce among the Asamiya Muslims in the Brahmaputra valley in Assam.

A FUNDAMENTAL DIFFERENCE

In striking contrast to the stereotyped notion of Islam, in Assam Islam is open, accommodative, inclusive and adaptive in its local specificity. Here Islam is strikingly different from that in north and western India, the core area of Islamic civilization in India, and the actual social practices of Asamiya Muslims may be inconsistent with the laws of any Islamic schools. This is, of course, not to say that Islam is not a force in the behaviour of Asamiya Muslims but that these societies are influenced and shaped largely by local and environmental factors foreign to any other part of the country.

> Unlike the Muslims of north Indian states, who are deeply involved in the problems related to the status of the Aligarh Muslim University and the status of the Urdu language or even the Babri Masjid-Ram Janambhumi tangle, by and large, do not affect the Muslims . . . (of Assam) . . . psychologically. This signifies their level of integration with the regional society (Hussain, 1993: 225).

Asamiya Muslims can, at best, be described as non-practicing Muslims. Their religious faith is dotted with several features peculiar to the region as a whole. They are not archetypal Urdu-speaking, orthodox Muslims. Most do not read the *namaz* five times a day. What is extremely significant is that there is no overt or covert form of purdah practiced by the women who are resplendent in their *muga* or *pat mekhela-sador*, the traditional attire of the women of the valley. Local practices like touching the feet of elders, greeting one another with a *namaskar* (and not an *adaab*) like the Hindus in whose midst they have lived for centuries, have become a part of the Muslim societies of Assam. In this sense, they are misfits in the broader Muslim society elsewhere. And significantly, unlike Muslims in many other parts of the country, they form an inseparable part of the evolving Asamiya nationality in the Brahmaputra valley in Assam.[1]

Urdu and Persian names sit uncomfortably on the Asamiya Muslims of Assam; most of them do not even understand meanings. In the villages and towns of Upper Assam it is not uncommon to come across Muslim women with names like Meera, Golapi (rose), Jonaki (glow-worm), Rupahi (beautiful) and the like[2] while Muslim men often take names like Mukuta (pearl), Sonai (gold), and Rupai (silver) (Saikia, 1967: 244-5). In the Nagaon district of Assam, Asamiya Muslims are said to have even joined the Hindus in the cattle-bathing ceremony which marks the beginning of *Bihu*, the spring festival of dance and music in Assam (Saikia, 1967: 248). Again, since a large number of Asamiya Muslims were, in later years, mostly converts, many continued to retain their Hindu names. For example, one of our Muslim respondents said that going through his property records he had discovered that the name of his great grandfather was Haji Soneswar Baruah which indicated that even after returning from the *haj* some Muslims continued using their Hindu names. Certain *Bihu* songs also refer to the skills of Asamiya Muslims in playing musical instruments and show that they participated in the group dances and made music along with Asamiya Hindus. Again, both the communities offer the *tambul* (a betel-nut preparation) as the first article of reception to their guests.

Asamiya Muslims, for all practical purposes, are Asamiyas first, and Muslims afterwards. They share a lot more in common with the Asamiya Hindus, from names, food habits, clothes, lifestyle to language and culture, than with the Muslims of Uttar Pradesh or Lucknow. *Biryani* and *sevai* are delicacies saved for festive occasions and the Asamiya Muslim lives on a regular diet of *masor-tenga* (river-fish in a light, sour gravy), *dali* (lentils) and *doi* (curds)—a light, low-spice diet suited to the climatic conditions of the Brahmaputra valley.

Also, what makes Asamiya Muslims strikingly different is the fact that they are an educated, upper-middle class, propertied and pedigreed community of Assam. It will not be an exaggeration to say that the rate of literacy here might be the highest among the Muslim communities of India. The professions commonly followed by them are teaching, medicine, engineering, civil services, academics, politics and the like.

Most Asamiya Muslims belong to aristocratic families of the pre-colonial era located in the Upper Assam districts of Dibrugarh, Sibsagar, Jorhat, Golaghat and Lakhimpur from where they, in time, migrated all over the region and outside. Generally, they are tall, fair-complexioned and with a hint of Mongolian features which can be explained in terms of inter-marriage with the Ahoms of Upper Assam. What is significant is the claim of Upper Assam Muslims that Muslims of Lower Assam are less respectable (except those of Goalpara) because of their divergence from the urbanite ideal of educated, cultured Muslims.[3] The claim to higher status of the Muslims of Upper Assam is based upon secular and religious titles denoting descent from 'foreign' settlers who migrated from the West and found employment as officials, scholars, religious functionaries, etc., and received land-grants in the countryside.

Contrary to popular opinion, they are more Westernized than Islamized. The proximity to the Upper Assam tea gardens and the legacy of the Raj brought several Western customs into this community. For example, playing golf, going to the club or cutting a layered wedding cake and throwing cocktail parties at a *nikah* or Muslim marriage party are a regular part of the Asamiya Muslim culture of Upper Assam now.[4] In its local specificity, then, Asamiya Muslim societies contrast sharply with the stereotyped notion of Islamic societies nurtured by the 'essentialist discourse'. Various differences can be seen fairly clearly in the field of everyday life of the Asamiya Muslims.

THE ORIGIN

Muslims have a history of more than seven centuries in Assam which has the second largest concentration of Muslims in India after Kashmir. The Census of 1991 puts the figure at 28.43 per cent of the total population of the state or a total number of 63,73,204 persons with a percentage increase during 1971-91 of +77.42. While in the north the Muslims (to use a 'homogenizing' term) arrived as conquerors or as a part of the ruling class and in the south as traders, Muslims came to Assam as internal migrants or prisoners of wars from the neighbouring provinces, especially undivided Bengal, from the thirteenth century. Almost all of them were Sunnis.

Hussain has divided the Muslims of Assam into four separate groups: Asamiya Muslims, also known as *Thalua Musalmans* or *Goriyas*; Bengali Muslims of the Barak valley in Cachar district; the *Na-Asamiya* or Muslims of East Bengal origin now considerably 'Asamiyaized'[5] and living in the Brahmaputra valley, and finally, north Indian Muslims living in Assam. In this study we confine ourselves only to the first group or Asamiya Muslims who constitute a very small community in the Brahmaputra valley.

The systematic propagation of Islam as a religion started only in the early part of the seventeenth century. This was largely the work of a Muslim mystic Shah Milan, popularly known as Azan Fakir, who came to Assam in about 1630 (see Hussain, 1993). It was Shah Milan who brought about the synthesis between Islam and popular

Asamiya culture and made this religion acceptable to many in the region.

When Shah Milan and his brother Nabi made Chunpora in Upper Assam their home, they found that the original Muslims living around Garhgaon and surrounding areas, had become far removed from the original principles and practices of their own faith. They were given more to local habits and customs as practiced by the non-Muslim population of the region. Shah Milan was quite dismayed to learn that local songs and dances were more popular than the usual prayer (*namaz*) (Malik, 1990: 7). This is echoed in the accounts of Shahabuddin Talish, the chronicler accompanying the Mughal General Mir Jumla, who led the siege of Assam in 1662-3. He wrote: 'As for the Muslims who had been taken prisoner in former times and had chosen to marry here, their descendants act exactly in the manner of the Assamese and had nothing of Islam except the name' (quoted in Malik, 1990: 7).

Shah Milan then started his mission of preaching the pure and unadulterated tenets of Islam in Upper Assam. With a handful of followers and disciples he built a mosque at Chunpora from where he gave the call to the followers of the Islamic faith to gather at the mosque to perform *namaz* five times a day (Malik, 1990: 7). It was because of this, it is said, that Shah Milan came to be known as Azan Fakir in Assam.

Azan Fakir composed many simple and colloquial songs full of local colour that are still cherished by all sections of people in Assam, particularly village-folk. These songs known as *Jikirs* were sung to the accompaniment of various musical instruments and dance, and introduced the Muslims of Assam to the contents of the Qur'an, the Hadith and other Islamic literature with which they were scantily acquainted. It is interesting that Azan Fakir did not forbid dancing as a part of the singing of devotional songs: 'The Muslims of those days, most of whom were converts from other religions, were used to dancing along with singing of songs, whatever the contents might be . . . the *Jikir* songs would lose much of their attraction and rhythmic tempo if dance were prohibited' (Malik, 1990: 16).

Jikirs occupy an important position in Asamiya folk culture. Bearing messages related to the Islamic way of life, their appeal was primarily humanitarian and secular.

> (F)rom all considerations (the *Jikirs*) were Assamese and nothing but Assamese. Even the Arabic, Persian and Urdu words that had to be used in the compositions, since no adequate and suitable words were available to convey the full sense of these words, were so used that they would appear to be familiar words of the Assamese vocabulary (Malik, 1990: 23).

This unique way of propagation suited the local conditions and helped in spreading Islam among the masses. This was further helped by the fact that brahmanical Hinduism had not yet grown too strong in this region and society continued to be multi-religious. This considerably cushioned the opposition to the forces of Islamization.

The chief objective of the *Jikirs* appears to be to reorganize Asamiya Muslims by regenerating their faith and love for Islam in such a way that there would be no discord in their age-old harmonious relations with their Hindu neighbours (Saikia, 1967: 266). Referring to the relations between the two faiths, the *Jikirs* declare:

> *Mor monot aan bhaab nai, O Allah*
> *Hindu, Mussalman, ek allar farmaan,*
> *Hinduk puriba, Musalmanak putiba*
> *Eke khani jaminor tolot.*

> (I do not make any distinction between Hindus and Muslims, O Allah . . . when dead, a Hindu will be cremated on fire and a Muslim will be buried under the same earth. . . .)

and,

> *santa, mahanta, awliya sakale eketi namote khate . . .*

> (The *sants* and *mahants*, that is, Hindu holy men, and *awliyas* all supplicate to one name, the name of God).

And again,

> *Sari Vede giyanake koi, Allah . . .*

> (The four Vedas also speak out knowledge, O Allah).[6]

Early Ahom rulers appointed only persons of their own stock to all the high posts from and above that of the Phukans, but from the time of King Jayadhwaj Sinha (1648-53) we find Muslims being promoted to high posts. The influence of Islam can further be gleaned from the fact that Queen Pramatheswari, in 1729, was the first to issue coins in the Persian script. It is said that the knowledge of gunpowder and the use of paper instead of agar wood bark, came from the Muslims.

Thus, in the pre-colonial phase of migration, the Muslims from the rest of India settled down in Assam and became naturalized citizens. Moreover, as most of them were prisoners of wars, they married local women which hastened the process of Assamization. A congenial social climate, royal patronage and the hospitality of the local people helped these new settlers to give up their separate identity and merge with the indigenous population. 'Influence of women-folk on the men, particularly in matters of social customs, rites and rituals, beliefs and prejudices, did not lead to conflicts in personal life, so long as they did not violate the basic tenets of Islam as professed by the men-folk' (Malik, 1990: 3).

Malik writes that there was no question of seeking or finding a Muslim bride.

> Any able woman was considered a fit wife irrespective of her caste, creed or the religion. It is not difficult to presume that those local women who had been taken as wives by the Muslim settlers, got converted to Islam. As against this process of conversion, the husbands had to adopt the language of their wives, that is, the Assamese language (Malik, 1990: 3).

Thus, a 'new' society with Islam as the religion and Asamiya as the means of communication began to emerge. This process of Asamiyaization was peaceful and almost unnoticed. More so, because in the pre-colonial years, the flow of migrants into Assam was very small and it was easy and natural for the few migrants who made their ways into the forests of Assam to mould themselves to the new environment.

Thus, what Shahabuddin Talish found to be a ground for reproof has been one of the finest aspects of a cultural miscegenation (Saikia, 1967: 311).

MARRIAGE AMONG ASAMIYA MUSLIMS

For Asamiya Muslims, marriage is more a sacrament than a contract. On the face of it, this might sound blasphemous and in striking contrast to Haniff's dictum on stereotypes: 'It is always necessary if you are writing in the Indian context to write somewhere the following sentence—"In Islam marriage is a contract and not a sacrament"' (Haniff, 1983: 185).

Significantly, this statement does not hold true for Asamiya Muslims inasmuch as marriage for them is a personal event and some informality is attached to the proceedings. Firstly, in most cases, the *nikahnama* or the 'contract' is not signed and the *mehr* is agreed upon orally. An overwhelming 80 per cent of the respondents admitted to not having signed a *nikahnama* at the time of marriage. Secondly, only rarely is qazi called upon to preside over the *nikah* ceremony. It is usual to invite a *junab* instead who recites prayers and blesses the couple. The ceremony is completed with the traditional assent of both the bride and the groom to the marriage.

There can be two reasons for dispensing with the *nikahnama*: one, the Asamiya Muslim community is very small and families are generally known to one another; two, like most small communities, they tend to be endogamous and most marriages take place between distant cousins and relatives.

Nearly 70 per cent of the respondents agreed that a marriage was for life and the possibility of a divorce is not entertained at the time of the *nikah*. An academician of Lakhimpur descent felt it would be 'in bad taste' to insist upon a *nikahnama* as it would betray mistrust. An entrepreneur, a lawyer and a teacher, all of them women, were surprised by the question on *nikahnama*. 'Why should we sign a *nikahnama*? There is no need for it', they agreed. Writing as far back as 1976, Irshad Ali felt that the practice of signing a legal document (*nikahnama*) to solemnize a marriage is becoming obsolete among Asamiya Muslims (Ali, 1976).

The wedding ritual consists of two formal ceremonies: *magni* or *angathi pindhua* (the ring ceremony) followed by the *nikah* (the actual wedding ceremony). At the time of the *nikah*, the proposal and acceptance is made in the presence and hearing of two adult male witnesses. Another person known as the *ukil* asks the bride and the groom for their consent to the marriage. As soon as the consent is obtained, the imam or *junab* recites verses from the Qur'an. Following this the imam or *junab* leads a supplication in which all the persons present also join. In some parts of Assam the customs of presenting *joran*, the ceremonial bath or *noani* and *ath mongola*, all Asamiya

Hindu customs, are also observed. Some also fix the date of the marriage in consultation with an almanac or *panjika* and sing *bianaam* or wedding songs like the Hindus.[7]

DIVORCE AMONG ASAMIYA MUSLIMS

In a similar vein, divorce among middle class Asamiya Muslims need not follow any legal procedure. It is usually backed only by social sanction. Though in the course of our fieldwork we found 24 instances of *talaqnamas* having been signed, almost all had been signed after the divorce had been socially accepted or after the man had remarried. This is not a universal practice among Asamiya Muslims and is not a constraint so far as remarriage is concerned. Our study revealed that only in cases where the women were married to non-Asamiya Muslims, like Muslims from Hyderabad, Bhopal or Bengal, had both the *nikahnama* and the *talaqnama* been appropriately signed and the *mehr* paid up.

Significantly, Asamiya Muslims of the Brahmaputra valley generally do not practice triple *talaq* or *talaq-e-bidat* like the Muslims of the Barak valley or Na-Asamiya Muslims, also of the Brahmaputra valley. For instance, *talaq-e-sunna* is practised by only a very small segment of Muslims, like the educated moulvis, maulanas and a small section of an Islamized middle class in the Barak valley. *Talaq-e-bidat* is the most prevalent type of divorce in the valley. There is a socio-religious organization called the Nadwa-ul-Tamir established by the ex-Jamiat-ul-Ulema leader, religious scholar and politician Maulana Abdul Jalil Chowdhury of Badarpur. This organization has its branches in various parts of the Barak valley and leadership is provided mostly by the Bengali-speaking maulanas. This organization has its local branches which act as *shar'iat* courts for settling cases dealing with divorces, alimony, payment of *mehr*, etc. On the whole, the Muslims of the Barak valley are more 'Islamized' and therefore more 'purist' even in the case of divorce. Similarly, the Na-Asamiya Muslims (of East Bengal origin) of the Brahmaputra valley commonly practice *talaq-e-bidat*. Polygyny is also prevalent among them. But this is one of the poorest communities of the world and they are driven more by the dynamics of survival rather than the dictates of religion.

Educated, middle class Asamiya Muslims on the other hand,

commonly practice *talaq-e-sunna* though there is no specific or established way for carrying out a divorce. No qazi or pir sahib is called to pronounce a divorce. Witnesses, though, are essential when the husband pronounces the third divorce in case he later on denies having given *talaq* to his wife. *Mehr* is generally paid in case of divorce given by the husband. But often the husband tries to avoid the payment of the *mehr* and the bargaining power of the wife becomes considerably reduced without a *nikahnama*. In that case the divorced wife is either compelled to go to court or resort to mediation by influential persons in order to get the *mehr*. Again, Asamiya Muslims of Lower Assam usually forgo the *mehr* amount, which is meagre in comparison to Upper Assam, by the bride even before the *nikah* is solemnized. In most cases of divorce the *iddat* period is observed. The *talaqnama*, as mentioned earlier, is not essential to a divorce. It may be noted that a divorced man or a woman can remarry without having formalized the divorce with a *talaqnama*. Our respondents were agreed that an oral understanding was good enough for a divorce and that it was unlikely that a socially divorced wife would come forward to reclaim her marriage.

CAUSES FOR DIVORCE

The primary causes of divorce among the population studied were bigamy/extra-marital love affairs and mental incompatibility. These were closely followed by barrenness, health problems, maladjustment with the husband's family and, significantly, demands for dowry. There were four cases of Asamiya Muslim women divorcing non-Asamiya Muslim men due to maladjustment because of religious differences.

THE CASE OF NIKHAT

Nikhat had an arranged marriage at twenty with the only son of a rich, propertied and pedigreed Muslim family settled in Guwahati. Asad Khan, the husband, was at that time an executive with a leading export house and was earning well. Within the next few years they had two sons and as she says, 'we thought we had settled down' when the problems started.

Asad was a remarkably handsome man and was not averse to

having occasional flings with other women. Initially, Nikhat was not aware of his philandering but with time it reached her ears. But by this time Asad was deeply involved with Marina, a rich and beautiful business woman who had already divorced her first husband. In vain Nikhat tried to win back her husband, reason with him, use the children to win his pity, but Asad was adamant that he would not leave Marina. According to Nikhat, he wanted the best of both worlds—his home, children, wife as well as his lover. As she was learning to accept her fate the bomb dropped. Marina wanted to marry Asad but would not do so unless he divorced his first wife. Nikhat even agreed to let him go ahead and have a second wife but Marina would not agree to such an arrangement.

After twelve years of marriage, then, Asad divorced his wife. Marina, being a modern, educated woman, was especially concerned that a *talaqnama* be signed so that all claims could be settled once and for all. The period of *iddat* was followed, the *mehr* returned and the divorce was formalized by a qazi. In three weeks time, Marina and Asad were married. Nikhat moved out to her parents' place with her two sons. Asad did not demand custody. Nikhat completed her postgraduation through correspondence after the divorce and now teaches in an English-medium school in Guwahati.

Marina and Asad continue to be married after ten years. Asad has never visited Nikhat or her children since the day of the divorce.

THE CASE OF SHAMA SULTANA

Shama Sultana hails from the Upper Assam district of Golaghat. A postgraduate of the Bombay University, she met and fell in love with Rahil, a Bihari Muslim also at the university. There was some opposition from her family to the marriage, but things were sorted out and in May 1979, they were married. An executive with a bank, Rahil was frequently transferred and for the first ten years of their marriage they moved from one city to another. There were no children. In 1989 Rahil managed to return to his home state with a posting in Patna. Living and coping with an extended family became difficult for Shama who could neither speak Hindi well, nor was accustomed to the social practices and the customs followed by her husband's family. 'We were not brought up as Muslims *per se*', said a dejected Shama in the course of the interview, 'and suddenly I found myself in a very staunch Muslim set-up to which I could not relate'.

In an attempt to spend less time at home, she decided to work. 'The frequent references to my childlessness were becoming intolerable and sometimes I would think about coming back home', she said.

It was exactly one year later that his family decided to have him remarry. Initially, Shama did not think this would actually happen. She pleaded with her husband not to remarry but he was completely under the influence of his parents and siblings. '"I cannot even defend you since it is true that you are barren", he would tell me', said Shama.

She pressured her husband to divorce her when he brought home a second wife. 'A second wife is unthinkable for Asamiyas. Nobody has two wives back home', said Shama. 'Maybe I would have accepted it if I, too, was a Bihari Muslim like him but this was too much.'

Her husband's family insisted upon a proper *talaq* with the qazi, witnesses, immediate return of *mehr* and a *talaqnama*. 'Everything was very proper. After all they were true Muslims, not like us.'

Shama has inherited a part of her father's property which is her sole source of income. She lives in a small rented house in an old Muslim locality of Guwahati ('I know many people here' she says) and is still trying to cope with the shock.

THE CASE OF NOOR JEHAN BEGUM

At 25, Noor was married to Suleiman Ali who worked in a government department. After five years of marriage it was discovered that she was barren. Her husband immediately decided to remarry. Since then she has been living separately. The husband has remarried and is living with his second wife. He refuses to maintain Noor Jehan. She has not yet approached the court for maintenance or a decree of divorce. It involves a lot of money which she cannot afford. She is a graduate but is not employed anywhere. Her father is a small businessman and looks after her quite well as she is the only child. Noor is still traumatized and is not very forthcoming on the matter.

Noor's father confided that he was looking around for a groom for his daughter. 'If her husband can remarry why cannot she?', he asked, 'What will happen to her when we die? She has no one but us to look after her.' We asked him if the *talaqnama* was not an imperative to a second marriage. 'Not at all', he replied. 'They have divorced mutually and that is final.'

THE CASE OF MARIUM

Marium, 34, was married to Sakin Ali, a middle level officer at the State Secretariat, in 1985. In 1986 she gave birth to a baby girl following which she was bed-ridden with post-partum problems. She also had a sudden attack of jaundice which took further toll on her health. After about seven months of severe illness she was taken to her parents' place by her husband. While she was recuperating there, Sakin Ali married another woman and stopped visiting Marium. Later, on being pressured by the parents and relatives of Marium to take her back, Sakin gave her *talaq* (orally) instead, in front of three witnesses. The message was then conveyed to her by the witnesses. But the *mehr* has still not been paid.

Marium and her little daughter continue to live with her parents in Guwahati. She is an Honours graduate but her failing health does not permit her to work outside the home. Being a certificate holder in cutting and embroidery, she runs a school from home and earns about Rs. 3,000 a month. Her father is a contractor who provides for her quite well.

Her only sister Sakira is married and lives in Dibrugarh.

These are a few examples from the cases studied in the course of fieldwork. The pattern is more or less same in each case. On the basis of the data collected, the following causes for divorce can be listed:

Desertion	2
Bigamy/adultery	10
Barrenness	16
Mental incompatibility	6
Family problems	6
Demands for dowry/money	5
Maladjustment due to religion	5
Total	40

From the evidence gathered it appears that barrenness and bigamy/ adultery are the most common reasons for a divorce among Asamiya Muslims in Guwahati. In some cases, however, it is not possible to pin point a clear-cut reason for the divorce as there may be more than one factor in operation as in the case of Shama Sultana for whom cultural differences played as strong a role as her barrenness.

TWO DEVIANT CASES IN GUWAHATI

In this section we talk about two deviant cases of divorce in Guwahati. The word 'deviant' is used in different meanings for the two women discussed here. While Zeenat Fatema Rashid fought tooth and nail for seven years to attain justice for herself and her son and finally filed a case in the Supreme Court to bring about changes in Muslim divorce law, Saba Anis is a woman who rose to eminence only after her divorce from her first husband, a Hyderabadi Muslim, created a very successful business for herself, remarried and continues to be happily married. Each in her own way, thus, challenges the traditional destiny offered to the divorcee and is a striking example of the Westernized, educated, pedigreed upper middle class Asamiya Muslim woman.

THE CASE OF SABA ANIS

Saba Anis is a strikingly beautiful woman in her early forties. She is tall, fair-complexioned, wears her hair short quite in keeping with the current trend in fashion and mostly wears designer *salwaar-kameez* to work. She is very interested in interior decoration and her sprawling hill-top house overlooking the river Brahmaputra in Guwahati bears ample testimony to her designing skills. Saba Anis is also one of the most successful entrepreneurs of the city. She runs one of the most popular English medium schools in Guwahati—a business that she started after her divorce from her Hyderabadi Muslim husband Khalid, about ten years back.

Saba, the youngest of three strikingly beautiful and educated sisters belonging to a highly pedigreed family of Sibsagar, was married at the relatively late age of 28 to Khalid. There was no opposition to the marriage at all because hers was a modern and Westernized family and her brothers and cousins were already married to Asamiya and Bengali Brahmins, Christians and Muslims from other states of India. Khalid and Saba had met socially and soon fallen in love. She was not working at that time and he was an assistant manager at an Upper Assam tea garden. They had a year-long courtship and finally got married.

From the day of her marriage Saba realized that she had married into an orthodox, '*pucca pucca*' Muslim household as her mother-in-law insisted on observing all the practices and rites of the *nikah*, including a *mehr* and the *nikahnama*. 'Among Asamiya Muslims, insistence upon a *nikahnama* would have been considered as a definite sign of mistrust by the boy's family and relations soured even before the *nikah* ceremony was completed', admitted Saba. But she was even less prepared for what lay in store for her ahead.

In a nutshell, admitted Saba, the main reason for the divorce was religious differences. On the face of it this sounds strange as both practiced the same religion but, Saba hurried to explain, 'In our society we were not brought up as *pucca* Muslims like Khalid was.' And that was the principal difference between the two. For Saba being a Muslim was just another aspect of her life, for Khalid it was the most important aspect of his life.

Saba was directed to say the *namaz* five times a day, observe all the Islamic festivals with the rituals and rites intact, fast compulsorily in the month of Ramazan and observe every other practice that a 'good' Muslim was supposed to. What rankled even more than the strict, unfamiliar regimen was that she was 'ordered around' as if religion was the most important thing in life. Saba felt highly pressured by all this and found that everything happened far too fast for her liking. 'I was not given enough time to adjust myself to the new environment. What they did not realize was that I came from an entirely different background where we prayed if we wanted to, observed *roza* if we wanted to ... there were no religious compulsions.'

Saba stayed married to Khalid for two years and then she could take it no more. She decided to divorce him. She wrote to her friends and sisters back home to come over to the tea garden where she was living with her husband. And one day when her husband was out on a tour, she packed her bags and left along with her sisters and friends for Guwahati.

Her sisters asked her to stay with them but she rented a small house in Guwahati and started living by herself. She still remembers with gratitude the enormous support given to her by her friends and sisters. 'They said why don't you start a school, and they sent me their little children', says Saba with a smile. She started her school with just two little children in the little house she had rented.

Meanwhile Khalid started divorce proceedings against her. 'Like the *nikah*, everything was *pucca pucca* about the *talaq*, too', said Saba. The *mehr* was returned and a *talaqnama* signed.

A few years passed. Saba expanded her school. She had more children coming to her for classes and not just her friends' children. She appointed some other teachers and her school began to grow.

It was then that she met Tarique, a tall and handsome Asamiya Muslim through some common friends. Friendship developed into love but there was a slight problem: Tarique was married, with two children. Saba gave him some time to think over his decision which took him almost two years to make. Tarique divorced his first wife and married Saba. A *nikahnama* was not necessary; they had faith in each other.

Ten years later, Saba Anis and Tarique Alam continue to be happily married. He is working with a tea company and as for her school, it is simply a great success.

THE CASE OF ZEENAT FATEMA RASHID

A frail, petite girl with curly hair reaching up to her shoulders and large watery eyes, Zeenat, thirty-three, is a tough woman. She fought for justice for herself and her seven-year-old son Zeeshan and her demand was for a change in the Divorce Law in Islam. The case was recently decided by the Supreme Court of India which ruled that a Muslim woman was entitled under Muslim Personal Law to maintenance even after divorce. Her voice is very strong and steady, eyes unblinking as she speaks.

In 1987 Zeenat was married, at 20, to a man who claimed to be working as a Forest Officer in the Assam Forest Department. Both families were from Guwahati and the marriage was arranged by common friends. On a humid August morning, the 23-year-old Zeenat arrived at her father's house clutching her infant son discarded by her husband and his family. The saga of her legal battle was about to begin, a battle which, over the next seven years, would turn into a lonely crusade for gender equality and a challenge against the very validity of the Muslim Personal Law (Shariat) Application Act, 1937.

Keeping her nine-months old son Zeeshan Anwar with her parents, Zeenat rushed that day to lodge an FIR with the police, accusing her husband and in-laws of torturing her for dowry. A fortnight later, on 29 August 1990, Zeenat filed a case in the court of the Chief Judicial Magistrate (CJM) in Guwahati seeking a maintenance allowance from her husband.

Producing a *talaqnama* to confirm he had divorced his wife by pronouncing the triple *talaq*, her husband, who was an employee of the Assam Forest Department, defended his case in the court on the ground that a Muslim divorcee is not entitled to maintenance from her husband. Zeenet, however, stuck to her claim that she was not divorced and that the *talaqnama* her husband produced in court was false and fabricated, prepared in collusion with a local qazi and two false witnesses.

Zeenat moved the CJM's court, challenging the *talaqnama* on the ground that it was fabricated. The court on 8 February 1991, dismissed the case saying that a Muslim husband need not prove a *talaq*. Undeterred, she moved the court of the Sessions Judge who ruled that since the wife had challenged the *talaq*, it must be proved.

The husband then moved the Guwahati High Court which, however, upheld the Sessions Court's ruling that the *talaq* has to be proved since the wife had challenged it, saying she was never divorced.

By this time, the Family Court had come into being and the case got transferred there. The Family Court ruled that the husband's written statement submitted to court amounted to a valid divorce even if it was not communicated to the spouse earlier. If this was to be the end of it, Zeenat was not to get any maintenance from her husband. She quickly moved a criminal revision petition in the High Court.

Her husband, in the meantime, had remarried on 28 September 1992, and Zeenat was now forced to fight her legal battle on a new front. She accused her husband of violating the Assam Government Service Conduct Rules, 1965, and filed a case in the Munsif Court, seeking an injunction to restrain the second marriage.

Rule 26 of the Assam Civil Service Conduct Rules, 1965, says that 'No government servant who has a wife living shall contract another marriage without first obtaining the permission of the Government, notwithstanding that such subsequent marriage is permissible under the personal law for the time being applicable to him.' The Munsif Court rejected Zeenat's petition and the case related to bigamy and the case was pending at the High Court.

It was the historic ruling of the Guwahati High Court on 5 May 1993, that altered the course of the case, converting it from a legal battle involving two persons to one with the wider ramifications where the legality of the Shariat Act was questioned. The court set aside her divorce and ruled that a Muslim husband cannot divorce his wife at his whim or caprice, and that the divorce must be for a reasonable cause and must be preceded by pre-divorce counselling to arrive at a settlement.

The two-member division bench consisting of Justice R.K. Manisena and Justice S.B. Roy, who primarily dealt with the question whether there had been a divorce duly effected in the case of *Zeenat Fatema Rashid* vs. *Md. Iqbal Anwar*, went back to a judgement made by a single judge of the Guwahati High Court in 1981 in the case of *Jiauddin Ahmed* vs. *Anwara Begum* and also the case of *Rukia* vs. *Abdul Khaleque*, in late 1981, where the judge had observed that the Holy Qur'an discouraged divorce, and that it permitted divorce only in extreme cases after pre-divorce conferences. The judges referred to the Qur'an, according to which the marriage had to be maintained as far as possible and that there should be attempts at conciliation before divorce, which according to the judges, also led to the conclusion that a Muslim husband could not divorce his wife at whim.

In the case of *Zeenat Fatema Rashid* vs. *Md. Iqbal Anwar*, the question of the pre-divorce conference became vital and the failure of the husband to produce any evidence that a pre-divorce conference was held in order to arrive at a settlement was also held by the judges as a failure of the husband to prove the alleged divorce.

The judges held that the court had to be convinced with evidence also to corroborate whether a divorce was effected orally in the absence of a written *talaqnama*, thus dispelling several myths about Muslim divorce. The Guwahati judges expressed their disappointment at some of the judgements passed from time to time by the High Courts of Bombay, Allahabad and Hyderabad where the courts had concluded that if divorce pleaded was not proved, then a statement in the written form itself operated as an expression or declaration of divorce. The judges held that any written statement regarding a divorce was simply a 'pleading'. A pleading, they stated, is a formal allegation by the parties of their respective claims and defense to provide notice of what is to be expected at trial, while proof is establishment of a fact by evidence or matters before the court or legal tribunal.

Zeenat's husband, as expected, moved the Supreme Court seeking a revision of the High Court's order. The Supreme Court granted special leave petition of the husband as an appeal but did not stay the High Court judgement. Zeenat's case was getting stronger every day.

Finally, she took the unprecedented step on 16 December 1994 of filing a writ petition in the Supreme Court for enforcement of her fundamental rights while challenging the validity of the Shariat Act, 1937, under the Constitution. She named the Union of India, the Assam Government and her husband as respondents.

On 9 January 1995 Justices R.M. Sahai and N.P. Singh referred this case to the Constitution Bench of the Supreme Court. A bench of at least five Supreme Court judges must now decide whether the Muslim Personal Law (Shariat) Application Act, 1937, was valid under the Constitution of India. Decisions had to be taken on whether the Muslim men's right to oral divorce, marrying a second time while the out-of-court proceedings were pending and their continuance in government service after such a marriage were legal.

Zeenat, who holds bachelor's degrees in science, education and law, has been teaching at a Kendriya Vidyalaya in Guwahati since 1991. The eldest of Abdur Rashid's three children, Zeenat questions the provisions of the Shariat Act in terms of which Muslim women were subjected to a civil court for getting divorce whereas the Muslim men could secure a divorce at will simply by pronouncing the triple *talaq*. She cited the Muslim Family Ordinance passed by the Ayub Khan government in Pakistan in 1961 which struck off the concept of triple *talaq*, stating that divorce cannot be given arbitrarily but has to be registered with the court.

Three years later, Zeenat is still awaiting a judgement.

AN OVERVIEW

In spite of Islam being open, accommodative and elastic in Assam, women continue to be divorced quite easily and even against their own wishes. Five cases, including that of Saba Anis, were the only instances where we found the initiative for divorce had come from the side of the women. In all the other cases, that is, 87 per cent of the respondents, had been divorced against their wishes. In fifteen cases the message of the divorce had been conveyed to them through only a third person. We found five cases of the triple *talaq* or the *talaq-ul-bidat* among Asamiya Muslims.

We observed that the bargaining power of women was considerably reduced due to the absence of a *nikahnama*, the focal point of a Muslim marriage. The amount of the *mehr*, thus, continued to be disputed and in most cases, was not paid up at all. Among the Lower Assam Muslims, a girl was considered to be a 'good girl' if she gave up her claim to a *mehr* even before the marriage was solemnized. In any case, the amount of *mehr* in the Lower Assam districts was pitifully low—about Rs. 200 or 300 only.

We found that most divorces occurred in the first ten years of marriage and consequently, most of the female divorcees were young women with small children and infants. In 80 per cent of the cases, the children remained with the mother. The most common reasons for divorce in the population studied have been barrenness and bigamy/ adultery.

In cases of love marriages (20 per cent of the respondents) the girl exercises her right to choose as much as the man. In cases of arranged marriages (80 per cent of the respondents) the proposal of marriage usually is initiated by a common friend. During negotiations informal assent of the girl is usually taken before finalizing the match. However, a bride is 'conditioned' to accept the choice of the parents as final.

Signing the *nikahnama* is an uncommon practice among the Asamiya Muslims of Guwahati. It is usually a 'verbal' *nikah* where the girl is required to give her consent by saying 'yes' in the presence of an *ukil* and two witnesses during the marriage ceremony in a large gathering. A marriage among the Asamiya Muslims is based on the principle of 'faith' and thus, is not a contract. In some cases even the *ukil* is not present and the consent is given simply before the gathering and the *junab* recites prayers and blesses the couple.

In 90 per cent of the cases, the divorced women considered the divorce to have been arbitrary and without reasonable cause.

As in the case of *nikah*, so in the case of *talaq*, the spirit is informal. There is no *talaqnama* signed after a divorce, the sanction for which is social rather than religious. The *talaq* is not sought through the court, nor are moulvis, qazis or pir sahibs called to finalize the divorce. In some cases family members try to arbitrate, but this is usually after the so-called divorce has been given by the husband. The *talaq* is usually pronounced in the presence of the wife alone. The *talaq-e-sunna* is the more favoured form of divorce though we came across five cases of triple *talaq*.

The men usually remarry soon afterwards and do not put forward claims to custody of their children from the first marriage as this may threaten the second marriage. The *mehr* is not commonly paid up though the period of *iddat* is followed. The most common problems faced by the divorced women are financial and that of social adjustment. Most divorced women go back to live with their parents except in the case of the professional women with a career of their own. None of the men tried to remarry his first wife and *halala* is a virtually unknown practice among the Asamiya Muslims of Guwahati.

CONCLUSION

If women continue to be divorced against their will in a society that has been historically an open, liberal and assimilative one, it says something important regarding the status of women in that society. In the case of Asamiya Muslims one thing is abundantly clear: religion here is only a means or an instrument of power over women and there is nothing overtly or covertly 'Islamic' about the condition of divorced Asamiya Muslim women in Guwahati. Asamiya Muslim society is a liberal, open and adaptive society with a very strong 'local' flavour. While instances of inter-marriage with the local Hindus are not very common, in the 'public' realm the two communities borrow heavily from each other. Every Asamiya Muslim interviewed agreed that she/he was 'different' from Muslims elsewhere. When asked to explain the 'difference' they unanimously said it was in their attitude towards their religion. 'If you find an Asamiya Muslim being fanatical about her/his religion', said an Asamiya Muslim Librarian, 'be sure that it is an artificial imposition and not something natural'.[8] Their informal attitude towards religion can also be gauged by their indifference to a *nikahnama*, the focal point of a Muslim marriage. In their dress, language, food habits and other outdoor activities there is nothing that differentiates an Asamiya Muslim from an Asamiya Hindu. In such a society when the triple *talaq* or an arbitrary method of divorce is practiced, it is difficult for the most insidious apologist to explain it in terms of religion. Again, even where the *talaq-e-sunna* was followed, the women themselves had been against the divorce and the reasons for remarriage had been barrenness or adultery by the men. What is important about the status of women in Islamic societies is not just the 'method' that is followed but that in practice, the right to divorce is invested primarily in the man and that it can be exercised unilaterally. In such a society, it is easy for men to take recourse to religion in order to rid themselves of 'undesirable' marital relationships.

Neither the condition of divorced Muslim women nor the causes for the divorces are strikingly different from those of the Hindu women of the city. Perhaps Islam is used by Asamiya Muslim men to exercise their power over the women more effectively and completely just as a Hindu man converts overnight to Islam in order to marry a second time if the first wife refuses to grant him a divorce.

The cases of Saba Anis and Zeenat Fatema Rashid, however, show that Asamiya Muslim women have begun to challenge the traditional destiny that society has churned out for a divorced Muslim woman. Increasingly, women from the educated sections of society are making themselves heard because in the end, it boils down to a question of right and wrong. Zeenat Fatema Rashid and Saba Anis are part of a definite trend within the community.

Liberalism can have its flip side. In not signing a *nikahnama*, the Asamiya Muslim women are making themselves more vulnerable. 'The signing of a *nikahnama* is an imperative in today's world', says Mahfuza Rahman, academician and social activist. She also feels that much more should be written on the Asamiya Muslims of Assam who are Asamiyas first and Muslims only later.

Last year at a conference in Bombay a lady admired my *mekhela-sador* very much and asked me where I was from.

'Assam', I said.

She turned to her friends and said, 'Look, doesn't she look like an Indian?' I was very surprised and asked her if she had ever visited India's north-east.

'Up to Siliguri', she replied.

'I think you need to go beyond that', I said.[9]

Islam has been, and in contemporary times, is a far more pluralistic religion than popular conceptions of it actually assume it to be (Ahmad, 1983: xxxv). Like any other major world culture, Islam contains in itself currents and cross-currents. Asamiya Muslims are a community where religion is exercised as an instrument of patriarchal power over women when it comes to issues like divorce and remarriage. Another Islamic society might assume a diametrically different manifestation in another part of the country, or even the state for that matter. Identity is not a stable or unchanging thing anywhere in the world and the essence of being a 'Muslim' does not exist anywhere. If it does, it can hardly bear analytical scrutiny.

NOTES

* The author would like to thank Dr. Mahfuza Rahman, Cotton College, Guwahati, and Dr. Monirul Hussain, Guwahati University, for their interest and help, whenever solicited, in the writing of this paper.

1. I am grateful to Mahfuza Rahman for suggestions and discussions on these points.
2. Verified by Monirul Hussain, Guwahati.
3. Based on intensive interviews with respondents and locally verified.
4. Verified by Monirul Hussain and other respondents.
5. Assamization and Asamiyaization are two analytical categories used by historian Amalendu Guha to conceptualize the different stages of assimilation experienced by migrants to Assam, especially, the Brahmaputra valley. Guha makes a conceptual difference between Assamization and Asamiyaization. The first takes place when migrants shift their homes to a new area and get acclimatized to the environment. Gradually, they develop changes in their habits of food, dress, social attitudes, etc. At this stage, however, they do not necessarily adopt the language of the dominant group of the receiving society but their dialects undergo changes. The second takes place when migrants make a conscious attempt to adopt the Asamiya language as a mother-tongue as well as the Asamiya culture (personal communication with the author, August 1995).
6. Collected from Malik (1990: 14) and Saikia (1967: 267, 274).
7. For details of an Asamiya Muslim marriage, see Ali (1976).
8. It is to be noted that only in cases where Asamiya Muslim women and married non-Asamiya Muslim men were all the rules of Islam, that is a *nikahnama*, payment of *mehr* and *talaqnama*, followed.
9. Narrated by Mahfuza Rahman, Cotton College, Guwahati.

REFERENCES

Ahmad, Imtiaz (1976), 'Introduction', in Imtiaz Ahmad (ed.), *Family, Kinship and Marriage among Muslims in India*, Delhi: Manohar.

Ali, A.N.M. Irshad (1976), 'Kinship and Marriage among Assamese Muslims', in Imtiaz Ahmad (ed.), *Family, Kinship and Marriage among Muslims in India*, Delhi: Manohar.

Haniff, Niesha Z. (1983), 'Muslim Women and the Minority Mentality', in Imtiaz Ahmad (ed.), *Modernization and Social Change among Muslims in India*, Delhi: Manohar.

Hussain, Monirul (1993), *The Assam Movement: Class, Ideology and Identity*, Jaipur: Rawat.

Malik, Syed Abdul (1990), *Ajan Fakir*, Calcutta: Sahitya Akademi.

Saikia, Mohini Kumar (1967), *Assam-Muslim Relations and its Cultural Significance*, Guwahati.

Strauss, Ansel and Juliet Corbin (1990), *Basics of Qualitative Research: Grounded Theory, Procedure and Techniques*, California: Sage.

2

Muslim Women's Divorce and Remarriage in a Town of Western Uttar Pradesh

Zakiya Rafat

Among the many aspects of a Muslim woman's life in India, the issue of divorce continues to be most hotly debated. On the one hand, it is commonly argued that the low status of a Muslim woman in India is exemplified by her extreme vulnerability in divorce. While she has no right to seek divorce (even if this right is guaranteed to her in theory), her husband can divorce her easily by simply pronouncing 'I divorce you' three time at one go. On the other hand, it is also argued that the allegation that a Muslim woman is extremely vulnerable to divorce is an exaggeration and that in reality the divorce rate among Muslims is comparatively low. Curiously enough, both these positions continue to be argued out without reference to any substantial body of empirical evidence.

Our aim in this paper is to adduce empirical evidence on Muslim women's marriage and divorce from a larger study of change and continuity in the status of Muslim women in Bijnor town in western Uttar Pradesh. Even though the study covered almost all aspects of Muslim women's life from their early socialization to education, place in the family and domestic space, their occupational role and political participation and ritual and religious life, I have chosen in this paper to focus on their divorce and post-divorce problems for two reasons. First, as already indicated, this is an aspect that lies at the heart of the controversy about the status of Muslim women in India. Second, as the subsequent discussion will show, divorce as a social phenomenon is closely related to a series of other aspects of society and has to be seen in a much broader context than is often done. This discussion should, therefore, serve as a corrective to the ill-informed perception that Muslim women are extremely vulnerable to divorce on account of their religious rules that admit the possibility of a woman being cast away by her husband at will and without assigning any reason. On to the contrary, our data suggests that, first, religion hardly enters into the discussion when divorces is contemplated, and second, divorce usually takes place after a long process of family disharmony and is resorted to only when the problem seems intractable.

THE SETTING

A town of roughly 73,900 inhabitants, Bijnor has a predominance of Muslims who account for 55.8 per cent of its population according to the 1991 census. At the time of Independence the Muslims of Bijnor town comprised a large landed aristocracy, a sizable service class as well as artisans and menials. Abolition of zamindari seriously weakened Muslim preeminence in the town, but the damage was more in terms of loss of social standing than loss of economic stability. Enlightened zamindar households had managed to distribute their urban and rural lands among a series of relatives and kinsmen and thus escape the loss of their economic assets. They also took advantage of burgeoning employment and business opportunities and retained their influence in the life of the city. Zamindars lacking education and the ability to anticipate the consequences of the abolition of zamindari on the contrary lost out on their lands and failed to take advantage of emerging opportunities for employment and business. Likewise, the more enterprising artisans and menials who took advantage of economic opportunities for employment and business in big cities, particularly Delhi, to which the town had been linked from early times, managed to escape the devastation caused by the loss of support from the landed aristocracy. The result is that while Muslim social standing has definitely suffered in the town since Independence, their hold over the economy has continued much as before. Old zamindar families have developed their real estates and created shopping complexes where they run their own businesses. Artisan families, which had migrated to big cities in the aftermath of the Partition, have brought back economic resources and invested them in new enterprises.

Five localities in Bijnor town are predominantly Muslim, among whom Kazipara, Chahshiri, and Mirdgan are particularly well-known. Kazipara is a prominent and relatively prosperous Muslim locality inhabited principally by 79 Kazi, 43 Syed and 7 Pathan households. Kazis are erstwhile zamindars and are engaged in professions and middle-level government services. Chahshiri is a middle class locality inhabited by 15 Syed, 22 Sheikh, 17 Mughal, 49 Pathan and 77 Sheikhzada households besides some lower caste households of Ansaris, Lohars, Kalals and Dhobis. Mirdgan is numerically the largest Muslim locality in Bijnor town inhabited very heavily by members of the lower Muslim caste communities most of whom are engaged in low-level government services, menial work and trade and commerce. Except for 14 Sheikh, 4 Pirzada, 5 Mughal and 26 Pathan households, the remaining 226 households belong to low caste communities.

Fieldwork for the study was conducted mainly in these three localities though the researcher carried out interviews to cross-check information in other localities as well. First, a detailed household survey of the three localities was carried out with a view to arriving at a social profile of the localities, their caste composition and the social and economic characteristics of the inhabitants. Frequent visits were made to the households in each locality and detailed interviews were carried out to collect ethnographic information about the composition of the households, the educational and occupational patterns of the different members of the households, the life styles of the households belonging to different caste and status families, their marriage patterns and practices and aspects of women's lives generally. Once the general ethnographic information had been collected, a detailed and intensive study of 150 households from the three localities was undertaken using the participant observation technique to obtain more reliable information and to cross-check the data gathered during the first phase of fieldwork. Since the object of the study was to acquire a 'holistic' understanding of Muslim women's lives, this mode of carrying out fieldwork was preferred over that of a survey based on a structured schedule. Subsequently, some of the data was quantified, but the account presented here relies both on field observations and interviews as well as case studies collected during fieldwork.

Among Muslims in Bijnor monogamy is considered the ideal form of marriage, and the predominant pattern is for a man to live with his wife for the rest of his life. Out of the 814 households surveyed, only 12 households were found to deviate from this general pattern. The remaining 802 households were monogamous with the man living with his wife continuously since marriage. Again, out of the 150 households taken up for detailed investigation, there were only 44 cases of men and 17 of widows and divorced women having entered into a second marriage. However, even in these cases a man had only one wife, although 2 men had entered into three or four marriages after a brief interval. For instance, one Jhojha rickshaw puller first married a Bihari woman. After six months, he found her sleeping with another man at night and divorced her. A year later, his grandfather and maternal uncle bought a south Indian girl for Rs. 3,500 and married him to her, but within a short time the maternal uncle again sold her to another man who took her to Delhi. Upon his filing a report with the police, the girl was recovered and brought back. She narrated the entire story whereupon he divorced her. With the aim of avenging the insult, he subsequently eloped with the daughter of his maternal uncle and married her, only to beat her and turn her out of the house. Finally, he entered into a secret marriage with a fourth wife with whom he was living at the time of the study.

This case goes to show that while the common pattern is for a man to enter into a marriage and to live with his wife for the rest of his life, divorces do take place. Out of the 812 households studied by this researcher, a total of 53 instances of divorce were found. This means that the rate of divorce for Muslims in the town works out to 6.5 per cent that is not particularly high and belies the common perception that Muslim women are exceptionally vulnerable to divorce on account of the prevalence of the practice of triple divorce in one go among Muslims. Subsequently, as we shall see, though this mode of pronouncement of divorce is undoubtedly prevalent among Muslims, whether this by itself prompts Muslim men to divorce their wives is a more open question in the light of our data. Often divorces take place only when there are other powerful factors also at work.

TABLE 1: NUMBER OF YEARS AFTER MARRIAGE WHEN DIVORCE TOOK PLACE

Period	Number	Percentage
6 months to 2 years	18	34.0
3 years to 5 years	16	30.0
6 years to 10 years	9	17.0
11 years to 25 years	9	17.0
Varied	1	2.0
Total	53	100

Table 1 sets out the period of marriage after which divorce took place. From the data set out in Table 1, it is clear that 18 women (34 per cent) were divorced within the first two years of their marriage, 16 women (30 per cent) were divorced between three and five years of their marriage and 9 women (17 per cent) were divorced between six and ten years after their marriage. Only 9 (17 per cent) women were divorced between eleven and twenty-five years after their marriage: 2 (3.8 per cent) after eleven years, 3 (5.7 per cent) after thirteen years and 4 (7.6 per cent) between seventeen to twenty-five years. In one case, a woman had been through divorce as many as 9 times. Each time the period of divorce after the marriage varied. Sometimes the divorce occurred within six months while at other times it came after as long as three years. It is clear that a women is most susceptible to being divorced within the first five or six years of her marriage. This comes out clearly if we take the age of the woman at the time of divorce into consideration. Of the 53 divorced women, 49 (92.4 per cent) had been divorced when they were between twenty to thirty-five years of age. Only 4 (7.6 per cent) women were divorced between forty-five and fifty-five years of age. After she has had children and has acquired a foothold in the household the chance of a divorce tends to reduce. Nonetheless, cases of women having been divorced after ten or more years of marriage, during which period she has had several children, are not entirely unknown. Such cases usually take place when the husband falls in love with another woman and there is quarrel over his attachment to another woman.

DIVORCE AND SOCIAL CLASS

Even though the possibility of breakdown exists in any marriage, the occurrence of divorce is not quite as random as is sometimes assumed. On the contrary, a detailed analysis of the data adduced by our study suggested that the occurrence of divorce has strong correlation with a number of social variables such as the status of the caste community of the spouses, the educational level of the husband and the wife, the occupation of the husband, etc. This implies that one can expect significant differences among different categories and groups of Muslims in terms of the incidence of divorce among them even if they are committed to Islam and are governed by its laws. If this indeed turns out to be correct, then the focus of the discussions pertaining to the position of Muslim women in India must shift from religion and Muslim Personal Law as causative factors in divorce to those social factors which are strongly correlated with the occurrence of divorce.

Let us begin with an examination of some of these correlations in greater detail. Table 2 presents the distribution of divorced Muslim women in Bijnor by their caste community. Since marriages among Muslims in Bijnor tend to take place within the caste communities,

TABLE 2: CASTE COMMUNITY OF DIVORCED MUSLIM WOMEN IN BIJNOR

Caste Community	Number	Percentage
High Status		
Syed	4	7.5
Sheikh Siddiqui	7	13.0
Pathan	1	2.0
Low Status		
Sheikhzada	14	26.0
Ranger	11	21.0
Ansari	5	9.5
Qureshi	1	2.0
Sunar	1	2.0
Dhuna (Mansuri)	1	2.0
Sakka (Abbasi)	1	2.0
Jhojha	5	9.5
Manihar	2	3.5
Total	53	100

TABLE 3: EDUCATION OF DIVORCED MUSLIM WOMEN AND THEIR HUSBANDS

Educational Level	Wife		Husband	
	Number	Percentage	Number	Percentage
Illiterate	14	26.0	13	25.5
Qur'an literate	14	26.0	8	16.5
Home educated	4	7.5	-	-
Primary level	1	2.0	1	2.0
Up to Junior School	6	11.0	8	16.5
Up to High School	13	8.0	5	11.0
Undergraduates	7	12.0	5	11.0
Graduates	4	7.5	9	17.5
Total	53	100	49*	100

Note: * Since 4 men divorced more than once, the number of husbands is 49.

this means that the caste community of the wife was also the caste community of her husband. From the data presented in Table 2, it is clear that while divorce takes place among all caste communities, as is to be expected, the incidence of divorce among the low status caste communities is much higher as compared to the high status caste communities. Out of the 53 cases reported, only 12 were from high status caste communities, 7 from the Sheikh Siddiquis, 4 from the Syeds and 1 from the Pathans. All the remaining cases were of women from low status caste communities. Among the low status caste communities, the largest number of cases came from the Rangers and Sheikhzadas.

Table 3 presents the educational level of divorced Muslim women and their former husbands. Whether we look at the educational level of the divorced woman or that of her former husband, it becomes clear that education is strongly linked to incidence of divorce. More divorces appear to have occurred where the educational level of the wife as well as that of her husband tended to be low while incidence of divorce tended to decline substantially as we moved up to higher levels of education of the wife as well as the husband. Certainly, the educational level of the wife is crucial.

From the data set out in Table 4, no clear nexus between divorce and occupation emerges. Even so, it is clear that incidence of divorce is higher among petty traders, menial and blue-collar workers than

TABLE 4: LISTS THE OCCUPATION OF THE FORMER HUSBANDS OF THE DIVORCED WOMEN

Occupation	Number	Percentage
Professional	2	4.0
White-collar service	4	8.0
Business	1	2.0
Blue-collar service	7	14.0
Petty trade	11	23.0
Menial work	16	33.0
Others	8	16.0
Total	49	100

among professionals and white-collar workers. It is not possible from the limited number of cases of divorced Muslims women found in the course of the study to assert with any degree of certainty as to why a strong association between incidence of divorce and status of caste community, educational level of the husband and wife and the occupational standing of the husband of the divorced wife exists. Nor can we decide with any degree of certainty whether any one of these factors is singly important or their influence is cumulative. Since social inequalities tend to be cumulative in India, it seems that those belonging to higher status caste communities are likely to be more educated and to be better placed in terms of occupational standing. Because the lifestyle and values of higher caste communities emphasize that a marriage is for life and their members are better educated and placed in higher occupations, husband-wife relationships are not subject to those stresses and strains of life which lead to tensions and quarrels that end in a divorce. Therefore, it appears that the influence of the status of the caste community of the couple, the educational level of the husband and wife and the occupation of the husband is cumulative.

Besides the status of the caste communities, educational level of the husband and wife and the occupational standing of the husband the composition of the household in which the couple were residing at the time of divorce too has an influence over the incidence of divorce. Of the 53 cases of divorced women surveyed, 13 (24.6 per cent) were living in nuclear households, 19 (35.8 per cent) were residing in joint households, and 18 (33.9 per cent) were living in extended families. Three women (5.7 per cent) were living in a transitional type of family, that is, their household was in the process of breaking up from a joint to a nuclear household. Our informants said that the joint or extended nature of the household limited the possibility of their coming close to their husbands. Besides, the other members of the joint or extended household influenced the husband who, caught between loyalty to the members of extended family and the wife, decided to take recourse to divorce. Several informants noted that their extended kin were indeed quite happy when the divorce took place. Even though we have no reason to question this, there is need to balance these statements with those made by other women who stated that their extended kin had often intervened in husband-wife quarrels and that this had made it possible for a divorce to be averted.

REASONS FOR DIVORCE

A divorce does not take place because of a single quarrel between husband and wife. It is usually a culmination of a series of developments and there is always a definite reason for a divorce to occur. Table 5 sets out the main reasons for divorce as articulated by the divorced women.

TABLE 5: REASONS FOR DIVORCE IN BIJNOR

Reasons for divorce	Number	Percentage
Sterility	4	7.5
Family quarrels	7	13.2
Economic reasons—Dowry	5	9.5
Inability to provide for wife	7	13.2
Indebtedness	2	3.7
Wife demanding jewellery	1	1.9
Relations with another woman	5	9.5
Relations with another man	7	13.2
Impotency	3	5.7
Husband's alcoholism	1	1.9
Chronic illness of husband	2	3.7
Desire for revenge	1	1.9
Ill treatment by husband	3	5.7
Ugliness of wife	4	7.5
Black magic by someone	1	1.9
Total	53	100

From the data presented in Table 5 it is clear that the reasons for divorce are varied. Infertility of the wife, family quarrels and economic reasons are the most prominent. Four women (7.5 per cent) were divorced because they could not conceive. Their husbands consulted doctors, practitioners of Ayurvedic and Unani medicine and even tried using talismans from holy men but they could not conceive. In a few cases, the husband wanted to take a second wife in order to have a child to which the wife did not agree. Finally, the husbands divorced them and took a second wife. Whether the childlessness was due to the sterility of the woman or the infertility of the husband is difficult to ascertain. What is clear is that the inability of the wife to conceive was attributed to her sterility, though in a few cases the man was unable to have children from the other woman also whom he had married after divorcing his first wife.

Often several women living together in a joint or extended family are not able to work out a mutually satisfactory relationship. There are bitter quarrels among them, all the more so if there is no mother-in-law to intervene and control matters. When this happens frequently, the wife has to tell her husband who gets worked up. Sometimes relations may complain to the husband which further aggravates matters. Finally, finding no other solution, husbands take the easy way out by divorcing the wife for the satisfaction of the members of the extended family. Seven women (13.2 per cent) were divorced in this way. Of these three had had a love marriage and the members of the extended family had not liked them from the beginning. In one case, divorce took place because the wife visited her paternal family often and her in-laws resented this. She recounted her feelings thus:

> My husband did not allow me to go to my parents' house. Whenever I went without his permission, he would quarrel with me, because my parents are poor and my mother-in-law complained to him that I took things for my parents. She, too, used to taunt me about the poverty of my parental family. One day my father came to visit me. My husband insulted him and turned him away. When I cried over the incident, my husband pronounced divorce and sent me away.

Among the economic reasons for divorce, dowry, the inability of the husband to maintain his wife and indebtedness are the crucial ones. Of the 15 women (25 per cent) divorced for economic reasons, two were wives of college teachers of the Sheikh Siddiqui caste community. In both cases the husbands were trying to get their father-in-law's property transferred in their names. Every now and then they would send their wives to their parental homes with a demand. When the parents of these women refused to oblige, their husbands divorced them. One woman was divorced because her parents wanted to usurp the jewellery belonging to her husband; while in three cases the divorce took place because the husbands had taken a loan from their wife's parents, which they were not able to return. As one Sheikhzada woman put it. 'My husband was unemployed. He had taken a loan of ten thousand rupees from my elder brother to start business. When my brother demanded the return of the loan, he refused to pay back. As quarrels used to take place over the issue, he decided to divorce me and sent me away to my brother's house.' Another Sonar woman said, 'At the time of marriage my husband's family had said that my husband had a jewellery shop of his own. When I came here after marriage I found that he was without work. For this reason he was not able to provide for my daily needs. Whenever I complained he would send me for months to my parental family. During this period I also had two children and family expenses increased. Tensions over money kept increasing and one day he divorced me.'

Five women (9.5 per cent) were divorced as a result of their husbands having a relationship with another woman. In one such case the woman had four children. She narrated:

> I was not very attractive and good-looking. My daughter was already betrothed. My husband developed a relationship with another woman. He used to be at her place all day long and gave her all his earnings. He was not giving any money even for the wedding of the daughter. One day he mooted the proposal of getting married to the other woman before me. This led to a bitter quarrel between us. He then divorced me.

In the case of seven women (13.2 per cent) the divorce took place either because they were interested in or eloped with another man or they were suspected of being interested in someone else. One woman each from the Manihar, Weaver, Jhojha and Sheikhzada caste communities eloped with someone else and their husbands divorced them subsequently. One woman having been divorced on suspicion of being involved with another man narrated her experience thus: 'My husband always suspected me. One day when he was away to Delhi my sister-in-law's brother came on a visit. When my husband returned he started taunting me. Even after the boy had left he continued quarreling over him and finally went away to Delhi. He sent me a letter of divorce from there.'

One case among the women surveyed was that of a wife who was divorced because she was suspected of having practiced black magic against her husband. She recounted her story in these words:

> My husband used to be chronically ill. One day my mother-in-law took him to a moulvi sahib who told them that I had practised black magic against my husband in order to bring him under my influence. Upon returning home, both my husband and my mother-in-law started quarreling with me. My mother-in-law suggested that I should go to my parents' house for sometime. When the husband got well they would call me back. I stayed with my parents for two months, but nobody came to call me. Finally, I decided to come back on my own. From that day onwards, both quarreled with me. My husband lay all day in our room and my mother-in-law would not allow me to enter the room. One day, finding an opportunity, I entered the room and my husband started shouting. Everyone gathered and started blaming me. I was turned out of the house and asked to go back to my parents' house. When my father and his brother came to enquire what had happened and to bring about a settlement, my husband pronounced divorce in their presence.

These experiences and narratives as recounted by the divorced Muslim women of Bijnor reflect the sad plight of women and their vulnerable position in the event of divorce. However, if these narratives are analysed in conjunction with the influence exercised by the status of caste community, educational and occupational levels presented earlier, they also underscore the complex tie up between a culture of poverty and marital stability. It is clear that most of the women whose narratives we have reported came from relatively poor backgrounds where their hold over economic resources was virtually non-existent. This made them dependent on their husbands in the extreme and opened them to pressures which threatened the stability of their marriages. Since the husbands themselves lived in relative poverty and were not able to provide well for their families, the wife became an easy target of family intrigues if she was living within a joint or extended household. If she was living in a nuclear household, the relative poverty of the household created tensions and quarrels which embittered her relations with her husband. She ended up as a divorcee either because her maternal relatives thought that she was controlling her husband who was the mainstay of their economic and social support or because the husband found her demands for economic support too difficult to put up with. On the whole, therefore, divorce as an event was ultimately traceable to a wider spectrum of forces at work in the lives of the families explored.

DISSOLUTION OF MARRIAGE

A Muslim marriage can be dissolved in three principal ways. First, a Muslim man can divorce his wife unilaterally by pronouncing divorce three times without assigning any reason for his action. This form of divorce can be both oral and written. The second method of divorce is *khula*. It is resorted to when a woman wants a divorce and the husband is unwilling to free her of the marriage bond. Finally, she can approach a court or caste panchayat to get the marriage dissolved. Table 6 presents the method of divorce used in the cases surveyed. It shows that the most common mode of divorce resorted to is the one where the husband pronounces a divorce. As many as 43 women (81.0 per cent) were divorced in this way. In 38 cases (72.0 per cent) the divorce was pronounced orally, in 7 cases (13.0 per cent) it was communicated in writing, in 1 case (2.0 per cent) it was

TABLE 6: METHOD ADOPTED FOR DIVORCE

Method	Number	Percentage
Pronouncement by husband	43	81.0
Asked for by wife (*khula*)	9	17.0
Through court	1	2.0
Total	53	100
Oral	38	72.0
Written	7	13.0
Announced in newspaper	1	2.0
Through *panchayat*	3	5.5
Through court	1	2.0
Mixed	3	5.5
Total	53	100

announced through a newspaper, and in 3 (5.5 per cent) a combination of different methods was used. Only in 9 cases (17.0 per cent) did divorce take place at the initiative of the wife and in one case the divorce was obtained through the court. Occasionally it happens, particularly where family relations are strained and the husband sees the demand by his wife for divorce as an affront to his honour or he is interested in subjecting his wife to harassment by keeping her tied, that a husband is unwilling to pronounce a divorce and thus free his wife of the bond. In such cases the parents of the wife take the matter to the caste panchayat, which then has to intervene and pressurise the husband to agree to pronounce a divorce in her favour. If he refuses to relent, the panchayat, on its own, decides to dissolve the marriage.

In all cases of divorce an attempt was subsequently made to get the divorce validated by a moulvi. Relatives on both sides approached the moulvi and narrated the sequence of events leading to the divorce. If the moulvi ruled that the divorce was a valid one, both parties were obliged to accept the verdict. Sometimes relatives and friends tried to convince the moulvi that he should declare a divorce void as there were small children and their rearing would pose problems. Sometimes women themselves put pressure on relatives on both sides to present the circumstances in a distorted manner before the moulvi so that he would invalidate the divorce. One Sheikhzada woman narrated: 'My husband told the moulvi one month after the divorce that he had pronounced the divorce when he had fever and heat had got into his head. The moulvi said that under those circumstances the divorce was not valid and my husband brought me back.' One Ranger woman said: 'The divorce had taken place but my husband told the moulvi a false story. What can the moulvi do; he decides only on the basis of what others tell him and he tells us whether the divorce has taken place or not.' However, out of the 46 cases where he was approached for a ruling on a divorce, only in two cases did the moulvi invalidate a divorce.

OBSERVANCE OF *IDDAT*

After a divorce has taken place, a divorced woman is expected to observe the statutory period of waiting (*iddat*) before the expiry of which she can not marry again. Our data show that 11 out of the 53 divorced women surveyed did not observe this period of waiting and another 2 started out to observe it but gave up before completing it. One woman said that she had gone to her parental home when she received a letter from her husband that he had divorced her. She started *iddat*, but after a few days her husband came with a *fatwa* along with his relatives and persuaded her parents to send her back as the divorce had not taken place. One woman, who also gave up observing the period of waiting, said that she did not have any relations on her father's side. So she started observing *iddat* in her husband's house. There was only one room. A curtain was put up and she stayed behind it in the same room. After fifteen days her husband moved the curtain, re-established physical relations and told her that there had been no divorce.

Among the women who did not observe *iddat* at all, one was the wife of an impotent man. She did not think it necessary to observe *iddat*. In another case the woman was divorced within six months of her marriage. Her brother was in Delhi and he wanted her to re-join college. Since observing *iddat* would have meant absenting from college, she decided not to observe the period of isolation. In the same way two women of the Sheikh Siddiqui caste community did not observe *iddat*. Both were teachers and they thought that observing *iddat* would require taking long leave which they could not afford. Thus, observance of the statutory *iddat* period is often violated but people in the neighborhood as well as close relatives often look down upon women who do not adhere to the prescribed period of *iddat*.

PAYMENT OF *MEHR*

Once the divorce becomes final, the divorced women's immediate concern is to ensure her economic security, all the more so if she has children. Her first step is to secure the payment of *mehr*. As is well known, *mehr* is an amount of money or property that a Muslim man promises to his wife in return for her consent to marry him. Usually, the *mehr* is expected to be paid before the consummation of marriage, but in India the husband either asks his wife to condone it or defers its payment until a future time. Given the precarious economic situation in which a divorced woman finds herself, her first step is to try to recover the *mehr*, particularly if it is a substantial sum of money.

Of the 53 cases surveyed, only 3 divorced women received the promised *mehr* after their divorce. The remaining women were either refused or preferred not to ask for it. One woman's former husband paid the *mehr* on his own, while in the other two cases the women got it only after putting a great deal of pressure on their husbands through close relatives and friends. Eight women could not claim their *mehr* because they had neither proof of their marriage nor knew the amount of *mehr* fixed at the time of marriage. Two divorced women who had grown-up children have continued to live in the house of their husbands with their children. They did not ask for the *mehr*. One woman whose husband was insane and had divorced her under madness, did not ask for the *mehr* as she saw no point in advancing her claim for it. Husbands of three women were unemployed. They, too, did not see any point in asking for the *mehr*. Three women were themselves educated. They did not ask for payment of *mehr*. One of them said that her *mehr* had been fixed at Rs. 25,000 but now that she hated him she did not want even to take his name; where was, then, the question of asking for *mehr*.

Four women had been made to condone *mehr* and could not ask for it. Three women subsequently remarried their former husbands and preferred not to take up the matter of payment of *mehr* before getting married a second time. Five women were promised a *mehr* of Rs. 400 to 500. Since it was a paltry some they, too, preferred not to raise their claim. Nine women had themselves asked for a divorce. Hence, they could not claim *mehr*. Four women's parents were well-off. They did not feel that they wanted *mehr*. Four women were seeking to secure the payment of *mehr* through the court. These cases go to show, first, that most women do not get the promised amount after divorce and second, sometimes they themselves prefer not to press their claim for payment of *mehr*. Thus, the Islamic obligation for payment of *mehr* to the wife notwithstanding, social practice in this respect is highly variable and depends on the feelings of the divorced women.

What is true of payment of *mehr* also holds good for the return of dowry (*jahez*). Only 11 out of the 53 divorced women were returned their dowry. Two women whose divorces took place on grounds of impotency were returned their dowry without much hassle, and in three other cases where the woman had been divorced within six months of the marriage the husband's family returned the dowry.

Three women succeeded in securing their dowry by pressurizing their husbands through their relatives and friends, and in two cases only a part of the dowry was returned. One Sheikh Siddiqui woman said that a truckload of dowry had been given to her. Much of it had been used and was broken. There was, therefore, no question of getting back old and broken furniture or crockery items. However, gold jewellery which she had been given could have been returned. This was not done. The four or five pieces of jewellery that she wore regularly were already with her. Other pieces of jewellery had been kept back by her in-laws.

Of the women who have not recovered their dowry, a large number did not ask for it for one reason or another. Four women had themselves eloped with other men and did not advance any claim for return of dowry while two women had had a love marriage and had not received any dowry. Twelve women decided not to claim their dowry and six women who had been divorced a long time after their marriage felt that the items of dowry were already so decrepit that there would have been no point in asking for their return. Eight women's parents or brothers tried to secure their dowry, but the husbands refused to return it. It is clear that in most cases where the dowry is considerable and could be helpful to the divorced women financially, the husbands and in-laws try to avoid returning it. Gold ornaments and similar valuable items were in any case hardly ever returned and what a woman got back in a few cases was far short of what she had brought with her.

Divorced Muslim women are traditionally not entitled to any maintenance from their husbands. Even though Muslim Personal Law entitles her to maintenance during the period of *iddat*, none of the divorced women surveyed received any maintenance during that period. However, in eight cases women did receive some amount after their divorce. One woman had a two-year old daughter. After the divorce she brought the daughter with her. Her husband paid her Rs. 250 every month for the maintenance of the child. Likewise, in the case of a Sheikh Siddiqui woman who had a small child the husband is paying maintenance. One Ansari woman had a grown up daughter who was engaged to be married. When her husband divorced her, her parents-in-law did not allow her to go away. Instead, they told their son that they would give him a share in the family property only if he provided at least Rs. 30 per day for her expenses. He has been paying her that amount since. One Ranger woman filed a case in the court for maintenance. The court granted her a monthly maintenance of Rs. 250. However, the husband paid that amount whenever the court put pressure on him. Otherwise, he tried to wriggle out of paying her anything. On the whole, while there are at least two instances where the husbands have been paying maintenance to their wives either because they regretted their action or because their wives had no relations to return to, women are left very much to fend for themselves in most cases of divorce.

Since a divorced woman's situation is quite pathetic as she has to revert to her parental family where her brother and sister-in-law resent her presence, her family usually tries to get her re-married. If she already has children from her previous husband, their effort is that the former husband himself should remarry her. If she is young, they try to get her remarried to another man. Usually the remarriage of a childless divorced woman is easier, but the prospect of her getting married to an unwed man are remote. More often than not, she can only be remarried to an old divorced man or widower. Even so, the incidence of remarriage is quite low. Only 17 out of the 53 divorced woman had remarried. As many as 12 of them were issueless. Four of them had had an affair with men already married and prevailed upon them to marry them after divorcing their first wives. Two got married to men who had divorced their earlier wives. Three married men much older to them, and two married widowers with issues from a previous marriage. Two women were quite young when they were divorced. They went on to study and took up jobs. One of them became a manager in a bank and was able to remarry a bachelor of her own age but having a lower ranking job. The other remarried a divorced man of her own age who agreed to marry her for the financial status of her family. Three women remarried their former husbands.

REMARRIAGE OF DIVORCED WOMEN

Under Islamic law a woman who has been irrevocably divorced can remarry the same person only after she has been married to some other person first who too has pronounced divorce on her. Under strict Islamic law that marriage should be consummated, but in the majority of cases where remarriage to a former husband is contemplated the effort is to find someone who would be willing to divorce her without consummating the marriage. Out of the three cases of divorced women who remarried their former husbands, two women reunited with their former husbands without a formal *nikah* ceremony. Only one woman fulfilled the condition for such a marriage. She had three children and was pregnant. Her husband had pronounced divorce in a fit of anger, but soon repented his action. He wished to rectify his mistake by remarrying his former wife. The moulvis advised that he could do so only after his wife performed *halala*, that is, she married someone else who would divorce her to enable her to remarry her former husband after the observance of the *iddat* for divorce. Her mother-in-law then persuaded her already married nephew to enter into marriage with her and divorce her the following morning. He was reluctant, but the mother-in-law pleaded with the nephew that he would be doing a meritorious act by helping the family from breaking up. Even the nephew's wife was not told of this arrangement. When his wife and mother-in-law came to know about this they quarreled bitterly with the divorced woman and her mother-in-law and relations between the two families have remained strained ever since.

POST-DIVORCE PROBLEMS

Usually, women face many problems after they have been divorced by their husbands. Out of the total cases surveyed, 17 women faced post-divorce problems for a brief period until they remarried. By contrast, 36 women were still facing these problems at the time of the study. Their post-divorce problems can be divided into five categories. The first set of problems have to do with their kinsmen to whom they generally revert once they are divorced. These are generally day-to-day problems of adjustment within the families of their parents or brothers and of finding a suitable place to live if their parents or brothers are unwilling to keep them. Generally, parents are quite considerate towards their divorced daughters, though we did come across many instances where the father and the mother were inclined to be unsympathetic towards their divorced daughters and blamed them for the predicament in which they had been placed. The situation is worse if her brothers and their families are also living in the same household or if she has had to move to the home of a brother who is also married and has a complete family. In such situations the sister-in-law, and at her prompting even the brother, tends to treat the divorced woman as an unnecessary burden on the family and its meager resources and expects them to do all domestic chores: cleaning the house, washing clothes, cleaning utensils, cooking and looking after the children, etc. They are virtually made to work like maidservants in the household. As most women undergo considerable psychological stress after their divorce, particularly depression and headaches, this opens them to taunts from their sisters-in-law. Rather than providing psychological relief or looking after them, the sister-in-law tends to perceive her sickness as a ploy to avoid working in the household and bullies them in varied ways. If she needs to see the doctor or otherwise visit the market, the divorced woman faces the problem of finding an escort. If she goes alone, usually the entire neighborhood, including her brothers and sisters-in-law point a finger of suspicion at her. She is accused of loose morals. Even divorced working women are obliged to do domestic work after getting back from work, in the homes of their brothers. Further, they are also subjected to taunts, all the more so as they are away from home for long periods.

Of the women surveyed, 48 (83.1 per cent) had gone back to live with their parents after divorce. Our finding compares well with that of Mehta's study of divorced Hindu women which also showed that most women had reverted back to their parents or relatives after their divorce (Mehta, 1975). Of the 9 women who did not go back to their parents after divorce, 5 (9.5 per cent) continued to stay in the house of their former husbands. Two women had adult children and stayed on with them after the divorce. Three women had remarried their former husbands. Thus, only 6 (11.2 per cent) women covered by this study can be said to have faced the problem of finding a suitable place to live after they were divorced. One of them said,

> Even during the period of *iddat* my parents and brothers troubled me a great deal. They had kept the gold given by my husband. This was why I had been divorced. Therefore, they did not agree to keep me in the house after the completion of the *iddat* period. After the *iddat* period was over,

they drove me out of the house. For a year I worked in the houses of neighbours and slept at night in their courtyards or verandahs. They, too, looked down upon me. Finally, I contacted my former husband and told him my problem. He, then, agreed to keep me.

Similarly, a Sheikh Siddiqui woman said:

My mother was also divorced. She stayed with her brother. After my divorce, I was quite worried about where I would stay, but my maternal uncle allowed me to stay with his family. After completion of the *iddat* period, my maternal uncle's children started to quarrel with me and eventually turned me out of the house. Then I, along with my daughter and my mother, went to stay with my widowed sister. We paid her rent, but she asked us to shift out within a year. At last, I had to find rented accommodation and I now live with my daughter and mother in that house.

Four women (7.5 per cent) whose parents were dead and whose brothers refused to keep them in their homes stayed in the homes of some relatives and did all the domestic chores for them. On ceremonial occasions and festivals, other relatives employed them for a few days. This way they eke out their pitiable existence.

As a rule, a man who divorces his wife is not particularly keen to keep the children. Of the women surveyed, 25 (45.0 per cent) were issueless at the time of divorce. The remaining 28 (52.6 per cent) had children. Of these, husbands of 5 decided to keep the children and had their custody of the children entered in the *talaqnama*, but in two of these cases the children decided to come and stay with the mother after their father contracted a second marriage. Another 2 women (3.7 per cent) who were divorced when they had reached middle age are living with their adult children in their former husband's home. Others have been faced with one problem or another related to their children. At the time of divorce 6 women (11.2 per cent) who were pregnant faced problems relating to delivery and childcare. Again, 14 (24.5 per cent) who had small children faced problems in raising them and providing them education. They had themselves to go to the schools for their admission and provide them school uniforms which was not always easy. Because they stayed with their brothers, quarrels broke out between their children and their brothers' children leading to tension in the household. Their children feel ignored and are prone to remembering their father which further depresses them. Usually, such women keep a distance from their children and scold them a great deal. This makes the daughters scared and sons obstinate and peevish. Outside the school or in the locality they often fight with other children or beat them up. This is a source of constant worry and anxiety for the women. As many as 6 women (11.2 per cent) whose children were grown up wished to establish contact with their father. This makes these women nervous. As one woman explained, 'Whenever my former husband comes to see my daughter, my heart begins to tremble. I cannot ask my daughter not to see him. Yet, I am anxious.'

The children's marital prospects are also adversely affected at times because their mother is a divorced woman. One eighteen-year old girl said, 'My engagement was broken because my prospective in-laws did not like my meeting my father. They had conveyed to me through my mother in so many words that I should not be meeting him. I did not want to stop meeting my father as he had started seeing me after fifteen years.' In two other cases women faced problems in arranging the marriages of their daughters. When they succeeded in arranging the marriages of their daughters, their former husbands came to know because of the close kinship networks and had the negotiations cancelled. There were a few cases in which a woman's divorce not only adversely affected the prospects of her daughter's marriage but also that of her unmarried siblings. For instance, in one case, whenever a marriage proposal for a boy whose sister was divorced was made the girl's side would reject the proposal saying 'when the brother is already burdened with the responsibility of his divorced sister how will our daughter be happy in the family'.

The large majority of divorced women have to face serious economic problems. The principal reason for this is that girls are poorly educated, especially in lower class homes, and the dominant social ethos tends to confine them within the four walls of the home. They are economically dependent upon their parents and brothers until they are married and after marriage they are supposed to be maintained by their husbands. Therefore, after they are divorced they usually end up becoming a burden upon their fathers or brothers and are exposed to severe pecuniary hardships, particularly in cases where the father or brothers are not well-off. Of the 53 divorced women, only 9 (16.9 per cent) did not face any economic hardships as a result of their divorce. In one case the son was earning and took care of his mother. In another case the former husband paid Rs. 30 per day to her for the maintenance of his children who were living with her. Before they were divorced 3 women were economically independent. They were working as teachers. They have not faced any serious economic hardships. However, 44 women (83.5 per cent), mostly illiterate and from relatively poor economic background, have had to face serious economic hardships after their divorce. These hardships were temporary in case of 20 women (37.7 per cent), because 17 women (32.0 per cent) remarried soon after and 3 (5.6 per cent) went on to complete their education and became economically independent. One of them is a bank manager. Facing acute economic problems are 25 women (45.2 per cent) because they found it difficult to remarry and the economic status of their families is low.

Economic hardships are generally more serious in the case of women who have children staying with them. Issueless women are able to curtail their needs so as not to become a burden on their parents or brothers. They will often not seek medical advice when they fall ill as they feel that this will put an unnecessary burden on their parents or brothers. Women with children are forced to face economic difficulties both because of the demands their children often make and the largely hostile and negative attitude of their sisters and sisters-in-law. For example, when sisters visit their parents or brothers they spend a good amount of money on shopping and buying things for their children. The same holds for their sisters-in-law. Seeing other mothers splurging on their children, the children of divorced mother too ask for the same things. This makes them unhappy and they end up beating their children for making unreasonable demands. Eventually, most of them try to start earning by doing some work. One of them does tailoring. She used her sister-in-law's sewing machine until one day the sister-in-law refused to allow her its use. Her father bought her a new machine. Another women goes door-to-door selling cloth. Only 4 women do domestic work for their relatives to eke out an independent existence. Most of these women do not wish it to be known that they are working as they fear that if the *biradari* comes to know of it the marital prospects of their daughters would be jeopardized.

For most women the utterance of *talaq* by the husband caused a mental earthquake. 'When the divorce took place,' one woman said, 'I felt acute pain throughout my body. I have not been keeping well since the divorce took place.' Another woman reported, 'When the divorce was pronounced, I was mentally devastated. Various kinds of thoughts came to my mind. How will I get my daughter married off? How will I support myself? In fact, the whole world seemed meaningless to me.' Childless women become depressed and cry alone at night; women with children constantly worry about their children's future. Life seems meaningless to them; they loose all interest in dressing well or in wearing jewellery or make up. Their social world gets confined to a few female relatives and neighbours The attitude of their relatives and society in general reinforces this tendency towards withdrawal. They are considered guilty and morally lax. What Mehta (1975) notes in her study of Hindu divorced women holds equally true for divorced Muslim women.

CONCLUSION

This paper has been concerned with divorce and remarriage in a township of western Uttar Pradesh. Evidence presented in this paper shows that the incidence of divorce is not particularly high among Muslims in this township. At any rate, so far as we can gauge from national data, it is lower than the national average. However, this should not detract us from other aspects of divorce which impinge directly on the status of Muslim women in general and within the marriage system in particular. On a careful and close look at the data presented, we are unable to escape the conclusion that Muslim women, much like their Hindu sisters, grow up in the belief that their proper place is in their husband's home and they should be sacrificing and obedient towards their husbands. When they are divorced their situation is generally pathetic.

A divorced woman has to revert to her parental family where she remains a source of worry to her parents and a cause for resentment for her brothers and sisters-in-law who see her presence as an intrusion into their lives and a burden on their limited economic resources. She has to work as almost a housemaid in order to sustain herself. If she falls ill or has to venture out of the house for one thing or another, she has to take the help of her father or brothers as she cannot go out on her own. If she decides to venture out on her own, she is made the target of adverse taunts by neighbours and relatives and doubts are cast on her integrity. Consequently, while Islam invests Muslim women with rights to *mehr*, dowry and remarriage, social and cultural mores rather than Islamic principles exert a greater influence in determining their actual social status in the event of divorce and separation from their husbands.

REFERENCES

Esposito, J.L. (1982), *Women in Muslim Family Law*, Syracuse: Syracuse University Press.

Mehta, R. (1975), *Divorced Hindu Woman*, New Delhi: Vikas Publishing House.

3

A 'Uniform Customary Code'? Marital Breakdown and Women's Economic Entitlements in Rural Bijnor

Patricia Jeffery

Drawing on research in rural Bijnor district, this paper focuses on aspects of everyday gender politics in western UP.[1] In particular, exploring marital breakdown enables me to raise questions about the relationship between formal law and theology on the one hand and the lived realities of Muslim and Hindu women on the other, about the efficacy of the law in protecting women's rights, and about strategic priorities in the struggle for gender equity in India—all issues that are raised by the Shah Bano controversy.

THE SHAH BANO CASE

Among the many activities initiated during the British colonial era one was the classification of the Indian population on the basis of religious allegiance and another the codification of indigenous legal systems and customary means of dispute settlement.[2] These included procedures for dealing with events in family life—such as marriage and marital breakdown, child custody, and property transfers within the family. Recent commentaries note that written texts were privileged over oral traditions and encoding the 'correct' legal framework entailed attempts to homogenize the diversity of 'customary practices'. Crucially, British civil servants who consulted (male) religious experts assumed that family life was governed by religious texts. Thus, distinctive systems of 'personal law' were codified, despite considerable evidence of cultural parallels and religious syncretism. Further, official policy was that family life should normally be regulated by the authorities of the different religious communities.[3] After 1947, despite opposition the Hindu Code was revised (Agnes, 1995; Kapur and Cossman, 1996; Kishwar, 1994; Parashar, 1992) but Indian Muslims are still (notionally) governed by the Shar'iat Law of 1937.[4] Thus, the multiplicity of 'personal laws' remains—enshrining religious or communal divisions through the differing procedures, rights and obligations for Indian citizens of different religions.

However, systems of civil and criminal law applicable to all citizens irrespective of their religious allegiance, including the Criminal Procedure Code (CrPC), were also developed and enforced by the British. The Indian government's 1973 revision of Section 125 of the CrPC enabled women who became homeless (after divorce, for instance, or being ousted from a son's house) to press for maintenance from their ex-husband or their son. In such cases, how would Muslim Personal Law and the CrPC come into play in relation to the rights of divorced Muslim women?

After being divorced, Shah Bano, an elderly Muslim woman from Indore (in Madhya Pradesh) appealed through the provisions of CrPC Section 125 for maintenance from her ex-husband. He contested the case, arguing that it would be un-Islamic for a Muslim man to provide for his wife beyond the *iddat* period. Eventually, the case came before the Supreme Court in Delhi in 1985.[5] Conservative Muslims argued that the (Hindu) Supreme Court judges had neither the competence nor the jurisdiction to try the Shah Bano case or to make adverse comments on women's position in Islam. Indeed, due to the hue and cry raised by the case Shah Bano felt compelled to dissociate herself from the judgement because she came to believe that it was contrary to Islamic law (Engineer, 1987: 211-12). Rajiv Gandhi's Congress government permitted an independent Member of Parliament to introduce the somewhat curiously titled Muslim Women (Protection of Rights on Divorce) Bill, which became law in 1986. Under its provisions, it seems that Muslim *men* were protected from maintenance claims by ex-wives because Muslim *women* could no longer make claims under CrPC Section 125.[6]

The Bill was widely debated but responses to it were largely framed by Congress and conservative Muslim rhetoric emphasizing the constitutional protection of the rights of the minorities to govern their own domestic lives, free from state interference and in accord with the (supposed) requirements of their religious beliefs. In opposing the Bill, the Hindu Right[7] also focused on minority rights, but to accuse the Congress of cynically refusing to intervene in Muslim family law in order to retain the 'Muslim vote bank'[8], and of 'appeasing' Muslims by according them more rights than the majority Hindu population had (for instance, by letting Muslim men evade the obligations entailed under CrPC 125); the conservative Muslim stance was viewed as confirmation that Muslim men victimize their womenfolk and that Islam is inherently oppressive to women (in contrast to Hindu men and the Hindu tradition). Soon, this was explicitly linked to the Hindu Right's increasingly assertive proclamations over the Babri Masjid in Ayodhya and to the wider communalization of politics, marked by Muslim vulnerability to physical and rhetorical attacks from the Hindu Right and by the electoral successes of the BJP in the 1990s. In terms of subsequent political developments, then, the reading of the Shah Bano case in terms of minority rights and communal politics clearly has considerable justification.[9]

Yet the Shah Bano case was certainly not simply about minority rights and communal politics. At its core are crucial issues of women's economic entitlements. Liberal Muslims opposing the Muslim Women Bill asserted that generosity to ex-wives would not be contrary to the spirit of Islam or signify that Islam was endangered. Various feminist organizations not only opposed the Bill because it disadvantaged Muslim women *vis-à-vis* other Indian women, but attacked the negative comments about Islam in the Supreme Court judgement and highlighted the paltry sums normally awarded as maintenance. Shah Bano herself was granted just Rs. 179.20 per month by the Supreme Court after a lower court had originally granted her Rs. 25. Feminists also contested the claims of the Hindu Right that Muslim women were especially disadvantaged and that the position of Hindu women was unproblematic. They argued that the furore distracted attention from the inability of Indian women in general to ensure their financial security outside marriage. Such voices, however, became increasingly marginalized in the unfolding debate because of the stridency of the Hindu Right's interventions.

Gender equity is enshrined in the Indian Constitution—but so too is freedom to practise religion. During the 1980s, the Indian government was swayed in turn by the contradictory demands of Muslim conservatives and the Hindu Right, for whom women were a crucial part of the terrain on which battles about minority rights and national identity were fought.[10] As the Shah Bano case demonstrated, religious freedom may be privileged over gender equity when the two clash: 'community' self-regulation on matters covered by personal laws is a core element of religious freedom, yet the protection of religious freedom can have an extremely detrimental impact on women's rights (Jeffery, 1999; Kapur and Cossman, 1995).

Accounts of the Shah Bano case, however, are marked by a focus on high profile political, legal and constitutional issues. Little attention has been paid to the implications of the case with regard to communal and gender politics at the grass roots, my central concerns here. I want to make three main points in this paper. First, crucial parallels in the everyday domestic lives of Hindu and Muslim women in rural Bijnor, combined with case material on marital breakdown, challenge the assertion of the Hindu Right that Muslim women alone are oppressed by their menfolk and by their religion. Second, the Shah Bano case and the Babri Masjid campaign were highly significant in terms of local-level communal politics in Bijnor (Basu, 1995b; Jeffery and Jeffery, 1994b and 1997). Yet, the Muslim Women (Protection of Rights on Divorce) Act, 1986; appears to have had no impact on the economic situations of ordinary Muslim women. And finally, as a consequence of the first two points, placing local-level gender politics alongside the communalization of politics exposes the dilemmas of feminist activists with regard to mobilizing rural women around issues of gender equity.

COMMUNITY AND GENDER IN RURAL BIJNOR

About a quarter of Indian Muslims live in UP. In 1991, according to the Registrar General and Census Commissioner 1996 (Table C-9) they numbered over 24 million or 17.33 per cent of the state's total population. Almost two-thirds live in the rural areas, compared with the overall UP figure of just over 80 per cent. Muslims are under-represented among the most wealthy sectors: town-dwellers tend to inhabit particular residential areas and are especially associated with artisanal activities such as weaving and metal work; rural Muslims are generally middle or poor peasants, landless agricultural labourers or semi-skilled labourers (mechanics, weavers, etc.). Within the same class, the domestic arrangements, property rights, linguistic and diet patterns of north Indian Muslims and Hindus, and the distinctively South Asian flavour to Islam, are strikingly similar despite the divisions connected with the aftermath of Partition and the recent communalization of politics (Ahmad, 1973, 1976 and 1981; Hasan 1991 and 1997; Mann, 1992).

Bijnor district in western UP seems less affluent than districts to its west, which have had canal irrigation since the end of the nineteenth century, but on most criteria of social and economic development it is rather more 'developed' than eastern UP. At about 32 per cent, the rural Muslim population in Bijnor district is proportionately one of the highest in UP.[11] Broadly speaking, kinship and marriage, residence and property ownership, gender politics and demography among Muslims and Hindus alike reflect what Dyson and Moore have called the 'northern demographic regime' (1983). What follows is an attempt to sketch the position of young married women, for whom marital breakdown by separation or divorce is most salient.

As throughout the region, productive resources, especially land, are owned (albeit inequitably) and managed by men. Women—whether as daughters or as wives—scarcely ever own land, irrespective of community or social class (Agarwal, 1994). A girl normally depends on her father and brothers to meet the costs of raising her and of arranging her marriage. At all levels of the class hierarchy, the most honourable form of marriage requires the bride's parents and their wider kin network to provide a dowry. This can entail major outlays for clothing and jewellery for the bride and members of her husband's family, household goods—bed, bedding, cooking utensils, etc.—and, among Hindus, cash.[12] On marriage the bride normally migrates to her husband's village. If the mother-in-law is alive, the new bride can expect to spend some years sharing a cooking hearth, subject not only to her husband's controls but also to those of his mother.

It is crucial that a woman bear children, yet the physiological processes associated with fertility and childbearing (sexual intercourse, menstruation, pregnancy, child birth and post-partum bleeding) are matters of shame (*sharm ki bat*) and/or of pollution (locally termed *gandagi*). Moreover, Muslims and Hindus alike readily express a preference for sons over daughters, largely grounding their views on parental anxieties about providing dowries for daughters and on the importance of having sons to ensure support in old age. This part of UP—and northern South Asia in general—is notable for a preponderance of males in the sex ratio, attributable to differential care of young boys and girls and high rates of maternal mortality.

Whilst a young married woman's work may be trivialized by her in-laws (and even by herself), she plays an important economic role in the well-being of her husband's household, cooking, rearing children, caring for livestock or working in the family fields. Variations in women's work relate to the class position of their husband's household, whether Hindu or Muslim, as well as to life cycle changes. In the wealthiest households, controls over women's mobility beyond domestic space are evidenced in seclusion practices known locally as purdah; women will work almost wholly in and around the home. Somewhat poorer households may endeavour to keep their womenfolk engaged in activities based around the home, generally unpaid work for the household, although some women earn small sums of money by spinning cotton thread or stitching clothes for neighbours. Women in the poorest households may be compelled to seek employment as domestic servants or field labourers for the richer households. Poor, and usually elderly, widows (or women whose husbands have low incomes) may practise as *dais* (traditional birth attendants), a low status occupation associated with pollution (Jeffery and Jeffery, 1993a). Most rural women are not well-placed to support themselves. Very few have the schooling or training that could enable them to earn enough to become economically independent.

Migration due to marriage has important social consequences for women. Unlike her husband, a young married woman generally has little 'social capital', because she is separated from the networks of kin and friends she established during childhood. Nevertheless, her parents and brothers continue to be concerned for her. Partly, this is reflected in the things they continue to present to her. Indeed, Hindu and Muslim women described their 'income' (*amdani*) as the foodstuff (grain, sugar products), jewellery, clothing and cash (and very occasionally livestock) sent by their natal kin after the rice and wheat harvests, at festivals (e.g. Id for Muslims and Holi for Hindus), when they give birth, when their children are married, and when there are marriages and births in their natal household. Usually, however, such gifts are neither regular nor sufficient to meet all their requirements and provide them with a route to economic independence. Indeed, women whose parents and brothers are financially straitened may receive little or no such 'income'.

Some features of domestic life in rural Bijnor suggest that many Muslim women may be somewhat better placed than the typical Hindu woman. While preferences for a son are expressed irrespective of religious community, maternity history and census data from the villages studied indicate that sex ratios are markedly less in favour of males among Muslims than among Hindus (Jeffery and Jeffery, 1997: 68, 230-5).[13] Among Muslims, the demand for dowry and harassment of young married women for more dowry, the fear of which plagues Hindus, is rare and Muslim dowries do not include cash, unlike those among Hindus. Hindus marry their children into villages usually at some distance from their own (25-30 km was common); women are usually married into households where they know no one and only rarely are two closely related women married into the same village. Muslims generally arrange their children's marriages within a smaller geographical radius (about 3 km or less, and even within the same village) and/or with people who are already closely related. This does not guarantee a woman's well-being after marriage but Muslim women are normally less cut off from their natal kin than Hindu women. Married Hindu women normally receive visits from their brothers: many are never visited by parents (particularly the mother) and they rely on their husband or brothers to accompany them to their natal village for visits. Many married Muslim women can walk to their natal village—maybe with their children or another married woman—and it is not uncommon for even their mothers to make the reverse trip. Dense marriage networks enable a Muslim woman's parents to have considerable information about a potential groom and his close relatives before agreeing to a marriage—and to exert pressure if their married daughter is mistreated, although many Muslim women see this as a rather ambiguous benefit because parents cannot easily be spared knowledge of their marital troubles.[14]

Basically, though, a married woman—whether Muslim or Hindu—is the responsibility of her husband and his kin, who should continue to provide for her throughout her life, meeting her daily expenses for food, clothing, medical care and so forth. Young married women are very unlikely to own productive resources or have incomes that permit economic independence. They continue to obtain some social and economic support from their natal kin, but are basically dependent on their husband and his kin. The room young married women have for self-determination in their affinal village is severely circumscribed by their lack of economic and social power in their own right (Jeffery and Jeffery, 1996a: 1-37). Being married closer to their natal home and lesser dowry does not add up to greater autonomy for Muslim women, but it probably does make the negotiation of dependency somewhat easier for them. Few Hindu or Muslim women in rural Bijnor, however, regard their dependency as problematic and many feared the 'responsibility' (*zimmedari*) that independence (*azadi*) would entail (Jeffery and Jeffery, 1994a, 1996b and 1993b). The limitations of what women think is a secure state, however, are starkly exposed by marital breakdowns.

MARITAL BREAKDOWN

Conversations with women in rural Bijnor suggest that marital bliss is a somewhat elusive state. Women often resented the treatment meted out to them by their husbands, their mothers-in-law and other in-laws. Many women complained that they cannot visit their parents as often as they wish, that they are required to work extremely hard and yet their efforts are inadequately appreciated, that marital violence is commonplace.

Nevertheless, few marriages end in separation.[15] Most separations occur in the first few years of a marriage, when there are few, if any, children. Beyond that, though, it is impossible even to hazard rates of marital breakdown. It is a 'shameful matter' (*sharm ki bat*) and we often learnt of separations or marital difficulties by chance, when querying gaps in women's maternity histories, or when old marital conflicts were dug up as part of people's weaponry in present disputes, or when young women returned to their natal village and became the focus of gossip. Our most detailed data relate to the eighty-eight key informant couples.[16] Of these, about 6 per cent of the key informant women had experienced separation: one Muslim woman and three Hindu women were in second (or later) marriages and another Muslim woman had been 'divorced' by her husband but had returned to live with him (see Jeffery and Jeffery [1996a: 142-54] for more details of her case). This figure cannot be extended to the populations as a whole, of course; nor can these cases give a firm sense of differential rates of marital breakdown, say by economic position or community, or which spouse is more likely to initiate the separation.

While these cases and the others we learnt about vary in their specifics, there are some common features, whether they occurred before or after the Shah Bano case. Formal divorce procedures are hardly ever deployed. Few people take marital disputes to secular law courts and Muslim couples are unlikely to take their case to a qazi. Rather, informal kin- and village-based mechanisms are central, both in trying to prevent marital breakdown and in dealing with it once it happens. These 'customary' and taken-for-granted procedures may not relate closely to stipulations laid out in theological treatises or in the statute books of the Indian state. Focusing on how people customarily respond to marital problems and marriage breakdowns further demonstrates important parallels between Muslims and Hindus in rural Bijnor.

AVOIDING MARITAL BREAKDOWN

Marital breakdown is far more than a 'shameful matter' and the economic as well as social constraints that separated women face help explain why women often devote considerable energy to avoiding it. Recent discussions emphasizing the importance of disaggregating the household and focusing on intra-household negotiations give some leverage here (Agarwal, 1997; Kandiyoti, 1988, and 1998; Sen, 1990). Sen views households as characterized by 'co-operative conflicts', because members have some interests in common and others which differs. Negotiations over conflicts reflect the parties' perceptions of their interests, contributions to the household and entitlements: the outcomes normally benefit those parties with the least to lose in the 'breakdown position' (when the household itself dissolves) because they have the greatest bargaining power. Similarly, Agarwal outlines the differential bargaining power and different 'exit options' of household members. Against Sen, though, she argues that women's failure to strike bargains seemingly in their interest should not be interpreted as acceptance of their situation, for there is evidence aplenty that South Asian women critique their situations. An 'overt appearance of compliance' is a 'survival strategy' (Agarwal, 1997: 24) for women who lack economic power (productive and other resources, independent income) and social capital (social support networks after marriage migration, socially sanctioned and gendered styles of bargaining) within the household and beyond. This is similar to Kandiyoti's view of the 'patriarchal bargains' struck when women weigh up the short- and long-term costs and benefits of complying with or resisting their situations. Gender inequalities change through an individual's life-time and the relatively powerless young married woman can anticipate a more powerful position as mother-in-law in later years—provided she toes the line in the meanwhile (Kandiyoti, 1988).[17]

Men do not lightly or frequently oust their wives from the marital home. The labour intensity of household work plus the gender division of labour mean that households need able-bodied adult women just as much as they need men. Men also need wives to bear sons to support them in old age. That said, a separated man does not lose his home or his land (if any) and he is not usually socially shunned in his natal village, unless he has a reputation for extreme violence or heavy drinking. A separated man can generally find a second spouse more readily than a separated woman—although parents may be reluctant to marry their daughter to a man with a record of marital breakdown and such men's second wives are generally widowed or separated women.[18]

These considerations apply to Muslim and Hindu men alike, yet a central element of the Hindu Right's anti-Muslim rhetoric is the 'triple *talaq*', which they allege means that Muslim wives are routinely repudiated on a whim (by implication, in contrast to Hindu women).[19] Crucially for my argument, such communal contrasts are not supported by the Bijnor data. Few men of either community initiate a separation; when they do so, it is generally through informal means such as despatching their wife to her natal village or failing to collect her after a visit there. The triple *talaq* is simply not part of Muslim men's everyday repertoire—any more than secular law courts are for Hindu men.

In rural Bijnor, however, women's exit options make marital separation even less viable for them. Remaining in an un-congenial marriage often seems less forbidding when set against their likely fate as separated women. Several key informants as well as others—Hindu and Muslim alike—perceived their marital problems as seemingly having no realistic option but to live with them. Take Anisa, for example (Jeffery and Jeffery, 1996a: 254-6).[20] After she was widowed her parents wanted to safeguard her future so they arranged her marriage to Ahmed. About four years later (in 1991) her situation became miserable because her in-laws taunted her about her second marriage, beat her, refused to let her visit her parents and insulted her relatives if they visited her. How could she escape this situation? She had virtually no contact with her parents and had little prospect of rescue from that quarter:

> If I didn't think of the children, I'd just die. But then I realize there's no one who would care for my children. They'd end up running from one place to the next being beaten. . . . My first husband never even slapped me with his four fingers, but this one beats me daily. . . . On occasion, I've considered taking poison. But then I think about the children. Anyway, the villagers would say it was an unlawful death.

Generally, it is considered inappropriate for parents to become involved in their daughter's marital problems. Indeed, unhappily married women often say nothing to their parents, because they are ashamed or wish to protect their parents from knowing about troubles from which they should remain aloof, as Kavita's account illustrates (Jeffery and Jeffery, 1996a: 229-30). Much before her marriage in the late 1980s, Kavita's husband had been having an affair with his older brother's wife. In order to avoid trouble from the couple, Kavita adopted a policy of silence—both, with her marital relations and with her parents:

> The last time I visited my parents, my husband complained to them that I fight with him a lot. So my mother asked me why I fight with him. She told me to remain silent and not interfere with him whatever he might do. But how could I tell my parents about my husband's affair and the beatings?

I've never said a thing about it to my father when he visits me here. How could I tell him about such a wicked matter? I couldn't tell my mother either. Even if I got the courage to do so, my mother wouldn't be able to say anything to my father. So what would be the point?

Parental interventions considered unwarranted or excessively frequent are roundly criticized and create annoyance among their daughter's marital relations: A married daughter is in 'her own' house and is expected to deal with her own difficulties. Nevertheless, parents often did become involved if they felt that their daughter could not resolve or escape her marital problems without their support—a clear recognition of the young married woman's lack of social and economic power. For instance, when news came one evening in 1990 that Brijpal's daughter had taken rat poison after a dispute with her husband, Brijpal took a party of his young male relatives to threaten his son-in-law (Jeffery and Jeffery, 1996a: 192-6).

Sometimes a woman's parents make considerable effort to achieve a reconciliation or to make it possible for their daughter to tolerate her lot. Shankar's sister, for instance, was married to a man who spent all his income on drink. Shankar and his two brothers provided her with money, grain after each harvest and clothing so that she could remain in her marital village with her children (Jeffery and Jeffery, 1996a: 190). Often, interventions were occasioned when a daughter visited her parents and refused to return to her husband's home until her marital family had been confronted. A violent husband would be remonstrated and told that his wife would not return to his house until he mended his ways. A man whose father made unseemly advances or whose mother stirred up trouble—criticizing his wife's work, demanding that she bring more goods from her parents, taunting her because she had failed to bear any sons—might be told that his wife would not return until he guaranteed good treatment in future.

It is not unusual for a young woman to live in her parents' home for several months while these negotiations and threats take their course: Afsana spent nine months in her parents' home in 1982; Zebunissa was in her parents' home for over a year throughout our fieldwork in 1990-1; Promilla reported staying in her parents' home for about a year in the mid-1970s, while Jayavati was back in her widowed mother's house during much of our 1990-1 fieldwork (Jeffery and Jeffery, 1996a: 159-60, 219-23, 178-9, 197-9). The husband and members of his close family may make several visits before the young woman returns to her marital home.[21] Occasionally, a prominent person from the woman's natal village may mediate: Kunwar Satya Vira in Dharmnagri has enabled several young women to stand firm in refusing to rejoin their husbands, as in the case of Sudesh's daughter (Jeffery and Jeffery, 1996a: 132-3). The pressure on a woman's marital family may include threats of legal action, though they are rarely implemented: local people fear involvement in the legal process, even when their case is strong, because they believe the police and the judiciary to be corrupt.

MARITAL BREAKDOWN AND WOMEN'S ECONOMIC VULNERABILITY

When marriages break down, they generally do so before the wife has sons of an age to support her. Irrespective of who initiated the separation, the woman must leave the home she has shared with her husband: it is his home, not hers. She cannot even remain in her husband's village. Separated women do not enjoy ownership or usufruct rights in their ex-husband's land (or other property), any more than they have rights in the marital home; nor do they receive maintenance from their ex-husbands or his family. Few women have the education to enable them to enter the labour force on favourable terms.

Formally, Muslim women seem better placed than comparable Hindu women because of the *mehr* (the cash settlement by a Muslim man on his wife, specified in the marriage contract). In principle, the husband should give some or all of the *mehr* immediately. In practice, the *mehr* is deferred and the husband is expected to give it only if he initiates divorce; the woman who initiates separation forfeits the *mehr*. In the event of divorce, the *mehr* notionally provides the separated woman with economic security. There is no parallel among Hindus, which is perhaps why *mehr* does not figure in the Hindu Right's anti-Muslim discourse.

Muslim women in rural Bijnor were, however, sceptical about the *mehr*.[22] Many saw little sense in claiming it while living with their husband, since it would be spent on the food and clothing they were already receiving. Moreover, even if the *mehr* were given on separation it could not provide long-term economic independence. A quarter of the key informants did not know what their *mehr* was. Of those who did, just one mentioned a *mehr* of Rs. 15,000; another ten mentioned sums between Rs. 1,000 and Rs. 8,000, and five said their *mehr* was the '*mehr Fatimi*'[23] comprising 125 silver rupees. For the remaining third, the *mehr* was less then Rs. 500 (for more than half of them it was under Rs. 100 and several it was just Rs. 25). Several women said they had already consumed far more than their *mehr* was worth in their husband's home. Others said that their *mehr* was the focus of banter: Hashmi (whose *mehr* is Rs. 125) said 'My husband laughs and says "How much is the *mehr* anyway? I can give it whenever I wish!"' while Khurshida told us 'My father-in-law teases my husband, saying "Give Khurshida her Rs. 25—it's a very heavy *mehr*!"'

In any case, one-third of the key informants (largely those with the highest *mehr*) had 'forgiven' or 'renounced' (*mo'af karna*) the *mehr*, mostly under pressure from their husbands. For instance, when Zubeida was being married to her deceased older sister's husband, the proceedings were delayed for four days because of her step-father's insistence that the *mehr* be Rs. 5,000: but Zubeida was forced to renounce the *mehr* later (Jeffery and Jeffery, 1996a: 111-12). Two women had forfeited the *mehr* voluntarily in order not to place their husband in debt, while nearly a quarter could not recall if they had renounced it or not. The general view was 'But the *mehr* is fixed only to be forgiven—whoever pays it?' and 'The *mehr*? Who gives it? They all make you forgive it!' Not one woman had received her *mehr*, either when her marriage was consummated or later: as one woman put it, 'No one at all gives it. Period [*bas*!]. There must be one or two men somewhere in the world who give it, but we haven't heard of them!'

Even after divorce, women claimed, the *mehr* is not given. Several said that people are now 'tying' their sons-in-law with a 'price tag' (*raqam*, meaning a large *mehr*) to prevent them from initiating divorce, particularly if the marriage is between non-kin—but they saw little point if wives are compelled to renounce the *mehr*. Others said divorced and separated women are unlikely to receive the *mehr*, even when they have not forgiven it: 'But what is the benefit of *mehr*? If a man is going to leave his wife, he'll do so, no matter how much *mehr* has been set.' The *mehr* was sometimes shrouded in uncertainty as well as cynicism: 'I forgave it on the first night. But I've heard that *mehr* forgiven on the first night is not understood to have been forgiven in law. If it is forgiven a few days after the wedding, then it is considered forgiven. I do not really know. But here in the village, who gives the *mehr*? They don't give the *mehr* even if they do give *talaq*!'[24]

In rural Bijnor, then, Muslim women are not protected from marital breakdown or from financial insecurity after it by the *mehr*. A separated woman could not live an independent life on the basis of the *mehr*—but none of the separated Muslim women we knew had received their *mehr* in any case. In practice, no woman—whether Muslim or Hindu—is likely to receive financial support from her ex-husband.[25]

In other parts of the world, where women's property rights, agricultural work or educational levels permit economic independence, women may establish households headed by a female after separation or widowhood (Chant, 1997). South Asia as a whole, however, seems to be characterized by procedures that prevent such households from arising. The northern areas, in particular, are marked by low levels of female headed households.[26] For women in rural Bijnor, separation usually entails returning to their natal kin, at least in the first instance.

DEPENDING ON THE NATAL KIN

While a woman's natal kin will probably contribute to her material well-being, the dowry and other items presented to her may not be accessible to her. Foodstuff is generally shared and cooking utensils may have been requisitioned by her mother-in-law. Clothing may have been worn out or presented to an affinal relative and jewellery sold to pay off a debt or buy medicines, or presented to her husband's sister. Cash may have been spent on daily expenses or on large-scale expenditures, such as installing a tube well or refurbishing the house. Sometimes, a woman's parents threaten reprisal, but there is generally little hope of retrieving even a small portion of the items they presented to her, even if they have not been consumed.

Further, the woman who visits her parents and tells them of her marital problems could not have carried enough with her—apart from her jewellery perhaps—to support her for more than a few days. Some, such as Dilruba, who fear that their marriage might collapse, persuade their parents to store the foodstuff and cash they wish to give her rather than send it to them in their husband's home:

> For the past two years, I've been leaving the things at my mother's house so that I could buy my own necessities there. . . . Last Eid, for instance, I received 2 kg of sugar, 10 kg of unrefined sugar, 5 kg of rice, and 2 kg of flour. I just brought the sugar and left everything else at my mother's house. When he [Dilshad] divorced me and put me out of the house, I went to my mother's home. I sold some unrefined sugar and rice so that I could buy what I needed. Now I'm returning after six days, and my mother and my brother each gave me 10 kg of wheat. I've left it all in my mother's house. What could I do with it if I brought it here? (Jeffery and Jeffery, 1996a: 151).

A few women store jewellery in their parents' home, because they suspect that their parents-in-law or husband had designs on it—but the woman whose husband fails to collect her from her parents' house is more likely to have nothing salted away. In any case, even Dilruba's forward-planning would not provide long-term economic independence. Basically, a separated woman, whether Muslim or Hindu, faces almost certain penury unless she can persuade her natal kin to support her. Certainly, they are the separated women's best source of support—though not necessarily a very good one. Women whose marriages break down are often blamed for failing to adjust to their marital family, for bringing shame on their natal family and for damaging the marriage prospects of their unmarried siblings—unless they can plausibly argue that the whole sorry affair resulted from the evil intentions of their marital family. Moreover, once a daughter has been provided with a dowry, it is generally believed that she should not make further substantial claims on her parents' property, and certainly not on her father's land (if any). Periodic outlays for gifts to her as a married woman are of a very different order—in quantity and in how they are perceived—from meeting the expenses of a separated woman living permanently in her natal village again. Food, clothing, medical expenses on a daily basis for her and any children who have accompanied her, their education, and marriages, would exceed her parents' and brothers' expectations of their financial obligations. She would be considered not simply a financial burden, but as wrongfully consuming the entitlements of her brothers, their wives and their children. Her natal kin, then, may provide shelter and support only grudgingly and temporarily.

DEPENDENCY IN ANOTHER MARRIAGE

Even women acting decisively to end an unhappy marriage cannot ensure their control over their destiny thereafter, for their natal kin generally make haste to place them in new 'marriages'. Among Hindus, these new unions do not involve full marriage rituals; among Muslims they may. Locally, though, the pair are usually regarded as married and their children are considered legitimate.[27] This, however, may not necessarily be an attractive prospect for either party.

The preferred marriage for men is with a previously unmarried woman whose natal kin will provide her with a dowry. The separated woman cannot meet the former criterion—and her natal kin may not meet the latter one at all or only to the extent that makes her an attractive match.

Sometimes, natal kin put together a modest second dowry, but they are unlikely to have retrieved any items from the first one and they may be unable or unwilling to foot another substantial bill. A few years after Chet Ram was widowed in the mid-1980s, he remarried. His second wife had earlier been married to an impotent alcoholic and had spent three years in her natal village after refusing to return to him. Chet Ram presented her with no clothes or jewellery at the time of their marriage but her parents presented him with Rs. 200, a watch and some cloth some months later. Of the separated key informants, however, she is the only one remarried like this. The separated (and sometimes also the widowed) woman is more likely to become a 'bought bride', when her new husband 'takes a bride for a price' (*bahu mol-lena*), particularly if her brothers or another male go-between organize her second match. In the late 1970s, Taslim (in Jhakri) bought Tahira from his sister's husband who lived in Tahira's natal village. In Dharmnagri, Rohtash paid Rajballa's brothers Rs. 800 in the late 1970s, while Lalit obtained seven wives in this fashion, including Lakshmi for whom he paid his cousin (MBS) Rs. 2,000 in about 1980 (Jeffery et al., 1989: 39-41; Jeffery and Jeffery, 1996a: 231-44). In 1981 Muni left her violent husband and took shelter in the home of a cousin whose husband sold her for Rs. 2,000 to her current husband in Nangal.

This is certainly not an approved method of marrying. Usually the man is unable to arrange a conventional marriage, because he is widowed and already has children or is considered too old by parents with young marriageable daughters, or because he has been deserted by a wife who accused him of mistreatment, or of some social or physical disability, or was extremely poor. The woman herself can expect little or no economic and social support from her natal kin. Bought brides come empty handed (*khali hath*), without a dowry or the other gifts associated with the typical bride. They rarely visit their natal kin or receive visits from them and are very poorly placed to protect themselves, whether from taunting neighbours or marital violence. Yet remarriage is the most likely outcome for the separated woman: in the four study villages, just three women had remained separated for several years without being remarried.

It is hardly surprising that women and their natal kin strive so hard to prevent marital breakdowns. The social and economic prospects for separated women pale in comparison with an approved dowry marriage—perhaps even in the face of considerable discord. The similarity in Muslim and Hindu women's experiences of economic dependency in marriage and economic vulnerability after marital breakdown is a key point here. Contrary to the assertions of the Hindu Right, Hindu women in rural Bijnor are not less vulnerable to being left in penury by their husbands than Muslim women are. The types of problems women report, the efforts they put into achieving reconciliation, their reliance on natal kin and the centrality of kin-based mechanisms for dispute resolution are common across the board. So, too, are the outcomes when the marriage breaks down: women's lack of entitlements in the ex-husband's household, their temporary reliance on their natal kin, and their probable remarriage in circumstances that may prove no better (and may even be worse) than the first marriage.

LEGAL REFORM AND GENDER POLITICS AT THE LOCAL LEVEL

Adherents of organizations such as Tablighi-i-Jamat work to expunge 'cultural' and 'religious' syncretism from Muslim practices in South Asia (Gardner, 1999; Metcalf, 1999). On the other hand, the loyalty of Indian Muslims to the Indian nation has often been questioned by the Hindu Right, whose rhetoric is replete with contrasting stereotypes of Hindus and Muslims (Bacchetta, 1993 and 1994; Basu, 1995a; Hasan, 1988). In rural Bijnor, ethnic differences are indeed signalled in numerous ways (such as dress styles, aspects of religious belief and practice, stereotyping [Jeffery, forthcoming]). Yet, if we focus on micro-level everyday life, any bald proposition that Muslims and Hindus are inherently different flies in the face of social complexity. Identifications cross-cut one another in confusing and conflicting ways. People's behaviour—for instance, with regard to gender politics—cannot be neatly glossed as 'Muslim' or 'Hindu'. In other words, there are 'multiple patriarchies' cutting across the boundaries of reified religious communities (Sangari, 1995).

Nevertheless, much of the discourse surrounding the Shah Bano affair—whether emanating from the Hindu Right, conservative Muslims or the state—played on assumptions that Muslims and Hindus are (or ought to be) essentially different. Moreover, the communalization of contemporary Indian politics has had severe consequences for the attainment of gender justice. I shall just touch on two of the issues that arise here: the role of legal reform and how feminists can engage with the state; and the mobilization of women at the grass root level around issues of gender equity.

Just after Independence in 1947 there was widespread optimism that the state would act to protect its citizens and that legislative reforms and government planning could achieve social justice, including for women. The disillusionment already in evidence by the late 1960s was exacerbated by the damning evidence of the gulf between women's constitutional rights and their daily lives, presented in the report of the National Committee on the Status of Women in India in 1974. Other events in the 1970s and 1980s—for instance, the notorious Mathura rape case—left many feminists deeply doubtful about the state's capacity to be an effective and reliable ally for women, not least because agents of the state—whether local policemen, national and state legislators or senior judges—have so often been implicated in actions inimical to women's interests. The stock-taking surrounding the fiftieth anniversary of Indian Independence sparked further analysis among feminists about achievements and failures to date, as well as about strategic priorities in the light not just of communalized politics but also the economic developments of the 1990s, such as structural adjustment, economic liberalization and consumerism (see Agnes, 1995; Agnihotri and Mazumdar, 1995; Butalia, 1997-8; Kapur and Cossman, 1995 and Cossman, 1996: 232-83; Sangari, 1995).

Throughout these debates, the Uniform Civil Code (UCC) has been a recurrent and contentious theme. The report on the Status of Women in India had addressed the matter in the mid-1970s (National Committee on the Status of Women, 1975: 57) and, until the Shah Bano case, the replacement of the separate systems of personal law by a single gender-equitable UCC was a central demand of feminists in India. The Hindu Right, however, appropriated the idea of the UCC during the Shah Bano controversy, a move that seriously compromised feminist positions on legal reform. If feminists supported the UCC and opposed the Muslim Women Bill, they would risk being co-opted to the agenda of the Hindu Right and antagonizing many Muslims by intervening in community affairs. Not to press for gender-equitable legislation pertaining to family matters, however, could leave unchallenged personal laws that are premised on gender inequity. Not surprisingly, feminist activists in India remain divided over how to define the key issues and how to campaign for gender equity.

Can they tackle gender issues without marginalizing other dimensions of inequality (caste, class, community)? Can they rely on reforms coming from within 'communities'? Should they concentrate on legal reforms and if so, what form should these take (Anveshi Law Committee, 1997; Gangoli and Solanki, 1997; Working Group on Women's Rights, 1996)? Should feminists focus on legal provisions within the framework of women's dependency in marriage, may be pressing for larger maintenance payments (which are notoriously difficult to enforce) or for once-off rights in matrimonial property which might be easier to enforce but would not be relevant for women married to poor men (Agnes, 1992; Parashar, 1997)?

There is also the fear that focussing inordinately on women's rights to maintenance may perpetuate the presumption that women are (or should be) dependent on their husbands. Perhaps, indeed, the demand for a UCC falls into the trap of framing issues of gender equity solely in terms of women's position in the 'private' sphere of the family. Maybe, the emphasis should be on enabling women to attain economic viability outside marriage for that would be a better long-term remedy for their disempowering dependency within marriage. The recent unearthing of the National Planning Committee's 1938 Report of the Sub-committee on Woman's Role in Planned Economy has highlighted how this (albeit contradictory) document contained not just recommendations for a UCC but also emphasized women's role as productive citizens whose work would give them economic rights as well as benefit the nation (Banerjee, 1998; Chaudhuri, 1996; Kasturi, 1996). Yet government policy since 1947 has largely been oriented towards women as members of families, as mothers and as targets for family planning and welfare measures, not as individual citizens and workers. So, should feminist activism target state policies on employment and training?

Then again, going beyond questions of which emphases are most appropriate in relation to government policy and legislation, are feminist activities best focused on the state, given its history of failures? Lest I be misunderstood, let me clarify that I am not advocating disengagement from the state. For one thing, it would give *carte blanche* to pressure groups unlikely to have women's interests at heart. Further, at the very least, the law plays important symbolic and normative roles in stipulating what is permissible and what intolerable and so it is vital that the many gender (and other) inequities still enshrined in the legal system be removed. Yet, it is also crucial to ask how much priority and energy should be focused on legislative reforms and on the state at the centre. Even when the framing of legislation apparently points towards the eradication of gender inequities, implementation that is gender-biased may undermine the intent of the legislation and prevent women from ensuring that their legal rights are met in practice.

Marital breakdown in rural Bijnor is just one case in point. Prior to the Muslim Women (Protection of Rights on Divorce) Act, 1986, Hindu and Muslim women alike had no customary right to maintenance after marital breakdown and they relied on support from their natal kin or from a new husband. None of the separated Muslim women we knew had received the *mehr* or received support from a qazi to enforce their claims. Few women, whether Hindu or Muslim, could afford to employ lawyers and make maintenance claims under CrPC Section 125; after all, Shah Bano herself exercised control over no funds and she could pursue her claims in the courts only because of financial support from her adult sons. The law played a very limited role in preventing women from becoming destitute after marital breakdown. In practice, then, the removal of the Act that enshrined Muslim women's right to appeal through CrPC Section 125 had little direct negative impact on the *economic* situation of Muslim women in rural Bijnor. Nor did the Act differentiate between the economic positions of Hindu and Muslim women in practice (formally, though, it clearly did, and the wider impact of the affair on local communal politics should not be under-estimated). Briefly, Muslim and Hindu women's economic insecurity in the event of marital breakdown has remained comparable.

In other words, what practical effect would a gender-equitable UCC—or indeed other legislation focusing on gender issues—have on ordinary Indian women's experiences of family life? Even in a situation of formal legal gender equality, there is no guarantee that *substantive* gender equality would result, without interventions in local-level social, economic and political processes beyond the legal domain, such as gender inequalities in accessing property, income and entitlements in everyday practice. In rural Bijnor, there is already a (fairly) 'uniform customary code' with respect to gender politics at the domestic level, one that stacks the cards against women, especially young women. Many feminists argue that empowering and mobilizing women is the most effective remedy for this sort of issue (see, for instance, Molyneux, 1998; Moser, 1989).

Yet it is a remedy difficult to enforce in rural Bijnor. For one thing, essentialized gender differences and the naturalization of many aspects of everyday family life limit the critical reach of women's complaints. Women do not question the propriety of migration through marriage, for instance, yet it seriously disempowers young married women in their husband's household. The efforts people put into preventing marital breakdown reflect women's lack of realistic options beyond dependency within the household: women are unlikely to mount far-reaching challenges to their best source of support and well-being—albeit not always a very good source, and one that is often felt to be a source of misery as well. Further, the interests of the various women within a household do not coincide and their individual perspectives shift in the course of the life cycle. Moreover, lack of social capital in their affinal villages puts women in weak positions in the wider community, making it difficult for them either to mobilize or to withstand backlash (Jeffery, 1999; Jeffery, forthcoming; Jeffery and Jeffery, 1996a: 1-37 and 1999: 136-8). Women's resistance, then, is largely on an individual level and sporadic 'everyday resistance' rather than organized activism (Scott, 1985).

Crucially here, the communalization of Indian politics and people's heightened awareness of communal identities means that mobilizing women across the communal boundary is no simple matter. The impact of the Shah Bano case and the Babri Masjid campaign was felt locally, through communal violence, Muslim fears and Hindu assertiveness. During our research in 1990-1, many Hindu men cited the Shah Bano case as evidence of Hindu victimization, of Muslim appeasement, and the justice of the Babri Masjid campaign. Indeed, Muslim women and men in Bijnor discussed the Shah Bano case in relation to communal politics, not the rights of Muslim women. In Bijnor town, women of the Durga Vahini (the women's organization affiliated to the Vishwa Hindu Parishad) were crucial in the events that led up to the communal disturbances and curfew in October 1990 (Basu, 1995b; Jeffery and Jeffery, 1994b and 1997). At the village level, Muslim and Hindu women and men engage in communal stereotyping and distancing (Jeffery, forthcoming). Gender and communal differences are marked in the accessibility to facilities provided by the local state, such as health care and schooling (Jeffery and Jeffery, 1999). Women's allegiances to their communal identities hamper the translation of their complaints about their everyday situations into feminist activism across communal boundaries. Moreover, unlike in some other parts of South Asia, there is little NGO activity, including women's groups, in western UP that might facilitate women's mobilization and empowerment and the workings of local political parties, whether communal or not, provide little scope for optimism either (Omvedt, 1993).

The Shah Bano case certainly had a momentous impact on India's recent political history: the constitutional dilemmas it raised are unresolved and the scars of communal disturbances remain. Yet the case has tended to divert attention away from the need to tackle gender politics at the grass roots, not just within the formal legal realm and by focusing on the state at the centre. Rights and obligations during marriage and after marital breakdown are not narrowly legal matters amenable to simple legal resolution. They are intensely political issues and customary procedures for dispute resolution reflect power imbalances at the micro-level. Crucially, women currently lack entitlements to economic resources and they are relatively powerless in the domestic arena and beyond. Without far-reaching changes at that level, women's formal legal rights are likely to remain a dead letter.

NOTES

1. This work has been done in collaboration with Roger Jeffery and I am grateful to him for comments on this paper. Our thanks go to all the people in Bijnor who were so generous with their time; to our research assistants (Swaleha Begum, Radha Rani Sharma, Savita Pandey, Chhaya Pandey, Zarin Ahmed and Swatantra Tyagi); and to colleagues in Edinburgh, Kuala Lumpur, Amsterdam, Oxford and Prague for comments on earlier versions of this paper. We are grateful to the Economic and Social Research Council (UK), the Moray Fund of the University of Edinburgh and the Overseas Development Administration (UK) for research funding; none of these organization is responsible for the opinions expressed here.
2. The British also codified vocabularies and grammars of local languages, systematized place names and engaged in extensive geographical and geological surveys. For more on this see, Appadurai, 1993; Cohn, 1987; Ludden, 1993; Pandey, 1990.

3. The state's non-involvement in the 'private sphere' was (and still is) notional, of course. Prior to 1947, several instances of state involvement generated widespread debate and opposition: on *sati* (widow immolation) and the age of consent see Parashar, 1992: 17-76; Sangari, 1995; Sarkar, 1993.
4. In Pakistan, by contrast, revised legislation passed in 1961 as the Muslim Family Laws Ordinance attempted to enhance the legal rights of Muslim women by reducing some of the most overtly discriminatory provisions of the 1937 Shariat legislation. Implementation and enforcement have, however, remained partial at best; see, for instance, Chipp-Kraushaar, 1981 and Mumtaz and Shaheed, 1987: 57-9. At the time of writing, the Ordinance has been challenged by conservatives (as it has been periodically since 1961) which is being counter-challenged by feminist organizations see Women's Feature Service, 1999).
5. The following provide useful accounts of the case: Chhachhi, 1991; Engineer, 1987; Hasan, 1989, 1993, 1994 and 1999; Kishwar, 1986; Kumar, 1993: Chapter 10; Mody, 1987; Palriwala and Agnihotri, 1996: 511-19; Pathak and Rajan, 1989.
6. Certainly, the most widespread interpretation was that Muslim women's rights were being undermined. There is some ambiguity, however, because the Act's requirement that a Muslim man provide his ex-wife with fair and reasonable provision allowed some legal decisions in which Muslim women obtained sizeable lump sum payments. In West Bengal, for instance, Mukhopadhyay (1994) reports that some women obtained legal aid and some successfully claimed maintenance through the Criminal Procedure Code. After the Muslim Women Bill was enacted, Muslim men facing claims from their ex-wives made counter-claims that they were under no obligation to pay maintenance. Engineer (1999) reports a case in Mumbai in which the judges used the Muslim Women (Rights on Divorce) Act 1986, to argue for long-term maintenance for a divorced Muslim woman. In response to outcomes such as this, Syed Shahabuddin introduced a private member's bill in the Lok Sabha to prevent this (see Agnes, 1996).
7. The 'Hindu Right' comprises several organizations also known as the '*Sangh Parivar*' or the family of the *Sangh*: the Rashtriya Swayamsevak Sangh (RSS or National Volunteer Corps), the Bharatiya Janata Party (BJP) and the Vishwa Hindu Parishad (VHP).
8. The notion of a somewhat mythical 'vote bank' revolves around the assumption that groups of people, such as Muslims, vote en bloc in local and national elections because their leaders can control their followers' votes. Indian Muslims tended to vote for the Congress until the late 1980s, but sizeable numbers have also voted for parties championing the interests of the urban working classes and the rural dispossessed, especially in recent years.

9. For discussions of the Ayodhya affair and the communalization of politics, see Basu and Kohli, 1998; Basu et al., 1993; Chakravarti et al., 1992; Engineer, 1991; Gopal, 1991; Hasan, 1997; Jaffrelot, 1996; Ludden, 1996; van der Veer, 1994; Vanaik, 1997.
10. Literature on this topic addresses how women are iconized in relation to the nation or community, the role of women activists in the Hindu Right, and how politicized religious organizations advocate conventional family roles for women, emphasize the importance of personal law in 'defining' community, and use gendered stereotypes in communal politics: see Bacchetta, 1993, 1994 and 1996; Basu, 1999, 1993 and 1995a; Hasan, 1989, 1993, 1994 and 1999; Jeffery and Basu, 1999; Kandiyoti, 1991; Sarkar, 1991; Sarkar and Butalia, 1995. The complex interplay between gender and national or ethnic identities is an issue not only in India but more generally (see, for instance, Anthias and Yuval-Davis, 1992; Moghadam, 1994a and 1994b; Yuval-Davis, 1997).
11. Since 1982, Roger Jeffery and I have been working in rural Bijnor, in two Hindu-dominated villages, Dharmnagri and Nangal (populations about 750 and 4,000) and two Muslim dominated villages, Jhakri and Qaziwala (populations about 350 and 3,000). For more details on Bijnor's economy, demography and social organization see Jeffery and Jeffery, 1996a; Jeffery et al., 1989; Jeffery and Jeffery, 1997. For other accounts of villages of the western UP plains, see Raheja, 1988, 1995; and 1994: especially Chapters 3 and 4; Wadley 1994. For northern India more generally, see also Chowdhry, 1994; Mandelbaum, 1986, 1988; Sharma, 1980.
12. Parents cannot always achieve this ideal and those who fail to save for their daughters' marriages are subject to widespread censure or pity. I am leaving dowry escalation and dowry harassment to one side here.
13. We should also note, however, that Muslim women generally experience high levels of fertility and child deaths (though not necessarily higher than low caste and poor Hindu women), largely due to their concentration in the lower levels of the economic hierarchy and their position as an ethnic minority. For more on this see Jeffery and Jeffery, 1999 and 1997.
14. I discuss *mehr* below, in the context of marital breakdown.
15. The term 'separation' covers cases of marital breakdown, including the minority of formal divorces. I leave widowhood on one side here as the antecedents and consequences are normally somewhat different from separation/divorce. Widowhood does not necessarily reflect acrimony between husband and wife (and possibly wider kin); a young widow may remain in her husband's village (and possibly be married leviratically to her husband's brother) or return to her natal kin, who may remarry her or permit her to remain with them as a widow. Widowhood, though, is more commonly experienced by older women, who will probably remain in their husband's village and expect to be supported by their adult sons. For

more on widowhood, see Chen, 1998; Chen and Dreze, 1992, 1995a, 1995b; Chowdhry, 1994: 74-120, 356-77; Jeffery and Jeffery, 1996a: Chapters 14, 15 and 16; Kolenda, 1987a, 1987b: 288-354; Vatuk, 1990 and 1995; Wadley, 1994: 25-9, 154-62, 1995a and 1995b.

16. In 1982-3 (with follow-ups in 1985 and 1990) we concentrated on Dharmnagri and Jhakri and selected key informant couples from a range of class and caste positions in which the wife had recently given birth or was pregnant; in 1990 we added Nangal and Qaziwala and selected additional key informant couples with the wife aged between 25 and 35 and who covered a range of educational experiences and marriage distances. There are almost equal number of Muslim and Hindu key informant couples. Among the key informants, four women and eight men had experienced widowhood by 1991. For more details see Jeffery et al., 1989: 233-7; Jeffery and Jeffery 1997: 32-4.
17. Agarwal and Kandiyoti both address 'rationality' and the extent to which women understand the bases of their subordination or are submerged in false consciousness, but I do not have the space to discuss this further here; see Agarwal, 1997; Kandiyoti, 1998.
18. The use of the term 'marriage' for such second unions is somewhat problematic as they rarely meet formal legal definitions of marriage, even though they are generally regarded as 'marriages' by local people. See below when I discuss second marriages from the woman's viewpoint.
19. Hindu Right discourse suggests that Muslim men are sexually rapacious and liable to replace their wives frequently and/or to indulge in polygamous unions. Polygamy is very uncommon in Bijnor, but is slightly more frequent among Hindus (for whom it is not legal) than among Muslims (for whom it is permitted). Polygamy is usually connected with the infertility of the first wife. The 'victimized Muslim woman' discourse also includes claims about seclusion and lack of education, as well as the specific issues central to the Shah Bano case. See, for example, Bacchetta, 1994.
20. The pseudonyms here are the same as in Jeffery and Jeffery, 1996a and 1997; Jeffery et al., 1989.
21. If the problem arises from disputes with the husband's parents or brothers and their wives, both the daughter and her husband may live in the woman's natal village to preserve their relationship (e.g. Mamta and her daughter Rani: see Jeffery and Jeffery, 1996a: 224-6).
22. This discussion is based on talks with our Muslims key informants as well as many other Muslim men and women in rural Bijnor.
23. This was the *mehr* specified when Fatima, the daughter of the Prophet Muhammad, was married; it is sometimes called *shar'ai mehr*. Silver rupees are more valuable than contemporary coins of the same face value.
24. It seems to be common for Muslim women not to receive their due

according to Islamic law. Other accounts of contemporary practices with respect to *mehr* in India include Agarwal, 1994: 227-8, 260; Agnes, 1996; Ahmed-Ghosh, 1994: 178-80; Engineer, 1992: 111-13; Husain, 1976: 119-37, 193-4; Jacobson, 1976: 185, 207 and 1995: 187; Jeffery, 1979: 57-9; Mann, 1994: 154-6 and 1992: 69; Papanek, 1982: 24-5; Singh, 1992: 81. For historical sources see Ali, 1832: vol. 1, 345; Blunt, 1969: 198; Crooke, 1921: 75; Kozlowski, 1989; Metcalf, 1992: 139-42.

25. We can note the irony of conservative Muslim claims to orthodoxy over the issue of maintenance of ex-wives during the Shah Bano controversy, when Muslim women commonly do not even receive financial entitlements over which there does not seem to be doctrinal dispute.
26. For instance, older widows hope for support from their adult sons, while young widows will probably either be remarried (either leviratically in their deceased husband's village or from their natal village). Widows occasionally inherit land, but most do not. In relatively wealthy families with daughters but no sons, a female-headed household is averted by the 'in-living son-in-law' (*ghar jamai*) who moves to his father-in-law's home and runs the farm. Typically, women who inherit land, either as widows or as daughters, cannot manage or cultivate their farm effectively: women cannot plough (although they do many other agricultural tasks) and their mobility beyond the home is limited. Thus, they normally rely on male kin.
27. By contrast, some widows had remained with their natal kin for many years without being pressured into remarriage.

REFERENCE

Agarwal, B. (1994), *A Field of One's Own*: *Gender and Land Rights in South Asia*, Cambridge: Cambridge University Press.

——— (1997), '"Bargaining" and Gender Relations: Within and Beyond the Household', *Feminist Economics*, 3, 1-51.

Agnes, F. (1992), 'Maintenance for Women: Rhetoric of Equality', *Economic and Political Weekly*, 27, 2233-5.

——— (1995), 'Women's movement Within a Secular Framework: Redefining the Agenda', in T. Sarkar and U. Butalia (eds.), *Women and the Hindu Right*, London and New Delhi: Zed Press and Kali for Women.

——— (1996), 'Economic Rights of Women in Islamic Law', *Economic and Political Weekly*, 31, 2832-8.

Agnihotri, I. and V. Mazumdar (1995), 'Changing Terms of Political Discourse: Women's Movement in India, 1970s-1990s', *Economic and Political Weekly*, 30, 1869-78.

Ahmad, I. (ed.) (1973), *Caste and Social Stratification among the Muslims*, Delhi: Manohar.

——— (1976), *Family, Kinship and Marriage among Muslims in India*, Delhi: Manohar.

——— (1981), *Ritual and Religion among Muslims in India*, Delhi: Manohar.

Ahmed-Ghosh, H. (1994), 'Preserving Identity: A Case Study of Palitpur', in Z. Hasan (ed.), *Forging Identities: Gender, Communities and the State*, New Delhi: Kali for Women.

Ali, Mrs. M.H. (1832), *Observations on the Mussulmauns of India: Descriptive of their Manners, Customs, Habits and Religious Opinions* (2 vols.), London: Parbury, Allen and Co. (rpt. in 1973 by Idarah-I Adabiyat-i Delli, Delhi).

Anthias, F. and N. Yuval-Davis (1992), *Recialised Boundaries: Race, nation, gender, colour and class and the anti-racist struggle*, London and New York: Routledge.

Anveshi Law Committee (1997), 'Is Gender Justice Only a Legal Issue? Political Stakes in UCC Debate', *Economic and Politics Weekly*, 32, 453-8.

Appadurai, A. (1993), Number in the Colonial Imagination', in C.A. Breckenridge and P. van der Veer (eds.), *Orientalism and the Postcolonial Predicament: Perspectives on South Asia* Philadelphia: University of Pennsylvania Press.

Bacchetta, P. (1993), 'All our Goddesses are Armed: Religion, Resistance, and Revenge in the Life of a Militant Hindu Nationalist Woman', *Bulletin of Concerned Asian Scholars*, 25, 38-51.

——— (1994), 'Communal Property/Sexual Property: On Representations of Muslim Women in a Hindu Nationalist Discourse', in Z. Hasan (ed.), *Forging Identities: Gender, Communities and the State*, New Delhi: Kali for Women.

——— (1996), 'Hindu Nationalist Women as Ideologues: The Sangh, the Samiti and Differential Concepts of the Hindu Nation', in K. Jayawardena and M. de Alwis (eds.), *Embodied Violence: Communalising Women's Sexuality in South Asia*, New Delhi: Kali for Women.

Banerjee, N. (1998), 'Whatever Happened to the Dreams of Modernity? The Nehruvian Era and Women's Position', *Economic and Political Weekly*, 33, WS-2-WS-7.

Basu, A. (ed.) (1993), *Women and Religious Nationalism in India* (Bulletin of Concerned Asian Scholars, 25 (4)).

Basu, A. (1995a), 'Feminism Inverted: the Real Women and Gendered

Imagery of Hindu Nationalism', in T. Sarkar and U. Butalia (eds.), *Women and the Hindu Right*, New Delhi: Kali for Women.

——— (1995b), 'When Local Riots Are Not Simply Local: Collective Violence and the State in Bijnor, India 1988-93', *Theory and Society*, 24, 35-78.

——— (1999), 'Hindu Women's Activism in India and the Questions It Raises', in P. Jeffery and A. Basu (eds.), *Resisting the Sacred and the Secular: Women and Politicised Religion in South Asian*, New Delhi: Kali for Women.

Basu, A. and A. Kohli (eds.) (1998), *Community Conflicts and the State in India*, Delhi: Oxford University Press.

Basu, T., P. Datta, S. Sarkar, T. Sarkar and S. Sen (1993), *Khaki Shorts, Saffron Flags*, Delhi: Orient Longman.

Blunt, E.A.H. (1969), *The Caste System of Northern India*, Delhi: S. Chand.

Butalia, U. (1997-8), 'Communalism: A New Challenge to the Women's Movement in India', *Journal of Women's Studies*, 1, 15-27.

Chakravarti, U., P. Choudhury, P. Dutta, Z. Hasan, K. Sangari and T. Sarkar (1992), 'Khurja Riots, 1990-91: Understanding the Conjuncture', *Economic and Political Weekly* 27, 951-65.

Chant, S. (1997), *Women-Headed Households: Diversity and Dynamics in the Developing World*, Basingstoke: Macmillan.

Chaudhuri, M. (1996), 'Citizens, workers and emblems of culture: An analysis of the First Plan document on women, in P. Uberoi (ed.), *Social Reform, Sexuality and the State*, New Delhi: Sage.

Chen, M.A. (ed.) (1998), *Widows in India: Social Neglect and Public Action*, New Delhi: Sage.

Chen, M.A. and J. Drèze (1992), 'Widows and Health in Rural North India', *Economic and Political Weekly*, 27, WS-81-WS-92.

——— (1995a), 'Recent Research on Widows in India: Workshop and Conference Report', *Economic and Political Weekly*, 30, 2435-50.

——— (1995b), 'Widowhood and Well-being in Rural North India', in M. Das Gupta, L.C. Chen and T.N. Krishnan (eds.), *Women's Health in India: Risk and Vulnerability*, Bombay: Oxford University Press.

Chhachhi, A. (1991), 'Forced Identities: the State, Communalism, Fundamentalism and Women in India', in D. Kandiyoti (ed.), *Women, Islam and the State*, London: Macmillan.

Chipp-Kraushaar, S. (1981), 'The All Pakistan Women's Association and the 1961 Muslim Family Laws Ordinance', in G. Minault (ed.), *The Extended Family: Women and Political Participation in India and Pakistan*, Delhi: Chanakya Publications.

Chowdhry, P. (1994), *The Veiled Women: Shifting Gender Equations in Rural Haryana 1880-1990*, Delhi: Oxford University Press.

Cohn, B.S. (1987), 'The Census, Social Structure and Objectification in South Asia', in B.S. Cohn (ed.), *An Anthropologist among the Historians and Other Essays*, Delhi and London: Oxford University Press.

Crooke, W. (ed.) (1921), *Islam in India or the Qanun-i-Islam*, Oxford: Oxford University Press (rpt. in 1975 by Curzon Press, London).

Dyson, T. and M. Moore. (1983), 'On Kinship Structure, Female Autonomy and Demographic Behavior in India', *Population and Development Review*, 9, 35-60.

Engineer, A.A. (ed.) (1987), *The Shah Bano Controversy*, Bombay: Orient Longman.

Engineer, A.A. (1991), 'The Bloody Trail: Ramjanmabhoomi and Communal Violence in UP', *Economic and Political Weekly*, 26, 155-9.

——— (1992), *The Rights of Women in Islam*, Delhi: Sterling Publishers.

——— (1999), 'Muslim Women and Maintenance', *Economic and Political Weekly*, 34, 1488-9.

Gangoli, G. and G. Solanki (1997), 'Towards Gender Just Laws', *Economic and Political Weekly*, 32, 854-5.

Gardner, K. (1999), 'Women and Islamic Revivalism in a Bangladeshi Community', in P. Jeffery and A. Basu (eds.), *Resisting the Sacred and the Secular: Women's Activism and Politicized Religion in South Asian*, New Delhi: Kali for Women.

Gopal, S. (ed.) (1991), *Anatomy of a Confrontation: The Babri Masjid-Ramjanambhoomi Issue*, Delhi: Orient Longman.

Hasan, M. (1988), 'Indian Muslims since Independence: in search of integration and identity', *Third World Quarterly*, 10, 818-42.

——— (1991), *Nationalism and Communal Politics in India*, Delhi: Manohar.

——— (1997), *Legacy of a Divided Nation: India's Muslims since Independence*, Delhi: Oxford University Press.

Hasan, Z. (1989), 'Minority Identity, Muslim Women Bill Campaign and the Political Process, *Economic and Political Weekly*, 24, 44-50.

——— (1993), 'Communalism, State Policy and the Question of Women's Rights in Contemporary India', *Bulletin of Concerned Asian Scholars*, 25, 5-15.

Hasan, Z. (ed.) (1994), *Forging Identities: Gender, Communities and the State*, New Delhi: Kali for Women.

Hasan, Z., (1999), 'Gender Politics, Legal Reform and the Muslim Community in India', in P. Jeffery and A. Basu (eds.), *Resisting the Sacred and the Secular: Women and Politicized Religion in South Asia*, New Delhi: Kali for Women.

Husain, S.A. (1976), *Marriage Customs among Muslims in India: A Sociological Study of Shia Marriage Customs*, Delhi: Sterling Publishers.

Jacobson, D. (1976), 'The Veil of Virtue: *Purdah* and the Muslim Family in the Bhopal Region of Central India', in I. Ahmad (ed.), *Family, Kinship and Marriage among Muslims in India*, Delhi: Manohar.

——— (1995), 'Women and Jewelry in Rural India', in D. Jacobson and S.S. Wadley (eds.), *Women in India: Two Perspectives*, Delhi: Manohar.

Jaffrelot, C. (1996), *The Hindu Nationalist Movement and Indian Politics 1925 to the 1990s*, London: Hurst.

Jeffery, P. (1979), *Frogs in a Well: Indian Women in Purdah*, London: Zed Press.

——— (1999), 'Agency, Activism, and Agendas', in P. Jeffery and A. Basu (eds.), *Resisting the Sacred and the Secular: Women and Politicized Religion in South Asia*, New Delhi: Kali for Women.

Jeffery, P. (forthcoming), 'Identifying Differences: Gender Politics and Community in Rural Bijnor, UP', in J. Leslie (ed.), *Gender Constructs in Indian Religion and Society*, Delhi: Oxford University Press.

Jeffery, P. and A. Basu (eds.) (1999), *Resisting the Sacred and the Secular: Women's Activism and Politicized Religion in South Asia*. New Delhi: Kali for Women (also published in 1998 as 'Appropriating Gender' by Routledge).

Jeffery, P. and R. Jeffery (1994a), 'Killing My Heart's Desire: Education and Female Autonomy in Rural North India', in N. Kumar (ed.), *Woman as Subject: South Asian Histories*, Calcutta and Charlottesville: Bhatkal and Sen and Virginia University Press.

——— (1996a), *Don't Marry me to a Plowman! Women's Everyday Lives in Rural North India*, Boulder: Westview Press.

——— (1996b), 'What's the Benefit of being Educated? Girls' Schooling, Women's Autonomy and Fertility Outcomes in Bijnor', in R. Jeffery and A. Basu (eds.), *Girls' Schooling, Women's Autonomy and Fertility Change in South Asia*, New Delhi: Sage.

——— (1999), 'Gender, Community and the Local State in Bijnor, India', in P. Jeffery and A. Basu (eds.), *Resisting the Sacred and the Secular: Women's Activism and Politicized Religion in South Asia*, New Delhi: Kali for Women.

Jeffery, P., R. Jeffery and A. Lyon (1989), *Labour Pains and Labour Power: Women and Childbearing in India*, London: Zed Books.

Jeffery, R., and P. Jeffery (1993a), 'Traditional Birth Attendants in Rural North India: the Social Organization of Childbearing', in S. Lindenbaum and M. Lock (eds.), *Knowledge Power and Practice: The Anthropology of Medicine and Everyday Life*, Berkeley: University of California Press.

——— (1993b), 'A Woman Belongs to Her Husband: Female Autonomy, Women's Work and Childbearing in Bijnor', in A. Clark (ed.), *Gender and Political Economy: Explorations of South Asian Systems*, Delhi: Oxford University Press.

——— (1994b), 'The Bijnor Riots, October 1990: Collapse of a Mythical Special Relationship?', *Economic and Political Weekly*, 29, 551-58.

——— (1997), *Population, Gender and Politics: Demographic Change in Rural North India*, Cambridge: Cambridge University Press.

Kandiyoti, D. (1988), 'Bargaining with Patriarchy', *Gender and Society*, 2, 274-90.

Kandiyoti, D. (ed.) (1991), *Women, Islam and the State*, London: Macmillan.

Kandiyoti, D. (1998), 'Gender, Power and Contestation: "Rethinking bargaining with Patriarchy', in C. Jackson and R. Pearson (eds.), *Feminist Visions of Development: Gender Analysis and Policy*, London: Routledge.

Kapur, R. and B. Cossman (1995), 'Communalising Gender/Engendering Community: Women, Legal Discourse and the Saffron Agenda', in T. Sarkar and U. Butalia (eds.), *Women and the Hindu Right*, New Delhi: Kali for Women.

——— (1996), *Subversive Sites: Feminist Engagements with Law in India*, New Delhi: Sage.

Kasturi, L. (1996), 'Development, Patriarchy, and Politics: Indian Women in the Political Process, 1947-1992', in V.M. Moghadam (ed.), *Patriarchy and Economic Development: Women's Position at the end of the Twentieth Century*, Oxford: Clarendon Press.

Kishwar, M. (1986), 'Pro Women or Anti Muslim?', *Manushi*, 6, 4-13.

——— (1994), 'Codified Hindu Law: Myth and Reality', *Economic and Political Weekly*, 29, 2145-61.

Kolenda, P. (1987a), 'Living the Levirate', in P. Hockings (ed.), *Dimensions of Social Life*, Berlin: de Gruyter.

——— (1987b), *Regional Differences in Family Structure in India*, Jaipur: Rawat.

Kozlowski, G.C. (1989), 'Muslim women and the control of property in North India', in J. Krishnamurthy (ed.), *Women in Colonial India: Essays on Survival, Work and the State*, Delhi: Oxford University Press.

Kumar, R. (1993), *The History of Doing: an Illustrated Account of Movements for Women's Rights and Feminism in India, 1800-1900*, New Delhi: Kali for Women.

Ludden, D. (1993), 'Orientalist Empiricism: Transformations of Colonial Knowledge', in C.A. Breckenridge and P. van der Veer (eds.), *Orientalism and the Postcolonial Predicament: Perspectives on South Asia*, Philadelphia: University of Pennsylvania Press.

Ludden, D. (ed.) (1996), *Making India Hindu: Religion, Community, and the Politics of Democracy in India*, Delhi: Oxford University Press (also published as 'Contesting the Nation' by University of Pennsylvania Press).

Mandelbaum, D. (1986), 'Sex Roles and Gender Relations in North India', *Economic and Political Weekly*, 21, 1999-2004.

——— (1988), *Women's Seclusion and Men's Honor*, Tucson: University of Arizona Press.

Mann, E.A. (1992), *Boundaries and Identities: Muslims, Work and Status in Aligarh*, New Delhi: Sage.

——— (1994), 'Education, Money and the Role of Women in Maintaining Minority Identity', in Z. Hasan (ed.), *Forging Identities: Gender, Communities and the State*, New Delhi: Kali for Women.

Metcalf, B.D. (1992), *Perfecting Women: Maulana Ashraf 'Ali Thanawi's Bihishti Zewar A Translation with Commentary*, Delhi: Oxford University Press.

——— (1999), 'Women and Men in a Contemporary Pietist Movement: The Case of the Tablighi Jama'at', in P. Jeffery and A. Basu (eds.), *Resisting the Sacred and the Secular: Women and Politicized Religion in South Asia*, New Delhi: Kali for Women.

Mody, N.B. (1987), 'The Press in India: The Shah Bano Judgement and Its Aftermath', *Asian Survey*, 27, 935-53.

Moghadam, V.M. (ed.) (1994a), *Gender and National Identity: Women and Politics in Muslim Societies*, London: Zed Books.

——— (1946), *Identity Politics and Women: Cultural Reassertions and Feminisms in International Perspective*, Boulder: West View Press.

Molyneux, M. (1998), 'Analysing women's movements', in C. Jackson and R. Pearson (eds.), *Feminist Visions of Development: Gender analysis and policy*, London: Routledge.

Moser, C. (1989), 'Gender Planning in the Third World: meeting Practical and Strategic Gender Needs', *World Development*, 17, 1799-1825.

Mukhopadhyay, M. (1994), 'Between Community and State: The Question of Women's Rights and Personal Laws', in Z. Hasan (ed.),

Forging Identities: Gender, Communities and the State, New Delhi: Kali for Women.

Mumtaz, K. and F. Shaheed (1987), *Women of Pakistan: Two Steps Forward, One Step Back*?', London: Zed Books.

National Committee on the Status of Women (1975), *Status of Women in India: A Synopsis of the Report of the National Committee (1971-74)*, New Delhi: The Indian Council of Social Science Research/ Allied Publishers.

Omvedt, G. (1993), *Reinventing Revolution: New Social Movements and the Socialist Tradition in India*, Armonk and London: M.E. Sharpe.

Palriwala, R. and I. Agnihotri (1996), 'Tradition, the Family, and the State: Politics of the Contemporary Women's Movement', in T.V. Sathyamurty (ed.), *Region, Religion, Caste, Gender and Culture in Contemporary India*, Delhi: Oxford University Press.

Pandey, G. (1990), *The Construction of Communalism in Colonial North India*, Delhi: Oxford University Press.

Papanek, H. (1982), 'Purdah: Separate Worlds and Symbolic Shelter', in H. Papanek and G. Minault (eds.), *Separate Worlds: Studies of Purdah in South Asia*, Delhi: Chanakya Publications.

Parashar, A. (1992), *Women and Family Law Reform in India: Uniform Civil Code and Gender Equality*, New Delhi: Sage.

——— (1997), 'Family Law as a Means of Ensuring Gender Justice for India Women', *Indian Journal of Gender Studies* 4, 199-229.

Pathak, Z. and R.S. Rajan (1989), 'Shahbano', *Signs*, 14, 558-82.

Raheja, G.G. (1988), *The Position in the Gift*, Chicago: University of Chicago Press.

——— (1995), '"Crying When She's Born, and Crying When She Goes Away": Marriage and the Idiom of the Gift in Pahansu Song Performance', in L. Harlan and P. Courtright (eds.), *From the Margins of Hindu Marriage: Essays on Gender, Religion and Culture*, New York: Oxford University Press.

Raheja, G.G. and A.G. Gold (1994), *Listen to the Heron's Words: Reimagining Gender and Kinship in North India*, Berkeley: University of California Press.

Registrar General and Census Commissioner, I. (1996), *Census of India 1991*, Series 1 *India*, Part IV-B (ii) *Religion*, Delhi: Controller of Publications.

Sangari, K. (1995), 'Politics of Diversity: Religious Communities and Multiple Patriarchies', *Economic and Political Weekly*, 30, 3287-3307, 3381-9.

Sarkar, T. (1991), The Woman as Communal Subject: Rashtrasevika Samiti and the Ramjanmabhoomi Movement, *Economic and Political Weekly* 26, 2057-65.

——— (1993), 'Rhetoric Against the Age of Consent: Resisting Colonial Reason and the Death of a Child Wife', *Economic and Political Weekly*, 28, 1869-78.

Sarkar, T. and U. Butalia (eds.) (1995), *Women and the Hindu Right*, New Delhi and London: Kali for Women and Zed Books.

Scott, J. (1985), *Weapons of the Weak: Everyday Forms of Peasant Resistance*, New Haven: Yale University Press.

Sen, A. (1990), 'Gender and Co-operative Conflicts', in I. Tinker (ed.), *Persistent Inequalities: Women and World Development*, New York: Oxford University Press.

Sharma, U. (1980), *Women, Work and Property in North West India*, London: Tavistock.

Singh, A. (1992), *Women in Muslim Personal Law*, Jaipur: Rawat.

van der Veer, P. (1994), *Religious Nationalism: Hindus and Muslims in India*, Berkeley: University of California Press.

Vanaik, A. (1997), *The Furies of Indian Communalism: Religion, Modernity and Secularization*, London: Verso.

Vatuk, S. (1990), '"To Be a Burden on Others" : Dependency Anxiety Among the Elderly in India', in O.T. Lynch (ed.), *Divine Passions: The Social Construction of Emotion in India*, Delhi: Oxford University Press.

Vatuk, S. (1995), 'The Indian Woman in Later Life', in M. Das Gupta, L.C. Chen and T.N. Krishnan (eds.), *Women's Health in India: Risk and Vulnerability*, Bombay: Oxford University Press.

Wadley, S.S. (1994), *Struggling with Destiny in Karimpur, 1925-1984*, Berkeley: University of California Press.

Wadley, S.S. (1995a), 'No Longer a Wife: Widows in Rural North India', in L. Harlan and P. Courtright (eds.), *From the Margins of Hindu Marriage: Essays on Gender, Religion and Culture*, New York: Oxford University Press.

Wadley, S.S. (1995b), 'The "Village Indira": A Brahman Widow and Political Action in Rural North India', in D. Jacobson and S.S. Wadley (eds.), *Women in India: Two Perspectives*, Delhi: Manohar.

Women's Feature Service (1999), 'Muslim Family Law under attack in Pakistan', in *Women Living under Muslim Laws Newsheet*, Lahore.

Working Group on Women's Rights (1996), 'Reversing the Option: Civil Codes and Personal Laws', *Economic and Political Weekly* 31, 1180-3.

Yuval-Davis, N. (1997), *Gender and Nation*, London: Sage.

4

Muslim Women in the Indian Family Courts: A Report from Chennai

Sylvia Vatuk

This paper is based upon a preliminary analysis of material collected over a seven month period in the Chennai Family Court, in connection with a study of how the Muslim Personal Law of India impacts women.[1] Despite all the rhetoric in India these days about the need for reform of personal law and enactment of a Uniform Civil Code, there has been very little research on the actual experience of Indian Muslim women living under the existing code.[2] A good deal has been written about how women suffer because of the freedom given to Muslim men to divorce at will and to marry polygamously. But most of this writing is anecdotal and journalistic. Rarely are the arguments put forward supported by substantive empirical data.

Unfortunately, statistics that might shed some quantitative light on how Muslim women are impacted by the two aspects of the law that are most often cited as oppressive to them—that is, polygamy and unilateral divorce—are virtually impossible to come by. As far as polygamy is concerned, an oft-cited figure for its incidence among Indian Muslims is 5.7 per cent. Only rarely, however, do those who cite this figure indicate its source: a 1961 study by the Census of India of one lakh marriages in a selected sample of Indian villages.[3] However valid this figure may have been for the time and the rural locations in which the cited study was conducted, it is of questionable value as a measure of the contemporary prevalence of polygamy in India at large.

The absence of any system of compulsory registration of marriage and divorce in India is a serious barrier to any attempt to estimate the prevalence of either polygamy or unilateral divorce.[4] It is true that most Muslim marriages are recorded by Muslim clerics (qazis, imams, etc.) who—in accordance with custom, though not by law—read the *nikah* at most Muslim weddings. But it would be virtually impossible to calculate the prevalence of polygamy from such records, even if one were able to obtain access to them. Whereas it is standard procedure at the time of marriage to enquire of the woman (or of her guardian) about her previous marital history, similar information is not sought from the man. Nor is he asked if he currently has another wife. Hypothetically, it might be possible to derive a polygamy rate by examining the marriage and divorce records of a largely closed population, by some process of cross-referencing, following the marital histories of individual men and women over time. But, putting aside the complex technical issues that an analysis of this sort would raise, it is highly unlikely that a suitably closed population could be found to exist anywhere in India today.

As far as measuring the incidence of divorce is concerned, the records kept by religious functionaries can be of some value, even though these records are certainly less complete than the corresponding marriage records. A man who divorces his wife by pronouncing *talaq* is not legally obliged to inform either the state or the clergy of this fact, and many do not. But a substantial number do so voluntarily, either before or after pronouncing *talaq*, either because they mistakenly believe that it is a legal requirement or because they simply wish to have an 'official' divorce document in hand, in the event that it ever becomes necessary to prove that their marriage has been legally terminated.

Divorces initiated by women (*khula*) or obtained through mutual consent of the parties (*mubarat*) are probably somewhat more likely to be registered with a qazi or other religious functionary than are divorces of the *talaq* type, especially in urban areas. In both of the former forms of divorce the spouses must reach a negotiated agreement. To accomplish this, more often than not, some individual knowledgeable in Islamic law, commonly a qazi or the like, is called upon to mediate, help the parties reach a financial settlement, and draw up a written divorce contract. Sometimes even a *khulanama* that has been drawn up privately is later registered, again either because the parties desire 'official' documentation or because of the erroneous belief that a divorce, to be valid, must have the imprimatur of a recognized Muslim cleric.

Notwithstanding their incompleteness, marriage and divorce records of the kind maintained by Islamic religious authorities can be of great value for answering some of the kinds of questions that are commonly raised about divorce in the Muslim community. Unfortunately, there is little evidence that they have been extensively used as source materials by scholars doing research in this field. While their existence is frequently mentioned in the social science literature, no one, to my knowledge, has published a systematic analysis of any substantial corpus of such records. Doubtless one important reason for this is that marriage and divorce registers and the copies of *nikahnamas*, *talaqnamas*, etc., that are kept by religious authorities are not public records. Access to them, thus, requires the willing cooperation of those who hold them in their personal possession. One of the priorities of Indian anthropologists and sociologists working on Muslim marriage and divorce should be to pursue opportunities to dispassionately examine and analyse records of this kind, in the interests of contributing some factual information to the plethora of unsubstantiated generalizations that are being bandied about so recklessly, from both sides of the controversy over reform of personal law.

One other point that I would make about unilateral divorce in the context of southern India is that most Muslim men and women in Chennai with whom I spoke in the course of my research claimed that in their own family and circle of relatives and acquaintances, divorce was practically unheard of; that they knew very few, if any, men who had divorced their wives, and that any divorces that they did know about had taken place quite recently. Such statements cannot, of course, be used as reliable indicators of the actual incidence of divorce in the Muslim community as a whole. They do provide some indication, however, that divorce was probably not very widespread in the past, at least in the relatively small, close-knit communities, whether in rural or urban settings, that most Muslims in this part of India lived in a generation ago.[5] Considerable social pressure was presumably exerted on both men and women to stay in a marriage, no matter how conflictual their relationship. Interviews also suggest that in the current social milieu divorce may be becoming more common than it was in the past, as a result of a loosening of social ties among relatives and neighbours and a gradual decline in the ability of the local jamat in a large and increasingly impersonal urban environment to effectively control the conduct of members. An increasing incidence of marriage outside of close kinship networks and the increasing prevalence and rising costs of dowries may also be related to what appears to be a rise in the rate of divorce in recent decades. All of these propositions are highly speculative at this point, however, and require further study.

One of my purposes in carrying out this research was to help to remedy the lack of empirical information on how women are affected, in practice, by those provisions of the Muslim Personal Law that relate to the institution of marriage and its dissolution.[6] In the interests of obtaining as comprehensive picture as possible of Muslim women's experiences with the law, I examined its operation in two different sorts of venues: (1) the state-sponsored family courts, and (2) a variety of religious sites where marital disputes are brought for resolution, marriage and divorce contracts are drawn up and certificates issued. These sites include the offices of qazis, *shar'ia* courts, jamat committees, madrasas, and so on. Although the two sorts of venues are in theory quite separate, and although they function independently, they are in practice part of a single field of action, interconnected and complementary in their functioning from the perspective of the individual woman and her 'case'. There is also much interaction, and even some overlap, among their respective personnel. Thus, for example, I found Muslim lawyers assisting in the resolution of marital disputes by serving on jamat committees at their local mosques, while also guiding clients through the judicial process at the family court. I saw Hindu lawyers referring prospective women clients, and even accompanying them when necessary, to the office of the chief qazi of Chennai to enquire about the possibility of obtaining *khula* or child support from an uncooperative husband. The qazi, in turn, routinely advises abused women whose husbands refuse to release them that if they are determined to end the marriage their only option is to sue in the family court. Documents such as marriage and divorce certificates and letters from a qazi or from the head of a local jamat, addressed to one of the parties to a legal suit, are routinely encountered in family court case files. As one would expect, the relationship between the civil and religious functionaries who share between them the task of administering Muslim Personal Law is not free of tension, suspicion and mutual stereotyping, the causes and consequences of which I intend to explore at more length in a future essay. Here I will limit my discussion to what I have learned about the administration of Muslim Personal Law from my research in only one of these venues, the Chennai Family Court.

MUSLIM LAW IN THE FAMILY COURTS

The Chennai Family Court began operating in 1988. Similar family courts function today in most large cities of India, pursuant to central government legislation passed in September 1984 as the Family Courts Act. Under this Act,[7] family courts have civil jurisdiction over all matrimonial suits, including property disputes between husband and wife, regardless of the religion of the parties. They are also empowered to decide cases registered under Chapter IX, Section 125 of the Criminal Procedure Code (CrPC), which covers orders for maintenance of destitute wives and children of all religions and for divorced women, except if they are Muslim.[8] Before the passage of the Family Courts Act these kinds of cases were adjudicated along with others in the regular civil and criminal courts.

The original impetus for the establishment of family courts came from women's groups that were critical of the adversarial nature of matrimonial proceedings in the existing civil courts, the complexity of legal procedures, and the lengthy delays in resolving cases. These drawbacks were felt to be particularly disadvantageous for women, who tend to be less well-informed about the law than men and to have fewer financial and other resources with which to fight a legal case.[9] However, since the passage of the Act many of those who fought for their establishment, as well as many legal activists who have had first-hand experience in the new family courts, have expressed disappointment with the way that they operate in practice.[10]

An important procedural feature of family courts is that clients can be represented by legal counsel only if granted special permission by the presiding judge.[11] In practice, it is the rare client who tries to navigate the complicated court system without the aid of an advocate. Advocates are needed to prepare petitions and other court documents in the proper form, provide legal advice, and accompany family court clients to court hearings to guide them through the procedure and give moral support. However, they rarely seek the special permission required to be allowed to legally represent a family court client.[12] Their role in family court is thus very much circumscribed in comparison to that performed by advocates in other civil or criminal courts. Most importantly, they cannot represent their client at a hearing in the latter's absence, nor are they supposed to speak on a client's behalf even when the latter is present, unless specifically asked to do so by the judge. Parties to a matrimonial dispute must attend all hearings in person if the case is to proceed. This requirement, whose original intent was to make the proceedings relatively informal and non-legalistic and to allow the parties to present their cases in their own way and in ordinary language, imposes considerable hardship in practice. Though matrimonial cases are apparently being handled more expeditiously under the new system than they were in the past, they are rarely concluded in less than a year and often drag on much longer. This means that before her case is finally resolved a typical woman must make a minimum of ten to twelve all-day visits to the court premises, incurring in the process many associated financial and other costs.

Judges in family courts administer the personal laws of all religious communities and also the Special Marriage Act of 1954, used principally by couples belonging to different religions. The Muslim Personal Law that they dispense is largely uncodified. For guidance on difficult or complicated issues they may refer to English-language texts on Islamic law, whose authors, in turn, have drawn upon their reading (usually in translation) of certain well-known classical treatises on Islamic law as well as on Indian case law dating from the early nineteenth century. But, in their day-to-day practice, few of the Muslim cases encountered by judges in the family court demand more than a grasp of the main provisions of the two codified laws relevant to Muslim matrimonial causes—the 1939 Dissolution of Muslim Marriages Act (DMMA) and the 1986 Muslim Women (Protection of Rights on Divorce) Act (MWA)—to supplement the intimate acquaintance with Section 125 of the CrPC that they acquire as a matter of course in their daily dealings with destitute women of all religions who come before them seeking orders of maintenance.

WHO COMES TO COURT?

My principal sources for the following discussion are case files and other records of the Family Court of Chennai for the years 1988 to 1997, inclusive.[13] The procedure employed was to first identify in the pertinent registers for these years all cases involving Muslim litigants, and then choose from these a sample of cases for more detailed examination.[14] No attempt was made to address in a systematic way the question of possible differences between Muslim women's experience in the family court and that of Hindus or Christians. However, in order to get an overview of the variety of cases that come to the family court and the circumstances that cause women of all religions to file (or find themselves required to respond to) legal suits in that court, the year 1996 was arbitrarily selected for a complete count, by religion of litigant and type, of all family court cases filed. I then read a number of randomly selected Hindu and Christian case files.

From this very cursory examination of non-Muslim matrimonial cases my overall impression is that Muslim cases are not in any way distinctive from those in which Hindus and Christians are involved. The problems that bring women of all religious communities to court appear to be essentially similar, revolving principally around issues of domestic violence, desertion, and/or failure to maintain the wife and children, often in association with dowry-harassment and extra-marital relationships. Patterns in the outcomes of cases are not very different either, despite differences among the three major bodies of personal law. Comparative questions about how women of different religions fare under their respective personal laws, which constitute a sub-text in much of the discussion about the need for a Uniform Civil Code, certainly require further detailed investigation. Unfortunately, I was not in a position to do this in conjunction with my research project.

My research assistant and I read and copied a total of 104 case files: all of the cases filed by Muslims in the years 1993 and 1996 and a random sampling of Muslim cases from other years. One caution regarding my source materials is necessary before I proceed. The petitions, counter-petitions and other statements of the parties that constitute the bulk of the material to be found in family court files are strategic documents, written to meet the requirements of the particular law under which a suit or complaint is being filed. Their purpose is to convince the judge that the petitioner has a valid case in law and should be given the relief asked for—or, that the petitioner or plaintiff is lying and his or her plea should be denied. Furthermore, these documents are almost always written by an advocate, and they are written in English, a language that very few litigants command.[15] While one can assume that they always contain some elements of a story that the client has told his or her advocate in the course of one or more interviews, that story has invariably undergone editing, in line with the latter's professional judgments about how much should be said, what needs to be highlighted, what suppressed, and what added, in order to win the case. There is no way to assess the absolute 'truth value' of any of these individual documents. Nevertheless, from them we can learn something of significance about the parties involved in the dispute, about the kinds of situations that cause marital conflict in this society and about the ways in which marital problems of various kinds are culturally conceptualized and dealt with. The documents can also be read for what they reveal about people's understandings of how a man or woman ought to behave in a marital relationship, what kinds of behaviour are blameworthy or admirable, and which kinds constitute culturally acceptable justification—quite apart from the issue of legal justification—for an individual to seek dissolution of the marital bond.

Since I am still in an early stage of analysing these materials, my discussion here will be a very general one, pointing out some of the major themes and patterns that I have been able to identify thus far. In the Chennai Family Court, Muslim litigants are represented at a much lower rate in proportion to their numbers in the population than are people of other religions. According to census figures, the city had in 1991 almost 4 million people,[16] of whom 8.7 per cent were Muslim. However, only between 4 and 5 per cent of suits filed in the family court in any year during the period 1988-97 involved spouses of whom one or both were Muslim.[17] These figures may indicate a greater reluctance on the part of Muslims than of Hindus to bring their family problems to the civil authorities for resolution. There is no doubt that to go to the family court is not considered a good thing for a woman—or man—to do, not least because it entails making public the kind of unpleasant matters that should ideally remain within the very private confines of the home and immediate family unit. But a more compelling explanation of why Muslims make less use than Hindus and Christians of the facilities provided by family courts is that in a Muslim marriage, when conflict escalates to the point that one or both spouses desires to terminate the union, they have available to them a variety of alternative avenues that are cheaper and more expeditious, as well as socially more acceptable, than filing a suit for divorce.

Of the approximately 540 Muslim cases filed in the family court during the ten years between 1988 and 1997, 70 per cent were filed by women, more than two-thirds of whom sought either a divorce (57 cases) or maintenance for themselves and/or for their children (approximately 232 cases).[18] Muslim women also filed, though in smaller numbers, suits for declarations as to the validity of a marriage or a divorce, for getting legal custody of a child, or for retrieving personal property in the possession of the husband or parents-in-law.

Cases filed by men were overwhelmingly for 'restitution of conjugal rights' (RCR), a legal remedy whose purpose is to compel a spouse who has left the matrimonial home to return to it and, in the formulaic phrase repeatedly encountered in court documents: 'restore to the petitioner the comforts and bliss of married life'. Theoretically, a person of either sex can file for restitution—Hindu and Christian women do occasionally make use of an equivalent provision in their respective codes of personal law—but in all of the restitution suits filed by Muslims in Chennai the petitioners are male.

The data show that, almost without exception, women who find themselves in a family court (whether as petitioner or respondent) are already living apart from their husbands and often have been living apart for a considerable number of years. Female litigants in the cases examined range in age from nineteen to the mid-sixties, but most are in their twenties and early thirties. The majority have been married a relatively short time before the separation from their husbands took place, but several years usually elapse between that time and the filing of a legal suit, whether by the woman herself or by her husband. Almost all of the women have at least one child and are living—usually with the child—in the household of their parents or an adult sibling. If a woman is living with another man, this intelligence is, of course, most unlikely to appear in any petition filed by her, but occasionally such an accusation is made by a husband in a plea for RCR or in a counter to a divorce or maintenance petition filed by his wife. A small number of older women are living independently, apart from natal relatives but usually with their own teenage or young adult children. Insofar as this kind of information is provided in the case files, few of the women are or ever have been gainfully employed and few have been educated beyond a minimal level. Family incomes are consistently low—rarely above Rs. 1,500 a month and in most cases considerably less than this. Court files reveal that in most cases various attempts have already been made by the spouses and/or their respective natal families to find some solution, short of civil litigation, to their marital problems. These have included attempts at mediation by relatives or friends and when that did not succeed, consultations with a Muslim cleric of some kind, a jamat committee or a community panchayat. A significant number of the women have on one or more occasion filed criminal charges against their husbands at their local police station or at one of Chennai's three All-Women Police Stations, whose principal function is to aid women victims of domestic abuse and/or dowry harassment.

In a sample of 30 cases that I have had time to analyse in most detail, the women involved reported having married at ages ranging from 12 to 49—for some in the higher end of this range, the marriage may not have been their first. Husbands were generally 5 to 10 years older than their wives. Since 1978 the minimum legal age at marriage for girls has been 18 years.[19] Almost a third of the women litigants sampled claim to have been younger than this when they married, 20 per cent having been under sixteen. The vast majority of the marriages were arranged by the respective parents or other elder kinsmen of the couple. Few women were acquainted with their husbands before the wedding ceremony, though there are a small number of marriages of personal choice in the sample. Typically the couples involved in these latter kinds of union were former neighbours, co-workers, or close relatives. Not infrequently the wife is a non-Muslim.

Despite a long-standing preference among Muslims for arranging marriages within a close circle of kin, very few court petitions give any indication that the spouses had a prior kinship relationship.[20] It is difficult to know how to interpret this silence. It is possible that information about a prior kin relationship has been left out of the documents because the parties—and/or the advocates—considered it irrelevant to the case. However, I am inclined to think that if such a relationship is not mentioned in connection with the narrative about the arrangement of the marriage or the events that followed it, it is probably because the parties are not close relatives. If I am correct in this conjecture, then the paucity of references to close-kin marriage in the case files suggests that spouses who are close relatives are both less likely to have some of the problems that bring others to a family court and, if they do have these problems, are less likely to resort to the law as a way of solving them. The data may also reflect a real decline in recent decades in the frequency of close kin marriages, a trend that is hinted at in some of the literature cited above.

At the time of marriage the parents of most of the women are described as having presented their daughter, her husband, and her in-laws with substantial amounts of cash, gold and/or silver jewellery, clothing, and other goods by way of 'dowry', as well as having spent liberally on the wedding celebration and associated feasts. Detailed lists of such items are sometimes found in case files, having been submitted to the court to substantiate a demand for the return of property rightfully belonging to the wife but allegedly being held in the possession of her husband or in-laws. Case files show that, after marriage, the new wife almost always joined the household in which her husband was already living with his parents and siblings. Only rarely did the couple move in with the wife's family or set up housekeeping on their own immediately following their marriage. This kind of patrilocal extended family living arrangement provides the setting for certain distinctive patterns of marital conflict, in which the respective sets of parents and siblings of the couple typically play active supporting—or, more likely, aggravating—roles.

CAUSES AND CONSEQUENCES OF MARITAL DISCORD

The nature and source of tensions within the households of female litigants in a family court naturally varies, but certain patterns recur.

A very large percentage of the women report domestic abuse by the husband and, in some cases, by in-laws, particularly the husband's mother and sister. Fathers-in-law are rarely mentioned in this connection. Charges of mental and physical abuse are frequently made in support of a petition for divorce on grounds of cruelty under the DMMA. This is the most frequent ground on which women base such suits, the second being desertion.

A common theme in suits alleging spousal cruelty is the husband's 'suspicion' of his wife. Thus, a woman reports that her husband suspects her of seeking or even engaging in sexual encounters with other men and punishes her with physical and mental abuse. One common form of abuse is to lock the wife inside the house whenever the man goes out, so that she will be unable to consummate her supposed desire to seek out male companionship in his absence. Men's petitions for RCR frequently include charges of adultery or attempted adultery by the wife, as do men's counter-petitions to women's pleas for divorce or maintenance on grounds of cruelty.

Interestingly, interviews with male lawyers, as well as with male members of the religious establishment repeatedly turned up this same theme. Early on, when I began asking such interviewees what kind of matrimonial cases they typically encountered or tried to elicit examples of cases with which they had dealt in the recent past, I was startled to be treated, time and again, to narratives that involved unfaithful wives. Later I began to expect them. Questions about the most frequent causes of divorce within the Muslim community were also routinely answered with remarks about women's propensity to be unfaithful.

This male preoccupation with women's alleged liberality with their sexual favours looms quite large in providing a background for matrimonial disputes. The idea that male respectability and honour is intimately tied up with women's sexual purity and must constantly be guarded by keeping control of one's women has often been described by scholars as dominating gender relations, not only among Muslims, but in Indian society more generally.[21] But its role in structuring legal discourse on marital matters in India has not really been investigated to date and requires further study.

While 'suspicion' of wives is a frequent source of marital discord, men's alleged infidelity is also often cited by female litigants as a reason for their unhappiness in marriage. Divorce and maintenance petitions very frequently assert that the husband is carrying on an adulterous affair with a neighbour, co-worker, close relative, or prostitute. While adultery on the part of the husband is not, per se, a ground for divorce, it can be cited in a divorce suit or as a valid defence against a suit for RCR if the extramarital relationship has contributed to the man's neglecting his wife's material and/or sexual needs[22] or has caused him to treat her with cruelty—as, for example, if he requires his wife to shelter and provide meals and other services for his paramour.[23] Likewise, if it can be shown that the husband has committed adultery in the context of 'associating with women of evil repute' or 'leading an infamous life', a woman may obtain a divorce on this ground.

Sometimes women complain that their husbands have contracted a second marriage and have either brought the other woman to live in the same home with her, or have established a separate household, using income and assets that she feels should be spent on her own needs and those of her children. Occasionally, a second wife petitions the court, claiming that she was unaware at the time of their marriage that the groom was already a married man, and that after marriage he failed to treat her on the same footing as his prior wife. While a Muslim man is legally entitled to marry a second wife while still married to the first, his failure to treat both women equally thereafter is considered a form of 'cruelty' under the DMMA.[24]

Other common complaints against husbands cited in divorce and maintenance petitions include alcoholism, drug abuse, addiction to gambling and keeping bad company. Allegations that a husband has taken away money or other valuables belonging to the wife are also frequent. In Muslim law, a wife is entitled to retain and control her own personal property after marriage. Such property is typically in the form of jewellery and/or cash and household goods. For a husband to take possession of it without her consent, to dispose of it, or to prevent her from exercising her rights over it, is also a ground for divorce. Women often allege such offences, which are regarded as especially heinous if the man has used his wife's property to feed his vices or satisfy the desires or needs of other women in his life.[25]

Problems with in-laws are also very often cited in divorce and maintenance petitions and in responses to suits for restitution of conjugal rights. Occasionally women who make such complaints explicitly exonerate the husband of fault and indicate a willingness to live with him in a separate household, apart from his parents and siblings, if given assurance that he will not permit his relatives to interfere in their relationship in the future . Usually, however, men in such a situation are unwilling to leave the parental home, typically citing an inability to support two households.

Complaints about in-laws tend to conform to certain patterns. Women report being harshly criticized by their husband's female relatives—mother-in-law, wives of his brothers, any sisters who might still be living at home—for their lack of competence in or their way of performing household tasks. They mention being overworked while other female members of the household are allowed to take their ease. Another common complaint is that the woman has been denied adequate food or is habitually given food of poorer quality than that consumed by other members of the household. Accusations of black magic performed by in-laws—either to make the younger woman ill, abort her foetus, or alienate the husband's affections—are also very frequently encountered in the case files.

Harsh treatment by in-laws is regularly associated with 'dowry harassment', whereby a mother-in-law and sisters-in-law—often in concert with the husband—subject the woman to recriminations for having brought insufficient dowry and repeatedly demand that she obtain from her parents additional money, jewellery, and other goods. This kind of harassment is usually alleged to have commenced very shortly after the marriage. In women's narratives, as found in court petitions, what begins as verbal harassment gradually escalates to physical abuse and culminates either in the woman's forcible ejection from the house or her escape from it, usually with the help of her father, brothers, or other members of her natal family. Again, whereas in-law problems do not, in themselves, constitute a ground for divorce under the DMMA, a husband's failure to protect his wife from abuse by his parents and siblings can be considered a form of cruelty for this purpose.

Another kind of in-law problem is cited by men in petitions for RCR or in response to divorce or maintenance suits filed by their wives: namely, alleged interference by the wife's parents in the life of the couple and/or pressure from the former to force the man to move into their home and live with them as an in-married son-in-law. In such cases, the man frequently charges that his wife's parents are motivated by greed, desiring to exploit his earning power for their own benefit. He may have even tried, unsuccessfully, to prevent his wife having contact with her parents and other family members, in order to ward off their demands or their alleged 'interference' with the relationship between himself and his wife.

HOW EAGER ARE MEN TO PRONOUNCE *TALAQ*?

Court files typically provide considerable information about the 'history' of the case, including previous attempts to resolve the problems that have given rise to the suit. My examination of a multitude of Muslim matrimonial cases raises some interesting issues in relation to the troubled question of unilateral divorce. Notwithstanding a widespread assumption that Muslim men are very quick to take advantage of their legal entitlement to divorce their wives at will and without providing any reason for their act, there is some evidence in these case files that, in fact, a significant proportion of men whose marriages have effectively broken down are somewhat reluctant to pronounce *talaq* on their wives. Most of the women who come into court seeking maintenance and, by definition, all of those who come seeking divorce or in response to their husbands' suits for RCR are still married, though no longer living with their husbands. The case histories suggest that, although *talaq* is recognized as an option by most men experiencing marital problems, they do not necessarily act upon it, for one reason or another. In some cases they may simply not bother, especially if the wife is no longer living in their home, they have ceased supporting her and have perhaps married again and begun to raise a new family. As long as the wives refrain from making any demands on them, the men are not motivated to take action to divorce them. Things may change when the man learns that the wife has filed a suit for maintenance, but even then many husbands hold back from taking this step.

There are a number of social and financial drawbacks associated with pronouncing *talaq* that may lead a man to deliberately avoid doing so, at least until things reach the point where he feels he has no other choice. In the Muslim community generally a man who pronounces *talaq*—unless he can show that his wife has committed some egregious fault, such as adultery—is not well regarded or respected for his act. Among other things, he may later have difficulty finding another wife, as parents will be reluctant to marry their daughter to a man who they know has divorced his first wife without good reason.

Case files show that it is not unusual for a man who wants to end his marriage to try to get his wife to approach the qazi and ask for *khula*.[26] In an interview that I conducted, following up on a case of RCR filed in the Chennai Family Court, one woman told me how she refused to cooperate when her husband went himself to ask the qazi to summon her and persuade her to initiate a divorce by *khula*. She explained that she wanted the marriage to continue. Furthermore, if she agreed to ask for *khula*, she would get a 'bad name' for taking the initiative in terminating her marriage. Then people would be able to say that she was a woman of 'bad character', instead of placing the blame where it belonged, with the husband who had abused her and thrown her out of the marital home.[27]

Another reason for some men's reluctance to pronounce *talaq* is financial. If a husband does so, he is obliged to pay his wife her *mehr* and maintenance for the *iddat* period of approximately three months, whereas if a *khula* is negotiated he will be relieved of this obligation. Of course, many men ignore this obligation anyway.[28] However, if the divorce is registered with a qazi, the latter will usually make some effort to see that the *mehr* and *iddat* amount is paid. Some qazis, before issuing a divorce certificate, require the man to deposit the appropriate amount to be handed over later to the wife. Obviously, many men—perhaps most—are not deterred from pronouncing *talaq* by the possibility of incurring social disapproval and financial loss. But if one wishes to understand the dynamics of the divorce phenomenon among Muslims in all its complexity it is important to recognize that these factors do enter into individual decision-making and into negotiations between spouses when a marriage seems headed for breakdown.

THE ROLE OF A WOMAN'S FAMILY

Case files show that women's natal families—parents and brothers in particular—play a major role in initiating and then pursuing the suits that were technically being filed by the women themselves. In fact, I would venture to generalize that if a young woman's family is not prepared to provide this kind of material and moral support, it is unlikely that she will come to court seeking legal relief. Indian parents, of any religion, very often pressure, or even compel, a daughter who is having marital difficulties to remain with her husband, fearing the social disgrace and, in some cases also, the financial burden, that they will have to bear if they allow her to return home. Even those who are prepared to shoulder these burdens often have legitimate concerns about whether the best solution for their daughter is to live out her life as a divorcee, forever tainted by disgrace, shame, and heightened sexual vulnerability.

Some Hindu legal practitioners whom I interviewed felt that Muslim parents are less likely than Hindus to insist that their daughter remain with an abusive husband. They felt that the stigma of divorce is minimal among Muslims, by comparison to that found among Hindus and Christians. They often pointed out that a divorced Muslim woman can remarry, something that is not socially acceptable among Hindus. However, many Muslim interviewees referred to the stigma of divorce as a serious problem for women locked in unhappy marriages, and, while praising their religion for allowing the re-marriage of divorcees, they admitted that in practice it is difficult to find a man willing to marry a divorced woman, especially if she has children.

DIVORCE SUITS IN FAMILY COURTS

Relatively few divorce suits are filed under the DMMA. This fact does not necessarily mean that few Muslim women initiate divorce, only that it is always much cheaper and more expeditious, provided her husband can be persuaded to cooperate, to get *khula*, either by making an agreement with him privately or by seeking the intercession of a qazi or other religious functionary. Any amount that she might have to pay her husband in order to obtain a *khula* will certainly be exceeded by lawyers bills, court fees, and transportation and other costs of attending a family court for a period of several months or years. Furthermore, the *khula* agreement would rarely involve an actual cash outlay on her part, since it is most unlikely that she would have already received the *mehr* amount that an agreement for *khula* would oblige her to forgo. Even lawyers practicing in the family court routinely advise prospective female clients to try to negotiate a *khula* before filing for a civil divorce.

Of the 57 divorce suits filed in the Chennai Family Court between

1988 and 1997, half were dismissed, either because the woman withdrew the suit or because she simply neglected to pursue it, for one reason or another. In some cases the record shows that the husband pronounced a divorce or the couple came to an agreement for *khula* while the case was still in litigation. Sometimes, the couple was persuaded by court counsellors or others to reunite. However, the women whose suits were not dismissed for one of these reasons invariably succeeded in obtaining a divorce decree.

I found no instances of a divorce suit dismissed by the judge for lack of evidence or failure to prove the grounds cited. Of course, it is quite possible that in some of the cases dismissed as withdrawn or not pressed the petitioner had been persuaded by the judge or by her advocate that the suit had little chance of success and for this reason decided not to pursue it further. This would be consistent with the judges' general reluctance either to issue a contested judgement or to deny any petition outright. Instead, the usual policy is to try to reach a compromise that, in the short term at least, both parties are willing to agree to, however reluctantly. Thus most divorce decrees that were issued involved some sort of compromise—presumably brokered by lawyers, counsellors, and judges—whereby the woman agreed to give up any financial claims against the husband (such as the return of her *mehr*, alimony for the *iddat* period, personal property, or future child support) in exchange for his dropping his opposition to the divorce or allowing her to retain custody of their children.

MAINTENANCE CASES

Maintenance cases are filed by Muslim women (as they are by Hindu and Christian women) much more often than suits for divorce. But Muslim women file such suits at a much lower rate than do women of other religions, partly for reasons of eligibility arising from the provisions of the MWA, detailed above, that deny divorced Muslim women the right to claim maintenance under Section 125 of the CrPC. A large number of successful maintenance suits are, however, filed by divorced Muslim women on behalf of their minor children.

Maintenance cases tend to be the most protracted of all types of cases that come before the family court. They occasionally drag on for several years. In repeated counselling sessions counsellors try to get the couple back together again or, if that proves impossible, to persuade the husband to offer some amount of support for his wife and/or his children. Judges and lawyers alike tend to be sceptical of the value of ordering a man to pay a specific amount, even where the evidence shows he can afford it, because such orders are almost impossible to enforce, unless the man is a government employee and therefore subject to salary attachment. Therefore, court personnel and lawyers for both parties usually work together to try and get a voluntary commitment from the husband for a modest amount, in the hope that under such circumstances he is more likely to actually come through with the cash each month.

RESTITUTION OF CONJUGAL RIGHTS

Suits for the restitution of conjugal rights are somewhat more common than divorce suits (63 in the period with which I am concerned), but the frequency of cases dismissed as withdrawn or not pressed is even higher—almost 85 per cent. This confirms the impression of some lawyers that such suits are generally filed as a form of harassment or threat, or to retaliate against a wife who has made a police report or filed against him for divorce or maintenance. The mere filing of a suit for restitution of conjugal rights may be enough to induce a wife to drop such a suit or even to return to her husband. Or it may convince her parents that they should use their influence to get her to go back to him. Such suits, even if not successful, may also provide moral justification for a man who is inclined to pronounce *talaq* but fears the social opprobrium associated with that act. This way, he can demonstrate that he was willing and eager to take her back, but because of her unreasonable refusal to return he had no other choice than to divorce her.

Though few cases in fact result in a decree ordering the wife to return to her husband, they are almost never denied outright. If the wife repeatedly refuses to consent to a reunion, there is little that a judge can do to force her to rejoin her husband even if he or she does hand down a restitution order. Her refusal to return can, however, result in the cancellation of a maintenance order that she may have previously been granted or cause the dismissal of an ongoing maintenance suit.

CONCLUSION

I have presented here some of my findings from a study of Muslim case files in the records of the Family Court at Chennai and have raised a number of issues that emerge from a preliminary analysis of the data. It is clear that the experience of Muslim women in the family court captures only one small part, from one limited perspective, of the much larger phenomenon which this volume is designed to address. The very nature of the material at my disposal, with its inherent limitations, makes it difficult to draw any definitive conclusions even about the extent to which Muslim women are benefited by the laws intended to protect their marital rights in the setting of a family court. It is, however, quite clear that when one begins to examine the actual practice, not just the letter of Muslim family law in India, one finds a situation that is far more complex than allowed for by those who castigate Muslim law out of hand for its oppressive impact on women. There is no doubt that the marital home is a site of great tension and even unbearable misery for large numbers of Muslim women—as it is for women of all religions—and that the law has shown itself incapable of providing satisfactory relief to a significant portion of them. But at this point, I feel that the major contribution that social scientists can make to the solution of these widespread problems is to continue to add to our empirical knowledge of the actual workings of the law that purports to deal with them. Only in this way will it be possible to decide how best to ameliorate the conditions that we deplore.

NOTES

1. This paper was written while I was a Faculty Fellow of the Institute for the Humanities at the University of Illinois at Chicago. My research in India was supported by a Fulbright-Hays Senior Research Fellowship and a sabbatical leave from the University of Illinois at Chicago. In Chennai I was affiliated with the Madras Institute of Development Studies.
2. Some recent exceptions include Mukhopadhyay (1998), Moore (1998) and Women's Research and Action Group (1997a, 1997b).
3. The source is a mimeographed report entitled 'Incidence of Polygynous Marriages in India', cited in Committee on the Status of Women in India (1974: 108). I suspect that most of those who refer to this figure are citing it from the latter secondary source, rather than from the original document

which is not readily, if at all, accessible to scholars. Without access to the original text it is not even possible to know how the figure is to be interpreted: does it refer to the percentage of (married?) men who have more than one wife, to the percentage of *marital units* that consist of one man and two or more wives, or to some other measure?

4. A recent book whose title holds out the promise of shedding some light on the former issue does not, in fact, address it at all. Instead, it reports the findings of a survey of a sample of divorced Muslim men and women in two Indian cities (Siddiqui 1996).
5. My own genealogical investigations among elite Urdu-speaking Muslims in Chennai and Hyderabad clearly substantiate the hypothesis that divorce was unknown before the 1950s, and even now is extremely rare. Khan maintains that in the Karnataka village where he carried out research in the 1980s, he found no cases of divorce (1994: 143-5).
6. My other goals were more theoretical in nature and cannot be dealt with in the space of this paper.
7. See, for example, Tiwari and Zaidi (1997).
8. This exception came into effect in 1986 with the passage of the Muslim Women's (Protection of Rights on Divorce) Act, following agitation resulting from the Supreme Court decision on the Shah Bano case. Under that Act, a Muslim man is not responsible for maintaining his divorced wife after the expiry of the *iddat* period. See Verma (1988: 474-84) for a more detailed discussion of the legal ramifications of this act. One of its practical ramifications is that it has become routine for men faced with a suit for maintenance under the CrPC to immediately pronounce divorce and thus evade further claims on their pocketbook. This tactic does not, however, absolve them of responsibility to pay child support.
9. An early statement of these problems and a recommendation that family courts be established came from the Committee on the Status of Women in India (1974: 141-2).
10. See, for example, Rameseshan (1989), and Nagasila (1991, 1992). Both writers have had personal experience in the Chennai Family Court.
11. See Chapter IV, Section 13 of the Act. Cf. Tiwari and Zaidi (1997: 37-42).
12. That is, by filing an official *vakalatnama*. One of the unfortunate consequences of this, from the point of view of the kind of research I carried out in the family court, is that the name of the client's advocate almost never appears in the file. This makes it impossible to obtain further details about a case by interviewing the person responsible for preparing and filing the suit and seeing the case through the judicial process.
13. For their cheerful assistance I am extremely grateful to my research assistant, R. Saraswathy, and to employees of the record room at the

Chennai Family Court, who patiently retrieved from their massive collection of materials the individual files that we required. I thank the then Chief Justice of the Chennai High Court for permission to carry out research in the Family Court and the then Acting Principal Judge of the Family Court for kindly arranging for me to consult the relevant files under her jurisdiction.

14. I limited myself to cases filed under the following three headings: (1) 'Ordinary Suits' (referred to by the shorthand 'OS'—almost all cases filed by Muslims fall under this heading), (2) 'Original Petitions' ('OP'—most of these are filed by Hindus and Christians, but a small number are filed by Muslims who married under the Special Marriage Act, usually because their marriage was an inter-religious one), and (3) 'Maintenance Cases' ('MC'—these can be filed by persons of any religion—most are filed by women against their husbands, either on their own behalf or on that of their child). Unfortunately, the MC registers for the years 1988 through 1991 could not be located.
The Family Court also entertains a number of other types of petitions and suits, such as for orders of execution, for interim orders, injunctions, etc. These, however, are almost always secondary to an earlier suit that falls into one of the categories cited above.
15. The language used in the court is Tamil. Native speakers of other languages who cannot speak and understand Tamil or English well enough to plead their cause in court are entitled to employ a translator. Most Chennai Muslims speak Tamil as their mother tongue, while others are Urdu-speakers. Most men and some women of the latter group are also conversant with spoken Tamil.
16. The precise number was 3,841,396 (*Census of India*, 1991. Series 23 *Tamil Nadu*, Part IV-B (ii) *Religion* (Table C-9: 4-5).
17. For example, in 1996 in only 4 per cent of the 1,442 original suits and petitions filed in the Family Court were one or both of the parties Muslim.
18. I have had to estimate this figure and that of the total number of cases, due to the fact that the MC register for the years 1988 through 1991 could not be located at the time of my research. In reaching this estimate I am assuming that the average number of total cases per year in the period 1992-7 (470), as well as the proportion of those cases that were filed by Muslims (5%), was the same in the pre-1992 period.
19. See the Child Marriage Restraint Act of 1978. The minimum marriage age for men is 21.
20. Cf. Mines (1976: 308-9), according to whom 61 per cent of Tamil Muslims surveyed in the early 1970s in the town of Pallavaram were married to kinsmen. Genealogical data that I have collected from Urdu-speaking Muslims in Chennai reveals an even higher rate of kin group

endogamy (see Vatuk, 1990). See also Khan (1994: 77-113); Fanselow (1986).

21. There is an extensive literature on notions of honor and its association with control of female sexuality in India and other parts of South Asia, much of which is cited and synthesized by Mandelbaum (1988).
22. Cf. DMMA Section 2 (ii): 'that the husband has neglected or has failed to provide for her maintenance for a period of two years' or (iv): 'has failed to perform without reasonable cause his marital obligations for a period of three years'.
23. Cf. Section 2 (vii) (a) of the DMMA: 'makes her life miserable by cruelty of conduct even if such conduct does not amount to physical ill-treatment'.
24. Cf. Section 2 (vii) (f): 'if he has more wives than one, does not treat her equitably in accordance with the injunctions of the *Quran*'.
25. See Section 2 (viii) (d) of the DMMA, according to which a Muslim woman can be granted a divorce on grounds of cruelty if her husband 'disposes of her property or prevents her from exercising her legal rights over it'.
26. Furthermore, more than one Muslim cleric with whom I spoke about this matter maintained that, in their experience, *khula* divorces are more frequent than *talaq*. They made this point in the context of trying to show that they facilitated women's needs by brokering such agreements when unhappy wives came to them for help. One such interviewee offered that in his opinion men do prefer to have their marriage dissolved by *khula* instead of *talaq*. However, he did not speculate as to their motives.
27. In the end, unable to get the family court to award a decree of restitution, he did pronounce *talaq*, doing so in the chambers of the judge who was presiding over his case.
28. For example, in a study of 100 divorced women in Bombay, Merchant found that 60 per cent had not received their *mehr* after divorce. Note that she does not distinguish within her sample those who were divorced by *talaq* from those who obtained a *khula* or a civil divorce (1992: 111).

REFERENCES

Committee on the Status of Women in India (1974), *Towards Equality*, New Delhi: Government of India, Department of Social Welfare.

Fanselow, F.S. (1986), 'Trade, Kinship and Islamisation: A Comparative Study of the Social and Economic Organisation of Muslim and Hindu Traders in Tirunelveli District, South India', Ph.D. Dissertation, Social Anthropology, London School of Economics.

India, Government of (1991), *Census of India*, Series 23 *Tamil Nadu*, Part IV-

B (ii), *Religion* (Table C-9), Directorate of Census Operations, Tamil Nadu.

Khan, C.G. Hussain (1994), *Marriage and Kinship Among Muslims in South India*, Jaipur: Rawat.

Mandelbaum, David (1988), *Women's Seclusion and Men's Honor: Sex Roles in North India, Bangladesh and Pakistan*, Tucson: University of Arizona Press.

Merchant, Munira (1992), 'Indian Muslim Women: Post-Divorce Problems, Social Support and Psychological Well-Being', Ph.D. Dissertation, Social Work, University of Illinois at Chicago.

Mines, Mattison (1976), 'Urbanization, Family Structure and the Muslim Merchants of Tamilnadu', in Imtiaz Ahmad (ed.), *Family, Kinship and Marriage among the Muslims in India*, Delhi: Manohar.

Moore, Erin P. (1998), *Gender, Law and Resistance in India*, Tucson: University of Arizona Press.

Mukhopadhyay, Maitrayee (1998), *Legally Dispossessed: Gender, Identity and the Process of Law*, Calcutta: Stree Publications.

Nagasila, D. (1991), 'Family Courts: A Step Backward?', *The Hindu*, 24 March.

——— (1992); 'Family Courts: A Critique', *Economic and Political Weekly*, 27, 1735-7.

Ramaseshan, Geeta (1989), 'Family Courts: Wide Gaps', *Indian Express*, 11 March.

Siddiqui, M.M. (1996), *A Preliminary Report of Incidence of Divorce among Muslims*, New Delhi: Institute of Objective Studies.

Tiwari, Devendra Kumar and Mahmood Zaidi (1997), *Commentaries on the Family Courts Act, 1984*, Allahabad: Alia Law Agency.

Vatuk, Sylvia (1990), 'The Cultural Construction of Shared Identity: A South Indian Muslim Family History', *Social Analysis*, 28, 114-31.

Verma, B.R. (1998), *Muslim Marriage, Dissolution and Maintenance*, 2nd edn., Allahabad: The Law Book Company.

Women's Research and Action Group (1997a), *Women, Law and Customary Practices*, Mumbai: WRAG.

——— (1997b), *Aspects of Culture and Society: Muslim Women in India*, Mumbai: WRAG.

5

Divorce and Separation among Muslims in West Bengal

Syed Abdul Hafiz Moinuddin

This paper deals with divorce and separation among Muslims in West Bengal. Women as a rule face more problems than men in the event of divorce and separation,[1] but the question is whether there are basic differences in this respect among women on account of variations in religio-cultural identity. Some problems can be common to all women, but some problems can vary from community to community depending upon their religio-cultural identities. The principal aim of this paper is to delineate the position of divorced and separated Muslim women by tracing out the operation of the system of divorce and the factors responsible for its prevalence in rural West Bengal. Specifically, it seeks to find out (a) the nature and magnitude of the problem of divorce and separation among Muslims, (b) how the system of divorce operates, (c) the social and other causes due to which the practice of divorce among Bengali Muslim women persists, and (d) the variations that exist between the textual and operational models of divorce and separation among Bengali Muslim women. The thrust of the paper is empirical and sociological. It is well-known that social traditions and practices play a vital role in shaping the attitudes as well as behaviour patterns of any human group and emerging trends in society cannot be viewed in isolation from them. This paper, therefore, seeks to look at divorce and separation in the context of social structure, cultural norms and value judgements as determinants of behaviour patterns in communities.

The paper is based on data drawn from two gram panchayats in the Barddhaman and Murshidabad districts of West Bengal. Muslims are distributed all over West Bengal and accounted for 17.60 per cent of the total population of the state as a whole according to the 1981 census. However, some districts have a greater concentration of the Muslim population than others. Murshidabad district accounts for 58.67 per cent of the Muslim population. Murshidabad was the capital of Bengal for a long time and contained a sizable aristocracy, a large service class and numerous artisans. Barddhaman district has 17.60 per cent Muslim population. On the whole, Muslims in West Bengal inhabit rural areas in larger proportion (85.8 per cent) as compared to urban areas where their proportion is 14.2 per cent. Concentration of Muslims in rural areas is particularly marked in agriculture-based districts such as Jalpaiguri, Coochbehar, West Dinajpur, Malda, Murshidabad, Nadia, Birbhum and Medinipur. Furthermore, rural Muslims are not prone to migrating to urban areas of Calcutta and other district towns. This is a function of their traditional ties with their land. Other than Calcutta, the highest concentration of Muslims is to be found in Howrah (32.77 per cent). Panchthupi Gram Panchayat in Murshidabad and Mongolkote Gram Panchayat in Barddhaman were chosen as they seemed to reflect the settlement pattern and economic and occupational characteristics of the Muslim population in West Bengal.

Fieldwork was carried out in the selected gram panchayats in two phases. First, in order to arrive at some areas of investigation, and to lay down guidelines, directions and tentative formulations regarding the subject, especially as no previous research existed, a pilot survey among 20 divorced and separated Bengali Muslim women in Mongolkote village in Barddhaman district was undertaken. The aim of this pilot survey was to gain insight into the problems of divorced and separated women as perceived by the affected women themselves. Questions asked at this initial stage of research were open-ended and interviews were relatively unstructured. This was followed by more intensive fieldwork. We interviewed 70 divorced and separated women in Mongolkote Gram Panchayat. Divorced included those women whose *talaq* or release from the marriage bond had occurred in the presence of legal authorities or local elders. Legal authorities included the maulana, moulvi and imam. Elders included those recognized by the community as responsible enough to be witnesses to such actions. Divorced also included those women whose dissolution of marriage had occurred in court. On the other hand, separated were those who did not have any relationship with their husbands and were at the time of the interview living with their parents. However, they harboured the hope that their husbands would some day give due recognition to them and take them back with honour.

Among the 70 women interviewed in Mongolkote Gram Panchayat, 31 were divorced and 39 were separated. We also interviewed 52 guardians in Mongolkote. These included 16 fathers, 28 mothers, 7 brothers and one elder sister. Eighteen women had no guardians. In Murshidabad district Panchthupi Gram Panchayat was selected for detailed investigation. A total of 58 Muslim women were interviewed among whom 36 were divorced and 22 were separated. We also interviewed 47 guardians among whom 17 were fathers, 27 were mothers and 3 were brothers. Eleven women had no guardians. The rationale for interviewing guardians was that as heads of households they controlled all channels of communication and were in a position to take important decisions regarding the women. We felt that interviews with them might tell us how they rationalized their actions especially as some of their actions were clearly at variance with Islamic injunctions. We also collected five case histories in each gram panchayat to obtain some supplementary information. The study being largely descriptive where the main emphasis was on uncovering the reasons for divorce and separation, it was ensured that the research design was flexible enough to permit consideration of as many aspects of the phenomenon of divorce as possible. In order to gather as much information as possible and to be able to make the study sufficiently 'intensive', both methods—interview and case studies—were adopted for data collection.

Experience in the field showed that considerable rapport with the respondents was called for as the study involved attitudes and sentiments and intimate, delicate and emotionally-laden personal facts were sought from the respondents. The modality of interview had to be one where the respondents could be persuaded to be truthful, frank and honest in answering questions and narrating their experiences. Intensive interviews proved to be very useful for this purpose. If the respondents were allowed to follow their trail of thought, answers to many questions were forthcoming on their own. For this reason, considerable time had to be spent with the respondents before beginning the interviews. Once rapport had been established, polite conversation slowly changed to serious and pointed questioning. Although long and time-consuming, this method appeared most suitable for the purposes of this study and turned out to be extremely useful in obtaining reliable data. On an average, it took us between 20 and 45 minutes to conduct one interview.

There is a popular belief that Muslims in India strictly follow the basic tenets of Islam as embodied in the *shar'ia*. This belief has been widely accepted by both sociologists and social anthropologists and by common people. But there is a need to remember that every world religion also has its own cultural variations. Local practices, rituals, belief systems and related forms of social behaviour have been incorporated in all world religions. No world religion has been able to root out local belief systems and practices and they have become a part of religions through the ages. There is, therefore, need to analyse such variations among the Bengali Muslims on the question of marriage, divorce and separation if we wish to understand Muslim divorce practices.

Like all other communities, Bengali Muslims, too, look upon marriage as essential for both males and females. Muslim parents are said to be 'not free' unless their sons and daughters are married. Marriage is contractual in Islam and both the bride and the bridegroom can stipulate conditions for marriage. A Muslim marriage has fixed and rigid rules that have been laid down and practised from the times of the Prophet. Some scholars argue that marriage between parallel and cross cousins is preferred because of the weak economic condition of the families. Others argue that Muslims prefer marriages between close relatives in order to keep family property intact. Shushtery (1992) argues that marriage between cousins, both paternal and maternal, is preferred in Islam. Among Arabs and Iranians, a man had the right to claim the hand of his cousin so that property remained in the family and, if the family were not rich, at least the purity of blood was preserved. Iranians preferred marriage with the first cousin on the grounds that where the husband and the wife were of equal status and possessed the same family background and ties, harmony of life and domestic happiness would be ensured. Our study suggests that most parents give greater weight to physique and occupation of the bridegroom rather than to kinship considerations in mate selection for their children. Out of the total 128 respondents interviewed, 29 had no guardians. Of the remaining 99 respondents, parents assigned the highest weight to the physical capabilities of the bridegroom in both districts. Next in order of preference was the ownership of property.

Table 1 sets out the characteristics of the bridegroom preferred by parents in selecting a mate for their daughters. Only in 5 cases (3.91 per cent) in the two gram panchayats was preference given to kinship. In 2 cases (1.56 per cent) preference was given to the job, and in another 3 cases (2.35 per cent) preference was given to the education of the bridegroom. Otherwise, in 56 cases (43.75 per cent) the primary consideration in mate selection was the health of the bridegroom and in 11 cases (16.41 per cent) it was property. A number of conclusions can be drawn from this data. First, it shows that a large proportion of the parents interviewed in the two districts placed a great deal of emphasis upon the health of the prospective bridegroom. Second, while importance was attached to his property, educational qualifications and the white-collar status of the bridegroom was hardly taken into account. This is a comment upon the overall socio-economic conditions prevailing among Muslims in West Bengal villages. The area of mate selection in all cases was also very much restricted to neighbouring villages due to the poor economic condition of the families.

In the past the age at which marriages were contracted was extremely low among Bengali Muslims. Many old Muslim women

TABLE 1: FACTORS CONSIDERED BY PARENTS IN SELECTION OF MATE FOR THEIR DAUGHTERS

Factors	Murshidabad		Barddhaman		Total	
	Number	Percentage	Number	Percentage	Number	Percentage
Health	24	41.38	32	45.71	56	43.75
Property	11	18.97	10	14.29	21	16.41
Daughter's choice	6	10.34	6	8.57	12	9.37
Relative	4	6.90	1	1.43	5	3.91
Education	1	1.72	2	2.86	3	2.34
Service	1	1.72	1	1.43	2	1.56
Not available	11	18.97	18	25.71	29	22.66
Total	58	100.00	70	100.00	128	100.00

TABLE 2: RESPONDENT'S AGE AT THE TIME OF MARRIAGE

Factors	Murshidabad		Barddhaman		Total	
	Number	Percentage	Number	Percentage	Number	Percentage
10 years	3	5.17	6	8.57	9	7.03
10-15 years	24	41.38	38	54.29	62	48.44
15-20 years	21	36.21	24	34.28	45	35.16
20-25 years	9	15.52	1	1.43	10	7.81
25-30 years	1	1.72	1	1.43	2	1.56
Total	58	100.00	70	100.00	128	100.00

speak of themselves and those whom they knew as having been married off at a very early age. The picture has not changed significantly today. Table 2 sets out the age of the respondents at the time of their marriage. It shows that in Murshidabad 3 (5.17 per cent) and in Barddhaman 6 (8.57 per cent) women respondents were, on an average, married off when they were ten years old. Again, 24 (41.38 per cent) in Murshidabad and 38 (54.29 per cent) in Barddhaman were married while they were in the age group 10-15 years. Of the remaining women respondents, as many as 21 (36.21 per cent) in Murshidabad and 24 (34.28 per cent) in Barddhaman were married between 15-20 years of age and 10 (9.37 per cent) in both the districts were married while in the age group 20-30 years. On the whole, thus, it is clear that child marriage or at least marriage before the legislated minimum age for marriage is widespread among rural Bengali Muslims. As many as 71 (55.47 per cent) women respondents in both the districts were married off before they reached the age of fifteen.

An important part of arranging a marriage is the making of a formal proposal of marriage. Traditionally, the woman herself does not negotiate or proposition her marriage. Bengali Muslims hold that the marriage of a girl should be arranged by her parents or by senior relatives in case her parents are not alive. In general the parents of the girl start the negotiations. This is done through close relatives or friends of the family and sometimes through the elderly people of the village. The practice of using the services of a *ghatak* (match-maker) does not exist among Bengali Muslims. Muslim law requires that the consent of the girl be obtained and, technically at least, her marriage depends upon her approval. However, among

Bengali Muslims the proposal for marriage comes from the groom's side and is accepted on behalf of the girl by her father or *wali* (marriage guardian) Modalities of obtaining the girl's consent are varied and differences exist among the respondents on the necessity of taking the girl's consent to her marriage.

Table 3 sets out the responses of the respondents regarding their parents' attitude towards taking their daughter's consent at the time of her marriage. It shows that 26 parents (44.83 per cent) in Murshidabad and 38 (54.29 per cent) in Barddhaman were in favour of taking their daughters' consent at the time of their marriage. However, this finding is inconsistent with the earlier finding that early marriage is widespread in both the districts. Clearly, there would be no point in seeking, and parents would not seek, a ten year old daughter's consent for marriage. What seems more plausible is that she is given into marriage by her father or *wali* and the mandatory consent sought from the bride at the time of *nikah* is considered equivalent to consent regarding her marriage. Engineer quite rightly observes: '. . . the *jahiliya* practice of contracting marriage by her *wali* on her behalf re-established itself and her approval was reduced to a mere nod or silence. From playing an active role in marriage she came to be relegated to a passive position' (1992: 108).

The most essential part of the wedding ceremony among Bengali Muslims is *nikah*. *Nikah* solemnizes the marriage and the form of this ceremony is the same as that prescribed by Islam. However, among Bengali Muslims the *nikah* ceremony is preceded and followed by different kinds of rituals and ceremonies. Women sing songs composed in their own dialect in the houses of both the bride

TABLE 3: PARENTS' ATTITUDE TOWARDS TAKING THEIR DAUGHTERS' CONSENT AT MARRIAGE

Attitude	Murshidabad		Barddhaman		Total	
	Number	Percentage	Number	Percentage	Number	Percentage
To be taken	26	44.83	38	54.29	64	50.00
Not to be taken	21	36.20	11	15.71	32	25.00
Felt no need	-	-	3	4.29	3	2.34
Not available	11	18.97	18	25.71	29	22.66
Total	58	100.00	70	100.00	128	100.00

and the bridegroom in the evening. Three days before the marriage the bridegroom's family sends *lagna* (a trunk-load of saris and cosmetics) to the bride's house. And the day before marriage the ritual of *tel halood* and *aiburo bhat* are held in both the houses. Women of all ages gather at a central place for the *tel halood* ceremony. In the bride's house the bride and in the groom's house the bridegroom is seated and women present in the house place their palms over the head of the bride or the bridegroom and the mother pours coconut oil. Women make seven rounds of the bride or the bridegroom and sing songs. Then the bride/bridegroom is anointed with *halood* (turmeric paste) while the mother distributes dry food among those who attend the ceremony. The *aibro bhat* ceremony is the ritual of having rice before the marriage. Whatever its socio-economic status, the family prepares the best possible food and serves it to the bride/bridegroom in the evening. Elderly male and female relatives as well as neighbours present at the ceremony feed the bride/bridegroom and offer gifts.

The *nikah* is a simple ceremony. The maulana or qazi sits in front of the bridegroom surrounded by all the invited guests and friends and performs the *nikah*. Two adult males must be witness and the amount of *mehr* payable to the bride is fixed. The witnesses first approach the girl who, dressed in her best, sits surrounded by her friends and the elderly women of the house. Her father or mother or elder brother usually tells her to give her consent after one of the witnesses announces the details of the marriage proposal. As soon as she gives her consent, the witnesses return to the bridegroom. It is announced that the bride has given her consent to the marriage and a similar affirmation is then sought from the bridegroom. Once the consent of both the partners has been obtained, the maulana or qazi recites a few passages from the Qur'an and the Hadith in praise of sexual relations and ends with blessings for both in which the others present join in.

The *mehr*, also known as *sadaq*, is an essential part of the *nikah* ceremony. Without *mehr* a *nikah* cannot be said to have been properly solemnized. The origin of *mehr* is pre-Islamic and tribal and it is essentially a brideprice, but Islam elevated it from merely being a brideprice to being a token of love, truthfulness and sincerity. Originally, there was a difference between *mehr* and *sadaq*. The former was paid to the *wali* and the latter to the bride herself (Maududi, 1955: 126). Today *mehr* is a sum of money or other property which the wife is entitled to receive from the husband in consideration of marriage. It has to be fixed before the solemnization of marriage though whether it is actually paid depends upon the circumstances of the bridegroom and his family. Usually, the amount of *mehr* is agreed upon but its payment can be deferred to a future date.

The *mehr* varies from one and a half *surkh dinar* (this is the amount fixed by the Prophet as an ideal amount for his daughter and is considered appropriate according to the *shar'ia.* It is, therefore, also called *shar'ai mehr*) to several thousand rupees. Our survey showed the highest amount to be Rs. 50,000. Families of maulana and moulvis and some religiously-aware people fix the *shar'ai mehr*, but in all other cases the amount of *mehr* depends upon the status of the girl's family. The more financially well-established and renowned the family, the higher is the amount of *mehr*. Some people consider *mehr* a security for women and try to fix a higher amount as *mehr.* 'Dower is often high among Mohammedans to prevent the husband from divorcing his wife, in which case he would have to pay the amount stipulated' observed the court in *Zakeri Begum* vs. *Sakina Begum* (1892). Therefore, bargaining over the *mehr* is common. Sometimes such bargaining leads to unpleasantness and even cancellation of marriage. The girl's parents always try to fix a high amount as *mehr* hoping that since the sum is beyond the means of the bridegroom their daughter will not have to face the threat of divorce from her husband in future.

There is no provision of dowry in Islam, but among Bengali Muslims the practice of dowry is widely prevalent whatever the socio-economic status of the family. The amount of dowry is fixed well before the fixation of the date of marriage and varies from family to family and place to place. If we go by the survey data, parents of as many as 103 respondents (80.47 per cent) in the two gram panchayats had to pay dowry. Again, the amount of dowry varied from cash and ornaments to land. Out of the 128 respondents, 54 (42.19 per cent) had paid cash and 42 (32.18 per cent) had paid both cash and ornaments. One respondent in Murshidabad and two in Barddhaman had given land as dowry. It is thus clear that the practice of dowry is very much prevalent among Muslim in West Bengal. Since our survey was conducted in a rural setting, the importance of land as a form of dowry is also very much in evidence.

This brings us to the question of divorce. *Talaq* (release from the marriage tie) is common among Muslims. Though the Prophet maintained that divorce is the most reprehensible of all things permitted, he allowed it as a last resort where there was no possibility of the husband and the wife living together in harmony and conjugal peace. There is nothing more displeasing to God than divorce. However, on the question of divorce the Qur'an is fettered with inequalities with the woman in every case being less equal. The Qur'an says, 'Women who are divorced have to wait for three monthly periods, and if they believe in God and the Last Day they must not hide unlawfully what God has formed within their wombs. Their husbands would do well to take them back in that case, if they wished to be reconciled. Women also have recognized rights as men have, though men have an advantage over them. But God is almighty and all-wise.' It cannot be gainsaid that some provisions and rights have been provided in the Qur'an and the Hadith for the benefit of Muslim women. However, it should always be remembered that the legal rights enjoyed by women in a society are not necessarily a true or complete index of their social status (Bhatty, 1976).

The Qur'an lays down an elaborate procedure for *talaq*. The two basic elements of that procedure are: (1) that where a divorce is contemplated there should be an effort at reconciliation before the *talaq* is allowed to take place, and (2) the *talaq* should be pronounced in such a way that the door to reconciliation remains open till the end. Towards these ends, the Qur'an explicitly states: 'When ye have to divorce women, pronounce divorce only when they are in a free state (i.e. free from menstruation or pregnancy). . . . Do not turn them out of their houses. . . . God may perhaps bring about a reconciliation between you' (Surah Al-Talaq: 1). Again, it reads: 'And when they have reached their prescribed term, either retain them with kindness or part from them in a just and gentle manner. Take two upright witnesses to the transaction. . . . God will show a way to the righteous for a honourable reconciliation or a honourable parting' (Surah Al-Talaq: 2). Elsewhere, in Surah Al-Baqarah, the

Qur'an clearly stipulates: 'When you have divorced your wives, and if they have reached the period of waiting, then keep them honourably (by revoking the divorce), or let them go with honour, and do not detain them with the intent of harassing lest you should transgress' (231). Later, this Quranic prescription for divorce was compromised through jurisprudential interpretation and pronouncement of *talaq* by the husband three times at one sitting was allowed.

Our study tried to ascertain the respondents' level of the knowledge and awareness about the rules and regulations about *talaq* as laid down in the Quran and the Hadith. It was found that only 9 interviewees (7.03 per cent) in Bardhaman had any knowledge of these. Strangely enough, none of the respondents in Murshidabad— all divorced and separated women—possessed any information about the religious rules about divorce though they had themselves experienced it. Again, we found that the respondents' families were neither aware nor interested in the Qur'anic rules to be followed in giving effect to a divorce. As a results there was a great deal of divergence between theory and practice on the question of divorce among Bengali Muslims. For example, despite the Qur'an's unequivocal pronouncement, 'When ye have to divorce women, pronounce divorce only when they are in a free state (i.e. free from menses and pregnancy) . . .' no husband waited for three menstrual cycles for the final pronouncement of *talaq*.

Wide divergence between theory and practice was also evident in respect of observance of *iddat* and payment of *mehr*. The Qur'an is very specific on the question of the observance of the *iddat* period. The requirement of *iddat* is dealt with not only in Surah Al-Baqarah (Chapter 2) of the Qur'an, but also in the Surah Al-Talaq (Chapter 65) where it is emphatically ordained, 'The prescribed term of waiting is three months except for pregnant women for whom time is extended till they have laid down their burden.' In our field study we found that no woman had observed *iddat*.

Wide variation was also found in the case of the payment of *mehr*. The *mehr* is a woman's right as a protection against indiscriminate *talaq*. Without *mehr* a marriage cannot be said to have been solemnized and *mehr* belongs to the wife alone. The Qur'an repeatedly exhorts men to give *mehr* to women. It says: 'And give women their dowries as a free gift. But if they of themselves be pleased to give you a portion thereof, consume it with enjoyment and pleasure.' It is usually believed that the *mehr* is a good security for women. In case of any difficulty in her marital life, and when she is divorced, the *mehr* has to be given to her. However, in our field study we found that only 2 out of the 128 women interviewed had received their *mehr* from their husbands after the divorce. This would seem to bear out Levy's observation that 'Where family life is concerned, in marriage, divorce and the distribution of inheritance, the presence of the *sha'r* would appear to be very widely neglected' (1962: 55).

Our study shows that Muslim women in West Bengal have to face the prospect of arbitrary divorce, and that religion plays a vital role in this. However, a divorce or separation is usually not the result of a sudden or isolated case of friction between the husband and the wife. It is the result of a long series of developments and there is usually a specific reason behind the occurrence of divorce or separation. Table 4 sets out the reasons as perceived by the respondents for their divorce or separation. It shows that extramarital

TABLE 4: REASONS FOR DIVORCE OR SEPARATION

Reasons	Murshidabad		Barddhaman		Total	
	Number	Percentage	Number	Percentage	Number	Percentage
Extramarital relation of the husband	26	44.83	28	40.00	54	42.19
Poor economic condition	1	1.72	1	1.43	2	1.56
Family quarrels	7	12.07	8	11.43	15	11.72
Dowry	5	8.62	8	11.43	13	10.16
Issuelessness	2	3.45	0	00.00	2	1.56
Second marriage of the husband	11	18.97	14	20.00	25	19.53
Reestablished relationship with former wife	00	00.00	7	10.00	07	5.44
Long absence of the husband	1	1.72	1	1.43	2	1.56
Not available	5	8.62	3	4.28	8	6.25
Total	58	100.00	70	100.00	128	100.00

relation of the husband (42.19 per cent), poor economic condition of both the parties (1.56 per cent) and family quarrels (11.72 per cent) are the most common causes for divorce. Other reasons for divorce are dowry (10.16 per cent), childlessness (1.56 per cent), second marriage of the husband (21.09 per cent), or re-establishment of the husband's relationship with the first wife (5.47 per cent). Some respondents' husbands used to stay away from the family for years together and they took divorce on that ground. In one case the respondent's family asked her to seek divorce due to her husband's regular involvement in anti-social activities.

Table 5 sets out the modality adopted in the exercise of the right of divorce. In 8 cases (6.25 per cent) the divorce proceedings were held in the presence of a qazi. Most divorces took place only in the presence of the local people who are usually not aware of the Qur'anic principles regulating *talaq*. It was also found that when a divorce occurred in the presence of local people the respondents were not present and no prior consent to the divorce had been taken from them. In one case divorce notice was sent through the mail and 18 respondents (14.06 per cent) said that their divorce had taken place in the court. It is to be noted that some of the husbands moved the court and subsequently informed the respondents by mail that they had been divorced. From our data three conclusions can be easily arrived at. First, the qazi is not considered indispensable for supervising *talaq* proceedings as in a large number of cases the divorce was formalized in the presence only of the local people.

TABLE 5: MODALITY ADOPTED IN FORMALIZATION OF DIVORCE

Modalities Adopted	Murshidabad		Barddhaman		Total	
	Number	Percentage	Number	Percentage	Number	Percentage
In the presence of qazi	1	1.72	7	10.00	8	6.25
In the presence of local people	26	44.83	18	25.71	44	34.37
In court	10	17.24	8	11.43	18	14.06
By mail	1	1.72	-	-	10	0.78
Other	2	3.45	-	-	2	1.56
Not available	18	31.03	37	52.86	55	42.97
Total	58	100.00	70	100.00	128	100.00

Second, even though the respondents all belonged to rural areas a fairly large proportion went to court to obtain their divorce. Finally, respondents' families in most cases were not interested in the Qur'anic rules being followed in a divorce. Most husbands took advantage of this fact.

Table 6 sets out the number of years of marriage after which divorce or separation took place. It shows that in 3 cases in Murshidabad (5.17 per cent) and in 6 cases (8.57 per cent) in Barddhaman divorce or separation occurred within a year of marriage. Again, in 62 cases (48.44 per cent) the divorce or separation took place within five years of marriage. In 45 cases (35.15 per cent) the divorce or separation took place within 10 years after the marriage. It is interesting that divorce or separation also occurred after a long period of marriage. There were 12 cases (9.38 per cent) where divorce or separation took place between 11 and 20 years after the marriage.

Breakdown of marriages and occurrence of divorce are shown by this study to have a strong correlation with low income and low status. As part of this study we attempted a statistical analysis to bring out this correlation (for details see Moinuddin, 2000). We used a slightly modified version of the measure adopted by Minhas (see Minhas et al., 1991) for measurement of poverty in West Bengal for determining income levels. On the basis of cost of living index constructed for agricultural labourers, which can be assumed to be relevant for all rural people, Minhas and others calculated the poverty line for West Bengal at Rs. 170.40 per month per person. We did not confine ourselves to this definition and considered all

TABLE 6: NUMBERS OF YEARS OF MARRIAGE AFTER WHICH DIVORCE TOOK PLACE

Year	Murshidabad		Barddhaman		Total	
	Number	Percentage	Number	Percentage	Number	Percentage
Within a year	3	05.17	6	8.57	9	7.03
Within 5 year	24	41.38	38	54.29	62	48.44
Within 10 years	21	36.21	24	34.28	45	35.15
Within 15 years	9	15.52	1	1.43	10	7.81
Within 20 years	1	1.72	1	1.43	2	1.57
Total	58	100.00	70	100.00	128	100.00

households having an income of Rs. 120 and less as low-income households. The main reason for this was that a monthly income of Rs. 600 per household with an average size of 5 members yields a per capita income of Rs. 120. Thus our cut off point (Rs. 120) lies below the line constructed by Minhas. As a result we can be reasonably sure that households having income levels of Rs. 600 per month can be considered as lying below the poverty line. It is to be noted that the data were obtained after interviewing all the divorced/separated Muslim women in the villages under survey. Hence, the question of any divorced/separated Muslim women from 'rich' or 'middle class' families to creep into the sample households does not arise, and the data can be said to provide a complete picture of the relationship between divorce and income levels.

Unlike income level, status is not a clearly definable term. It denotes the social standing of people but we ought to remember that social standards can vary significantly in inter-temporal and inter-spatial terms. Further, it depends on who is talking. To a rickshaw puller a taxi driver may appear to belong to a higher stratum though the latter may be just another 'cabbie' to the person sitting inside his taxi. Therefore, we first identified the occupations or professions that allegedly make a person belong to a 'low-status' group. We included menial occupations like those of a day labourer, rickshaw puller, gardener and *bidi*-maker in the low status category. To be more specific, jobs which need little or no formal training or which involve mostly raw physical labour or which offer little remuneration or a combination of the above were treated as wreckers of social prestige. With this in mind, we were able to easily exclude blue-collar workers, whole-sellers, students, masons, etc., for the purpose of establishing the relationship between marital breakdown and social status. Further, we also omitted people listed under the head 'agriculture' (excluding agricultural labour) because cultivation does not relegate a person to the lower rung of the social ladder in a rural setting.

It is to be noted that we considered the occupation only of the husbands of the divorced/separated women in determining the socio-economic status to their families. Lest it be thought that we suffer from a chauvinistic myopia, we also took into account the occupations followed by the parents and guardians of our interviewees. Nearly 40 of the interviewed guardians of the divorced Muslim women (22 in Murshidabad and 18 in Barddhaman) were housewives. This does not tell us much as this is a most non-descript and non-informative category of occupation. Leaving aside these 40 and another 29 guardian-less divorced/separated women, we find that 28 out of the remaining 59 guardians practiced low-status occupations, i.e. nearly half of the relevant figure.

On analysing the data from our survey we find that divorce among Bengali Muslims is more prevalent among people of low income and low status. Of the interviewed families, at least 78 per cent in Murshidabad and 51 per cent in Barddhaman belonged to the low-income group. Again, 26 out of 58 (44 per cent) of the husbands of the divorced and separated women covered in our survey in Murshidabad belong to the low-status category. The corresponding figure in Barddhaman is 38 out of 70 (54 per cent). This suggests that: (1) divorce among Muslims is more prevalent among low-income group. Both Murshidabad and Barddhaman districts show a distinct, positive relationship between lack of income and incidence of divorce/separation among Bengali Muslim women, and (2) divorce is more prevalent among the low status groups. However, there is a marked divergence between Murshidabad and Barddhaman as far as the economic condition of the divorced/separated Muslim women is concerned. Incidence of divorce is more widely prevalent among the low-income groups of Muslims in Murshidabad as compared to Barddhaman. On the other hand, there is no reason to suspect such divergence between the two districts as far as the relationship between status and divorce is concerned.

CONCLUSION

This discussion suggests that divorced and separated Muslim women in West Bengal are leading a miserable life. Their general condition is very pathetic. Those who hold that the provision of *mehr* in the Qur'an can be a source of maintenance are shutting their eyes to the reality of the position of Muslim women. Our survey shows that Muslim law as well as practice is fettered with inequalities, women in every case being less equal. Divorced Muslim women have not only been oppressed by the patriarchal bias in our society, they are also exploited by the non-availability of any legal protection. Our survey data suggest that besides the practice of arbitrary divorce that Muslim women have to face, there is the possibility that a husband will move the court and inform the respondent subsequently that she has been divorced. Anderson rightly observes:

> It is true that there are parts of the Muslim world where divorce is commendably rare, but elsewhere it is appallingly common. The Muslim wife indeed has always lived under the ever-present shadow of divorce, a shadow mitigated only in comparatively rare cases by precautionary devices— the unjustified repudiation of a wife is regarded by the jurists as a sin, but it is nonetheless held to be legally effective (1959: 132).

Any attempt at the betterment of the position of the divorced and separated Muslim women in West Bengal, as indeed in other parts of the country, demands positive attacks on poverty and socio-religious restrictions which presuppose male superiority and domination. Women's economic independence is an important factor in the emancipation and betterment of women's status. Muslim women in general and divorced or separated women in particular constitute an integral part of our society, and it is palpable in contemporary times that erecting barriers in their path to development is a serious mistake. We ought to remember that as long as we remain blind to the legitimate rights of women in respect of education, free movement and participation of women in economic activities a vital organ of our society will remain non-functional and oppressed.

NOTE

1. This is a well-researched finding. One of the points that emerges from extant studies on divorce in other societies and in urban centres in India is that a women who has been divorced takes far longer to stabilize than men.

REFERENCES

Anderson, J.N.D. (1959), *Islamic Law in the Modern* World, New York: New York University Press.

Bhatty, Zarina (1976), 'Status of Muslim Women and Social Change', in B.R. Nanda (ed.), *Indian Women: From Purdah to Modernity*, Delhi: Vikas Publishing House.

Engineer, Asghar Ali (1992), *The Rights of Women in Islam*, Delhi: Sterling Publishing.

Levy, Reuben (1962), *The Social Structure of Islam*, Cambridge: Cambridge University Press.

Menon, Indu (1981), *Status of Muslim Women in India*, Delhi: Uppal Publishing House.

Minhas, B.S. et al. (1991), 'Declining Incidence of Poverty in the 1980s: Evidence versus Artifacts', *Economic and Political Weekly*, 6-16 June.

Moinuddin, S.A.H. (2000), *Divorce and Muslim Women*, Jaipur, Rawat.

Shushtery, A.K.A. (1992), *Outlines of Islamic Culture: Philosophical and Technological Aspects*, Bangalore: The Bangalore Press.

6

Personalizing Islam in Communicating Divorce

Mohammad Talib

Divorce among Muslims is a complex subject where aspects of Islamic jurisprudence, customary regulations of gender roles, prescriptions of Qur'anic verses and related aspects of everyday living inextricably intertwine. The event of divorce in the fields of biography, society and history scarcely offer easy determinants and designs.

Based upon two long letters which a Muslim husband and wife in Delhi exchanged communicating to each other the reasons and reactions which the act of divorce generated before and after the separation, this paper seeks to capture one brief moment in the complex trajectory of divorce. The husband is a university teacher whose wife manages the household. The husband is addressed as Mausoof and the wife as Khatoon by the predominantly Muslim neighbourhood in the teachers' colony. The material from the letters is supplemented by the observations and responses of the neighbours of Mausoof.

The general precept that guides the present analysis is that the appropriation of Islam by Muslims follows the logic of the social and the cultural context as well. But it is difficult to say if a given act demonstrates the consummation of Islam by the Muslim or the Muslim by Islam; whether Islam is personalized or the person Islamized, words contextualized or context verbalized. Perhaps the dichotomy is unwarranted, and depending on the premise chosen as the starting point different trajectories can be represented: text of the stated logic or the context of the individual's biography.

As a curtain raiser, let the present description begin from the point where Mausoof's predominantly Muslim neighbours collectively confronted him to ask him why he had locked his wife in a room for weeks before sending her back to her parental home. Mausoof remained reserved and withheld obvious expressions of displeasure and disapproval. In Mausoof's own perception of himself, there was nothing about his life that could be termed 'private'. Islam had taken over his life completely not merely as a personal creed but also as the paramount mission of his life. One reason why public criticism scarcely upset him was because he was always ready to explain, defend, advocate and clarify his views of Islam's position in his behaviour.

To the critical neighbourhood, Mausoof's one line defence was that everything he did in his home was in strict conformity with the dictates of Islam as laid down in the holy Qur'an and some authentic *ahadees* (traditions of the Prophet). 'I am well within the sphere of Islam in all that I have done to my wife', he stated in response to the neighbours' upbraiding. One fellow Muslim teacher who was not convinced retorted, 'Are you within the sphere of Islam or is Islam within your sphere?' He then drew two circles on the muddy ground. One represented the small point in the centre as the individual and the rest of space as Islam. The other circle had Islam as the small point in the centre and the surrounding space as the individual. The unrelenting critic then pointed his stick to the circles in an effort to pin down the insurmountable. 'Are you this or that?' he enquired. The question amused the audience but put Mausoof off completely. Mausoof turned away from the group saying that there was no ground between them for a proper dialogue.

II

Mausoof explained his position in a long letter he wrote to his wife Khatoon in the month of Muharram 1417 Hijri (June 1996). The letter was handed over to her when she was sent back to her parental home. As she left, she had no inkling that she had been finally divorced.

Khatoon's response to the letter as well as Mausoof's letter is presented here in juxtaposition. While Mausoof's letter is presented without any significant deletions (except where a theme is repeated verbatim), Khatoon's response was more problematic. I must confess at the outset that I had never met Khatoon (hereinafter K) and

Khatoon's letter to Mausoof (hereinafter M) and her friends' comments and opinions were all that I had to go on.

The main text of the letters is as follows:[1]

M: Between 1981 to 1983, I received innumerable proposals of marriage. As I had a permanent teaching position, I was much sought after by wealthy parents of educated and beautiful daughters. My father's celebrated position in the missionary circles improved my status as a prospective groom for families well-known for religiosity. But I had told *ammi* (mother) that I was fully aware of the ways of educated girls in the university. As they didn't observe purdah, they were lacking in *sharm-o-haya* (sense of shame and modesty). They are invariably blunt and mulish. They have a poor understanding of *din* (personalized Islam). Therefore, my preference would be for a girl who should be religious and good looking but not particularly educated. This was my simple criterion for selecting my prospective bride. Your maternal uncle, who shared a common missionary background with my father, brought the proposal of marriage with you.

Your uncle was persistent. We were diffident in view of my sound financial position in the university. But in accepting your proposal, we recognized the merit of your case in the following terms: due to poor education, you would not be overbearing or headstrong. Instead, you would be compliant and sensitive to your husband's moods and manners. This proposal also had an immense demonstrative value for the mission, viz., Islam does not recognize considerations of caste and clan. Your proposal, if accepted, had the potential to be a 'pure' case in projecting the universalistic position of Islam in conjugal alliances as well as the ceremonial aspect of marriage.

K: *You give the impression that you had a choice in the matter of your matrimony and that you selected me with lot of reservation. But why do you forget that you were hardly acceptable to the families of the university employees. You say that my uncle pleaded for my acceptance. But your father was no less enthusiastic in clinching the* rishta *(conjugal alliance). We were told about your epilepsy. But the criterion in selecting you was that you seemed very religious. We took it for granted that all your actions would match your words. We were sure that an individual living by Islam would never be cruel.*

M: Remember how austere our marriage was: simple *nikah*, only a handful of *baratis* (the group of relatives and associates of the bridegroom), no dowry, no vulgar parade of the gifts exchanged on the occasion, *mehr* (dower approved by Muslim Law) paid to you at the time of our first meeting after the *nikah*, and no common customary practices unknown to Islam observed. None of our family members, yours and mine, tried to show off our economic position. And we consciously evolved this as part of the Islamic way of marriage.

K: *Austerity in the marriage ceremony! You had sent us a menu for the* baratis *and when you learnt about the single-bed being given as part of the dowry you wrote to us that you wanted a double-bed according to a specific design.*

M: The first few years of our married life were spent in getting to know each other. But as soon as I began to alter our routine in the family according to Islam, our relationship turned sour. From your tantrums and periodic ill-tempers, I realized that you and your relatives seemed to remember only one point about Islam, viz., that Islam does not recognize caste and clan and enjoins its believers to keep the marriage simple and materially austere. The rest of Islam was outside your ken. Perhaps, at the time of our marriage Islam suited your family more in material terms. Regarding Qur'anic clarity on what constitutes a wife, what is her real status in the family, what is the qualitative nature of the relationship she ought to maintain with her husband, how she should obey and attend to her husband, bring-up children, manage household affairs, relate to her husband's parents, I inferred that your parents had not taught you the Islamic precepts for a woman.

K: *You don't have to say that I am ignorant about many aspects of Islam and have always been clumsy as a wife and mother. What about you? Do you know the Islamic injunctions for a good husband? Do you have no role to play in the upbringing of your children? You found me uneducated but always expected me to motivate the children to study. I supervised their homework without qualification, but why did the children have to put up with your absence in their studies despite your doctoral degree?*

M: I do not believe ignorance to be a problem. The real problem was that you were scarcely prepared to accept or follow anything Islamic. I wish you had known the Qur'anic verse:

> And among His Signs
> Is this that He created
> For you males from among
> Yourselves, that ye may
> Dwell in tranquility with them
> And He has put love
> And mercy between your (hearts)
> Verily in that are signs
> For those who reflect (Surat Ar-Rum; 30: 21)[2]

I even reminded you about an instructive observation from *Sahih Muslim*, 'everything in the world is a temporary arrangement in which the most appropriate, pious and perfect is wife'.

K: *As I draw upon some commonly available* Tafseer *(interpretations of the Qur'an) I find that both husband and wife are required equally in bringing up the offspring. Both are necessary to nurture affection and tenderness in them. One* Tafseer *tells us that as women are the weaker vessel, the protecting tenderness which the strong should give to the weak may be likened to mercy.*

M: Rather than acquiring the requisite traits in your personality, you adopted a life style inimical to Islam. For instance, you pressurized me into purchasing a television set and not enforcing strict purdah on you. Our children were not instructed in Islamic values, and their constant misdemeanour towards *abbu* (father) and *ammi* (mother), a defiant posture towards my authority in my own family, befriending of neighbours without *din*, who ridiculed Islam and were opposed to my views pained me. You drew special pleasure in controlling the household affairs and leaving me perplexed and in quandary. At the time of accepting your proposal for marriage, I had the vain hope that you were steeped in the Prophet's quotation about the perfect wife: 'The husband feels sheer joy upon seeing her. She readily conforms to her husband's instructions and relates to worldly possessions only through the husband's concurrence.'

But your knowledge of Islam turned out to be grossly insufficient in domestic matters. Were you not aware of my passion for Islam? If you knew about my mission, why did you and your family members spoil my life?

Subsequently, I sought the indulgence of your uncle and explained every thing about you in the presence of my parents. Don't you remember even my father had a complaint against you. He found your behaviour lacking in decency. Your uncle warned you about the negative consequences of non-compliance. I was extremely patient with you. I kept your misconduct private and consistently projected a good image of you among our acquaintances so that you would not be maligned. This also gave you ample time to reform your self in deference to Islam's chosen values and practices.

Months and years went past but your wayward style continued unchanged. The children became estranged from me. At the slightest pretext they would slip out of the house without my knowledge. They got addicted to watching the TV, wore unwashed clothes, had unkept hair, uncut nails and had no fixed schedule for breakfast and other meals. Don't you remember how much time I wasted searching for the children in neighbours' homes or outside the locality.

When the children were at home they were hardly ever supervised or controlled. There were virtually no regulations or restraints in the family. Whenever I reprimanded you for the children's unruly behaviour, you would always retort sarcastically that there were too many children and disciplining them was beyond your capacity. You even derided me by saying that the numerous children were no fault of yours. It is partly true that you loathed childbearing. You not only spoiled the children but even allowed them to stray away from *din*. You ignored their laxity in offering prayers. You were slack in teaching them the Qur'an. One never heard a word of Allah and his Prophet from your children. When the children clamoured for bedtime stories you would be engrossed in reading your favourite magazines. I even fetched some story books of Islamic literature but you cared two hoots for these. Your fervour for watching TV infected our children and they, too, rallied round you. I disliked TV viewing but I relented and procured a television set unwillingly. I laid down certain conditions for TV viewing which you initially accepted but soon began to violate. After seven months I disposed it off. Pandemonium reigned in the house. You would beat up the children or they would beat each other. Where was the affectionate mother sharing her thoughts and feelings with them?

K: *I am surprised that whenever I disagreed with you, you always called it an opposition to Allah and Islam. Have you ever asked as to what was your role in spoiling our children? How have you contributed to their character building? When I was busy in the kitchen and with other household chores, your presence was most vital for the children. The propagation of Islam made you indifferent to everything else in the household. When I argued with you that the good upbringing of children was also the propagation of Islam, you became annoyed.*

You talk about our children slipping out of their home without our knowledge. But do you ask why the atmosphere at home was so boring for them? In a way, these children were without a father. And you know it for sure that such situations bring no comfort to the mother either.

I was not against having children but I objected to having unwanted children. The birth of every child should have made us more responsible, but you showed no signs of change.

The dependence on TV was largely due to your absence. As ever, you had a mission to fulfil, but I had to keep the family in good order, do the cooking, serve meals and attend to you and the children for everything. After the day's schedule, even you preferred to sleep than tell bedtime stories to children.

Disposing off of the TV was hardly a solution because you were, as usual, not available to the children. You lived in the house as a guest and I had to play the perfect host. Obviously, keeping the house clean was my responsibility. But you were supposed to merely enjoy it. And if ever your casual attitude towards the family was pointed out, you began to remind me for not doing my duty.

M: Our house had no internal decor. It was not just disorderly but dirty as well. I always felt that I would fall sick any time. The neighbours gossiped about our filthy house, but I always defended you. 'What if the house is dirty, she has a clean character', was my usual refrain. But you scarcely learnt anything or showed any improvement. One had expected that you would overcome your lack of education in the company of your husband or father-in-law (such well-known teachers otherwise). But you became estranged from us. Instead, you were more impressed by those who discredited us or the Islamic ethos of our house.

I repeatedly drew your attention to the worsening situation, but for you it was a laughable matter. As our domestic life began to turn sour, I would show my displeasure but you were least bothered. I would not take my meal at home or would not talk to you for days together. But surprisingly you would not even notice it. And in the end, my male weakness would make me give in. Without waiting to have your apologies, I would tender mine, unconditional and unqualified. This made you even more headstrong. *Ammi* was upset with you, *abbu* was vexed.

Despite my clear instructions, you would never serve food to *ammi*. I repeatedly reminded you that *ammi* was the one who had brought you to this house as a *bahu* (daughter-in-law). I warned you to restrain yourself for your sons' wives could ill-treat you similarly. But you were not deterred. Our family was rapidly being overtaken by a strongly un-Islamic, in fact a satanic, impulse. As I drew close to a complete adoption of Islamic life, your resistance to it grew correspondingly. Your defenders in the neighbourhood were growing in numbers and so was the intensity of gossip against me. It shocked me whenever the most intimate conversation between us was quoted publicly in a loud voice.

Only two solutions appeared possible, as two divergent pulls caught me in a difficult paradox: should I divorce you? Or else with your consent perform a *nikah* with a woman who could assist me in minimizing the damage and restore the Islamic atmosphere in the family. If you recall, immediately after our *nikah*, I had briefed you that for a variety of reasons, I favour a second *nikah*. You endorsed my views instantly, even showed a lot of interest in the matter. Sometimes you would badger me as to why I was delaying the second *nikah*.

K: *You and your parents always thought that you had done a great favour to me in marrying me. Because I lacked formal schooling I was treated virtually as a slave in your family. I was not supposed to object to anything, answer back and always be on my toes as a good waitress. If a minute was lost in complying with a request, then you would invariably remind me of Allah's wrath.*

As the atmosphere in the house began to worsen I was held responsible for it. You were the protagonist in implementing Allah's will, while I was the stooge of Satan. You became the crusader, while I was the problem to be overcome. I adjusted to you through two strategies: (i) ignored your misbehaviour, and (ii) I sought to please you within my means. This pushed me into an awful absurdity when I approved of your proposal for nikah-e-saani.

I did not know what was in store for me. But I always noticed that a discussion on nikah-e-saani *gratified you beyond description. I broached the topic, off and on, in order to put our relationship on a pleasant level. The liberal use of the strategy ultimately backfired.*

M: But the second *nikah* (*nikah-e-saani*) was a more complex matter, though not too difficult to arrange. But the acrimony after the first *nikah* was too bitter to be ignored. I told you that to perform the second *nikah*, we needed to conform to well laid conditions. Without fulfilling the conditions, the second *nikah* would not be possible. I explained to you clearly that the second woman in the house would be your partner. She would share her life with you more than me. I constantly reminded you that the final choice would be yours. You always volunteered to hunt for a suitable girl for me. Subsequently, I published an advertisement in the matrimonial column of an Urdu daily. The content of the advertisement *zaroorat-e-rishta* stated my preferences in no uncertain terms. In retrospect, I realized that the advertisement listed all the traits I desired and preferred in a woman and which were, in fact, conspicuously lacking in you. The advertisement stated the following:

'Wanted a Muslim girl for *nikah-e-saani* who is willing to be the proposer's *rafeeqa-e-hayat* (life partner), his wife's peer, and an aunt of his children. A girl who is interested in Islamic missionary work, who is beautiful, religious, amenable and educated; who can stand as a fortress for her husband against a degenerated atmosphere and has the ability to protect the faith and has proper conduct; who is indifferent to the world's colours and costumes; instead she longs for Allah's favours in the *akhirat* (the day of the last judgement) and is currently struggling hard to save herself and others from *jahannum* (the fire of hell); preference would be given to a madrasa graduate. Those interested should send their biodata at the given address. But before doing so a careful reading of Surat An-Nur (24), Surat Al-Ahzab (33), and Surat Al-Tahrim (66) is mandatory.

The advertisement served the required purpose. The woman with whom I performed the *nikah-e-saani* possessed the virtues listed in the advertisement. The *nikah* followed the precept of Islamic austerity where the girl's family was not allowed to spend a single paisa. You had shared with me all the letters that I exchanged with the girl and her parents with respect to the *nikah*. You remained my partner in all the decisions we took during the second *nikah* as well as the future chalked out for our changed family. How you and my second wife would share the task of upbringing our children, the regulation and management of household chores as well as the activities required for missionary work. You always had the choice to opt out of our conjugal relation just in case you found my interests cumbersome. After all, the Islamic practice of divorce is impressively simple.

After the second *nikah*, your status improved considerably. You received applaud for sharing your domestic space with my second wife. On one occasion you, me and my second wife's family members shared a glorious moment where everyone cheered the two women who shared a common conjugal space without jealousy and with mutual consent. This was upheld as *qabil-e-taqleed misaal* (an ideal model for others to emulate).

Recall the five categories of girls whom I regard as the victims of circumstances, viz., (i) the divorced, (ii) the widowed, (iii) the unwed who have passed the marriageable age, (iv) the ugly, and (v) the destitute.

The alleviation of these categories of women is possible through plural *nikahs*. This is how I understand the Islamic prescription. But the obstacles in implementing the idea are invariably the first wives. They lack the required readiness of mind. Don't forget that everybody was looking at us. If our experiment succeeded then it would make all of us hopeful. But if it failed then every one would close their mind to the possibility of a second *nikah* for ever. Perhaps, they would rightly conclude that if the advocates of the Qur'an and Sunnat could not make second *nikah* practicable, then no one else could. Our position was precarious. The adversaries of the second *nikah* are well organized. They would pounce on us at the slightest mistake; we should not give them a chance.

In the beginning you took my second *nikah* sportingly. But everyone else in the neighbourhood was dumbfounded. Every one was terribly intrigued, 'Who is this audacious man who could enliven a Sunnat amidst hostility and in full public view?' At first there was a great deal of gossip and condemnation. The tremors of the event were felt in several families, however different from each other with respect to their attitudes towards *din* (Islamic faith) and *duniya* (the secular world). One was not surprised to see the commotion among women who lived without purdah and whose daughters wore skirts and who paid scant respect to Islamic prescriptions. But the *harum* (womenfolk) of families of the custodians of *din* were also badly shaken.

'What if our husbands follow suit?' was the general alarm. They were helpless in their own spheres so they directed all their misgivings by poisoning your ears against me about the second *nikah*. They made a victim out of you. You, too, fell prey to their prejudice easily.

This was the time when my university and the children's school were closing for the summer vacations. You wished to spend the vacation at your parents' place in Rampur. I supported you, even added that you could stay beyond the vacations, but only if your parental family, who had rebelled against Allah's dictates mended their ways. They were TV addicts and the suppliers of a cinema magazine called *Shama* (a popular Urdu monthly magazine). The magazine is full of glamour and nudity. The magazine also promotes lucrative contests with attractive prizes. This is clearly un-Islamic as it promotes a lure for easy money and gambling. But you paid little heed to my comments. You turned more stiff in your position, even disrespectful towards my views.

K: *After your second marriage, you became further estranged from me. Perhaps you were lost to me completely. I turned out to be a double villain. I was constantly reminded of my educational backwardness, particularly in comparison to your new wife who was evidently more educated and more aware of Islam and the precepts of Allah and His Prophet. You divided the domestic labour between the two of us. I was allotted the role of bearing and rearing of children, looking after the kitchen and household management. Your second wife was given the task of educating the children and organizing Islamic study circles among women.*

By this time I was becoming sick of my role as a maidservant. There was no equality of work among your wives, and you even treated us differently. You were deferential towards your second wife but indifferent towards me and when I was bored and broken, your second wife always joined you in reminding me about my poor and disorganized upbringing.

M: After the second *nikah*, I worked hard to create an atmosphere of conviviality. I tried eating our meals from a common plate, made social visits together. Even purchases from the market were equally shared. Although your bedrooms were separate there was a mutually agreed upon schedule which bound me to share your rooms equally by turns. But you were the first to break the sanctity of the schedule. Even when it was not your turn, you would clamour for me. You turned menacing as never before, made mountains out of molehills, leaked out private matters to the neighbours. You intimidated me, maligned me, refused to do household work, mismanaged the dining schedule. We had breakfast at lunch time, lunch in the evening and dinner late into the night. You distorted facts, befriended my opponents, did not offer *namaz* and always looked out for an opportunity to teach me a lesson. For days together you would not serve meals to me, would not talk to me, would visit neighbours despite my strong disapproval.

K: *Whenever women folk from the neighbourhood came to visit me, you always turned suspicious of them. You were always curious to know what transpired between me and my friends. You were irked to see me in the company of other women who would cheer me up.*

You had your ways in controlling me. There was either one or the other stick in your hand which I was shown whenever you found my behaviour objectionable: (i) the unclean room, (ii) the prayer not offered, and (iii) the bedtime story not narrated to children.

You used the name of Allah so copiously that most of the time I found it difficult to understand if the command was issued from you or Allah. You are so erudite in Arabic and Qur'anic expressions that you never had any difficulty in cloaking your thoughts in the Qur'anic idiom.

M: Most of the time you remained taciturn but when you chose to express yourself, you poured out venom on me. The following is a small sample of your vituperations hurled at me:

This is my way of doing things. If you order me to do something I will simply not do it./You want your will to rule the house./I will not offer prayers out of fear of my husband./ What if I love the world and worldly ways./Are children your servants?/I can not serve my husband all the time./ Yes, I will side with the evil and the immoral. Do what you can.

I explained to you that a caring husband should be valued and that Allah disliked ungrateful people. And those in the neighbourhood who were posing as your well wishers, were in fact enjoying the break-up of our marriage. Your sister and mother counseled you to return to me. But it was of no avail.

In the end, I gave you the last choice, the one which the Prophet of Islam in conformity with Allah's command, offered to his wives:

O Prophet ! say
To the Consorts:
'If it be that ye desire
The life of this world,
And its glitter,–then come!
I will provide for your
Enjoyment and set you free
In a handsome manner

But if ye seek Allah
And His messenger, and
The Home of the Hereafter,
Verily Allah has prepared
For the well-doers amongst you
A great reward' (Surat 33: Al-Ahzab, 28-9)

K: *These verses relates to* azwaj mutahrarat *(consort of purity)—the wives of the holy Prophet. Here they are told that they had no place in the sacred household if they merely wished for worldly glitter. If such was the case, they could be divorced and amply provided for. While they were asked to deny themselves some of the ordinary indulgences of this life, they were reminded of the greater reward in terms of spiritual satisfaction for rendering higher services. But the easy resemblance that you see between their household and ours is beyond my imagination. Do you really think that the worldly possessions you have gathered in our house due to my insistence actually become an excuse for divorcing me?*

M: You had ten days to consider the bindings of the Qur'anic verses. But your behaviour continued to deteriorate. Your brother intervened, concerned for the harmony in our conjugal relations. I told him that the past could not be changed but if compensation for damage was made it would still be possible to patch up if you observed the following:

(i) Repent and show guilt for your past misdeeds.
(ii) Seek *tauba-o-astaghfar* (forgiveness) from Allah.
(iii) Apologize to me and *ammi*.
(iv) Recognize me as the head of the family and then obey and serve me.
(v) Build-up the family according to the Qur'an and the Sunnat.
(vi) Be pleasant with all the family members especially my parents and my second wife.

Subsequently your brother urged you to apologize to me but you stuck to your guns. As I understand it, you had already entered the domain of *nushooz* (defiance against the husband-Mausoof's translation). In a case like this, I conveyed to you Allah's injunctions:

Men are the protectors
And maintainers of women
Because Allah has given
The one more (Strength)
Than the other, and because
They support them
From their means
Therefore the righteous women
Are devoutly obedient, and guard
In (the husband's) absence
What Allah would have them guard
As to those women
On whose part ye fear
Disloyalty and ill-conduct

Admonish them (first)
(Next), refuse to share their beds
(And last) beat them (lightly)
But if they return to obedience
Seek not against them
Means (of annoyance)
For Allah is Most High
Great (above you all)
If ye fear a breach
Between them twain
Appoint (two) arbiters
One from his family
And the other from hers
If they seek to set things aright
Allah will cause
Their reconciliation
For Allah hath full knowledge
And is acquainted
With all things (Surat An-Nisaa, 4: 34-5)

In dealing with a woman's defiance and disobedience Allah has recommended four strategies for correction: (i) make the other see reason through advice and counselling (*samjhana bujhana*), (ii) leave them alone in their beds, (iii) batter them, and (iv) get arbiters from the family of the husband and the wife to intervene in order to sort out the discord.

Quite often, I used these strategies. This time, while remaining within the sphere of the Qur'an and the Sunnat, and with a lot of diffidence, you were thrashed. This was necessary as I apprehended Allah interrogating me on the day of *qayamat* (Last Judgement Day) as to why I refrained from using the Qur'anic option and instead followed my own assessment about you. Moreover, in your case your father had recommended that you be battered in the event of non-compliance with the husband's wishes. Subsequently, arbiters from your family were sent for. I used the speedpost so as not to lose time.

When I beat you up for the purpose of correction, you created a lot of commotion. You maligned me and threatened to quit the house. I reminded you of my status as your husband and that my permission was mandatory in case of your wanting to step out of the house. But you responded by smashing your bangles. (You knew already that bangles are broken at the husband's death.) You threw out my clothes from your suitcase, and in the morning, without seeking my permission, and despite my strong disapproval, you left the house with your brother. While leaving, you even commented, 'When I have decided not to return, every thing else is irrelevant to me.' You stayed at your brother's place for four days, doing every thing that disgraced both of us.

K: *Our neighbours in the teachers' colony and your colleagues in the university will testify that I never willfully damaged your possessions or reputation. Your total boycott among your university colleagues is enough proof that you had smeared dirt on your face after opting for the second* nikah *and simultaneously estranging me from my home. You branded me as a deviant with respect to Islamic practices. I would not dispute this matter with you but what troubles me is that you seem to be the sole interpreter of the Qur'an. You also know that there is no one in your vicinity who understands the Qur'an with comparable proficiency. When you are hell-bent on implementing a Qur'anic verse according to your own interpretation, I expect trouble. You mention four steps for correction. The first one was used practically everyday as it strengthened your authority. The second was automatically enforced when you had a second wife. The third one was your easiest temptation. Not only you but your second wife also joined you in giving me sound physical correction. My complaint is not that you hurt my body. Such pains are a part of my routine. What pained me was that the beating heralded a falling apart of my family and children. You are an educated person and specially educated in Islamic literature. It was very easy for you to find a simple Islamic scapegoat. I saw myself sinking in the pit but could do nothing about it. I don't believe that beating a wife is an easy prescription. And if every thing we do in life is in the presence of Allah who watches over us, don't you think that in physically thrashing me, you were petty and contemptible in Allah's presence?*

My sense of survival asserted itself, although it was not part of my upbringing. You took special pleasure in hitting me in front of your second wife. I was not too sure as to what to expect in the future. Most of the time I thought that this was like bad weather, that subsequently everything would be fine once again. I was forced to think like this as I had no other place to go to. You knew very well that my brother and father were already in a tight financial position. They couldn't look after themselves properly, how long would they support me if I fell back on them? My helplessness made you feel stronger.

M: Our children who sided with you, were used to publicize our private matters. Are these the ways of a *shareef* (noble) woman. In a way, this was your declaration that Islam is not a decisive principle between you and me. Even my understanding that *nikah* and Islam were the foundation of our relationship turned out to be unwarranted. Your behaviour after the beating was clearly un-Islamic. Was I not a complete loser in marrying you?

K: *I increasingly found myself in a hostile and alienating atmosphere in the family. I was a derelict, but you possessed the corrective measure. Islam was on your side, while I was the deviant from Islam. You were clearly right; I was the confirmed wrong. You had spelt out unilaterally the proper code of conduct meant to correct me. For you,* nushooz *is a wife's rebellion against the husband. But what about your* nushooz—*your violations of marital duties, your brutal treatment of me? It will take me years to be able to read the Qur'an as fluently as you do. But meanwhile could you help me in locating the Qur'anic verses that indict you for your* nushooz?

M: I explained everything to your father. I suggested to him that his daughter should not be forced to adopt the Islamic life, that Islam disfavours imposition and if, contrary to her wishes she was bound to me again, then He would be accountable to Allah. However, one last possibility was still open: With guilt and repentance, with apology and atonement, with a pledge and resolve to reform her behaviour, his daughter would be welcomed back as if nothing had happened. Otherwise, let her make a choice according to her inclination. Finally, he should be mentally prepared for a complete separation.

I sent you back with your father to spend a day thinking the matter was over. You returned the next day. You were sent inside the house to apologize to my mother. Rather than apologize, you had a heated argument with her. Still, we decided that you should stay on.

K: *My apology was probably the last proof you needed from me in justifying your Islamic posture. I, therefore, decided to withhold my last asset. Helplessness makes one infinitely strong even to face death. I was aware that I had no other place to go to, except the present one. Yet something in me declared that enough was enough. I don't even know what awaits me as I walk out of this family. But something in me says 'do it now and don't turn back'.*

M: During the three weeks time you remained here you continued as you were, perhaps changed for the worse. Far from apologizing, you did not even speak a word to me or my parents. There was no dearth of good advice from various quarters. Your father, your brother, your *bhabi* (sister-in-law), my second wife and her mother, your sister and her husband, tried to make you see reason. But you were hardly bothered. All we could gather from you was the oft repeated refrain: 'I cannot follow Islamic precepts. All I want is separation.' Clearly, the limits prescribed by Allah's injunctions were infringed. You were publicly defiant.

K: *In your law court you were always a self-styled judge and a clever advocate while I was always the accused. In a jiffy, I would be convicted on the basis of unilateral judgements. In your view, I neither had an argument nor did my case need an advocate. Is your law court an Islamic law court?*

M: I began to fear the consequences of postponing Allah's command. What if I, too, am implicated for non-conformity to the divine dictate?

> Say: If it be that your fathers
> Your sons, your brothers
> Your mates, or your kindred
> The wealth that ye have gained
> The commerce in which ye fear
> A decline: or the dwellings
> In which ye delight
> Are dearer to you than Allah
> On His Messenger, or the striving
> In His cause; then wait
> Until Allah brings about
> His Decision: and Allah
> Guides not the rebellious (Surat Al-Tauba, 9: 24)

Let me give you a brief synopsis of your derelict ways with respect to our family: in important decisions of the household you followed your judgement rather than mine. You refrained from attending to me in the house. You were casual towards saying the *namaz*. You were openly critical of living according to the edicts of the Qur'an and the Sunnat. You were too lax about purdah. You always indulged in double speak and misrepresentations. You ridiculed the *dindar* (those steeped in Islamic values). You showed complete indifference towards your husband's meals and dress. You were a shirker of household chores. You were rude towards the children, yet pampered them excessively. You either spoke foully with me or snapped the conversation at your will. My displeasure meant nothing to you.

These deviances eroded the trust so necessary in a marital relationship. I can't trust you any longer in family matters. In my understanding there are three factors that led to our mutual estrangement, viz., (i) your father's fondness for viewing popular films and his support in procuring a TV set, (ii) his taste for cheap popular magazines, and (iii) his inability to distinguish between *mehrum* (unmarriageable individuals) and *na-mehrum* (marriageable individuals). Don't forget that your family shared a common residential space with one of your father's friend's family from your childhood.

The male members of the other family never observed any Islamic rules of 'privacy' and purdah. Your parents found nothing objectionable in the unrestrained heterosexual intermingling.

This mishmash in your upbringing influenced your character and attitudes. You were so charmed by your *maika* (parent's family) that you sought to replicate the atmosphere in your husband's family as well. My objections to your un-Islamic ways caused so much commotion and opposition in you that our entire family was upset; children's deviance, wife's disobedience and a disrespect to Islamic norms without qualms became routine features.

In this scenario, I had only two options. One was to tolerate the violations of the precepts of Allah and His Prophet and to somehow let you remain as a part of the family without upsetting our relationship. The second was to opt for the last step in repudiating the rebellion against Allah, and to initiate your separation from me and to rely on Allah to help me face the trials and predicaments which separation was likely to bring. Here, I drew strength from the following:

Thus when they fulfill
Their term appointed
either take them back
On equitable terms
Or part with them
On equitable terms
And take for witness
Two persons from among you
Embued with justice
And establish the evidence
For the sake of Allah. Such
Is the admonition given
To him who believes
In Allah and the Last Day
And for those who fear
Allah, He (ever) prepares
A way out
And He provides for him
From (sources) he never
Could expect. And if
Any one puts his trust
In Allah, sufficient is (Allah)
For him. For Allah will
Surely accomplish His purpose
Verily, for all things
Has Allah appointed
A due proportion (Surat Al-Talaq, 65: 2-3)

I repose fully in Allah who supports his followers and transforms their trials into triumphs. You have shut out the various options available except the one which I hate to choose. But I also shudder to allow anyone to share my life who is otherwise a rebel against Allah. With much serious contemplation, I have resolved to divorce you from our contract of *nikah*. This separation is called *talaq rajai* (revocable divorce) where the husband has the option of resuming connubial intercourse. I am pronouncing the *masnoon* (most approved) *talaq* in the state of *tuhr* (purity, wherein the woman is free from her menstrual courses and the husband observes abstinence). The duration of the *talaq* is three menstrual cycles. At the culmination of the third period, your *iddat* (period of confinement following the pronouncement of *talaq*) will come to an end. Even our contract of *nikah* which we had signed thirteen years ago would stand annulled. The period between the three menstrual cycles would also be the period of your *iddat*. During the period of *iddat* the husband is responsible for the wife's board and lodging. But a woman undergoing *iddat* is forbidden to step out of the house. Allah has a clear command in this respect:

> O Prophet! When ye
> Do divorce women
> Divorce them at their
> Prescribed periods
> And count (accurately)
> Their prescribed periods
> And fear Allah your Lord
> And turn them not out
> Of their house, nor shall
> They (themselves) leave
> Except in case they are
> Guilty of some open lewdness
> Those are limits
> Set by Allah: and any
> Who transgresses the limits
> Of Allah, does verily
> Wrong his (own) soul (Surat Al-Talaq, 65: 1)

K: *By this time you had cleared most of the obstacles in your way. Not that you hadn't committed a wrong, but in your own perception you were incapable of committing a wrong. Most of the time you would be frowning at me. But suddenly you turned very gentle towards me. This confused me again. Has Allah changed your heart, I wondered. But the next day I was locked in a room and you told me that I could leave for my parents' place after spending a period of three menstrual cycles and that this was strictly according to the command of Allah. I wanted to return to my parents but I had no intention of violating the Qur'anic saying you had shown me, particularly the given* ayat *(Qur'anic verse). I told myself that if this was so then so be it. This was my first experience of being locked in a room for three months. There were moments when I thought that I was completely wrong but in the next moment my anger would take over. I was confused. For the first time in my married life I became your guest. Your second wife cooked for me, but did it grudgingly. Did you eat the same food that you offered me? Or was it a different one? If I had cooked similar food in the past, you would have created hell in the house and quoted half a dozen verses from the Qur'an to say that a virtuous wife should cook good food. But why were you so complacent this time?*

I survived in the locked room for three months because of the support of my caring neighbours. The food your wife cooked had no taste for me. It was usually cold and not what I wanted to eat at the particular moment. My neighbours took great care of me. I was virtually their guest for weeks together till you discovered the mystery of my 'hunger, strike' as I wouldn't eat the food cooked by your wife. Thereafter, the ventilator and the back window of the room (my only link with the outside world) was virtually sealed. My room now turned darker and colder. It smelt of stale air and rotting food crumbs. I felt nauseated. My body began to wear down. My sickness would not spare me for a minute. You discovered my high fever only when I collapsed physically. I was rushed to a hospital where the doctor diagnosed tuberculosis. It was during this time that our concerned neighbours reported to the police that a husband had locked his wife in a room against her wishes. I was too weak to respond to the queries of the investigating officer. To tell the truth, I had no strength to open another front against you, that too with the help of the police. I only told them that they had been misinformed. You thought I still had a hope, but believe me I had chosen to repose in Allah for every thing. Let Him deal with you. The police and the law courts would ultimately have provided you with an escape route.

M: Due to the *talaq rajai* the husband has the option to review his judgement and revoke the decision. In Islamic *shar'ia*, the father is the custodian of the children and looks after their upbringing and upkeep. Don't bother about them any longer. I shall take care of them, if Allah permits. Please note that in deference to Allah's command, I shall arrange to give you *muta* (gifts to a divorced wife on final divorce). One clarification before ending the letter is that your behavioural impairments and ill treatment towards me outweigh their description in the letter.

K: *In the entire episode, I lost my family, my children (you kept them with you on the plea that Islam holds the father to be the custodian of the children) and even my meager material possessions. You recited Qur'anic verses fluently but you always showed, even to an illiterate person like me, that all was not well when you used them practically in your life, for you were either cruel or ridiculous. There are hundreds of examples but let me just quote two of them from my recent experience. A few days before my departure from the house in the teachers' colony, you spread the impression that we had finally patched up and resolved everything. You needed to do so as you wanted to stall the possible unpleasant reaction of the neighbours at the time of my departure*

The muta *consisted of a new suitcase and some new clothes, a towel and a pair of shoes. This is the height of your literally correct implementation of Allah's command. Don't forget that Allah has noted numerous other instances in your life.*

I don't have the strength left to turn to the court of law and allow myself to be interrogated in the vulgar and obscene language of the advocates and the jury. But I do hope that someday a judgement will be pronounced against you and your misdeeds and manipulations, leaving you high and dry and without avenues of escape.[3]

III

The present article is essentially based on the two letters that were exchanged with reference to an intimate event which both a husband and wife went through. In the process of exchanging their thoughts, they conveyed their insights into the generalized symbols of Islam and their bearing on the specific aspects of concrete encounters. As they constructed their understanding of life in relation to each other as well as to the normative structure which regulates their routine behaviour, certain serendipities come to the fore.[4]

The analysis of letters considers the specific context wherein intimate thoughts are written and exchanged. These letters, which were exchanged in a moment of acute acrimony, add colours of prejudice and personal predilections to data. But at the same time, the data also gains in validity as most references cited by the two individuals are cross-checked and critically evaluated by each other.

The debate thus generated also evokes the context to the two letters.

The two letters present contesting worldviews and individual defenses of their biographies. They not only point to the plurality of existential positions but also pluralistic readings and interpretations of spiritual Islam and its codified injunctions. For a student of Islam and society, it is important to capture the arena of contestation where individuals are drawing upon their common discursive resources of traditional faith to find meanings, negotiate explanations, and defend present positions as well as their concept of life as it ought to be.

The contestation between Khatoon and Mausoof is not between equal partners. The asymmetry of powers is couched in their literary idiom as well as the idiom of gender, civility as well as class. While Mausoof displays confidence and lays a claim to firm foundations, Khatoon tends to accept most of the stereotypes and prejudicial categories hurled at her. The only certainty in Khatoon's narration is an acute uncertainty which besets her and challenges her to respond with all her meagre resources of culture and tradition. Mausoof is like a craftsman who knows his craft as well as the tool at hand. He has even repudiated various breakdowns in meaning as well as the suspended moments of biography in the rites of passage. One reason why the serious blanks in meaning are easily circumvented is because there is a non-falsifiable (more appropriately non-relinquishable) theodicy at work which can withhold internal inconsistencies even when confronted with an anomalous experience or an unpremeditated happening. Khatoon, on the other hand, is only clear about the degradation and damage to herself. She is typically unable to make clear her point of view in her petition. Her narration represents her will to overcome the malaise of her life. This puts her again in sharp contrast to Mausoof whose narration represents the truth of something that has been already there for ages. But Khatoon is seeking to make sense of the non-recurring, of something never dreamt of before. Mausoof is privy to the various discursive instruments owned by orthodoxy. Khatoon, on the other hand, is only groping in the dark without known conceptual contrivances but seriously challenged. She is constrained to find a way out of the present impasse in her life. From the letters one infers Mausoof's remarkable proficiency in making connections between his experiences and that of many others who have lived their lives in the mirror image of Qur'anic regulations. While Mausoof finds continuities all the time, Khatoon exhibits stark discontinuities in equal measure. Concerned individuals on her side are not the legitimate interpreters of Islamic traditions and merely end up by providing ready tools to Mausoof.

Mausoof's worldview does not recognize its own cleavages nor even internal disharmony. He merely has to overcome Khatoon's idiosyncrasies for which she can scarcely garner support from the resources of Islam. Khatoon relents and willingly abjures many positions in contestation but firmly holds on to and concedes paramount reference to Allah and His Prophet. This reference is so tightly held on to that she even becomes suspicious of existing institutions of justice and remedy. Khatoon is able to see through the deluge of verbiage in Mausoof's questions and references. Her travail is so poignant that all she knows of is the single contest of her own life which confers upon her its own truth as well as a way of knowing and interpreting sacred regulations. Mausoof's mission is to find a single and universal context for all human beings, true for all times. Khatoon's truth searches for words but she is ultimately forced to describe and create her own independent of easy references to wider relations. But the contingent character of her experiences paves the way for newer interpretations as well as new metaphors and meanings.

The line between Mausoof's strength and Khatoon's weakness is also the line between a narrative with claims to familiarity and universality and one which has to engage in the act of production in an unfamiliar and idiosyncratic language. Yet, it would be simplistic to evaluate Khatoon's account in terms of triumph or tragedy. To social researchers she offers an account of an active, will(ing), individual in a perpetual drama of self-overcoming.

Here Khatoon finds a way to describe her life which the life never knew and thereby create her self which her antecedents and precursors never knew was possible. In a way she discovers secular roots to sacred symbols by tracking divine injunctions to the familiar context of the family without excluding the various contingencies around.

Mausoof's privileged position should not be explained away with reference to patriarchy or class superiority alone. It is true that he derives his power from a constant identification with the common resources of the Qur'an and the Hadith which he shares with representative sections of his community. It is not as if Mausoof's position is without anxiety or pain or even lacking in sensitivity. He represents to us a case of an individual possessed by a mission which seeks to create a replica among individuals according to *one right description* which subsumes all other descriptions.

Most of the time Khatoon is resigned to and submits to her mute despair and mental anguish. But when she responds, she juggles with several descriptions and contrary interpretations without insisting on *a priori* questions. Her narrative hinges on expanding repertoires of contending descriptions. In her contestations she does not adopt the powerful instruments of her husband but evolves her own manner of recognizing the condition of pain and the contingency of her situation. Her victory lies in her ability to create a language for self-creation and self-overcoming. She is condemned by her husband not only for breaking free of the common life space but the case is built up on her repeated failure to practice the generalized Islamic precepts.

The present paper offers a vantage point to rethink the discourse on Muslim divorce law. It allows the analytical gaze to shift from a case of patriarchy or male oppression versus female subordination to that of gender relations. Khatoon's voice foregrounds the case of women's agency.

Writing an ethnography of divorce persuades us to capture the realm of active contestation and work out the interplay between life encounters and discursive resources. Of course, the writing is incomplete without locating how meanings are created and negotiated in a scenario where Islamic resources are treated as pure externality with a sardonic refusal to recognize contingency or life outside the fold of established sacred symbols. In the same vein, there is also the tendency to conflate what is right according to scriptural Islam with the customary injunctions. Islamic prescriptions are also harnessed to legitimize prevailing principles of domination. An ethnography of divorce tracing the track from codified symbols of Islam to the interactional-situational dimension of the routine life of a Muslim should carefully document various operationalizations/instantiations or generalizations which hinge on various social and cultural principles in the constitution of relationships and their network.

NOTES

1. The intimate nature of personal letters publicized in the present paper poses an ethical challenge to the researchers. While the classical justification of sociological intrigue furnishes instant license to enter private procincts of biographies, the present article takes care not to push the characters of our narrative into greater vulnerability by changing certain pronouns in the presentations. It also uses pseudonyms both for the names of individuals and actual places.
2. The English translation of Qur'anic verses is taken from *The Holy Qur'an: English Translation of the Meanings and Commentary*, revised and edited by the Presidency of Islamic Researchers, IFTA, King Fahd Holy Qur'an Printing Complex, n.d.
3. Latest information from the field tells us that Khatoon suffers from an advanced stage of lung cancer. Mausoof weds the third time after divorcing the second wife. Mausoof, however, feels upset that he had not still been able to demonstrate an ideal model of polygamy according to his view of Islam.
4. Mausoof's voice is empirically singular but backed by age-old discursive resources that have been kept in animation by a community spread over generations. In sharp contrast, Khatoon's voice is empirically pluralized but refers to experiences which scarcely find parallels or congruence in the already codified resources of the Islamic tradition. Even if literal support is garnered for a particular experience, it is liable to be contradicted by some acceptable interpretation.

7

Cunning, Deceit and Vindictiveness: Case Studies of Divorced Muslim Women and Men in North India

Sabeeha Bano

The recent outcry over the system of triple divorce prevalent among Muslims in India has tended to colour our perception of the phenomenon of Muslim divorce in several ways. First, it has tended to reinforce the image of the Muslim woman as a vulnerable and pathetic being who has to submit to the whims and fancies of her husband for fear that he might pronounce divorce on her at the slightest pretext. Second, it has tended to create the impression that whenever a divorce takes place it is always the man who is to blame for using the provisions of Muslim Personal Law to get out of a marital union without in any way having to pay for his action in psychological, social or material terms. It is hardly ever contemplated that at least in some cases women can also take advantage of the law to get out of the marriage bond with substantial benefits to themselves. Finally, it has led to the widespread belief that Muslim Personal Law is so remarkably one-sided as to render it impossible for a woman to use it to subject her husband to different degrees of psychological and material oppression and hardships.

There is no doubt that certain in-built inequities exist in Muslim Personal Law as they, indeed, do in all laws operating within a broadly patriarchal social arrangement. The provision of triple divorce as it has been allowed to be practiced in India is an acute expression of that built-in inequity against women in the marriage system. There is by now ample evidence to show that this system is often used by unscrupulous men to get rid of an unwanted wife without assigning any reason or being called upon to account for their action to their wives or to the community of which they are invariably members. However, the mere presence of this system should not lead one to the conclusion that the situation of the Muslim woman is always necessarily that of a passive recipient of what is handed out to her or that the principal responsibility for a divorce can always be placed on the shoulders of the husband. It is possible to contemplate a situation where the wife takes the initiative to use the law to achieve an advantage over her husband. Therefore, any careful analysis of divorce among Muslims, as indeed in any community, must recognize that divorce is something that results from a complex web of factors for which either the man or the woman might be responsible. Either partner might then attempt to use the law to advantage to put the other to difficulty and hardship.

The dominant tendency in studies on divorce among Muslims in India, though they are few and far between, has been to concentrate on social and legal dimensions. Generally speaking, the effort has been directed towards ascertaining socio-economic and demographic profiles of the spouses, the number of years after which divorce takes place, the procedure followed in giving effect to the divorce, the reasons for divorce as articulated by whosoever has provided the data and whether the obligations imposed under the law by way of settlement of *mehr* (dower) in the case of husband and observance of the *iddat* (statutory period of abstinence) in the case of wife were fulfilled. Occasionally, an attempt is also made to explore the problems which divorced women face in the process of adjustment to the situation created by their divorce. There has been relatively little effort at analysing the dynamics of the relationship between the alienated partners and the working of their mind as they go through the divorce experience. Consequently, we know relatively little about the psychological dimensions that are crucial for an understanding of the way individuals behave in a martial conflict leading to divorce. This is an aspect that needs to be carefully explored in future studies on divorce whether among Muslims or other social communities.

One reason for this aspect to have been neglected so far appears to be that the methodological procedure usually followed in the study of divorce among Muslims has been that of the social survey.

There is no doubt that the social survey is an extremely useful methodological procedure and can be applied fruitfully to the study of divorce. However, there is need to recognize that this methodological procedure also suffers from certain in-built limitations both as to the dimensions that it can explore and the nature of the data that it can generate. The utility of the social survey consists in that it can yield data on a number of social axis and can lead to generalized statements about a phenomenon where little previous knowledge can be said to exist. For example, the social survey can suggest regularities of distribution of divorce cases along a number of demographic, social and economic variables and enable classification of divorces into a number of types depending upon whether the divorce was pronounced by the husband or demanded by the wife; the reasons for divorce as articulated by the parties and whether the various injunctions enjoined upon the wife or the husband in the event of a divorce were followed. But it is a poor methodological procedure when it comes to an exploration of the complex processes through which a divorce usually comes about or the various maneuvers the husband and the wife adopt to secure advantages for themselves before a divorce is allowed to occur. Case studies as a methodological procedure offer us the advantage of exploring some of these dimensions of divorce in greater detail than is possible in a social survey.[1] Consequently, this paper relies upon detailed interviews with a limited number of divorced Muslim women and men as the basis for discussion.

Before we take up the case studies for detailed discussion, there is need to be clear about the dimension that is of interest to the study of divorce and remarriage among Muslims in India. It is not simply that divorces take place among Muslims; breakdown of marriages is a fact of life in all societies and Muslims in India do not differ significantly in this respect from other communities and societies. Nor is it that Muslim Personal Law, by which Muslims claim to be governed, and locally prevalent social customs allow for relatively easy divorce. Societies differ considerably with respect to their attitudes towards divorce. Some societies regard marriage to be a sacrament or a sacrosanct union that has to be maintained throughout life. Other societies stress the desirability of keeping a marital union going as far as possible, almost condemning its dissolution at the level of moral principles, but recognize that there may be situations where it would be more desirable for an unsavoury marital union to be dissolved rather than force it to be continued with spouses feeling suffocated and stifled. Certainly, Muslim attitudes to divorce fall on that side of the continuum where divorce is discouraged but allowed to take place without serious hassles once it has been established that the couple cannot lead a harmonious and satisfactory life in wedlock.

Even the practice of triple divorce does not really constitute the most significant dimension of divorce though a considerable public rhetoric has been wasted on it. As far as can be ascertained from a careful reading of the Qur'an, which Muslims consider to be the primary and most authoritative source of canonical law, this practice did not originally constitute a part of the body of rules that were supposed to govern divorce among Muslims. It came to be permitted only subsequently, as the relatively liberal principles of early Islam came to be compromised to accommodate deviations from the prescribed principle. This happened not only in the sphere of divorce but in a variety of other spheres of life as well. There is a powerful line of reasoning among Muslims that does not fight shy of asserting with uncanny aggressiveness that Islam offers a complete blueprint for life for all times and cannot be changed. This fact should be instructive by itself in that it goes to show, contrary to the conviction which Muslims commonly espouse, that they are adhering to what had been originally revealed to them through the Qur'an. On the contrary, what this demonstrates is that what Muslims today hold to be the original body of formal rules and prescriptions has been changing historically in response to social developments through accretion of deviations superceding the originally enunciated Qur'anic principles and rules. Therefore, if the practice of triple divorce persists and is not being allowed to be changed, the reasons for its persistence have little to do with religion. If it persists, the reason is that it is convenient to men within the patriarchal framework of the Indian Muslim social organization.

The primary purpose of all world religions has been to shape human nature for orderly social life. All religions recognize that man is a combination of both good and evil tendencies and, unless the propensities for evil and mischief are controlled and regulated, orderly social life would be almost impossible. Accordingly, all religions lay down moral principles and norms so that the human propensity for evil is constrained and a basis for orderly social existence is created. However, one of the greatest predicaments of the human situation is that the propensity for evil often asserts itself and prompts human beings to defeat the moral principles that religion ordains. This has been so from time immemorial and is so today. What is, therefore, of particular interest for the study of divorce among Muslims in India is not the elaboration of rules and laws worked out under Islam for the regulation of marriage and divorce or assessment of adherence to them. What is really interesting is how the elaborate body of rules worked out under Islam for the dissolution of marriage is twisted and turned by the partners to a marriage or their close kinsmen, once the marriage has soured, to consolidate material gains for themselves and to put the other partner to harassment and psychological persecution.

This paper seeks to approach the issue of divorce among Muslims from an essentially neutral perspective and tries to explore the ways in which both men and women tend to use the provisions of existing laws to maximize their social and material advantages or to inflict psychological and material damage upon the other once one of them has made the decision to break the marriage and get out of the matrimonial home. Once that stage has been reached human proclivities for deceit, cleverness, vindictiveness and persecution are pushed to the fore and have free play. The parties then try to use the law to consolidate their material advantages and to satisfy their psychological urges to damage their partner to their heart's content. In this virtual tug of war, sometimes men and at other times women have an upper hand. Only rarely are men and women able to part in a decent manner where neither side is sought to be psychologically assailed or materially damaged. On balance, therefore, divorce takes on the character of a psychological and material combat where each side tries to keep the initiative to oneself and to dismantle and damage the other with the result that the final outcome is always fraught with serious implications for both. This is the broad perspective from which divorce among Muslims is approached in this paper, but it is necessary to point out that looked at from this perspective divorce among Muslims would not appear to be materially different from that in any other community or society.

THE CASE OF SHAGUFTA

Shagufta comes from a well-off zamindar family. Her father was a lawyer in a township of western Uttar Pradesh. She is the youngest of six children in the family. Her three brothers are engineers. One works in Saudi Arabia and one is settled in the US. The third brother works in an oil refinery in Assam. Both sisters are post-graduates and are happily married. Shagufta did Ph.D. in chemistry and worked as a part-time teacher in a women's college.

Shagufta was married in 1985 to Nahid. Nahid had a Ph.D. in geography and was working as a post-doctoral fellow at the time of their marriage. The marriage was an arranged one. Shagufta's *mehr* was fixed at Rs. 60,000 and she received a very large *jahez* at her wedding. She was extremely well-looked after by her in-laws. Her mother-in-law and sister-in-law usually cooked and served all the meals. She went to the college as soon as she was ready and stayed there for long hours. If family friends or relatives visited the house, her usual practice was to go to her supervisor or to the college or her department where she continued with her research. She often told her husband that they should live separately. He was the eldest son of the family and had to shoulder the family responsibility after his father's death. He did not listen to her and this brought about the estrangement between them.

On her first visit to her parental home, Shagufta carried with her a part of the dowry which had been given to her by her parents. Subsequently, whenever she visited her parental home she usually carried a few items with her. Her refrigerator and television was kept packed in some friend's house. After six months, Nahid's brother-in-law came to visit them. After a few minutes of his arrival, she clung to him and started shouting, 'Save me! These people will set fire to me, they will kill me!' One of Nahid's friends and his wife were also present in the house. All of them tried to talk sense into her, but she would not listen to them. Immediately after this she went to the police station followed by Nahid, his brother-in-law and his friend. Meanwhile, Nahid also called his supervisor and a few other friends. All of them tried to placate her, but she was in no mood to listen to them. At the police station she asked for immediate divorce. Nahid pronounced the divorce. Nahid's friends and supervisor collected the money and paid the *mehr* due to her in terms of the marriage agreement. She went from the police station to a friend's house.

Shagufta shifted to Delhi a few months after her divorce and took up a senior administrative job in a university. She stayed for some time in the university guest house and finally moved to a working women's hostel attached to the university. Almost after a year or so she got a temporary lectureship at another university, but she continued to stay at the hostel. After almost twelve years, she married again. The proposal was initiated by one of her friends. Her second husband has an MBA and is running his own factory. He was a divorcee. She has no affinal relatives staying with him, but she does not appear to be particularly satisfied and happy even with the second marriage. She seems to take her dissatisfaction with her second marriage with a degree of resignation.

THE CASE OF KHATOON

Khatoon comes from a business family. Her father was a lawyer, but her three brothers are engaged in the transportation business. Her sisters are educated and married. She is postgraduate with a bachelor's degree in education. After completing her B.Ed. in 1983 she was married to a boy who had his own business. Within a short time, her marriage began to sour. Her mother-in-law was very strict. She made Khatoon do all the household chores, but did not give her enough to eat. She was given leftovers after all other family members had eaten. Since the mother-in-law had a great hold on her son, she often prompted the son to torture her physically. She bore all this for sometime, but finally decided to return to her parental home.

Khatoon had been selected for a schoolteacher's job. She had not joined it as she was getting married, but the Director of Education had told her to think things over and take more time, if she wanted, before refusing to take up the job. Within months of reverting to her parent's home, she shifted to Delhi and joined the school teacher's job in the corporation. Her husband periodically came to visit her at Delhi and asked for money. If she refused, he would threaten that he would kidnap her nephews. She felt quite hapless and paid him money. Her parents wanted her husband to divorce her, but he was unwilling to oblige though he had married in the meantime. It took a few years before her divorce came through. After a few years, her former husband died.

Khatoon works as a school teacher and lives in a working women's hostel. She has built two houses and is well-off financially. She is going steady with a professor who is himself a widower. Her anticipation was that once the professor had married off his younger daughter, he would marry her. However, the professor has so far pleaded his inability to formally marry her as he says that his children do not want him to get married again. This has become a source of acute tension between them, though neither has taken the initiative to break off the relationship. She goes about telling her close friends that the professor had entered into a secret *nikah* with her, but does not have the courage to tell his family that he has married her. She also says that she will not break off relationship with him as this way she can keep him harassed and agonized. She has developed health problems as a result of the tension that this uneasy relationship involves.

THE CASE OF NAJMA

Najma hails from a well-off, middle class family. Her father was in a good government job. Her two brothers are also well-settled and married. One works as a scientist and the other is employed with the Home Ministry. Her mother was an educated but highly religious woman. She believed that daughters should be educated and allowed them to receive as much education as they could secure. At the same time, she insisted that they should have a religious upbringing. She made her daughters walk with their eyes lowered and their head covered. All the three sisters of Najma are well-educated, but they did not marry. Her eldest sister was an education officer with the government until her death a few years ago. One sister has been missing for the past few years. The third sister stayed with the eldest sister until her death and now lives with her brother. Najma earned a large number of degrees in science, law, homeopathy, ayurvedic medicine and education. She worked as a teacher in a private school and lives in a working women's hostel.

Najma married a man settled in the US. He had already been married to an American girl. He said his mother was a religious-minded woman and wanted that he should marry a religious-minded girl. Accordingly, he had divorced his American wife and was now looking for a match in India. The marriage was arranged by one of Najma's father's friends who had also settled in the US. He had come with the proposal to Najma and tried to persuade her to marry the man. He assured her that the man was a manager in a good firm in the US and he knew him personally. 'Since I am your father's friend, I would like you to get married to a good man. This man is good and you will be happy. Therefore, if you are willing you should meet this man and decide whether you want to get married to him,' he said. The very next day the man came to visit her at her friend's house where she lived at that time. She saw him but did not talk to him yet gave her consent to the marriage. She was married from her friend's house after three days as her brother was out of station. He came just in time to be present at the marriage. She herself paid for all the preparations for the marriage.

Her husband brought her rich dresses and a good amount of jewellery. After the *nikah* he took her to the hotel where he was staying. He told her that his mother had sent the clothes and jewellery especially for her. He had the marriage registered and assured her that after a few days stay at the hotel he would go back to the US and arrange to send her visa and ticket so that she could join him. He also told her to get a passport in the meantime.

For sometime after his return to the US he would call her and assure her that he would call her to the US soon. This continued for five to six months, but thereafter he stopped calling her. Najma's salary was just about Rs. 1,600. She could ill-afford to make calls through to the US, but she called him often to enquire why he was not calling her and when would he send the ticket and visa for her to join him. Whenever she got through and asked for her husband, the person who picked up the phone at the other end denied that anyone by her husband's name stayed there. She then tried to contact her father's friend who had brought this marriage about. He would tell her that her husband was very busy as he was planning to start another work, but he would call her soon. When she persisted in calling him from time to time, he admitted that he had not met her husband for quite sometime and he had no idea of his whereabouts. Nearly one year passed in this process after which she received a letter from her husband communicating that he had divorced her.

When Najma consulted her brother about what she should do, he told her to start practicing law so that she can file a case against her husband. However, her friends advised to continue with her school-teaching as her brothers did not support her and she would face an uncertain future if she started practicing law. Caught up in this predicament, Najma wrote a letter to Hillary Clinton narrating her story and asking her to intervene on her behalf with her husband. She received an acknowledgement of her letter, but nothing else came out of her plea. She entertains all kinds of strange ideas for what has happened. Sometimes she thinks that her husband has been murdered as he ran his business in partnership with other friends. Sometimes she entertains the illusion that the children of her husband's American wife might have faked the letter of divorce. She tried to find out the truth, but she could find no one who would take the trouble to search out her husband and communicate the reality to her. Under the circumstances, she sustains herself as best as she can without support from her brothers and other family members.

THE CASE OF NARGIS

Nargis belongs to the Meo community of Haryana. Her father was in the army. He educated his daughters and Nargis was sent to an English medium school. She was married after she passed class ten into a well-off landowning family. The boy was moderately educated.

Nargis's elder sister was studying for a post-graduate degree at a prestigious university in Delhi. There she became interested in a non-Meo boy. This alliance was bitterly opposed both by the members of her own family and that of Nargis's matrimonial family on the ground that the boy was not a Meo. She eventually did not marry him. After sometime, Nargis's in-laws wanted to marry

Nargis's sister-in-law to the same boy. He was a friend of Nargis's husband who did not like this alliance. He intervened and stopped this marriage. However, Nargis's in-laws thought that the marriage negotiations had been stopped at the instance of Nargis's sister.

This brought about alienation between the families. They stopped interacting and visiting one another. Whenever Nargis wanted to visit her parental family she had to do so entirely on her own. No one escorted her or went to bring her back as custom required. Soon thereafter, piqued at what they thought was a negative role played by Nargis's sister, her in-laws started ill-treating Nargis. Her husband was a bit of a crank and they used to quarrel often. He provided no money to her for buying clothes or meeting other contingencies. He would say, 'Why do you need money? Food is available in the house. Two sets of clothes are enough for a year. What do you want money for?' Meanwhile, three children were born to them.

This continued for sixteen years. Harassed and distraught, one day Nargis left her matrimonial home along with the three children and went to live with her elder sister. Her in-laws prompted her husband to bring back the children. One day he went to Nargis's sister's house. Nargis had in the meantime sent the children to play in the park with the intention that if the children were not at home the husband would not be able to take them away. However, Nargis's sister and mother secretly told the husband where the children were playing. He picked up the children and took them away. After the husband had left, Nargis went to call the children from the park. When she did not find them there, she looked around all over. Later she learned that her sister and mother had told her husband where the children were playing and he had taken them with him.

Nargis then shifted to a working women's hostel. She took up whatever part-time work she could find in order to meet the hostel expenses. She also started legal proceedings against her husband. Her advocate was a lady. She gave her the name of some women's organization and advised her to approach them for divorce. Nargis contacted the organization and narrated her story. It sent several notices to Nargis's husband asking him to come to its office. When the husband came, the organization functionaries asked him to divorce Nargis. In about six months the divorce materialized but she neither got the children nor the *mehr*. The husband admitted two children to an orphanage in Delhi. The third child has been taken away by the husband's sister to Rajasthan. Nargis visits the children in the orphanage once every week. After some time, her parents came to the working women's hostel and took her to stay with them.

Nargis' mother was a traditional and conservative woman. She cursed her every day for walking out of her marriage and taking divorce. Finally, tired of her mother's frequent curses she again left her parental home and came back to Delhi. She has taken up a small job and shares a small apartment with four other girls.

THE CASE OF SURAIYA

Suraiya hailed from a small town in central Uttar Pradesh. Her father was a famous professor of mathematics at a central university. He went almost every year to lecture in Canada. His wife was illiterate and stayed in the town. On one of his annual visits he was struck by paralysis and stayed on in Canada for treatment. After he recovered partially, he was given an assignment by the Canadian government and he settled down in Canada. He also married the nurse who looked after him when he was undergoing treatment. His first wife also joined him in Canada, but did not stay long. She was treated almost like a servant so she returned to India and stayed at her father's house. Her husband sent money from time to time for her and the children who were studying in India. As his sons grew up he called them to Canada and settled them there. Suraiya was the only child left behind in India.

Suraiya's father wanted her, too, to marry someone settled in Canada or the US. He found a boy who hailed from a village in Uttar Pradesh but had taken Canadian citizenship. He was an engineer working with a leading firm in Canada. Suraiya was interested in marrying a boy in the neighbourhood, but she could not have her way. She was married to this boy from Canada. Suraiya's husband had come on leave from Canada to get married. He overstayed in India after the marriage and his employers decided to terminate his services. He tried to secure another job, but was not successful. As a matter of fact, he could not find a permanent job.

Suraiya, who had accompanied him to Canada after the marriage, then decided to take up a job in order to run the household. Meanwhile, she had had two children. However, she was not satisfied with her life and the pattern of her relationship with her husband. She started complaining that her husband did not work, did not pay attention to her and did not spend time with her. She suspected that he was interested in someone else. Finally, after sixteen years, she filed a case in the court for the dissolution of her marriage and was divorced. Asked why she took so long to ask for a divorce, her explanation was that the children were small and she did not want them to grow up without their father. Since they were now grown up, she went in for a divorce.

THE CASE OF MUNNAWAR

Munnawar comes from an average middle class family in Patna. His father was a retired government servant. His eldest brother works in the railways. One brother and sister had migrated to Pakistan and are now living there. Munnawar got an MBBS from Bihar Medical College and then went on to do his MS in ophthalmology from a prestigious central university in Uttar Pradesh.

Munnawar was married while he was studying for his MS degree. One of his friends had recommended the girl saying that she was beautiful and nice and her parents were very fine people. Munnawar met and talked with the girl, Mussarat, and the marriage was arranged. Mussarat was a post-graduate.

The marriage was an elaborate one. The girl's side gave an enormous dowry that included utensils for daily use, a refrigerator, a television and furniture, etc., besides curtains for the home. The curtains were of the size of the doors and windows of a room in Mussarat's parental home which Mussarat's parents said they wanted to give for their exclusive use. As Munnawar was at that time studying for his MS and was living in a hostel, the dowry was kept in that room on the pretext that it would be sent wherever Munnawar established his own residence. However, their real intention was that Munnawar should come and stay with them in their house. This was, perhaps, why the curtains were of the size of the doors and windows of a room in their house.

Within months of the marriage both Mussarat and her parental family started asking Munnawar to come to Patna and set up private practice. However, he was reluctant. He told them that he wanted to go in for higher studies and progress in his career and settling down in Patna would not be particularly helpful from this point of view. Meanwhile, Munnawar and Mussarat had two children. Mussarat stayed with Munnawar for barely four to five months during these four to five years. Once in a while she would go for short periods, stay with him and then return to her parental home. She also did not spend any length of time with her in-laws though they were living in Patna.

Around 1981 Munnawar went on an assignment to Iran. He thought of taking Mussarat along, but she was not willing to accompany him. She told Munnawar that he should go first and after he had settled down she would join him. After he settled down, he asked her to come to Iran. However, on one pretext or another she refused to join him. Munnawar wrote many letters to persuade her to come, but she always refused and flatly told him that she did not want to shift to Iran. Finally, she wrote to him that she wanted a divorce. Munnawar again tried to dissuade her, but she was quite insistent. Munnawar came to India hoping that he would be able to convince her to see reason and agree to go with him to Iran. Others also tried to convince her, but to no avail.

The matter went to the local qazi who also tried to convince Mussarat that she should join him in Iran and not insist on a divorce. She did not listen to the qazi either. Ultimately, Munnawar had to agree to divorce her. As the divorce had taken place at Mussarat's initiative, the *mehr* did not have to be paid. Further, since both their children were small, the qazi said that the children would stay with their mother. After they attained the age of fifteen years the father would be entitled to take them. However, he would be entitled to meet them whenever he wished to do so.

After a couple of hours after the divorce Mussarat realized that she had made a mistake in asking for and forcing a divorce. She approached a few of Munnawar's friends asking them to explore with Munnawar if there could be a possibility of a reconciliation with him. The qazi was approached for advice, but he said that since the divorce had been finalized there could be no reconciliation. If the pronouncement of divorce had occurred over a period of three monthly cycles, as indeed the Qur'an lays down, there might have been a possibility of a reconciliation. Since three pronouncements had been made one after another the divorce was now irrevocable. She could remarry him after first marrying someone else and getting divorce from the second husband. This process is known in Muslim Law as *halala.* Neither side was prepared for this.

As soon as the divorce materialized, Munnawar's relations started insisting that he should remarry. Actually, by the evening a few proposals had already arrived. However, Munnawar left home and went to Mughal Sarai where his mother's sister lived. There his aunt talked him into getting married to her daughter. Munnawar saw and talked to her and returned to Patna. His aunt sent someone the following day to find out his response to their proposal. Munnawar gave his consent and within three days of the divorce he was married again. The girl's side was rather poor and the marriage was a simple affair. No dowry was given. Only the *nikah* was performed. A few days later he left for Iran. His wife joined him after a month.

Whenever Munnawar visits India he goes to see his children from the first wife. Mussarat allowed him to meet the children a few times, but then started putting obstructions in his meeting the children. She would tell Munnawar that he could come to see the children at such and such time, but when he went there she would send word through someone in the house that the children had gone out to some relative's or friend's house. She fears that he might take the children away. Munnawar keeps sending clothes and money for the children from time to time.[2]

THE CASE OF SHUJA

Shuja belongs to an average middle class family in Delhi. His father was a lecturer in education in the university. Shuja did civil engineering and worked for some time in the Punjab and then decided to go to the Gulf and explore opportunities there. On his return from the Gulf after seven years, he started living with his father, two brothers and his married sister who worked as a school teacher. Shuja started construction business.

Shuja wanted to get married. Through a matrimonial advertisement he found a girl from Almora who was postgraduate in psychology. Shuja, his father and elder sister and her husband went over to the girl's house to finalize the marriage. Shuja's two brothers shared the house but had separate hearths. Shuja's father, married sister and her husband had a common hearth. After the marriage, Shuja's wife started objecting to this arrangement. She believed that since Shuja was still trying to establish his business he did not have much money. She reasoned it out to herself that perhaps this was the reason why he was living with his married sister and was dependent on her. She wanted him to set up a separate establishment and they started having arguments over this. Finally, when she went to visit her parental family, she stayed on and did not return. Shuja went to bring her back, but his in-laws refused to send her.

Soon thereafter, Shuja's wife filed a case for divorce in court alleging mental and physical cruelty and torture as reasons. The litigation went on for several years. Finally, a compromise was reached between the parties. It was agreed that Shuja would return the dowry and other gifts which had been given to his wife and give divorce and her family would return whatever gifts Shuja's family had given her at the time of marriage. One day, some people from the wife's family came to collect the dowry and other gifts. What Shuja's family had given as gifts at the time of marriage was not returned. Shuja pronounced divorce in their presence. Since the divorce had been demanded by the wife, the *mehr* was not paid.

About two years after the divorce, Shuja married again. His wife had studied up to the intermediate and was working as a typist in his office. She had fallen in love with Shuja and wanted to marry him, but he was reluctant. Finally, he reflected over the matter and came to the conclusion that out of all the proposals that had come she might be the best choice for him. He married her and they now live separately. His sister has since shifted out.

What do these case studies tell us about divorce, about the reasons why marriages breakdown, about Muslim divorce practices, about how Muslim personal law is used by both husband and wife once their marriage has soured, and about the implications of the Muslim provision for triple divorce for Muslim women. It is clear that divorce is not a sudden occurrence but a culmination of a prolonged process in which the husband or the wife comes to realize that adjustment with the spouse is seemingly difficult and any further investment of effort in sustaining the marriage is a waste. As a rule, the efforts of both husband and wife are required to sustain a marriage.[3] However, when it becomes clear that the differences and conflicts between them are either irresolvable or one of the spouses is indifferent to or unwilling to recognize and negotiate those conflicts and differences that the precipitate step of pronouncing a divorce or walking out of the matrimonial home in the hope of securing divorce later on is taken by the aggrieved spouse.[4] There are strong individual differences and some spouses reach the threshold of their patience and tolerance sooner than others. Nonetheless, divorce comes about only after that threshold has been reached.

The personal commitment of the spouses is a key factor in the sustenance of a marriage. Where that commitment is initially weak, and the reasons for this can be legion, the prospect of a marriage lasting out are considerably poor. This is eloquently illustrated in the case of Shagufta and Mussarat both of whom had strong preconceived notions of how and where they wanted to live after their marriage. Even though Shagufta's husband's kin were caring and solicitous, doing all household work which would otherwise have been her responsibility, she failed to sustain her marriage because she had strong feelings about living with her husband in a nuclear family. Her emotions for and commitment to her husband was not strong enough to allow her to adjust to the inconvenience of living in a joint household whose responsibility her husband was bound by custom and a personal sense of obligation to shoulder. Mussarat, on the other hand, wanted her husband to live at her parental home in Patna. When she realized that the husband was unwilling to accept that arrangement she decided to opt out of her marriage along with her three children and live with her parents. She obviously did not have a strong emotional attachment for her husband that would have prompted her to adjust to the prospect of living with him.

Divorces can result from very mundane reasons when one of the spouses takes the other's insistence on living in a particular way or refusal to do something as an affront to personal ego.[5] Shuja's and Munnawar's case illustrates this very well. In Shuja's case his wife was unhappy at having to live with his married sister and wanted to live separately. Shuja did not accommodate her by moving out and setting up an independent establishment though he did precisely that after he remarried. In the case of Munnawar, his wife wanted him to live with her parental family. Munnawar apparently found this insulting and was unwilling to accommodate her demand and her ego was deeply hurt when he refused to pay heed to her insistence on this count. A hurt ego also served to alienate Suraiya from her husband. It is quite clear that in a majority of these cases the spouses would not have been pushed to the point of asking for a divorce if the other partner had shown a degree of understanding and patience and tried to accommodate the other's point of view. Usually, the situation is rendered all the more difficult where the parents or other kin pamper or prompt the spouse to persist with a demand.

As soon as the alienation between the spouses surfaces and one of the partners decides to walk out of the matrimonial home or go in for a divorce, the finer emotions and other human sensibilities usually recede into the background.[6] If a spouse decides secretly to break the marriage and succeeds in keeping that decision secret, it is easier to consolidate material and social interests. Again, the cases of Shagufta and Mussarat illustrate this eloquently. Shagufta had reached a decision in her mind right at the start that she was not going to be able to, or was not probably interested in, sustaining her marriage. Therefore, on her visits to her parents she would take a part of her dowry with her. She also kept a few items packed in her friend's house so that she could have easier access to them when she decided to walk out on her husband. Mussarat, on the other hand, was so sure that her husband would abide by her request, or she would prevail upon him to live at her parental home, that she even got the curtains to fit the size of the doors and windows at her parental home. She also left most of the dowry that had been given to her at her parent's home. Once she woke up to the realization that she was not going to be successful in her designs, she simply left her matrimonial home never to return.

From personal knowledge we know that men as much as women move quickly into action to consolidate their material gains once they realize that their marriage has soured. There is a difference on this point between women and men that ought carefully to be noted, however. Since men are in control of the resources of the family, including property, there is no need for them to engage in elaborate maneuvers to consolidate their assets. On the other hand, since customary law and social practices do not vest any right to ownership of property in women or of even what she might have brought with her from her parental home as *jahez* or acquired by way of payment of *mehr*, the pressure on a woman to engage in obvious maneuvers to consolidate hold over at least some assets is greater. This has given rise to the stereotype of the cunning wife typified in our case studies by Shagufta and Mussarat. Otherwise, both women and men would appear to be remarkably similar in their behaviour when it comes to the consolidation of their material interests. Equally, where attachment to the spouse is strong, neither is likely to bother much about material interests.

There is overwhelming evidence in our case studies of the key role that family members play in the sustenance or otherwise of a marriage. This role can be both positive and negative. Shagufta's case illustrates their positive role in both caring for the daughter-in-law and trying to bring about a reconciliation when she raised a hue and cry that her in-laws would set fire to her or kill her. It is another matter that in this case the couple could not be reconciled, obviously because the wife had already made up her mind to terminate the marriage bond. Other cases—particularly those of Nargis, Mussarat and Suraiya—illustrate the negative role that family members sometimes play in causing the breakdown of a marriage. Mussarat's family acted negatively as it refused to prevail upon her to live with her husband wherever he wished to stay rather than attempt to bring him to stay with her family in Patna. Nargis' in-laws started torturing and harassing her once they could not succeed in arranging the marriage of their daughter with the boy in whom Nargis' sister was at one time interested. Given that finding another wife for a man is considerably easier in Indian society, it is not hard to imagine that in a large number of cases where a family has nursed grievances against a daughter-in-law, the husband's family would not hesitate to encourage him to divorce his wife or at least to send her away. At any rate, the critical role of the family in the sustenance or breaking up of a marriage cannot be gainsaid in the light of the evidence provided by the case studies.

Children are the greatest causality of a broken marriage. Our case studies afford powerful evidence that the children are put to a distinct disadvantage because their parents cannot sustain their marriage. The extent of this disadvantage varies according to the position the spouses take with respect to the children. The primacy accorded under Islam to the husband in respect of the custody and guardianship of the children notwithstanding, the damage is always less severe and grievous when the children stay with the mother who is more likely not to remarry. When the husband decides to assert his right to keep the children, whether he genuinely wishes to do so out of affection or merely acts out of vindictiveness towards the wife, the situation can be truly traumatic. This is pathetically demonstrated by the case of Nargis. Out of vindictiveness towards his wife, Nargis's husband took the children away. He was helped in this by Nargis's elder sister and mother who had their own axe to grind. They did not want to bear the cost of having to bring up someone else's children. Ultimately, two of the children landed in an orphanage and the third one was taken away by the husband's sister.

The case studies offer insufficient basis for generalization about divorce practices among Muslims. However, the little evidence they provide clearly suggests that Islamic stipulations about observance of *iddat* and payment of *mehr* are adhered to more in their violation rather than in their observance. Except for Najma, none of the women observed the statutory waiting period after the divorce. Again, there is no indication in these case studies of any eagerness on the part of the husbands to settle the *mehr* on their own. As Shagufta's case suggests, a wife can hope to secure it only by deceit or by coercion. She manoeuvered a situation in which the husband was coerced into making instant payment of the dower. Otherwise, husbands invariably try to get away with a divorce without paying the dower.

Finally, whether the initiative for divorce came from the wife or was taken by the husband, the mode of dissolution of the marriage in each case was that of triple *talaq*. Even where the woman herself demanded divorce, the formalization of the divorce required that the husband pronounce triple divorce. Whether this mode acted to the detriment of the women depended upon the peculiarities of the situation in each case. In some cases where, for whatever reason, both the husband and wife had come to realize that they could not, or did not want to, live together as husband and wife, this mode allowed a relatively hassle-free termination of the marital relationship. In other cases, it worked to the detriment of the woman as she found herself divorced without having any say in the matter. This was pathetically so in the case of Najma whose husband sent her a divorce notice after having assured her that he would soon arrange for her to join him in the US. Those campaigning for a ban on the system of triple divorce must seriously and carefully reflect on two aspects: whether the ban on triple divorce would make the situation of women who are today able to negotiate and secure a divorce from their husbands without much hassle difficult and complicated, and whether it would substantially strengthen the situation of those hapless women who are cast away at present by the unscrupulous use of the triple divorce formula in terms of the rights and advantages which should normally come to them. No definite and settled answers to these questions are available.

NOTES

1. Cf. 'Ultimately of course, most sociologists aspire to general descriptions and explanations of the social phenomena that they study. However, the representativeness of research findings is often restricted, particularly when the topic for investigation is relatively unexplored and when it involves the subjective feelings of ordinary people. Large-scale extensive questionnaire surveys may provide much valuable empirical data about whole populations, but they are incapable of yielding sensitive information about personal circumstances and perceptions and they may only be used to test hypotheses that have already been developed. When one's field of study is fairly novel, it is necessary to resort to more intensive techniques of investigation' (Hart, 1976: xii).
2. Cf. 'When custody was awarded to the mother, her husband's access to his children often became severely restricted. Sometimes the mother felt that visits from the children's father were disruptive and emotionally disturbing and she tried to discourage them. Wrangles over access to children tended to

be one of the main themes of an estranged couple's relationship, and this was destructive of both parents and children. Men who paid maintenance resented that they had no control over how income transfers were spent and that they received virtually no return for supporting their children. Some accused their wife of poisoning the children against them in their absence; and parents often competed for their affection, through material gifts and the dispensation of privileges' (Hart, 1976: 175).

3. 'For the partners to a marriage the union is conceived of, at least initially, as a life-long commitment to another person. Apart from the emotional investment which this entails, the married couple usually enter into a system of reciprocal financial obligation involving home formation, budgeting, and the accumulation of property. The size of this undertaking varies between different socio-economic groups, as do life-styles; but, for many people, the small surpluses over subsistence requirements which are gained from salaries and wages are invested exclusively in the home and its contents. *At any moment the accumulated goods of the conjugal pair may therefore represent a lifetime's savings. In terms of time, energy and available funds, therefore, the marital relationship must be the repository of a large share of any individual's investment resources, and hence we can infer that it occupies an important place in the role-identity hierarchy and that, as such, it carries a high level of commitment*' (Hart, 1976: 13-14; emphasis added).

4. Cf. '. . . the most significant determinant of an individual's behaviour . . . concerns his own subjective attachment to the marriage, for, unless he recognizes that the marriage is finished for good, he is unlikely to develop viable strategies for building an alternate future' (Hart, 1976: 105). Hart makes this point more elaborately when he writes, 'In the early phase of married life, when the normative framework for the conjugal relationship is laid, potential conflicts based on a dissimilarity of background or expectations may remain unresolved. At this time the relationship is at its strongest and, in the romantic aura of that envelops the newlyweds, basic conflicts of this kind may seem like details which should not be allowed to mar their happiness. Later, when the conjugal relationship has become more routinized, sublimated differences may remain a source of resentment or annoyance, which in time can develop into deep hostility. However, the domestic circumstances of marriage are not static. As the couple move through the developmental cycle great changes may occur in the major preoccupations of the two partners. For this reason the conjugal relationship must be sufficiently flexible to make adaptations to internal pressures for change in the marriage. If it is not, then conflict between husband and wife is more likely to be manifested' (1976: 83).

5. This point has been affirmed by Becker and Hill. They write, 'Each young man who married brings with him, both consciously and unconsciously, his idea of the part to be played by himself as husband and the part to be played

by his wife as his wife. Similarly the young woman enters marriage with a preconceived notion of the roles of husband and wife. . . . If the conceptions of both are reasonably fulfilled, we can expect a satisfactory adjustment. . . . We should remember however, that we enter marriage with definite expectations, and if reality falls short of them, dissatisfaction follows' (Becker and Hill, 1942: 316-17). It is also affirmed by Phillips: 'Marriage breakdown can be thought of as condition or behaviour on the part of one spouse, which one or both spouses regard as wholly inappropriate to their marriage. More formally we might describe it as an irremediable incongruence between the marital expectations of one or both spouses and the preconceived state of the marriage' (1991: 96).

6. Cf. 'Although the husband and wife have shared interests as a couple, as independent individuals they also have selfish goals and aspirations. Thus, there exists a dialectic between the "we" of the conjugal pair and the "I" of the self-interested, independent being, a dialectic that must be worked out in accordance with the changing exigencies of married life' (Hart, 1976: 55).

REFERENCES

Becker, H. and R. Hill (eds.) (1942), *Marriage and the Family*, Boston: Heath.

Hart, Nicky (1976), *When Marriage Ends: A Study in Status Passage*, London: Tavistock Publications.

Phillips, Roderick (1991), *Untying the Knot: A Short History of Divorce*, Cambridge: Cambridge University Press.

8

Chowdu (Divorcee): A Study of Divorce among the Rajamundry Muslims of Andhra Pradesh

Shaikh Abdul Azeez Saheb

This paper is concerned with a discussion of divorce among the Muslims of Rajamundry town in East Godawari district of Andhra Pradesh. The Muslims of the town, comprising roughly 40 per cent of the population, are divided both culturally and ethnically and in terms of sectarian affiliation and adherence to different schools of law, which leads to innumerable divisions among them (Ahmad, 1981). One expression of this extreme degree of social and religious differentiation is the presence of a large number of mosques. Some of these mosques are attended by Muslims of all ethnic groups and religious persuasions, while others, established by members of particular castes, ethnic groups or sects, are attended largely by people of that particular ethnic or caste groups (called *qaum*) or adherents of sects or schools of law and theology.

There are ten mosques in Rajamundry town. The Royal mosque is the oldest and was built by Sultan Muhammad bin Tughlaq during his visit to the town. The Railway Colony, Danvaipet and Rajendra Nagar, Waterline, Mallaipet, Ammavari Satram and Al-Baksh mosques had been either established by individuals or people of particular residential localities irrespective of their ethnic or sectarian affiliations. These mosques are not associated with the members of any particular caste or ethnic group or followers of distinct sect or school of law and theology. The Choti, the Jampet Labbai, Ah-le-Hadis Gai Khasab, and Bakra Khasab mosques were established by members of particular caste, ethnic or occupational groups and are associated with them. The Choti mosque was constructed with the help of contributions made by the traders of the city and is so-called because it is smaller than the Royal mosque. The Jampet Labbai mosque was built with the donations made by the Labbai (dealers in skin and hides) merchants of the city whose mother tongue is Tamil. The Friday sermon is delivered at the Jampet Labbai mosque in Tamil. Therefore, it is used exclusively by Tamil-speaking Muslims. The Ah-le-Hadis Gai Khasab mosque was built by contributions from the Gai Khasab (beef butchers) who are an endogamous ethnic group and belong to the Ah-le-Hadis sect. The Bakra Khasab mosque, as the name itself indicates, was built by donations from the Bakra Khasab (goat butchers) who constitute a distinct endogamous ethnic group within the Khureshi (butcher) community in the town.

The mosque is primarily a place of worship where Muslims gather for congregational prayers. However, where a mosque is associated with a particular caste, ethnic or sectarian group, it also has a social significance which goes beyond the performance of prayers and provision of religious education as mosques often also have a madrasa attached to them. It serves as the headquarters of the *jamat* where marriages, divorces, social disputes and internal religious questions of the members of the caste, ethnic or sectarian group are settled by the *jamat mutawalli* (head of the *jamat* or association president). Of course, not all mosques associated with a particular caste, ethnic or sectarian group are seats of such *jamats*, nor do all such groups necessarily have separate mechanisms for settlement of marital, social or religious disputes. The members of the Bakra Khasab group consult the qazi designated by the state and do not rely for settlement of marital and social disputes on the prayer leader of their mosque or their *jamat mutawalli*. On the other hand, the prayer leader of the Al-Baksh mosque, which was originally built by a leading steel-merchant of the town after whom it is named and is not associated with any particular ethnic, caste or sectarian group, settles matters of marriage and divorce. He is a highly educated and wise man and is widely respected. People go to him for quick settlement of marriage and divorce disputes though he is not a state-designated qazi. He maintains records of marriage and divorce just as does the state-designated qazi.

This paper is based on data drawn from four different sources:

individual and group interviews conducted by the author, records available with the state-designated qazi, records maintained by the *jamat mutawallis* attached to mosques where people prefer to consult their *jamat mutawalli* in matters relating to marriage and divorce, and FIRs relating to divorce and dowry cases available with the local police. The data drawn from the examination of the records maintained by the state-designated qazi as well as the *jamat mutawallis* highlight dimensions that have so far received little treatment in discussions of divorce among Muslims in India. For example, one common presumption has been that the divorce process is extremely ad hoc and arbitrary and can be set in motion without necessarily having to follow any recognized authority or agency. The data drawn from these sources point to the existence of fairly well-worked out mechanisms of settlement and adjudication of marital disputes as well as formal dissolution of marriages where the parties to a marital union are determined to dissolve their marriage bond. Again, the data drawn from police records throw interesting light on how laws such as the Dowry Prohibition Act, 1961, are interacting with Muslim Personal Law and are being used by Muslims in matters relating to divorce and separation. These are areas that require further detailed treatment and discussion and are only briefly indicated here in the light of the data collected.

MARRIAGE AND *MEHR*

Marriage is a civil contract in Islam. The core marriage rituals among Muslims are, first, seeking the consent of the prospective spouses to their marital union in the presence of two *vakils* (witnesses) on assured payment of *mehr* (dower) to the bride, and, second, sealing the marital union through *nikah*, which consists of the recitation of holy verses from the Qur'an. The *mehr* is a custom that can be traced to pre-Islamic Arab society where it was customary to pay a price for the bride. Islam continued this custom in a slightly modified form as the sum payable to the bride in consideration of her consent to marry the man. *Mehr* can be of two kinds: *muajjal* (prompt) and *muwajjal* (deferred). The former has to be paid at the time of *nikah*. The latter can be settled at any time during the lifetime of the spouses. Except in rare cases, deferred *mehr* is the norm.

Rajamundry Muslims cite four reasons for the importance attached to *mehr* in marriage. First, it can serve as a security deposit for the wife in the event of adversity or her husband deciding to leave her. Second, it can help the girl's parents to meet the marriage expenses. Finally, it can be used by the newly weds to settle down in life. None of these reasons hold for the Muslims of Rajamundry. The practice of settling the *mehr* before the marriage ceremony does not obtain in Rajamundry. Therefore, *mehr* is considered by Rajamundry Muslims as a debt that the wife can claim at any time in the future. Whether it is actually paid is, however, an open question, and the limited evidence we were able to gather in the town shows that *mehr* is often denied to the wife on one pretext or another even after divorce. The payment of *mehr* is often a bone of contention in a divorce when the woman advances her claim that her husband pay it.

In Islam a man has more rights than a woman in the matter of the dissolution of a marriage. Under certain conditions such as adultery, barrenness, chronic illness and disobedience, he can divorce the wife against her will. However, an aggrieved or alienated wife can take *khula* (redemption). The case studies recorded in the field suggest that divorces take place through three different modalities: *talaq* pronounced by husband, *khula*, and a decree of dissolution of marriage passed by a court. Of the divorce cases recorded, 29 took place through *talaq*, 21 through *khula* and 2 through court decrees.

Talaq is pronouncement of divorce by the husband and can take place without the consent of the wife. Purely from the point of law, the possibility exists for a husband to pronounce *talaq* even when he is alone and the marriage is deemed to be dissolved. Courts recognize such dissolution to be entirely valid and do not as a rule interfere. However, whether a divorce by *talaq* is always so unilateral and arbitrary is an open question. It is possible that even in cases where the divorce pronouncement takes such unilateral and arbitrary form there may be a background with both the husband and the wife knowing that the marriage would eventually end in a divorce. Only the actual dissolution may be abrupt, unilateral and arbitrary as the husband may take the initiative to pronounce *talaq*. Our research was not able to go into this complex question because we did not gather the information directly from the respondents who might have been involved in the divorce process. Our data were gathered through interviews with a cross-section of respondents and focused more on the patterns that obtained rather than on the specificities and intricacies of the nature of the intimate relationships that existed between couples before they were divorced. This is a possibility that requires to be carefully explored in studies on divorce among Muslims. Where a divorce takes place by *talaq*, the husband is obliged to pay the *mehr* at the time of divorce if he had not paid it at the time of marriage, but whether it is actually paid is again an open question and has not been established in studies on divorce among Muslims.

Khula is a form of divorce wherein the initiative for the dissolution of marriage comes from the wife. She may take this initiative on her own or may do so at the prompting of her husband. Where she takes the initiative to start *khula* proceedings at the behest of her husband or after he has expressed his consent for it, the divorce process can be relatively easy. Where this is not the case, *khula* can be a difficult and arduous exercise for the wife. Technically, *khula* is the prerogative of the wife and she is entitled to it even if the husband is unwilling to concede it. However, in practice *khula* requires that the husband pronounce divorce or an external agency charged with the responsibility of settling marital disputes issue a decree of divorce even if the husband is unwilling for *khula*. Where such an external agency does not exist or is not recognized, the only course left to a wife desirous of *khula* is to appeal to the husband to grant her release from marriage or to bring community pressure upon him so that he agrees to free her of the marital bond. In a *khula* divorce the wife is obliged to return the *mehr* if it had been paid at the time of marriage or forego it if she had not received it at the time of marriage.

CAUSES OF DIVORCE

There can be two ways of looking at divorce as a social phenomenon. One is to regard divorce as a sudden and spontaneous occurrence without any antecedent conditions that can be said to have brought it about. The other is to regard divorce as the culmination of a long process of marital discord. This distinction is important as it is likely to exercise a significant influence over how we view the causes of divorce and the exercise of the provision of triple divorce that has been a subject of some debate. Underlying this debate is the assumption that triple *talaq* takes place without any reason. Under this mode of divorce, the husband exercises the unilateral right to cast away his wife without having to necessarily divulge a reason. There is no doubt that in a triple divorce a husband can break off his marital relationship without assigning a reason and the wife has no legal right to be told why her husband has chosen to cast her away. However, conceding to a Muslim husband the right to unilaterally divorce his wife without assigning a reason for his action, which Muslim divorce law currently does, is not to say that the triple divorce is a sudden and spontaneous outburst without a tangible reason. Even a triple divorce may have behind it a history of marital breakdown.

Where the process of the dissolution of a marriage takes the form of triple divorce, the cause of divorce is not a part of the divorce proceedings. Careful questioning of the spouses after the divorce has already taken place is also unlikely to yield an understanding of the reasons. What one is likely to get as a result of such questioning would be conflicting versions from the two spouses as to why the divorce occurred. Pressed to account for his action, the husband would try to offer a rationalization of why he took the precipitate action of pronouncing a triple divorce. The impulse on the part of the husband would be to heap all kinds of blame upon his wife so that his own action appears justified. On the other hand, the wife would either repudiate her husband's contention or cook up her own rationale for the husband's action. Her impulse would be to project herself as the innocent victim of her husband's malice and arbitrariness. Whether the husband's account is as credible as he is likely to make it appear and the wife is quite as innocent as she is likely to project herself is difficult to ascertain in such cases.

Probing close relatives, neighbours or friends of the family can sometimes provide the background to the action of the husband, but even here there are serious limitations that may prevent the real reason for the divorce from coming out. A considerable body of available sociological research on divorce suggests a strong tendency on the part of kin, neighbours and friends to take partisan positions on a divorce depending upon the strength and closeness of their bond with either the husband or the wife. Under the circumstances, the prospects are that those likely to be in the know of things, in the large majority of cases, merely relay the version or the point of view of the spouse to whom they are close. If they are close to the husband, they simply end up reiterating and reinforcing the version that the husband may have chosen to advance. If they were close to the wife, they will most likely reiterate and reinforce the projection of the relationship made by her. Thus, the cause of divorce in most cases of triple divorce is likely to remain obscure and hidden even if a powerful reason for the divorce to have occurred may indeed exist.

The situation is entirely different where the dissolution of marriage comes about after proper divorce proceedings supervised by an agency—the qazi, the *jamat mutawalli* or elders in the family or the local community. Where this mode of divorce is relied upon, the cause of divorce is a part of the divorce proceedings and can be easily ascertained and analysed. Table 1 sets out the causes of divorce as given by the husband in the divorce proceedings conducted by the qazi, the *jamat mutawalli* or court records where re-

TABLE 1: REASON GIVEN BY HUSBAND IN *TALAQ* CASES

Reason for Divorce	Cases settled by state qazi	Cases settled by *mutawalli*	Cases settled/ pending in court	Total
Chronic illness of wife	1	-	-	1
Wife's disobedience of elders	2	-	-	2
Wife guilty of adultery	4	1	-	5
Wife's quarrelsome nature	4	2	-	6
Wife's refusal to observe purdah	1	-	1	2
Wife's abortion	1	-	-	1
Wife's doubtful character	1	-	-	1
Wife's barrenness	3	1	-	4
Wife's wilful overstay at her home	1	1	-	2
Wife's disobedience of husband	2	-	-	2
Husband wanted second marriage	2	-	1	3
Total	22	5	2	29

course was taken to the court for the settlement of divorce. Table 2 sets out the causes of divorce given by the wife in cases of *khula*. It is clear from these tables that the causes of divorce in the cases settled by these agencies were ones that normally exist universally in all communities and societies. As al-Ati (1977: 217) has noted in another context,

> . . . they apply to human society irrespective of time, place or level of civilization [and they range] from the unavoidable death of a spouse or involuntary barrenness to the trivial cooking mistake of burning the husband's food or putting too much salt in it, not to mention the man's arbitrary dislike of his spouse or capricious preference for another woman who seems more pleasing to him.

There is one problem, however, with the figures presented in the tables. It is that the cause of divorce as given by the husband or the wife to the qazi or the *jamat mutawwali* and shown in the records maintained by them does not quite capture the precise manner in which it worked itself out, in the life of the couple, eventually leading them to go in for the termination of their marriage. In order to get at the details we tried to construct the profiles of a few cases from the records available with the qazi and the *jamat mutawallis*. These records contain complete details about the names and

TABLE 2: REASON GIVEN BY HUSBAND IN *TALAQ* CASES

Reason for Divorce	Cases settled by state qazi	Cases settled by *mutawalli*	Cases settled/ pending in court	Total
Husband's refusal to repay loan taken from wife's parents	1	-	-	1
Husband took a second wife	3	1	-	4
Husband's adulterous nature	1	-	-	1
Husband's inability to maintain	1	5	-	6
Husband's incurable illness	1	-	-	1
Husband's inhuman treatment	-	3	-	3
Husband untraceable for 3 years	-	1	-	1
Husband's impotency	-	1	-	1
Poor economic condition	1	-	-	1
Husband cheated	-	1	1	2
Total	7	12	2	21

addresses of the spouses and their parents, the date of marriage, and the number of children, but the information contained in them as to the details of their martial relationship are perfunctory. This prevents us from forming a comprehensive idea of what went wrong with the marital relationship in each case. Where such details were provided in the documents or were recorded by the qazi or the *jamat mutawallis*, they have been used to construct the profile of the divorced couples. There was no way of ascertaining whether the reasons given by the spouses seeking the divorce were correct as doing so would have required going back to the couples and their families and asking them questions independently. This we could not have done given the constraints of our study. However, even the sketchy profiles of the cases that we have pieced together are useful in showing that divorce is neither a spontaneous outburst nor a sudden occurrence, but the end result of a process where one or another cause has been responsible for bringing about the alienation of the spouses or leading them on to decide to terminate the marriage in self-interest.

Chronic or incurable illness of the spouse was the ground for divorce in two cases as shown in Tables 1 and 2. One of the cases on which the records provided the details involved a couple which had been happily married for a year and had a daughter. However, after sometime the wife developed chronic anaemia. She had suffered from this disease from childhood. After marriage the problem recurred and she could not sustain her married life. She stayed with her parents most of the time. This vexed the husband's parents. Finally, they decided that their son's marriage should be dissolved and conveyed their decision to his wife's parents. Both sides then approached the state-designated qazi who granted *talaq*. This was a case of divorce by mutual agreement. The daughter was given into the custody of the wife and, at the suggestion of the qazi, the husband deposited a sum of Rs. 10,000 in the name of his daughter in a bank as a security measure for her.

There was another case in which divorce took place because the husband suffered from leprosy. His parents had kept the fact of his affliction secret. At the time of the consummation of the marriage the wife discovered that her husband suffered from leprosy. She refused to consummate her marriage and told her parents who instantly filed a case of cheating against the husband. Finally, the matter landed up with the qazi who called the parents of both the spouses and granted *khula* to the girl as she could not have lived with her husband. After the *khula* proceedings, the wife's side demanded that the husband also pay the marriage expenses as he had cheated them into spending on the marriage by withholding information about his affliction. When the husband's family refused to pay the Rs. 50,000, which the wife's parents claimed they had spent on the marriage, the wife's parents moved the court. Finally, a compromise was reached between them through police intervention and the husband's parents paid a sum of Rs. 22,000. The court also confirmed the divorce.

Most parents like to give some dowry to their daughters at the time of marriage. What is actually given is determined by the economic status of the family and varies a great deal across the social or class spectrum. Unless the girl comes with a huge dowry, a great deal of bickering is an almost essential feature of marriages in the traditional system. Taunt and pinpricks to the effect that the girl had not brought adequate dowry would be made but as time passed these eventually ceased. Rarely was any kind of pressure mounted on the girl to bring in additional dowry. This has now changed to such an extent that in many cases the girl is subjected to cruelty or harassment to get her to bring in additional dowry. In one case parents had paid a sum of Rs. 5,000 besides giving ten items as *jahej* (dowry) which included one pair of gold bangles, one pair of silver anklets, one *beruva* (wooden almirah), one wooden bed, one wooden cot, one iron trunk, one set of glass tumblers, one dinning set, one *marachembu* (steel jug), two *bindelus* (steel pans) and one steel tray. This may not seem very much by contemporary standards, but it was quite a great deal for the girl's father. However, the boy's side was not quite satisfied and started making additional demands soon after the marriage.

The couple led a disturbed married life for three years. As the girl's father was a poor man and could not afford to meet the demand, the husband used to beat, abuse, and tease the girl almost daily to get more money from her parents. Unable to tolerate the inhuman treatment meted out by the husband, the girl along with her parents made a complaint to the state-designated qazi. Based on the complaint filed by the girl, the qazi sent summons to the husband's parents to confirm the facts. He then called both sides to his office and tried to reconcile them. His efforts were in vain. Finally, he issued a decree of *khula* through a deed known as *khulanama*. Her *mehr* and *jahez* were returned to the girl's parents. As per the procedure laid down for *khula*, the wife was required to declare that she was in a conscious state and sound mind and repeat three times in the presence of the qazi '*main khula deti hun*' (I, so and so, give *khula* to my husband). Later, the husband acknowledged ill-treating his wife and received a copy of the *khulanama*. As a precautionary measure, the husband and his parents were asked to affix their signature to the *khulanama*. This made the settlement of divorce by *khula* final and irrevocable.

Occasionally sharp differences in the cultural or socio-economic background of the spouses also lead to alienation, resulting in divorce. This was the ground for divorce in one case of intermarriage between a Shaikh boy and a Pathan girl. As a rule, Shaikhs and Pathans are endogamous and, following the common restriction on inter-caste marriage, do not intermarry. However, in this case the marriage took place because the boy and the girl had fallen in love. The boy was handsome, educated, cultured and good-natured but belonged to a poor family. He was Telugu-speaking. The girl, who belonged to a well-off family, was Tamil-speaking. Because of socio-cultural and linguistic differences they were unable to establish a stable marital relationship to begin with. As the girl came from a well-off family, she also could not adjust to the relatively poor conditions in which she was now obliged to live. She wanted to go to the Gulf so that she might earn money and obtained a passport and visa. Her husband refused to let her go. The issue became contentious and, finally, the girl decided to ask for *khula*.

The inability of the wife to have a child is a common ground for divorce, especially in societies where a great deal of emphasis is placed on the birth of a male child. This was the reason for divorce in one case where both the husband and the wife came from the same village. The marriage lasted for nearly seven years without any apparent signs of marital friction. However, as the wife could not have a child, the husband's parents decided to terminate the marriage and approached the girl's family to agree to the proposal for divorce. Once agreement between both sides was reached, they approached the *jamat mutawalli* of Al-Baksh mosque to bring the marriage to an end. The *jamat mutawalli* asked the boy's side to pay the girl her *mehr* fixed at Rs. 16,500, which they readily settled. The *jamat mutawalli* then asked the couple to sign a *talaq-nama* (divorce deed), copies of which were given to the parties to avoid future complications.

Where a husband has been missing or absconding for a long period of time a legitimate case for the dissolution of marriage exists. Such was the ground for divorce in a case of *khula*. A boy was in love with a Hindu girl whom he wanted to marry. However, his parents forced him to marry his maternal uncle's daughter in the hope that once the marriage has been solemnized the husband would get over his attachment to the Hindu girl. This did not actually happen. After some time the boy left the house and disappeared with the Hindu girl. The wife thought at first that her husband had gone to the city to get the monthly rations. However, he did not return home. Finally, after waiting for three years at the home of her in-laws, she returned to her parents who approached the state-designated qazi for a *khula*. The qazi conducted investigations and on finding the wife's complaint to be genuine, issued a *khulanama*. The *khulanama* was signed on the husband's behalf by his parents. After a month, the wife married another man.

Suspicion about the character of the wife or the husband can often lead to alienation between spouses and can result in divorce. In one case a couple had been married for several years. However, the husband was of a remarkably suspicious nature and constantly doubted the wife's fidelity. He would tease and taunt her for small incidents. As the wife was submissive and good-natured, she put up with this situation. Soon she had a daughter. One day she was breast-feeding the child in the house in the presence of some relatives. The husband took exception to this and scolded her. On another occasion, she was breast-feeding the child in the presence of her husband's brother. This angered the husband who felt that she was probably having an affair with his brother. He instantly pronounced triple divorce in the presence of his parents and brother. Subsequently, he approached the qazi to formalize the divorce. At first the qazi tried to reunite them, but when the husband refused to take back his wife the qazi told him to pay her *mehr* which had been fixed at Rs. 15,000. He also stipulated that the daughter would stay with the mother until she was five and he would be obliged to pay a sum of Rs. 500 per month for the daughter's maintenance. The daughter would revert back to the father after she attained the age of five. The qazi also asked the wife to observe *iddat*. At the end of the *iddat* period he issued a *talaqnama* that was signed by both parties.

There was one case in which the divorce came about, ostensibly, as a result of the wife's abortion soon after marriage, but the real reason was quite different. Both the spouses in this case came from rich and highly educated families, but differed in their religious outlook. The wife's family was extremely liberal and modern and she had been used to a great deal of freedom in her parent's house. The husband's family was orthodox and religious. It started placing restrictions on the daughter-in-law and wanted her to observe purdah. Meanwhile, she conceived. She was reluctant to have a child so soon after marriage, but the husband's family wanted her to bear the child. She defied them and had an abortion. This led to tensions between her and her husband and his family. Finally, she went without the husband's knowledge to her parental home and settled there permanently. When the husband's parents asked her to return, she refused. Vexed by her defiant attitude the husband pronounced triple divorce before the qazi. However, the wife's parents refused to accept the divorce and filed a complaint of harassment for dowry against the husband. The case is pending in court.

There were two cases of divorce involving a second wife. In one case, a man whose wife had died leaving three children took a second wife. He was prevailed upon to do so by his parents who advised him to remarry as the children were too young and it was impossible for him to look after them on his own. After a few months problems began to crop up between his children from the first wife and his second wife and she started ill-treating the children. He could not tolerate this as he was greatly attached to the children. He tried to persuade the wife to be kind to the children, but rather than abiding by his wishes she would quarrel with him and abuse him. Unable to put up with her irritating behaviour, the husband finally approached the qazi and pronounced divorce in his presence. She did not accept the divorce approved by the qazi and instead moved the court for maintenance and a share in his property. The case is pending in court.

The second case is that of a civil engineer settled in Saudi Arabia. He married into a rich family and was given a dowry of Rs. 2 lakh. The marriage seemed to be working well until the wife came to her parent's house for the delivery of the first child. After the delivery, the husband wanted her to go and live with his parents until she joined him in Saudi Arabia. However, the wife's sisters and mother persuaded her against going to live with her parents-in-law. This angered the husband. He sent her the first pronouncement of *talaq* through the Saudi court.[1] Subsequently, when he came on home leave, he called up his wife to say that he was going to take another wife. He did so later and stayed with his second wife for a month before returning to his job in Saudi Arabia. He left with the intention of sending her visa to join him there. Meanwhile, however, the first wife came to her senses and moved to her parents-in-law's house. This forced the second wife to return to her parental home. She filed a case of cheating against her husband and asked for maintenance and refund of marriage expenses. Her case is pending adjudication in the Andhra Pradesh High Court.

CONCLUSION

This paper has been concerned with a discussion of divorce among the Rajamundry Muslims of Andhra Pradesh. Our discussion has focused on the institutional mechanisms available to Muslims for the settlement of marital disputes. This should not be taken to mean that all divorces either take place or are regulated by these institutional mechanisms. Many divorces may be taking place outside of these mechanisms. What this paper has tried to show is that while a great many divorces may be taking place outside any institutional framework, institutional mechanisms do exist for the settlement of marital disputes. People can either go to the state-designated qazi or the *jamat mutawallis* of a mosque for the dissolution of their marriage or settlement of marital disputes. Our data does not allow us to arrive at an understanding of how the choice in favour of going to the qazi or the *jamat mutawalli* is really made, except to indicate the possibility that in case of some caste or occupational groups caste rules may require that marriages be dissolved through the *jamat mutawalli* of the mosque established by the caste. However, it is clear that a large number of cases of divorce do land up with the qazi or the *jamat mutawallis* who try to settle the cases as amicably as possible.

Leaving aside cases where husbands may have arbitrarily used the provision of triple divorce, divorces usually result from definite causes. The principal grounds for divorce suggested by our analysis were the barrenness of the wife, the chronic or incurable disease of the spouse, socio-cultural differences between husband and wife, wife's failure to abide by the wishes of her husband or husband's parents and tensions arising out of the husband having more than one wife. There is nothing specifically Muslim about these causes. They are common to all communities and societies.

From the limited details available of cases settled through institutional mechanisms, it is clear that the qazi and the *jamat mutawallis* usually try to bring about the settlement of divorce cases as amicably as possible, keeping the interests of both spouses and their children in mind. They ensure the payment of *mehr* and the maintenance and the return of the dowry to the wife where the dissolution of marriage has been forced upon the wife because of a failure or lapse on the part of the husband. Where the marriage has to be dissolved at the initiative of the wife or her parents, payment of *mehr* is usually not insisted upon. This is understood to be the position in the *shar'iat* (canonical law of Islam) and is commonly accepted by Muslims in Rajamundry.

There is clear indication in the data collected that the effort of the qazi and the *jamat mutawallis* is to ensure that all the religious formalities laid down for divorce are adhered to. Thus, the qazi insists that the wife observe *iddat* (period of seclusion) before issuing the *talaqnama* or *khulanama*. However, there is also evidence to the effect that in the process of imposing adherence to the *shar'iat* as they understand it, they also sometimes bypass the prescribed conditions for divorce to suit the exigencies of the prevailing situation. For instance, we were often told in Rajamundry that in the cases adjudicated by the *jamat mutawallis* women's observance of the obligatory *iddat* is not insisted upon.

Our study suggests that reliance upon the institutional mechanisms of the qazi and *jamat mutawallis* does not foreclose the option of using formal judicial processes. When a party is not satisfied with the settlement worked out by the qazi or the *jamat mutawalli* as well as when they lack the power to enforce their direction, people do take recourse to the formal judicial channels of adjudication. However, this mostly happened in cases where the spouse was well-off and could meet the cost of prolonged litigation. For the large majority of the poor Muslims, the institutional mechanisms of the qazi or the *jamat mutawalli* serves as a hassle-free means of settling marital disputes without the element of adversarial procedure and mutual recrimination of parties coming into the divorce process.

NOTE

1. This calls for an elaboration for those not familiar with Muslim divorce law. Under Qur'anic law a man is required to pronounce divorce three times spread over three menstrual cycles and the divorce becomes final and irrevocable only after the third pronouncement of divorce. Until then the spouses can reunite and the pronouncement of divorce stands automatically revoked. If the husband pronounces divorce three times at one go, the three pronouncements are to be counted as only one pronouncement of divorce under this procedure. This provision was originally provided to encourage reconciliation as there is always the possibility that if the husband and wife live under the same roof they might resume their conjugal relationship. This rule degenerated later when three divorces pronounced at one time came to be counted as final and irrevocable. Under the law in Saudi Arabia, a man must follow the procedure of pronouncing divorce three times at intervals of one month. Since the husband in this case had approached a Saudi court for divorce, he was allowed to pronounce the first divorce. He could have gone ahead and pronounced divorce on two other occasions and his marriage with his wife would have stood irrevocably and finally dissolved. He did not complete the process and instead took a second wife. This allowed the first wife to return to his parent's home and reclaim her standing as a wife to the discomfiture of the second wife.

REFERENCES

Ahmad, Imtiaz (1981), *Caste and Social Stratification among Muslims in India*, 2nd rev. edn., Delhi: Manohar.

al-Ati, H. (1977), *The Family Structure in Islam*, Indiana: American Trust Publications.

9

Muslim Women and Divorce: Two Case Studies

Malika B. Mistry

Existing literature on Muslim women in India is acutely deficient in empirical information on divorce and related issues. This paper is an attempt to fill this gap by presenting detailed case studies of two divorced Muslim women from Pune city in Maharashtra.

Pune is the second largest city in Maharashtra, the first being Mumbai. Traditionally, Pune has been an important centre of education and culture in India. In recent decades, it has also become an important industrial centre. Historically, Pune is famous for its freedom fighters like Gopalkrishna Gokhale and Bal Gangadhar Tilak. It is also known for its social reformers such as Jyotiba Phule, Maharshi Karve and Pandita Ramabai who fought for the liberation of women and depressed classes.

The current population of Pune is twenty-five lakhs. Muslims are a minority in the city and account for about one-tenth of its total population. Historically, Pune Muslims, too, participated in the freedom struggle. After Independence, prominent Muslims migrated to Pakistan. Even then the Muslims of Pune can be considered more progressive than their counterparts in other areas because Pune itself is known for its progressiveness.

When I first undertook the research on which the present paper is based, I approached, through a common friend, one divorced young Muslim woman who had later remarried. Initially, she agreed to tell me her story. Later, because of her father's fear, she sent a message through her aunt that she did not want to tell her story. The point to be noted is that the topic of divorce cannot be easily discussed in Muslim societies and people usually try to hide cases of divorce within their families. I, therefore, approached the Muslim Satyasodhak Mandal, an organization which has been fighting for the abolition of oral and unilateral divorce for the last twenty-five years. In spite of all the hard work, it has not been very successful in achieving its purpose. Mainstream Muslim society treats this organization as an outcast but divorced and abandoned Muslim women approach it in search of justice. The work of this organization needs to be appreciated in this context.

Through the Muslim Satyasodhak Mandal (hereafter referred to as Satyasodhak) I approached two Muslim women who had been coming to it in search of help. Interviews with these two respondents were conducted in great detail at the Satyasodhak Centre. Their parental homes were also visited so that we could meet their family members and gauge their attitudes and behaviour towards these women and obtain supplementary information. The first case study is of Kaleemun and the second case study is that of Rafat. The case studies are first presented separately and then a combined analysis of these two divorce cases is undertaken.

THE CASE OF KALEEMUN

Kaleemunnisa Shaikh (Kaleemun) is the only daughter of her parents. She studied up to the third standard in an Urdu medium school but is illiterate for all practical purposes. She has two younger brothers. Mother Noorbi Shaikh works as an ayah in a private hospital (N.M. Wadia Hospital) run by missionaries. Noorbi is a smart and bold woman who studied up to the fifth standard in a Marathi medium school, which is the vernacular of Maharashtra. Father Shaikh Abdul Satter is illiterate and sold *papad* at one time. Presently he does sweeping and swabbing in a low-grade hotel. He also does petty jobs for the hotel where he is employed. Kaleemun's two brothers, Anwar Shaikh and Akhtar Shaikh, sell cloth on the footpath. Both the brothers are married and their wives look after the house. Both the brothers have two daughters each. Kaleemun's parents are natives of Pune and belong to the Shaikh community. Kaleemun's natal family belongs to the lower socio-economic stratum of society. Kaleemun's parents live in a small dilapidated house in Nana Pet, a Muslim locality in one of the crowded areas of the old city of Pune.

Kaleemun's parents got her married at the age of fifteen, not unusual in a community where marrying young girls is the norm. Since Kaleemun was her only daughter, Noorbi spent generously on her wedding. She gave Kaleemun gold earrings, gold *lachcha* (marriage necklace), silver toerings, sixty to seventy utensils and bed. The bridegroom was given a watch and a gold ring. The marriage was performed lavishly, of course, in keeping with the bride's economic status.

After marriage, Kaleemun went to live with her husband and his family. The matrimonial home was located in another crowded area of the old city of Pune within walking distance from her mother's house. Her husband Abdul Lateef Shaikh had two elder brothers and one younger brother. Both the elder brothers were married and had two sons each. Their wives were housewives. The younger brother got married fifteen days after Abdul Lateef. Abdul Lateef's father had married another woman and used to live with her, but he had died long before Abdul Lateef's marriage. Abdul Lateef's parents, too, were natives of Pune and were Shaikhs.

Kaleemun's mother-in-law (Abdul Lateef's mother) sold *sovri* (goat feed) for a living while one brother-in-law sold bananas on a handcart and another worked as a peon in a government hospital. Her husband had studied up to the eighth standard in an English medium school and used to paint motorcars for a living. Thus, Kaleemun's husband's family, too, belonged to the lower socio-economic stratum of society.

The first year of marriage was smooth for Kaleemun. She gave birth to a girl child. In the second year she became pregnant again. One day a woman came to the house. Her mother-in-law said that she was like her daughter. She started visiting the house often and everyone in the house was nice to her.

Kaleemun got suspicious and started questioning her husband and in-laws about her. She eventually learned that her husband was in an illicit relationship with another woman. This woman wanted to marry Abdul Lateef, but his mother did not approve of it because she was poor. She wanted a good dowry, which Kaleemun's parents were willing to give, and so Abdul Lateef was married to

Kaleemun. After some time Abdul Lateef married this other woman. He continued having children from both wives and had two children from his second wife.

Kaleemun was subjected to harassment and verbal abuse as Abdul Lateef and his family wanted to get rid of her. One day Abdul Lateef demanded Rs. 5,000 from Kaleemun's parents to go to Dubai. He threatened to divorce Kaleemun if his demand was not met. Around this time her mother-in-law and sister-in-law poured kerosene over her and were about to set her on fire when her neighbours got in touch with her mother. Barefoot, Noorbi rushed to Kaleemun and rescued her. She took her to the police station and registered a criminal complaint against Kaleemun's husband, mother-in-law and sister-in-law. She and Kaleemun also filed a case against them in court. Kaleemun stayed with her parents and delivered a baby boy.

All this frightened Abdul Lateef and he made a compromise with his parents-in-law. He came to his mother-in-law's house, celebrated the birthday of his elder daughter and took Kaleemun back to his house promising that he would behave properly.

During her third year of marriage, Kaleemun became pregnant again. The second wife, however, was a bone of contention between Abdul Lateef and Kaleemun. When she was two months pregnant he left her at her mother's house saying that he wanted to go to the Gulf in search of greener pastures. He said that he did not need funds from his in-laws. All that he expected was that they should take good care of his wife and children. He further requested them that, since he was well behaved towards their daughter, they should withdraw the case against him and his relatives. Believing him, they agreed to withdraw the case.

One day he came and told Kaleemun that he was taking her to a cinema house to watch a film. Instead, he took her to the court. He told her that he had bought a house and wanted to register it in her name. He took her signatures on a number of papers. She, being semi-literate, did not know what she was signing. Most probably the papers were meant to withdraw the criminal cases against him and his relatives. After this incident Kaleemun twice received a registered letter but she refused to accept it. The third time when the letter came, she accepted it and it turned out to be a letter of divorce. Her husband had given her a unilateral divorce through a registered letter. She was not even told that she was being divorced. Though she was furious with the husband over his second marriage, she had never wanted a divorce.

At the time of divorce, she was yet to deliver her third child.

After the divorce, her *mehr*, a paltry amount of Rs. 125, and provision of Rs. 675 for the *iddat* period of three months, a total of Rs. 800, was sent to Kaleemun by her husband. A part of the dowry was given back after much bickering. Not even thirty utensils were returned. The bed had broken and was therefore given back.

Kaleemun's brother was associated with the Satyasodhak Mandal that helped divorced and abandoned women seek justice. With the help of her brother, Kaleemun approached this group. The Satyasodhak helped her to file a suit in court for maintenance. In the meantime she delivered a baby girl. The court awarded her maintenance of Rs. 150 for herself and Rs. 50 for the baby boy.

Kaleemun was very hurt and upset after her divorce. Since she had no other place to go to except her parental home, she has been living with her parents. There were some problems initially but now her father treats her and her children with kindness. Her mother has been very supportive. After her brothers got married there were unpleasant arguments between Kaleemun and her sisters-in-law. Later, they went to live separately. Sometimes, when the mother longs for her sons, she blames Kaleemun for her sons and daughters-in-law living separately.

After the divorce, Kaleemun started working as a maidservant in the neighbourhood. Till very recently she was working as a maidservant, washing clothes and utensils to supplement her parents' income who are maintaining her and her children. Her father's elder brother and his children sometimes give her some money and old clothes. They are sympathetic to her plight. Now she is planning to go to Dubai to work as a housekeeper in one of her cousin's home. She hopes to save enough money by working in Dubai so as to buy a house for herself and her children. Her mother is willing to take care of her children in her absence.

At the Satyasodhak, a philanthropist once donated Rs.1,000 to Kaleemun to start some self-employment project. She spent that money on necessities for herself and her children. Once, somebody gave her a few notebooks for her children.

Today, it is more than twelve years since her husband divorced Kaleemun. Now her children are teenagers. The first child, a daughter, is fourteen years old. She is studying in eighth standard. The second child, a son, and the third child, a daughter, are both in class five. All are studying in Urdu medium schools. Now Kaleemun is about thirty-two years old. Overall, she maintains good health but sometimes she suffers from abdominal pains. Perhaps it is a psychosomatic pain. Doctors have told her that she has a low haemoglobin count. Perhaps her nutrition is deficient.

In the court, Abdul Lateef had stated that he would take custody of both the daughters but till today the daughters are living with Kaleemun and their grandparents. He paid maintenance till 1992. In 1993 he went to Dubai. His second wife also went with him. It is said that they are both working there. In 1993 he stopped paying maintenance to Kaleemun and their son. Kaleemun approached the court once again. When Lateef's second wife came to India, she deposited the maintenance money in the court. In 1997, Abdul Lateef again stopped payment of maintenance. Kaleemun once again approached the court. She has engaged a lawyer who is sympathetic to women's cause and is associated with Satyasodhak. This time she has pleaded for an increase in the maintenance amount for herself and her son. She has also asked for maintenance for her two daughters. She is expecting to get a maintenance amount of Rs. 500 per person, thus, a total of Rs. 2,000 per month for herself and her three children. The litigation continues. Abdul Lateef's second wife threatened Kaleemun that if she asked for maintenance for her daughters, Abdul Lateef would not bear the expenses of Kaleemun's daughters' marriages. Also, she told Kaleemun that Lateef had developed some heart problem and he would die soon. After his death, Kaleemun would have to bear the expenses of her daughters' marriages herself. If Kaleemun persists with the case for maintenance for the daughters, she would not allow her to get it. In spite of all these threats, Kaleemun is fighting for an increase in maintenance as well as award of maintenance to her daughters. She is very likely to win the case.

After her divorce Kaleemun's parents wanted to remarry her.

There were four to five proposals, one from a bachelor. The rest were either from divorced or married men. Some were sound but Kaleemun did not favour the idea of remarriage.

According to Kaleemun's mother, the blame for divorce should be placed more on the mother-in-law than on the husband. In her view, the mother-in-law as the head of the family should not have allowed another woman to visit her son's family. In that case, divorce could have been avoided.

THE CASE OF RAFAT

Rafat Mohammad Ahmad is one of nine children. She has six brothers and two sisters. Father Mohammad Ahmad Shaikh was a *hafiz* (one who has memorized the Qur'an by heart). He comes from a religious and old fashioned family. For a living, he conducted *namaz* at different mosques in Muslim localities. His income was not sufficient to maintain his large family. The children were brought up in poverty. Rafat's mother was a housewife, mostly restricted to the home. This family lived in Ravivar Peth, a crowded and mixed area in the city of Pune. Rafat studied up to the fourth standard in an Urdu medium school. But she is effectively illiterate.

At the age of fourteen she was married off. Her husband was much older than her, between thirty to thirty-five years, a government servant working in the Public Works Department (P.W.D.). He was also a moneyed man. He was a *patwegar* (from a lower social stratum) whereas Rafat was a Shaikh, i.e. from a higher social stratum.

After her marriage Rafat lived in Pune for a week with her matrimonial relatives. Later she was taken to Satara, a town two and a half hour's journey by bus from Pune. Most of the time she was made to sleep with the children in the family. Rafat noticed that her husband was not interested in her sexually. When her father came to know about this, he was upset but kept quiet.

Later Rafat learnt that her husband had sexual relations with his elder brother's wife and that his elder brother was impotent. Rafat did not protest.

One day Rafat fell sick and giddy and fell down. That night, her in-laws took out her gold jewellery, earrings, bangles and silver anklets. After a few days, she was left at her mother's house. She had stayed in her husband's house for only seven weeks. For two years she stayed with her mother. Then one day Rafat's husband and his relatives called Rafat and her parents to an advocate's office in Pune. In front of the advocate, the husband pronounced oral *talaq* thrice in one sitting. The relationship was over. Rafat cried a lot, as she felt helpless. She did not want a divorce. Yet she was divorced unilaterally by way of oral *talaq* in front of an advocate. Her dowry was not returned and no *mehr* was paid even though it was only Rs. 125.

After the divorce, Rafat lived with her parents for ten long years. Her parents were poor and so to survive, she started working as a maidservant. She also acquired some proficiency in stitching. She has received about twenty to twenty-five proposals for marriage. Two were from bachelors, the rest were from widowers, divorced or even married men. Some were good. One was from a man around forty-five years old, older than Rafat by twenty-five years. He rejected Rafat because he found her too young.

One Yakub Husain Shaikh, aged about thirty years and educated up to the seventh standard, used to visit Rafat's brother to get his auto-rickshaw repaired. He noticed that Rafat, though poor, was of good character. One day he offered to perform *nikah* with her. He was already married but his wife could not have a child as she had had three spontaneous abortions in two years. Also, his wife had quarrelled with him and had gone to stay with her mother. He was active in the Tabligh-i-Jamat. So, thinking that it was a good match, Rafat's marriage was arranged by her elders. In 1985, Rafat remarried.

After her second marriage, Rafat went to stay with her second husband. Like in the first marriage, some dowry was given, and her *mehr* was fixed at Rs. 251. For her present husband, it was a polygamous relationship. After Rafat came to Yakub's house, his first wife Sumayya came back to stay with him. Sumayya had studied up to the seventh standard. Sumayya would rest all day and Rafat, being the second wife, had to work like a slave. Rafat conceived her first child in 1987. Then Sumayya also conceived. Both of them delivered baby girls. There were celebrations in the family because two children had been born in the family. Immediately after delivery, Rafat started working and soon she fell ill. Sumayya went to her mother's home for rest and recover. Rafat's mother also came and took away Rafat for rest and recovery to her house.

Yakub was of a suspicious nature. After the second marriage Yakub's first wife often quarrelled with him for having married the second time. To pacify her, he made gold earrings and bangles for her. Rafat too wanted some jewellery for herself. She had saved some money out of her earnings before her marriage. Using this money, she made earrings for herself. When Yakub saw them, he was furious. Also, once she went to a Sufi saint's tomb with her uncle. Yakub did not like it. Reminding her of these incidences, he harassed her.

After some time Sumayya and Yakub started mistreating Rafat. Yakub started abusing her. He also resorted to wife beating. Meanwhile, Rafat became pregnant for the second time in 1988. There was a marriage in the family. Yakub was well behaved till the marriage got over. Then one day, he beat her on the leg with a hockey-stick. The leg became swollen. Rafat showed this to her mother and brother and went to stay with her parents. Soon after, Sumayya too conceived. Rafat delivered a baby boy at her mother's place while Sumayya delivered a baby girl. Yakub was very happy when he came to know that Rafat had delivered a baby boy. He came to visit her at the hospital, gave her two packets of biscuits and left. After some time he took her to his flat at Yerawada. He bought a new *burqa*-cloth and a gold pendant for her. For some time Rafat was happy. She did not want to have any more children. So she started taking pills on the doctor's advice. When Yakub came to know this, he was furious and so she discontinued.

Rafat became pregnant for the third time. She wanted to abort. When she told Yakub about this, he was furious and threatened to throw her out of his house. In the mean time, Sumayya also came to the flat and started staying with Rafat. Once again the misery started. Yakub would buy only one toy between two children, Rafat's son as well as for Sumayya's daughter. The children would fight. Rafat got fed up of their fighting and broke the toy into two and gave one part to each child. When Yakub saw this, he beat up Rafat and tried to strangulate her. Somehow, she was saved. From Yerawada he brought both the wives to his old house and the flat was given on rent.

Sumayya went for the subsequent delivery to her mother. In her absence the husband was nice to Rafat. When she came back after the delivery it was the holy month of Ramzan. Rafat's second child had fever. For some reason Yakub was angry and poured cold water on the child. Rafat protested. After she had broken the fast, he beat her up on her nose so badly that she urinated. She had to take the help of her sister-in-law to change her clothes. Then he sent her away to her mother's house. Even today a part of her nose is numb.

On small matters, Yakub used to pick up a quarrel with Rafat and beat her up. He also used abusive language. Rafat delivered her third child at her mother's place. For nine months Yakub neither visited her nor saw the child. When relatives informed him he came and took her to his house. Since Rafat had three children, she wanted to undergo sterilization. Yakub prevented her from doing so, saying that it was a sin.

Over the next four years, there was no pregnancy. Life was miserable, as usual. Sometimes the misery seemed to increase as the following incident shows. Her father-in-law would consume liquor and under its influence try to molest his daughters-in-law. One night he secretly tried to enter Rafat's room when Yakub was out of station. Rafat was very upset, but managed to push him away and locked her bedroom. Next day she reported this to her sister-in-law (husband's sister). Rather than sympathizing with her, she advised Rafat to go and stay with her parents. Rafat kept silent and did not report this incident to her husband. Then she became pregnant for the fourth time. She wanted to abort the child as she did not want any more children, but Yakub would not allow her to do so. During the eighth month of her pregnancy, he beat her up with a wooden log on her abdomen, hand and other parts of the body. She had to be hospitalized for four days. Yet she continued staying with him. Before delivering her fourth child, Rafat had fever, cold and abdominal pain. She had to be hospitalized once again. She was not provided food for two days. Yet, Yakub criticized and nagged her. Even the doctor and nurses expressed concern about her ability to deliver the child without having eaten as she had gone weak. She requested them to perform a sterilization after the delivery. She had a normal delivery, but developed complications afterwards. As a result she had to stay in the hospital for two weeks. The doctors did not perform sterilization on her. From the hospital she went to her husband's house.

When the child was five weeks old, Yakub fought with a man and beat him up till he bled. So a criminal complaint was lodged against Yakub with the police. In some land dispute he, along with his brother Ayub, murdered a man and seriously injured another man during the month of Ramzan. As a result, Yakub was imprisoned along with his brother for nine months at the Yerawada Central Jail. When they were released, the other party involved in the land dispute murdered Ayub.

As we have noted, Rafat was not harmed physically for only the first year after her marriage. From the second year onwards, she was regularly beaten up at least once in two months. After the hockey-stick incident in 1988, with the help of her brothers she had complained to the police. This had angered Yakub. So, after the compromise he took her home and in the privacy of the bedroom pronounced *talaq* once and later sent her with the children to her mother's house. Later, when he was in a good mood, he brought back Rafat and the children and started living with her. After this incident of one pronouncement of divorce, which happened after three years of marriage, Yakub totally forgot about it.

Again, when there was severe beating and she started bleeding from the mouth, Rafat went and complained to the police. She was tired of his beatings and did not want to stay with him. So she came away with her children and started staying with her mother in May 1995. The police inspector asked for a medical certificate, which she provided after visiting the government hospital. Around that time Yakub had committed the murder and criminal proceedings were on against him. So he was afraid. He tried to compromise with Rafat at the police station. He agreed to keep Rafat separate and provide maintenance for her along with the children. He gave in writing at the police station that he would construct two rooms for Rafat and her children on land which he owned at Katraj, a distant suburb of Pune, and pay Rs. 3,000 per month towards maintenance. He also agreed to give her a gold necklace and bangles.

Later Yakub was jailed. By this time he had nine children, five from the first wife and four from Rafat. He had also performed *haj* (pilgrimage) twice, the first time with his first wife and the second time alone. But the *haj* did not reform him. Rafat, with her children, went to stay at Katraj. For some time he provided maintenance but he did not give her any jewellery. Perhaps this was the most peaceful period of her married life! She bought a machine and started stitching clothes. For three months he provided maintenance but then he stopped. She waited for three more months. She was doing petty business by selling peppermints, kites, etc, but the income was not enough. In the mean time, he came out of the jail and totally stopped giving her maintenance or even visiting her. So she started staying at her mother's house, which was closer to her children's school. Once she met Yakub at the school and asked for maintenance. He shouted that she was a bad wife who took advantage of the criminal proceedings against him and that he would never take her back.

She approached the Satyasodhak Mandal. The chief of Satyasodhak tried to talk to Yakub to bring about a compromise. Yakub threatened him and asked him to stay out of their affairs. Rafat's relatives approached a *mutawalli* to bring about a compromise. Yakub told the *mutawalli* that he had divorced Rafat. Rafat's relatives also approached a prominent member of the Tabligh-i-Jamat to bring Yakub to sense. This effort too failed. Let us recall that after the hockey-stick incident Yakub had taken Rafat inside a room and in anger pronounced *talaq* once. Then he had sent her with the children to her mother's house. Afterwards Rafat was brought back to his house. He slept with her many times and begot two more children. No *halala* was performed.

Rafat's brother asked Yakub how he could have divorced Rafat when he continued to sleep with her thereafter and beget children. Rafat too asked how divorce could be unilateral when marriage required the consent of both.

Ultimately, Rafat decided to approach the court for justice. Through Satyasodhak, she filed a case against Yakub for maintenance. Rafat's economic condition is very poor. Her mother's family is also poor. Sometimes there is no food in the house. Many times there is no money. She tries to earn some money through tailoring. She has become weak as a result of years of beating by her husband. Her condition is really pathetic. While narrating her story Rafat wept many times. She feels helpless; she thinks that the relatives of the first wife have performed some black magic over Yakub to get rid of Rafat and her children so that the first wife and her children inherit all that Yakub has.

Rafat regularly wears the *burqa.* From the time she attained puberty she has been wearing the *burqa.* After her first marriage she continued this practice. After her first divorce, she worked as a maidservant and so stopped wearing the *burqa.* Since her second marriage she has resumed the practice of wearing a *burqa.* As she is staying with her mother and her brother is struggling for her and her children's survival, people advise her to stop wearing the *burqa*, but she continues to wear it religiously. This, perhaps, gives her emotional security.

ANALYSIS OF THE CASES

The analysis of these two cases of divorced Muslim women reveals many things. The educational level of the respondents and their spouses is not high. Also they hail from a low economic stratum. In case of Rafat both her spouses were from the middle-middle class. In both cases, the parents were supportive though the marital family was uncaring. Neither woman wanted a divorce for economic, social and emotional reasons. In spite of unhappiness, the women wanted to continue their marriages. In both cases divorce was given unilaterally. In Kaleemun's case, the divorce was given by way of a registered letter. However, *mehr* and maintenance during *iddat* was paid. In Rafat's case, her first husband divorced her in the office of an advocate in one sitting. In her second marriage, divorce has become contentious. The husband says he has divorced her and Rafat says that divorce has not taken place because he pronounced *talaq* only once and that too when he was angry and in the privacy of the bedroom. Rafat's co-wife, who is the first wife of her husband, says that Yakub pronounced *talaq* thrice. So we really do not know the marital status of Rafat. In our view, technically speaking, Rafat should not be classified as a divorcee with regard to her second husband. The husband, being a bad character and a criminal, contends that he has divorced her in order to shirk the responsibility of maintaining Rafat and her children. Chapter 65 of the Qur'an entitled 'Al Talaq' clearly sets out the circumstances under which divorce may be granted. Abdullah Yusuf Ali's 1989 translation of the Qur'an also implores to 'keep the tie of marriage sacred, but when it must be dissolved, use all precautions to ensure justice to the weaker party, protect the interests of the unborn or newborn lives, as well of social decency and close not the door to reconciliation'. Obviously, in the above cases, the Qur'anic spirit has been blatantly violated both by the husbands and their relatives.

After the divorce both women were devastated economically as well as emotionally. For their and their children's survival, they had to depend on their parents and other siblings. It is felt that if strong institutional support in the form of women's organizations or community organizations were available, perhaps the divorces could have been prevented or at least the bargaining power of the women in the process of divorce or after the divorce could have been increased. Now they have no bargaining power. On the other hand, if the women were educated and economically independent, perhaps they themselves would have divorced these men because any way they were not good husbands. They failed to provide love, understanding and faithfulness, basic values for growth and sustenance of marital relationship.

Coincidentally, and unfortunately, in both cases the 'other woman' was instrumental in ruining the marriage of the respondents. In the case of Kaleemun, had the husband married his girlfriend, or at least did not keep relations with her after marriage, Kaleemun's marriage would have been a normal and happy one. In the case of Rafat's first husband, were he not in an illicit relationship with his sister-in-law, perhaps he would not have left Rafat. Also, with regard to Yakub, the second husband of Rafat, if the first wife were not around, Rafat's misery could have been reduced considerably. In view of the above, it is felt that polygamous unions are against the interests of women and therefore measures should be taken to prevent or at least discourage such unions.

Both Kaleemun and Rafat approached institutions of justice, i.e. the police and the courts as a last resort, that too with the support of their parental family. There must be so many cases of divorced and harassed women who do not resort to legal action because of lack of parental support.

Discussions were also held with the advocate whom both Kaleemun and Rafat approached, through the Satyasodhak, to represent their cases in court. He takes on quite a few cases of marriage, divorce and maintenance of Muslim women. He observed that he files cases of Muslim divorced women for maintenance mostly under Section 125 of the CrPC because when cases are filed under Muslim Women (Protection of Rights on Divorce) Act, 1986, judges become suspicious and judgements are affected. Further, advocates do not usually like to accept cases of Muslim women regarding divorce and maintenance because of prejudice against Muslims. I suspect that only about 2 per cent of all such cases are fought under the Muslim Women (Protection of Rights on Divorce) Act, 1986.

It also seems that family planning would be in the interest of women because in case of a failed marriage, the woman is usually burdened with the responsibility of bringing up the children. Therefore, if the number of children is less her responsibility, too, is reduced.

CONCLUSION

In this paper an attempt has been made to fill the gap in empirical data on divorce among Muslims in India by undertaking case studies of two divorced Muslim women from Pune city. An analysis of these cases reveals that both were unilaterally divorced. The divorce devastated them economically and emotionally. With help and support from the parental family, both resorted to legal action to claim maintenance to ensure their and their children's survival. They find the legal battle lengthy and hard. They have also tried to be economically independent, but their lack of education and skills prevented them from attaining economic independence. Also, divorce further reduces the already low status of women in society. The Muslim Women (Protection of Rights on Divorce) Act, 1986, does not help Muslim women much. Social organizations like the Satyasodhak are more useful in helping these helpless women.

The following recommendations are made for the upliftment of divorced Muslim women. First of all, education and skills necessary for gainful employment need to be imparted and promoted among Muslim girls on a war footing. Also, economic opportunities for regular employment and income need to be provided to Muslim women. Besides these, community organizations, especially of Muslim women, have to be established and promoted to rehabilitate divorced Muslim women both economically and emotionally. Also, setting up of legal aid centres is necessary to fight the legal battles of these helpless women to get justice. Most important, unilateral and oral divorce has to be banned totally. Polygamy among Muslims also needs to be discouraged. This, too, requires legal reforms. Family planning must also be promoted among Muslim women to reduce their burden. To put the above recommendations in practice, Muslim women need the help of women as well as men both from within and outside their community. It is a long journey requiring patience and perseverance but at the end of the journey success is assured.

10

Male Privilege, Female Anguish: Divorce and Remarriage among Muslims in Bihar

Sabiha Hussain

This paper has a twofold aim. First, it seeks to analyse divorce on the basis of case studies of Muslim women from Darbhanga town in north Bihar. The central thrust of this analysis is to show how progressive Qur'anic injunctions are interpreted by the various schools of Islamic law and theology to suit the patriarchal norms of society and act as detriments to women's rights in marriage and divorce. There is thus a wide gap between theory and practice, between law and facts. It also tries to show how the event of divorce changes the whole life of a woman for her status is influenced more by socio-cultural and economic factors than religion. Evidently, the social stigma and economic hardship a woman has to live with after she is divorced or initiates divorce has not been taken into consideration by the interpreters of Muslim law. Second, the paper seeks to examine the working of an institution whose services are availed by Muslims in matters relating to marriage and divorce. This discussion is intended to show that divorce among Muslims in Bihar is not an entirely ad hoc process but operates mostly through institutional mechanisms.

THE QUR'AN AND DIVORCE

Talaq is an Arbic word which means 'undoing of or release from a knot'. It comes from the root '*tallaqa*' which means to release (an animal) from tether. Muslim jurists used this word to denote the release of a woman from the marriage tie. From a legal point of view it signifies the absolute power a husband possess of divorcing his wife at all times, for 'the matrimonial law of Mohammedans, like that of every ancient community, favours the strongest sex' (Ali and Ahmad, 1983: 19).

Talaq or divorce is strongly condemned in Islam but is permitted to avoid evils. The Qur'an states: 'with Allah the most detestable of all the things permitted is divorce' (13: 3). The Qur'an in verse 4: 19 further explicitly discourages divorce by saying: 'on the contrary live with them on a footing of kindness and equity. If ye take a dislike to them it may be that ye dislike a thing, and god brings about through it a great deal of good.' Before the advent of Islam, the husband had absolute power to divorce his wife at the slightest provocation. Islam did not only forbid this absolute right of divorce but also put limitations on its unfettered use. Not only this. Islam granted an equal right to women to divorce, which in turn raised their status. The Qur'an in verse 2: 228 explains the position of women by saying: 'And women shall have rights similar to those against them, according to what is equitable.'

Islam forbids the use of the right to divorce without the intervention of *hukkam* (arbitrators). The provision for reconciliation and for witnesses to oversee the divorce process has been clearly spelt out in the Qur'an. The Qur'anic verse 4: 35 suggests how reconciliation should be used between the parties to avoid final separation: 'If ye fear a breach between them twain, appoint two arbiters, one from his family, and the other from hers; if they wish for peace, God will cause their reconciliation'. Commenting on it Ahmad writes: 'If all hopes of reconciliation fail, a divorce is allowed but the final decision rests with the judge who is legally entitled to such judgement' (Ahmad, 1994: 152).

Likewise, verse 65: 2 indicates that witnesses be brought to oversee the divorce: 'And take for witnesses persons among you imbued with justice and establish the evidence as before God.' It is true that the grounds for divorce have not been specifically mentioned in the Qur'an. This is because reasons would vary in each individual case. As far as pronouncement of *talaq* is concerned, the Qur'an says in verse 2: 229: 'A divorce is only permissible twice. After that the parties should either hold together on equitable terms or separate with kindness.'

Thus, in the matter of divorce no distinction is made on the basis of sex. Both the sexes are placed on an equal footing. The term '*shiqaq*' or breach between husband and wife indicates that both the husband and the wife can break the marriage agreement. '*Talaq*', '*khula*', '*mubarat*' and '*fask*' are the various terms used in the Qur'an for the process of divorce. In all these processes each partner is required to appoint a *hakim* (arbitrator).

Talaq can take three forms: Ahsan, Hasan and Biddah. The first two forms of *talaq* are called *talaq-e-sunna* because repudiation can take place neither at a single sitting nor during menstruation. The role of arbitrators is very significant in this form of *talaq*. The third form of *talaq* is called *talaq-e-bidat* because under this form divorce takes place after the pronouncement of *talaq* three times in one sitting, which is disapproved of by the Qur'an. Some schools of Islamic law do not permit this form of *talaq*. For instance, Shia and Ahl-e-Hadis schools consider this form of *talaq* illegal. However, the Hanafi school, to which a large majority of Muslims in India subscribe, regards this form of *talaq* to be perfectly legal. The justification for allowing this form of *talaq* is drawn from certain traditions of the Prophet (Hadith) many of which are either self-contradictory or weak, and therefore are not considered authentic. I shall quote a few of them and on their basis argue that a conclusive argument for the validity of divorce by pronouncing *talaq* three times in a single sitting cannot be made.

The tradition often used to justify the legal validity of the pronouncement of *talaq* three times in one sitting relates to Uwaimir Ajlanee in which the reference to *liaan* (mutual imprecation) is made. It states that when both husband and wife had undergone the procedure of *liaan* (swearing), Uwaimir said: 'If I still keep her with me then I shall prove to be a liar and again he uttered divorce thrice before the Prophet had ordered it' (Ali and Ahmad, 1983: 50). Those supporting *talaq-e-bidat* (hereafter triple *talaq*) very often cite this hadith (tradition) to argue that, when Uwaimir pronounced *talaq* three times in the presence of the Prophet and the Prophet did not forbid him, his approval of Uwaimir's action is clear. What is overlooked in this case is the 'context', which is that after *liaan* parting is a must and no question of reunion can arise. Thus, Uwaimir's pronouncement was merely a confirmation of *liaan*. This could have been the reason for the Prophet not forbidding his action.

Contrary to the authority attributed to this and similar traditions, there are certain verses of the Qur'an which seem to call into question the legality of triple divorce. For example, verse 2: 229-30 reads:

> Divorce must be pronounced twice and then a (woman) may be retained in honour or released in kindness. And it is not lawful for you that ye take from women out of that which ye have given them except (in the case) when both fear that they may not be able to keep within the limits (imposed by) Allah. And if ye fear that they may not be able to keep the limits of Allah, in that case it is not sin for either of them if the woman ransom herself. These are the limits (imposed by) Allah. Transgress them not. For whosoever transgresseth Allah's limits, such are wrong doers. And if he hath divorced her (the third time) then she is not lawful unto him thereafter until she hath wedded another husband.

In this verse the word '*marrataan*' has been used. It means 'two times' which would suggest that *talaq* has to be pronounced on two separate occasions rather than that the word '*talaq*' merely be repeated three times on one single occasion. Arabic dictionaries render the word '*marrataan*' as 'one after another' and not merely as 'thrice'. This is confirmed by the interpretation made of the Qur'anic reference to the order of throwing of the seven pieces of stone at the time of *haj*. The majority of the ulema hold that if a person throws all seven pieces together this would not be in compliance with the command (Ali and Ahmad, 1983: 45). Maulana Sheikh Mohamad Thaanvi writes: 'The Qur'anic verse "Al Talaq Marrataan" means that one divorce should be followed by the other (second divorce)'. Therefore, the valid divorce is that which is pronounced at different intervals in different *thurs* (menstrual cycle) and not at a time in a single sitting' (quoted in Ali and Ahmad, 1983: 59).

It is clear that the entire question of the validity of triple divorce revolves around the interpretation of the word '*thalath marraat*' by the jurists of the different schools of law. Some interpret it to mean mere repetition of the word *talaq* thrice in one sitting and thus, regard triple divorce as a valid form of *talaq*. Others interpret it to mean that the word *talaq* should actually be pronounced three times on three different occasions. As Tyabji argues, 'by the deplorable development of Hanafi law the sinful or abominable forms of *talaq* (*talaq-e-bidat*) have become the most common for men always have moulded the law of marriage so as to be most agreeable to themselves' (1968: 163). Abdur Rahim also writes, 'I may remark that interpretation of the law of divorce by jurists, specially of the Hanafi school, is one flagrant instance where because of literal adherence to mere words and a certain tendency towards subtleties they have reached a result in direct antagonism to the admitted policy of the law on the subject' (quoted in Ali and Ahmad, 1983: 31). Therefore, in spite of Qur'anic injunctions which are relatively more favourable and just towards women, husbands got the power of unilateral divorce without having to follow the prescribed procedure of conciliation, witnesses and the appointment of arbitrators. This shows the patriarchal orientation of Muslim law.

EVIDENCE FROM FIELD SURVEY

Let us turn now to the evidence from Darbhanga town of north Bihar to understand how this patriarchal orientation of Muslim law translates itself in the lives of women. This evidence consists of the responses of a sample of 250 educated Muslim housewives, college-goers, wage-earners and women professionals whom we interviewed to ascertain Muslim women's changing attitudes towards education, employment, marriage, divorce, dowry, widow remarriage as well as their level of awareness about their constitutional and legal rights under Islam (see Hussain, 1998). We also made case studies of divorced women. First I present the responses to show the prevalent marriage and divorce practices that prevail in society today and women's responses towards them. Then I present the case studies to indicate the reality of women's post-divorce lives.

There is a clear-cut division between the Ashraf and the non-Ashraf in Bihar and hardly any marriage alliance takes place between the two, except in cases of love marriages. Few cases of love marriages or inter-religious marriages were found. The marriage proposal (*paigham*) is generally sent by the bride's family. Once the bridegroom's side has accepted it, a number of rituals are performed before the *nikah*. These are more influenced by local culture. The bride's consent to the marriage is not sought. She is not expected to express a liking or dislike for her prospective husband. She remains a silent spectator to the whole episode of marriage. Even at the time of the *nikah*, the elderly ladies surrounding the bride make her nod her head and proclaim that the bride has accepted her *nikah*. The qazi does not even bother to listen to her voice and goes away. Unmarried girls are not allowed to be present when the qazi comes to take the bride's consent. A *chaddar* (bed sheet) is used as curtain (*purdah*) and the qazi stands on the other side of the *chaddar*. An overwhelming majority of women (98 per cent) whom we interviewed had been married in this traditional way. What is significant is that they also approved of this traditional practice. They said that it was the duty of parents to arrange the marriage of their daughters and daughters have inevitably to agree to what their parents decide.

The amount of *mehr* (dower) has to be settled before the marriage ceremony can take place. Usually, it is settled between the families well in advance to avoid any last minute hassles at the time of the performance of the *nikah*. *Mehr* is indispensable because without it being stipulated a Muslim marriage is neither legally nor socially recognized. The amount settled usually depends on the social and economic status of the families, but this is not always true. There are instances where well-off families have fixed what is called *fatami* or *shar'ai mehr*, which is the equivalent of 1.25 *surkh dinar*, which the Prophet had fixed for his daughter Fatima. Similarly, there are instances of very poor husbands fixing a higher amount as *mehr*. In 98 per cent cases the *mehr* is settled in terms of cash. Under Muslim law, the *mehr* should be paid to the wife at the time of the *nikah* or within a stipulated time thereafter. More than two-thirds of the women (71.2 per cent) we interviewed felt that the *mehr* should be paid at the time of marriage or within a stipulated period because it is a right guaranteed to them by Islam. However, 28.8 per cent women thought that if a wife gets the *mehr* at the time of marriage or within a stipulated period, there will be no binding on the husband and he would be free to divorce his wife. Hardly anyone pays the *mehr* at the time of marriage and no time is stipulated for its payment when the marriage is solemnized.[1] Nearly

42 per cent women interviewed did not know the amount of their *mehr*. As many as 89 per cent were not in favour of demanding their *mehr* because they perceived it to be a security against divorce. Older women had condoned their *mehr*. Only 5 per cent women had received their *mehr* in the form of land, house or jewellery.

Very few women were familiar with the Islamic rules of divorce. Only 38 per cent women were aware of the Qur'anic provision of *talaq-e-sunna* and considered it to be the most desirable form of divorce as it allowed for the possibility of reconciliation. They also held that the pronouncement of divorce should not take place in a state of anger and the wife should be allowed to stay on in her husband's house during *iddat* (seclusion). Others had no clear idea of the intricacies of Muslim divorce law. However, the level of their awareness with respect to the *khula* form of divorce was better. As many as 57 per cent women knew that under Islamic rules of divorce a woman enjoyed the right to divorce and how this right could be given effect. They were aware that women could exercise this right by persuading their husband to agree to a divorce upon surrendering their right to the *mehr*. If this procedure failed, a woman could approach an authorized qazi or a *shar'iat* court for the dissolution of her marriage. One point made by women interviewed was that neither the right of *talaq* granted to Muslim men nor the right of *khula* available to Muslim women ensured the economic, social and personal security of women. Because of men's right to pronounce divorce at will, women have to live with a sword hanging constantly over their heads. On the other hand, they are deprived of *mehr* if they themselves initiate divorce proceedings.

The common form of divorce prevalent among the Muslims of Bihar irrespective of differences in education, caste (the Ashraf—non-Ashraf distinction), social class and rural-urban background is *talaq-e-bidat*, whereby a divorce becomes irrevocable if the husband pronounces divorce three times in one sitting. Of course, the women interviewed did not feel comfortable with this system of divorce and would like it to be changed. Nearly 70 per cent women were in favour of changing this system. The remaining 30 per cent held that the system was unfair to women but it could not be changed, as it was a privilege granted to men under Muslim Personal Law. Muslim Personal Law was in their perception the revealed Islamic Law that could not be altered. The majority of those favouring a change in this system of divorce maintained that it lowered the status of a Muslim woman. They said that even when a husband divorces his wife without any fault she is always blamed and looked down upon. She has to undergo a long phase of psychological trauma and destitution. Moreover, the privilege given to men to divorce their wives makes women feel insecure and hurts their self-respect and dignity.

Most divorces in the sample studied took place within two to six years of marriage after the couple had had one or two children.[2] Usually, women reconciled themselves to the divorce quietly as they mostly belonged to educated, middle class Ashraf families for fear of social stigma and loss of family prestige. The case studies show how and in what circumstances they were divorced. A man can divorce his wife in the name of religion if she is unable to produce a male child, is not cooperating with her in-laws, resiles from sex against her husband's desire, takes up a job to avoid economic hardships, refuses money to her husband for liquor or is not educated up to the mark of her husband's status. Neither the drunken state of the husband nor the woman's physical state can invalidate a divorce and qazis, too, will support it. I once pointed out to a member of the Muslim Personal Law Board that if a man divorces his wife in a state of anger or when he is not in a sound state of mind it ought not be considered a valid divorce in terms of Islamic injunctions. His pat reply was: 'Whether a man pronounces a divorce in anger, in old age or in the middle of the night, the divorce has taken place.' The Qur'an does not discriminate against women, but the law as practised favours men.

CASE STUDIES

Let us now detail some of the case studies of divorced women in the sample studied to show how and in what circumstances husbands pronounce *talaq*. In one case both the husband and the wife worked as labourers. The husband asked his wife to give him money for liquor. When she refused him money the husband pronounced *talaq*. In another case a man ran a teashop. His wife made snacks and brought them to the shop. One day the wife had fever and could not bring the snacks. Her husband divorced her in sheer anger. Afterwards, when the wife went to the qazi and recounted the circumstances he declared that the divorce was irrevocable.

In a third case a man divorced his wife after he had used the money his wife's family provided to go to the Gulf. He came from an Ashraf family and was working as an executive with a reputed multinational pharmaceutical company. He wanted to go to the Middle East to earn money, could not afford to do so because of his poor economic condition and his responsibilities towards his unmarried sister. Believing that the boy had a good background and since he was working with a reputed company, a business family made proposal of marriage for their daughter who was a graduate. He readily accepted it and the marriage was solemnized. The girl's family gave a huge dowry and much cash in marriage. Within a year of marriage he went to Dubai with the financial support of his in-laws. Soon after a daughter was born. He then pronounced *talaq* on telephone without giving any reason to his wife. The wife's father approached the local qazi and asked for his opinion. The qazi said, 'Yes, the divorce is final.' He also consulted the qazi of the Jama Masjid and he, too, gave the same opinion.

The wife neither received the *mehr*, nor the dowry. When her father approached the husband's family for the return of dowry, he learnt that it had been given away in the marriage of their daughter. The wife lived with her parents along with her six month old daughter. On a subsequent visit I found her still living with her parents along with her daughter, who is now four years old. She got her *mehr* back after one year, but was not given maintenance for the *iddat* period. She wanted to give the daughter to her father. He refused to take the daughter, but promised to give maintenance for the child. She refused it. After the divorce, she got a B.Ed. degree and is now working as a school teacher in a private school to keep herself busy and become economically independent. I asked her parents if they had contemplated marrying her again. Their reply was, 'Our family's honour has been compromised. Who will marry her now?' When I put the same question to the girl (she was then 27 years old), she said: 'Unmarried girls find it difficult to get married in our society. After the stamp of a divorce having been put on me, who will be willing to marry me? Will you get me married? Are there any organizations or ulema to stop this kind of divorces or get divorced women remarried?' I was dumbfounded.

There were two cases in which women were divorced because the wife was less educated than the husband. The first is of a not too well educated non-Ashraf girl from an economically well-off family. She was married at the age of seventeen to a boy who was a lecturer at a leading Muslim university in north India. Because of the relatively conservative orientation of her family, which insisted on her observing the purdah and did not allow her to pursue higher studies, she gave up studying after the middle school. However, the marriage took place because the boy was given a large dowry. After marriage, the husband did not take her with him. He left her behind with his parents on the plea that he would be returning during the vacations. Soon, a daughter was born to them and the wife expressed the desire to join her husband and live with him. At first the husband kept on postponing taking a decision on one pretext or another. When the wife insisted on accompanying him he became furious and asked her not to raise the matter again. Finally, when the wife reiterated her demand to go with him, he divorced her. She was shocked and started crying. Her in-laws came and, instead of dissuading the husband from such precipitate action, they supported him. They said, 'You misbehaved with your husband. This is why he has divorced you.' She kept pleading with her husband to take back his words, but to no avail. She was left with no option except to go to her parents. Her fault was that she wanted to live with her husband. When she was divorced, she was only twenty-two and her daughter was three years old.

The woman did not get back any of her dowry, including jewellery. It was later given to the former husband's new wife, a girl doing graduation at the university where he worked. The woman's father took the matter to the *biradari* panchayat in an attempt to get back the dowry but in vain. She was paid *mehr* four years after the divorce, that too after a great deal of pressure from the *biradari*. She received no maintenance for the *iddat* period. Maintenance for the daughter was paid for one year. Her husband was not ready to take the custody of the daughter as he got married after one year. She is now enrolled for Ph.D. and is also working as school teacher. Her father built a house for her before his death, which is her only source of security. Her brothers do not take much interest in her. She had entertained the idea of remarriage after the divorce, but could not find a suitable match. She remarked ruefully during the interview, 'Who marries a divorcee in our society?'

Another Ashraf woman was married at the age of eighteen. A large dowry was given to her considering that the boy was a lecturer at yet another leading Muslim university. Like the non-Ashraf woman, her husband refused to bring her to live with him. His excuse was that his job was temporary. After a daughter was born, he was informed, but did not go to see his wife and daughter. After much persuasion by the wife's family, he visited them briefly. When his wife asked him to take her and the daughter with him to Delhi, he curtly told her 'I do not wish to lose my respect by keeping you with me. You are hardly educated. What do you know about the lifestyle of a big city'.

The wife conveyed what he had told her to her parents. On a subsequent visit, when they insisted that he take their daughter with him, he brought the wife back to his parental home. When she told him later that day that if he refused to take her with him she would go to Delhi with her father, he became furious and divorced her. She was shocked and went crying to her mother-in-law, who was very sympathetic to the girl, but could do nothing. She came back to her parents. At first, they could not believe what she told them. Later, when they went to meet the boy they learnt that he had gone to another village to meet his relatives without informing his family members. Since the girl's family were landlords and enjoyed a great deal of prestige in the area, they had to passively accept the divorce. They neither asked their son-in-law to return the dowry nor the motorcycle they had given him on his insistence. The husband also did not offer to return the dowry or the motorcycle. He settled the *mehr* of Rs. 21,000 after two years, that too in instalments. Neither maintenance for the divorced wife for the *iddat* period nor for the daughter was paid. The wife remains confined to the house. She neither goes out to meet her relatives or friends nor likes to meet visitors. When I interviewed her, she pathetically said, 'I wonder what will become of me. Who will marry me?' Her parents are opposed to the idea of her remarrying. They said, 'Remarriage is not a practice in our family. It is against our prestige and honour.' They are willing to support their daughter and her child. Her former husband has married a Ph.D. scholar whom he had known for a few years.

There was one case in which the wife took *khula* after eighteen years of marriage. Both she and her husband were highly educated and were in the teaching profession. They had two children. The reason for asking for *khula*, as stated by the wife, was her husband's licentious nature. Sensing that this might not have a positive influence over the children, she sent them out of Bihar for studies. This infuriated him. He started misbehaving, abusing and beating her every now and then. Unable to bear such treatment, she complained to her in-laws. Instead of showing sympathy, they sided with their son. She then initiated *khula* proceedings, but many elderly people, including her colleagues and neighbours intervened, assuring her that her husband would not mistreat her in future and prevailed upon her to change her mind. Things worked well for a few months, but soon her husband started misbehaving with her again. She asked her husband to divorce her which he refused because he did not want to pay the heavy amount of *mehr* nor was he willing to take the blame for the divorce on himself. Since he kept torturing her, finally, despite a great deal of opposition, she obtained *khula* from the Imarat-e-Shar'ia at Bihar Sharif. *Khula* was granted on condition that no maintenance for her or her children would be given and she would also not be entitled to *mehr*. Her husband remarried a non-Muslim. She now lives on her own and suffers from depression and acute health problems. Most of her relatives and friends (mostly males) put the blame on her: 'She was mad to ask for divorce at this age. Highly educated women sometimes go out of their mind.' She does not, however, regret her decision.

Yet another case of *khula* relates to a woman from an educated middle class Ashraf family. The reason for *khula* as given by the wife was that she was badly treated by her husband who expected more dowry. She refused to go back to her husband's house after her initial visit after the marriage. Pressed by her parents, she confided that her husband wanted Rs. 50,000 by way of dowry and that he had told her that if she returned without the money she would be tortured and humiliated. Her parents went to see him and he reiterated the same demand to them. Since they were not in a position to pay that much money, they decided that the girl take *khula*. The husband readily agreed to *khula* on condition that the wife condoned the *mehr* which had been fixed at Rs. 51,000. Thus, she was divorced within three months of her marriage. She is a graduate and a trained teacher. She has since been looking for a job. Her parents also want her to secure a job in a school. If she had the inclination, they would find a suitable match for her. She is reluctant to marry and wants to become economically secure. About marriage her terse comment was, 'It was a frightful dream that has ended'.

Then there is the case of my school teacher. While at school, I had heard other teachers saying that she was not a good woman and that that was the reason her husband had divorced her. When I reached class IX she became our class teacher and I was made the monitor of the class. In this way I came close to her and one day I invited her to my house. She became friendly with my mother. When I was in college she would visit me and encourage me. I would often wonder why people did not like her. She was the only Muslim lady teacher in school and lived with her two sons.

When I undertook the survey of educated Muslim women of Darbhanga town, I selected her as a subject. When I asked her to narrate her story, she said:

> I belong to an educated Syed family. We were two sisters and my father was in the railways. We are originally from Patna. I was the eldest and I got married at the age of seventeen to a graduate boy who was a clerk in the Railways. I had just finished higher secondary. My husband's home was in the village, so I went to live there with my in-laws. Since I was educated, they would taunt me, saying I could do no housework since I was an educated woman, though I did all kinds of work from dusting, washing clothes and utensils to cooking. They were not happy with me. My husband used to come once in a week and never gave me a penny. I used to get two sarees in a year. My husband asked me to give all my jewellery to his mother for safekeeping. I had three children in three years. I was the last one to eat and had to be satisfied with leftovers. I could not breastfeed my children as I did not get adequate

food to eat. I was not allowed to go to my parents or meet them except when my husband was present. I was not supposed to meet the neighbours or any visitors. I would be locked inside the house whenever my in-laws went out. I decided to send a letter to my parents and promised to pay a woman fifty rupees if she would post the letter for me. Unfortunately, my mother-in-law caught me handing over the letter to her. When my husband came back, he started beating me. I was helpless. One day a friend of my father-in-law saw me. He was a school teacher. He was quite impressed with me and suggested that I should continue my education privately. He promised to help me. My husband agreed with him, but as soon as he left my husband started abusing and pulling my hair. 'You want to work. I will make you work just now', he shouted and tore off my school certificate. This was the turning point for me.

I took my children with me and came back to my parents. Seeing the situation in which I was placed, I was encouraged to continue my education. I did a course in teacher training and got a job in a government school. During this period my husband never came to see his children nor gave any money for their maintenance. My daughter died at the age of three. He came for the last prayer (*janaza*), but left immediately after. One day he came and asked me to leave the job and go back to the village. When I refused, he pronounced *talaq* and forcibly took away the younger son who was then five years old. For a whole year he did not allow my younger son to return nor did he give any maintenance for the eldest son. He did not give maintenance for the *iddat* period, but paid the *mehr* which was just Rs. 551. When my father approached the village panchayat for return of dowry, mainly jewellery, my in-laws blamed me of stealing everything. My husband remarried within one year of the divorce. After his remarriage, my youngest son escaped and returned to me. My husband filed an FIR charging me with having kidnapped my son. Since he was a minor, the matter went to court and I got the custody of the children. He never gave any maintenance for the children, so I went to court. That became a hot topic for the town. People started criticising me and I was declared a 'bad woman'. I gave tuitions because my salary was not adequate for us. My mother wanted me to remarry, but the social stigma of being a divorcee is a real obstacle, more so if there are children.

She concluded: 'All laws relating to women remain confined to law books. Our society is a creation of men. So also are the laws. We must take the blame for everything and be sacrificed. If a woman fights for her rights, she is socially boycotted. People do not treat her with respect. She is socially ostracized.'

There were two cases of *fask* of women from Ashraf families. The reason in the first case was humbuggery on the part of the husband, which created problems of adjustment for the wife. The reason in the second case was the impotency of the husband. Both charges were difficult to prove. The husband in the latter case refused to accept the allegation and put the blame instead on the wife. When she managed to get the medical report of her husband, she was physically tortured. She applied to the Imarat-e-Shar'ia for *fask*. Both women complained that the way the qazis at the Imarat-e-Shar'ia conducted the proceedings created feelings of fear and anger. First, the qazi took the husband and wife into a separate room and insisted that the wife take back the case. This was sometimes done in very harsh and commanding tones. If she hesitated or showed nervousness, they maintained that the claim had not been proved and postponed the proceedings. Again, the same process was repeated. If she succeeded in proving her case, *fask* would be granted. Otherwise, she is asked to go back to her husband. A woman who has been granted *fask* is entitled to receive *mehr* and maintenance. She can also condone both.

THE IMARAT-E-SHAR'IA

The concept of Imarat-e-Shar'ia was given by the great religious thinker late Hazrat Maulana Abul Mahasin Mohammad Sajjad. The Imarat-e-Shar'ia was established in 1921 at a meeting presided over by Maulana Abul Kalam Azad at Mohalla Patthar ki Masjid, Patna. Maulana Syed Shah Badruddin Qadri, *sajjada nasheen* of Khanqah Majibia at Phulwari Sharif was its first head (*amir-e-shar'ia*) and Maulana Abul Mahsin Mohammed Sajjad was its vice chief (*naib amir-e-shar'ia*). The aims and objectives of the Imarat-e-Shar'ia were to:

(1) ensure application of Islamic laws, as far as possible, particularly laws relating to marriage, divorce, inheritance, *khula*, trusts, etc., in their original Islamic juridical form.

(2) establish the Islamic system of life on the lines laid down by the Prophet so that Muslims may live within the framework of Islamic laws.

(3) safeguard and to look after Muslim interests and rights.

(4) unite all Muslims strictly on the basis of the *kalima*, even if they adhered to different schools of law.

Some of the services rendered by the Imarat-e-Shar'ia are:

(1) Preaching and propagation of Islam.
(2) Religious Education.
(3) Publication of religious literature.
(4) Humanitarian services to Muslims.
(5) Establishment of institutions for modern education for Muslims.
(6) Rendering of *ifta* (religious legal opinion).
(7) Provision for the settlement of legal disputes according to the *shar'ia* through the Darul Qaza (Islamic court of judicature).

There are 33 branches of the Darul Qaza all over Bihar, West Bengal and Orissa of which 28 operate in Bihar. The services rendered by the Darul Qaza include:

(1) Settling claims for separation on the ground of non-payment of maintenance and other violations of women's rights.
(2) Settling claims for separation on the ground of disappearance of the husband (whose whereabouts are not known).
(3) Settling claims for separation on the ground of cruelty by the husband.
(4) Settling claims for separation on the ground of impotency of the husband.
(5) Settling claims for separation on the ground of leprosy, leucoderma and other infectious diseases.
(6) Settling claims for separation on the ground of insanity of husband or wife.
(7) Settling claims for separation on the ground of husband's minority.
(8) Settling claims for separation on *khair-e-blugh* (puberty).
(9) Settlement of claims for separation on the ground of *hurmat-e-mosaherat*.

(10) Settling claims for separation on the ground of non-compliance of the order of Darul Qaza for the maintenance of the wife.
(11) Settling claims for separation on the ground of *hurmat-e-razaat* (prohibited conjugal relations).
(12) Settling claims for *khula* (demand of divorce on compensation).
(13) Confirmation of divorce.
(14) Settling claims for restoration of conjugal rights.
(15) Settling claims for *haqq-e-hazanat* (the right of the mother to rear her children).
(16) Confirmation of the validity of a *nikah* and certificates of marriage.
(17) Settling claims for *mehr*, alimony and maintenance.
(18) Settling claims for the return of articles given in *jahez* (dowry).
(19) Settling disputes relating to the protection of the interests of minors.
(20) Issuing certificates of legitimacy.
(21) Settling partition suits.
(22) Settling title suits.
(23) Authorization of *nikah*.
(24) Recording the authorization of *talaq-e-tafawiz* (divorce to a wife by mutual consent).

The Imarat-e-Shar'ia generates resources to cater to its clients through three means:

(1) *Qaumi mahsool* (community contribution) realized by asking every adult Muslim who makes use of its services to contribute Rs. 5 per month to the Imarat-e-Shar'ia as a regular donor member.
(2) Voluntary donations from individuals and organizations from within the country as well as from abroad.
(3) Funds collected as *zakat* (poor tax), *ushr* and other charities imposed on Muslims under Islam (*bait-ul-mal*).

The annual budget of the Imarat-e-Shar'ia is estimated to be around Rs. 3 crores. It is used for providing the various services listed above as well as for rendering help to the destitute and needy.

Every year more than 300 widows are provided with money (approximately Rs. 60,000). Poor children studying in madrasas as well as in institutions of higher learning, such as medical and engineering colleges and universities are paid scholarships and approximately Rs. 1,000 to 2,000 each is paid for the marriage of poor girls.

The naib nazim of the Imarat-e-Shar'ia, Mufti Naseem A. Qasmi, claims that approximately 70,000 judgements (35,000 by the headquarters and another 35,000 by the different branches) were delivered by the Darul Qaza between 1921 and 1999 in matrimonial matters. The Darul Qaza charges Rs. 150 for each application made to it and the judgement is usually given in three to four months. This is far less than what is usually required to be spent if a person goes to court. This may be one of the reasons why Muslims approach the Imarat-e-Shar'ia for settlement of matrimonial disputes. However, not all Muslims approach it for settling divorce or other matters. This would still leave out a large number of cases where divorce is given informally or though the intervention of family or community members without the involvement of any outside agency.

Official statistics available with the Imarat-e-Shar'ia at Phulwari Sharif, Patna, with respect to the nature of cases settled year-wise between 1994 and 1999 are set out in Table 1. These statistics

Year	*Fask-e-nikah*	*Khula*	Demand of *rukhsati*	Demand for non-payment of maintenance and women's rights	Demand of *mehr/ jahez*	Marriage certificates issued
1993-4	239	8	69	25	4	145
1994-5	203	8	39	11	4	132
1995-6	294	7	55	23	6	147
1996-7	182	8	57	9	4	198
Total	1,004	33	248	73	21	717

Source: Imarat-e-Shar'ia, Phulwari Sharif, Patna, Bihar.

reveal that 432 men in 1994-5, 485 in 1995-6, 572 in 1996-7, 572 in 1997-8 and about 206 in 1999 sought *fatwa* (judicial ruling). Naib Nazim Naseem Ahmad, Imarat-e-Shar'ia, Phulwari Sharif, claimed that almost 60 per cent people who came to seek a *fatwa* wanted to take back the wife they had divorced. The most common reason for the divorce was anger or an argument. He also pointed out that other reasons like differences between the mother-in-law and daughter-in-law, negligence of duties towards each other, preferential marriage, expectation of more dowry, mistrust, high expectations about the beauty and education of the girl are equally important reasons for divorce.

One of the oldest branches of the Imarat-e-Shar'ia is located at Madrasa Jame-ul-Uloom, Muzaffarpur. The regions covered by this branch include Muzaffarpur, Sitamarhi and Vaishali districts. Qazi Mohammad Yakoob of Jame-ul-Uloom, Muzaffarpur, also agreed that in cases of divorce almost 70 per cent men come seeking a *fatwa* about how they can take back their wife and almost 90 per cent agree to *halala* to be able to take back their wives. Most of the cases brought before the Muzaffarpur Darul Qaza relate to couples between the ages of 20 and 30 years who have been married for 2-8 years. Cases of instant divorce are very few. As to the socio-economic background of those who came to the Imarat-e-Shar'ia, he observed that mostly couples from the lower and lower middle classes, who were either illiterate or semi-literate came to the Imarat-e-Shar'ia with their problems. Literate people from the upper classes preferred to settle their divorce matters themselves for fear of loss of social prestige. Consequently, very few cases were from literate Ashraf families. Further, since a good number of Ashrafs of the area are of the Barelvi persuasion, they settled their divorce cases through the community panchayat rather than approach the Darul Qaza. He pointed out that an interesting phenomenon these days was that women had started using the Prohibition of Dowry Act to recover their dowry in cases of breakdown of marriage. To counter this and to save themselves from the net of the Prohibition of Dowry Act, men would approach the Darul Qaza in advance and file an application for *rukhsati* (bringing back their wives from the parental home). Further, he pointed out that cases of *khula* had increased over the past two to four years on account of the Prohibition of Dowry Act. Almost 20 cases of divorce (*khula*, *talaq* and *fask*) were filed each month with the Darul Qaza.

His observation was that *khula* is easier because it takes place with mutual consent with certain terms and conditions like condonation of *mehr*, maintenance for the *iddat* period, maintenance for children, return of dowry given at the time of marriage. The principal reasons for *khula* were failure of the husband to maintain his wife, drinking, gambling and cruelty by the husband. Asked if women also came back asking if they could remarry the same person after taking *khula*, he said that 5 per cent women come back and the Darul Qaza allows them to remarry. As far as *fask* is concerned, the procedure takes 6 to 8 months. The wife applies for *fask* with reasons and, if the qazi finds them valid, he calls both the parties. If the husband does not turn up, he is given two notices at an interval of two months. If he does not turn up even after two notices, a judgement is given in favour of the woman. She is provided with papers to claim maintenance for herself and her children from a civil court. However, in 90 per cent cases the husband comes and, if the allegations against him are proved, he is asked to give *mehr* and other valuables along with maintenance. He agreed that a *nikahnama* facilitates the return of *mehr* in case of a *talaq* or *fask*. There is a *nikah* Register in each district of Bihar and the fee for the *nikah* is Rs. 50. However, the bridegroom's family often does not like to get a qazi from the Darul Qaza for performing a *nikah* because the *nikah* would then be recorded in the register. They call other moulvis or qazis to perform the *nikah*.

In cases where the wife claims maintenance for her children the Darul Qaza fixes the amount according to the economic condition of the husband. It is deposited by the husband with the Darul Qaza every month and passed on to the wife. The amount normally fixed is Rs. 400. In case of payment of *mehr*, the Darul Qaza insist that it be paid at the time of the settlement of the case. If the husband is unable to settle the *mehr* at that time, he is given 2 to 4 months to make the payment. If he fails to make payment, the Darul Qaza provides papers to the woman to claim it through a court. The papers are valid in a civil court. In the case of working women only maintenance for the *iddat* period is given. If she wishes or if the husband so requests, she can waive the amount.

CONCLUSION

This paper suggests that a large number of socio-cultural factors determine the breakdown of marriage. Arriving at a general conclusion about the rights given to women in Islam without a contextual or situational analysis of the various factors responsible for marital breakdown is likely to lead us to a faulty understanding of divorce in Muslim society in India. The manner in which divorces usually take place is not in accordance with the Qur'anic injunctions. The position of divorced women, the stigma attached to them, the mental agony they undergo, their economic insecurity, and the poor prospects of remarriage are due more to societal norms which in turn are influenced by local culture. No woman interviewed had remarried although Islam permits remarriage of divorced women three months after divorce. Muslim women, thus, live under dual principles: those laid down by Islam and those dictated by local culture.

A woman can be divorced without any valid reason, in anger or under intoxication. The children born to her become her responsibility. She is denied *mehr*, her belongings and maintenance. She rarely remarries and ends up by becoming a liability to her parents, who in a majority of cases blame their daughters for their failure to adjust to the husband's family. If she herself initiates divorce on valid grounds, she is discouraged, severely criticized and ostracized for her action. She is reminded that a woman is supposed to go to her husband's home in a palanquin and leave it only in a coffin. Such beliefs are not in accordance with Islamic injunctions, but they are dinned into her from early childhood. No ulema or religious organizations ever try to weed out these un-Islamic norms so that a woman can realize the rights guaranteed to her in Islam. They are instead reinforced by interpretations of Islamic texts or by patriarchal norms of the society. In this kind of a contradictory situation women cannot be expected to get their due and are likely to continue to be the second sex.

Most women hesitate to go to either the civil court or the Imarat-e-Shar'ia to claim *mehr* or maintenance for themselves or for their children. If she approaches the civil court, the process of securing relief is so prolonged and prohibitive that she usually stays away. The Imarat-e-Shar'ia does not enjoy statutory powers to ensure implementation of its decisions. It, too, ends up giving papers to a woman to recover her *mehr* or maintenance from a civil court. Most husbands produce fake documents to show that their economic status is not too good and so deny *mehr* or maintenance to their wives. The majority of divorced women in the present study were dependent on their parents. Only a few educated women were economically independent, but even they had to live at their parental home for reasons of security. Finding a job is not an easy task. Even if they want to start a tailoring, cutting or embroidery centre, they need to make an initial investment. Nearly 94 per cent of the women interviewed did not know that under the current law, the Waqf Board had a responsibility towards a divorced woman who had no social support. Most of them had no knowledge of the civil codes or how to approach family court to claim their *mehr* or maintenance; nor were they well informed about their legal rights under Muslim Personal Law or the Constitution and civil codes. They also cannot differentiate between the existing customary laws applied to them and Muslim laws. This lack of information is a serious shortcoming for it prevents them from challenging wrong interpretations of Muslim laws.

There is an urgent need for more thoroughgoing empirical research on the way Islamic provisions of divorce are being used to short-charge women and also to arrive at some solution and modification of procedures for divorce within an Islamic framework. There is also an urgent need to provide materials in Urdu and regional languages about the Qur'anic injunctions relating to divorce so that women are not misguided by the predominantly pro-male interpretations of Islamic rules moulvis are prone to offering. There is a need to make both men and women aware about the differences that exist between principles laid down in religion as opposed to those propagated in the name of religion by moulvis or ulema who are often inclined to interpret Islam to justify misogynist cultural practices (Tallawy, 1997: 128). The naib qazi of the Imarat-e-Shar'ia emphasized that a movement should be launched to educate Muslims about the proper Qur'anic way of *talaq*. Marriages should be registered with the Imarat-e-Shar'ia so that in the event of a *talaq* the proceedings are easier. The system of registration of marriages was started by the Imarat-e-Shar'ia almost 15 years ago, but hardly 20 per cent marriages are registered. He further advocated the need for making a *nikahnama* so that in the case of a divorce the terms of the payment of *mehr* can be ascertained and the husband can be made to pay the actual amount, which is difficult to ascertain at present as many women do not remember the *mehr* stipulated at the time of their marriage. The qazi of Durul Qaza, Muzaffarpur, admitted that social issues directly related to women are not discussed in the sermon read out at the Friday congregations. The main focus of the *khutba* (Friday sermon) is on either religious observance or how to preserve minority identity. Divorce, the importance of education for women, women's rights and the increasing demands of dowry are never taken up as issues for discussion during religious congregations. These aspects have to be focused on to create a more balanced and egalitarian society. Towards this end, a network for information, solidarity and support of Muslim women is urgently required (WLUML Dossier, July 1988). The religious knowledge of men has to be increased as well.

NOTES

1. One important feature of Muslim marriages in Bihar is that in 95 per cent cases no *nikahnama* is made. A *nikahnama* is made mostly in those cases where the husband is employed outside India. This may be because the *nikahnama* is a documentary proof of marriage and anyone working outside India would require such proof to secure a visa for the spouse if he wishes her to join him abroad. More than 50 per cent women interviewed did not know anything about a *nikahnama*.
2. Various studies on divorce have shown that the chances of divorce are greater in the early years of marriage (Kenkel, 1966: 320).

REFERENCES

Hussain, S. (1998), *The Changing Half: A Case Study of Indian Muslim Woman*, New Delhi: Classical Publisher.

Imarat-e-Shar'ia (1975), *An Introduction: Imarat-e-Shar'iah*, Phulwari Sharif: Imarat-e-Shar'ia.

Marvat, Tallawy (1997), 'International Organisations, National Machinery: Islam and Foreign Policy', in Mahanaz Afkhami and Erika Fridt (eds.), *Muslim Women and the Politics of Participation,* Syracuse: Syracuse University Press.

Ahmad, Furqan (1994), *Analytical Studies with emphasis on Socio-Legal Aspects*, New Delhi: Regency.

Ali, Firast and Furqan Ahmad (1983), *Divorce in Mohammedan Law*, New Delhi, Deep and Deep Publications.

Tyabji, F. Badruddin (1968), *Muslim Law*, Bombay.

Appendix

ORDER FORM

Court Darul Qaza, Imarat-e-Shar'ia, Bihar and Orissa

Case No. ………………… Date………………..

Daughter/Son…………………………………………………………

Place…………………………………………………………………

Post Office……………………………………………………………..

Police Station…………………………………………………………..

District…………………………………………………………………

Complainant/Defendant………………………………………………

To

Son/Daughter…………………………………………………………

Place…………………………………………………………………

Post Office……………………………………………………………..

Police Station…………………………………………………………..

District…………………………………………………………………

Complainant/Defendant………………………………………………

Date ………………… Nature of Filed Case…………………………

Date of Judgement……………………………

Date Order Signature of Issuing Authority

NOTICE

To

Defendant..

Court Darul Qaza...

Case. No.............. Date...................

Complainant...

Defendant/Defendants...

Village/Post Office...

District...

The complainant has filed a case against you in Darul Qaza (Shar'iat Court) a copy of which is sent to you along with this notice. The date for hearing of this case has been fixed on ....

You are requested to submit a written statement in your defence on the above-said date.

Signature Deputy Qazi, Shar'iat Court

Date..............month............year.

Translated copy of the Judgement order of Khula Central Darul Qaza Imarat-e-Shar'ia, Bihar and Orissa, Phulwari Sharif

Case 70/1079 Date.................

Through Darul Qaza, Muzaffarpur
Complainant - Wheeda Khatoon D/o Shoaib
Defendant - Md. Arzoo
S/o Md. Akhtar Hussain

To, Maulana Md. Yaqoob, Deputy Qazi, Madrasa Jame-ul-Uloom, Muzzaffarpur

Received the proceedings of the case. Parties have solved the case of *khul* in your presence at the Court. Thereby, in the light of this, by issuing the following orders dated 11 Safar Hijri 20th, the proceedings of the case are closed. And the complainant is being informed with the following orders:

ORDER

Dated 9 Safar, 20th Hijri, the complainant Wheeda Khatoon D/o Md. Shoaib has condoned her *mehr*, maintenance for the *iddat* and all her claims of matrimonial rights. And defendant Md. Arzoo S/o Md. Akhtar Hussain has pronounced one *talaq bateen*.

Now complainant is no longer wife of the defendant. After Completing her *iddat* she is free to remarry and the defendant owes no responsibility of her *mehr* and maintenance for *iddat* period.

Translated Copy of the Judgement order for *FASK*

Central Darul Qaza, Imarat-e-Shar'ia, Bihar and Orissa, Phulwari Sharif

Case 37/1046 1419 Hijri Date 15 Safar 1419 Hijri

Through - Darul Qaza, Muzaffarpur

Complainant - Hajra Khatoon

Defendant - Md. Yunus

This is to inform you that the judgement in the aforesaid case has been given and the parties concerned have been informed about the following court order:

ORDER

Today on the ground of non-maintenance, other violations of the women's rights, disappearance of husband (whose whereabouts are not known), cruelty by the husband, dissolved (*fask*) the marriage alliance of Hajra Khatoon, daughter of Mohammad Haneef, with Mohammad Yunus, son of Mohammad Ramzan. The complainant is no longer the wife of the defendant. After completing the *iddat* she is free to remarry.

Darul Qaza
Imarat-e-Shar'ia

11

Divorce and Remarriage among Muslims of Jammu and Kashmir: A Socio-Legal Study

Nisar Ahmad Ganai

The institution of divorce has existed, in one form or another, from time immemorial. Bertrand Russel (1959: 3) says:

> divorce as an institution has been permitted in most ages and countries for certain causes. It has never been intended to produce an alternative to the monogamous family, but merely to mitigate hardships, where for special reasons, the continuance of a marriage tie was felt to be intolerable. The law on the subject has been extraordinarily different in different ages and places.

Islam also makes provisions for the dissolution of marriage (Hussain, 1971: 138). The Qur'an confers on the husband the right to divorce his wife without assigning any cause and even without any misdemeanour on her part. However Prophet Mohammad counselled moderation on the part of the husband. He showed his dislike for divorce in no uncertain terms and is reported to have said that 'with Allah, the most detestable of all things permitted is divorce' (Ali, 1944: 284), for it prevented conjugal happiness and interfered with the proper bringing up of children. Therefore, he restrained the powers of divorce possessed by the husband. Divorce was permitted only 'if the parties fear they cannot keep within God's bounds' (Kapadia, 1966: 203). It is said that 'toward the end of his life he went so far as practically to forbid its exercise by the men without the intervention of arbiters or a judge' (Ali, 1985, 2: 471-2). The Prophet also gave women the right to obtain separation on reasonable grounds though this was not so easy in practice. In India, the Dissolution of Muslim Marriages Act, 1939,[1] gave Muslim women the statutory right to seek divorce in several specific instances.[2] However, 'these rights are difficult to enforce and, howsoever aggrieved the wife may be, it is not as easy for her to get a divorce as for the husband, who merely has to pronounce a few words' (Tyabji, 1972: 145).

The man can, on his own accord, divorce the wife even against her will. On the other hand, the woman is not given such freedom. There are differences of opinion regarding this Qur'anic treatment of women in the matter of divorce.[3] Some think that a Muslim husband does not enjoy an arbitrary, unilateral power to inflict divorce upon his wife. Justice V.R. Krishna Iyer specifically states: 'It is a popular fallacy that a Muslim male enjoys under the Qur'anic law, unbridled authority to liquidate the marriage. The Holy Qur'an specifically forbids a man to seek pretexts for divorcing the wife so long as she remains faithful and obedient to him' (1972: 17).[4] Indu Menon is of the opinion that 'the reforms instituted by Mohammad effected a vast and marked improvement in the position of women. Islam improved the status of women by reorienting the Arab law of marriage and divorce in favour of women' (1981: 7). Shustrey believes: 'Islam contributed to the status improvement of woman by giving her the right of claiming divorce on certain grounds' (1938: 674). On the other hand, some writers are of the view that the law of divorce asserted man's domination over his wife in Islam and thus the status of woman is affected. Kapadia observes: 'a system where the wife has continually hanging over her head apprehension of a divorce cannot but prove an abiding source of uneasiness for her' (1966: 205). Unilateral divorce has always been detested as harsh and unjust to Muslim women. Anderson has aptly observed: 'It is the Islamic law of divorce, not polygamy, which is the major cause of suffering to Muslim woman. The Muslim wife indeed has always lived, so far as the law is concerned, under the ever-present shadow of divorce, a shadow mitigated only in comparatively rare cases by certain precautionary devices (1959: 51-2).

The Qur'anic law on divorce does provide for separation by women, but not on terms reasonable to them (Kapadia, 1966: 205).

As the formula for dismissal had to be repeated three times before the divorce was complete and became irrevocable, a woman could be kept in a state of being neither wife nor divorcee. In order to save herself from this state of suspense it was open to her to ransom herself from her husband for a sum agreed upon by both of them once the husband had pronounced divorce against her. Similarly, when a wife was desirous of divorce, and if her husband agreed to it, she could pay back the dower and get freedom. These provisions enabling a wife to buy her freedom were commonly called *khula* even among pre-Islamic Arabs (Sukri, 1971: 108-9).[5] The difference between pre- and post-Islamic practices lies in that, while in pre-Islamic Arab law the father could easily secure the freedom of his daughter by returning the dower, the bride price, in Islam a wife could secure her freedom by relinquishing her dower only if the husband agreed to it.[6] The law clearly aims at making it as easy as possible for men to give divorce and as difficult as possible for women to secure it (Kapadia, 1966: 205). A woman can secure a divorce only if she can persuade her husband to agree to it.

It is against this legal background that an attempt is made in this paper to determine the incidence, causes and modes of divorce among Muslims in Jammu and Kashmir. In recent years there has been a profound transformation with regard to approaches towards legal research. Law is increasingly being recognized as a social phenomenon and legal processes are understood and explained in a sociological context. In short, the emphasis has shifted from 'law in the books' to 'law in action'. Matters relating to divorce are no longer the subjects of arm-chair discussion. Empirical studies have become imperative. Therefore, in order to ascertain the attitudes of the Muslim community in the state of Jammu and Kashmir toward the dissolution of marriage, a field study was undertaken. Methodologically, the spatial concern of this field study should have been the entire state, comprising fourteen districts, but it was not possible to take up so vast an area due to the paucity of time and resources. Accordingly, the field study was confined to one district of the state, that is, Anantnag. This district was chosen because the investigator belongs to this district and it was hoped that access to Muslim households to make enquiries regarding the delicate questions of marital relations would not be as difficult and problematic as it would have been in other districts in which the investigator did not have many contacts.

The district of Anantnag has a population of 8,32,280 out of which 7,89,224 are Muslims, constituting 94 per cent of the total population of the district. For purposes of the survey, a sample of 600 Muslims was chosen. Respondents were selected randomly out of four socio-economic strata and included:

(1) agriculturists comprising cultivators, agricultural labourers and intermediaries;
(2) members of business groups comprising shopkeepers, contractors, industrialists, transporters and hotel owners;
(3) professionals comprising three sub-groups, namely, (a) highly qualified persons such as judges, advocates, doctors, professors, and executives; (b) less qualified persons such as administrative staff and school teachers; and (c) self-employed, skilled persons comprising barbers, carpenters, potters, tailors, weavers, drivers and mechanics;
(4) low caste persons such as sweepers, maidservants, midwives and chowkidars.

Every respondent selected was personally interviewed on the basis of a structured interview schedule. The interview situation consisted of the interviewer and the respondent. On an average, the interview lasted between 10 and 20 minutes. The data thus collected is analysed here.

As already pointed out, 600 Muslims were selected as subjects for this study. Of these 410 were men and 190 were women. Again, 250 men and 150 women were married. Table 1 sets out the responses with regard to the incidence of divorce. It shows that only 4 per cent of the 250 married males and 2.6 per cent of the

TABLE 1: SEX-WISE DISTRIBUTION OF DIVORCED RESPONDENTS

Sex of respondent	Sample Size	No. of Divorced Respondents	Percentage
Males	250	10	4.00
Females	150	4	2.60
Total	400	14	3.50

150 married women had been through a divorce. Thus, the incidence of divorce (3.50 per cent) was low.

Many factors are responsible for the low incidence of divorce among the Muslims of the state. For one thing, most Muslims in the state are averse to divorce and consider it to be a family dishonour. On marriage a Muslim girl is grafted on to the husband's family just as a Hindu girl and the father of the girl would rather prefer a life of penury or extreme hardship for his daughter than that she be separated from her husband. This is no doubt a relic of familial relations obtaining among Hindus and shows that despite their conversion to Islam the Muslims of the state have not given up their age-old customs (Ganjoo, 1959: 43). Second, the conditions of rural living also contribute toward keeping the incidence of divorce low. As a rule, parents like to arrange the marriage of their daughters in the same or a nearby village. In many cases the spouses are near relations. This makes it possible for family elders and relatives within the village to intervene effectively in case of family discord. Since joint families are still common in the rural areas, conventional notions of respect force the spouses to listen to the saner advice of their elders.

Table 2 sets out the response of Muslim husbands with regard to the reasons for the divorce initiated by them. The main reasons for divorce are sterility (30 per cent) and wife's doubtful character. Other significant reasons were disobedience on the part of the wife (20 per cent) and negligence toward the husband (10 per cent). A few divorces also took place because of the quarrelsome nature of the wife (10 per cent). These were the reasons stated by the husbands but we know that the decision to divorce arises from a complex web of factors which may not be necessarily those that are

TABLE 2: REASONS FOR DIVORCE GIVEN BY HUSBANDS

Reasons for Divorce	Response Frequency	Percentage
No issue	3	30.00
Wife disobedient	2	20.00
Wife negligent	1	10.00
Wife's doubtful character	3	30.00
Wife's quarrelsome nature	1	10.00
Total	10	100.00

TABLE 3: REASONS GIVEN BY THE WIFE FOR DEMANDING DIVORCE

Reasons for Divorce	Response Frequency	Percentage
Physical ill-treatment by husband	2	50.00
Husband's failure to maintain wife	1	25.00
Second marriage	1	25.00
Total	4	100.00

subsequently given to account for the fact of divorce. Even so, we would perhaps be not far wrong in concluding that Muslims do not dissolve a marriage without a justifiable reason.

As already pointed out, divorce was demanded by the wife in only four cases. Table 3 presents the reasons given by them for seeking dissolution of their marriage. It indicates that in two (50 per cent) cases divorce was demanded by the wife on the ground of physical ill-treatment by the husband. In one case (25 per cent) the wife demanded divorce for non-maintenance by the husband. In another case (25 per cent) the wife demanded divorce because the husband had contracted a second marriage. Thus, the main reason for a wife to demand divorce was physical assault by the husband. The economic factor, that is failure on the part of the husband to maintain his wife, is another powerful reason for divorce. The third reason, which in some cases leads the wife to demand a divorce, is the husband's action of contracting another marriage without taking her into confidence. It is worth noting that Muslim women will no more put up with physical ill-treatment by their husbands nor will they tolerate their husband taking on a second wife.

A Muslim marriage may be dissolved either (a) by the husband at his will without the intervention of the court, called *talaq*,[7] or (b) by the mutual consent of the wife and husband without the intervention of the court, called *khula*[8] or *mubarat*,[9] (c) or by a judicial decree at the instance of either the husband or wife. Table 4 sets out the mode of dissolution of marriage among Muslims in the state. In three (21.42 per cent) cases the marriage was dissolved as a result of the *talaq* pronounced by the husband. In 11 (78.57 per cent) cases the divorce took place by *khula*. There is not a single instance of divorce by *mubarat* or by judicial process. Thus, Muslims in the state generally take recourse to the dissolution of

TABLE 2: REASONS GIVEN BY THE WIFE FOR DEMANDING DIVORCE

Modes of Divorce	Response frequency	Percentage
By *talak*	3	21.42
By *khula*	11	78.57
By *mubarat*	–	–
By *judicial process*	–	–
Total	14	99.99

marriage by *khula* and rarely resort to divorce by pronouncement of *talaq*. The principal reason for this is that on pronouncement of *talaq* the husband becomes liable to payment of *mehr* (dower) to his wife. Therefore, in the case of disharmony and discord between the spouses, the husband, in order to avoid the liability of having to pay the *mehr*, prefers to keep the marriage in suspension and thereby compel the girl's side to ask for *khula*. As a general rule, in *khula* divorce the wife pays some compensation to the husband or relinquishes her right to *mehr* as part of the agreement to secure her release from the bondage of marriage. Sometimes, the parents of the girl are compelled to pay large sums of money in order to get their daughter released from the marriage bond. The procedure followed in *khula* is that the negotiations are conducted by common friends of the families or relations who try their utmost to bring about reconciliation between the parties. But if the parties cannot bear to live with one another, then the marriage tie is brought to an end on payment of the agreed upon consideration by the wife or her family.

The Jammu and Kashmir Dissolution of Muslim Marriages Act, 1942, confers a statutory right on a Muslim wife to ask for the dissolution of her marriage. It is open to her to press into service the grounds set in Section 2 of the Act.[10] Table 5 sets out the response of women by professional category with respect to their awareness of this provision in law. Although the Act has given to Muslim women in the state the right to seek release from marriage on a number of grounds, an overwhelming majority of women (98.95 per cent) are unaware of this piece of legislation. Not a single woman from the agriculturist, business and low caste groups is aware of her rights under the Act of 1942. Only 3.7 per cent

TABLE 5: RESPONSE OF WOMEN WITH RESPECT TO AWARENESS OF THE PROVISIONS OF JAMMU & KASHMIR DISSOLUTION OF MARRIAGE ACT, 1942, BY PROFESSIONAL CATEGORY

Professional category	Sample size	Response frequency	Percentage
Agriculturists	75	-	-
Business	35	-	-
Professional	65	2	3.7
Low caste	15	-	-
Total	400	14	3.50

women from professional groups, whom one expects to be educated and informed, are aware of this enactment. Muslim women in the state are, thus, overwhelmingly ignorant of their legal rights under the Act of 1942 which can provide them relief against unscrupulous husbands.

Leave alone women, even men are not aware of this important and progressive legislation. Table 6 sets out the response of men with respect to their awareness of this legislation by occupational category. It reveals that 1.21 per cent men from agriculture, 7.27 per cent men from business and 21.37 per cent men from professional groups were aware of this legislation. Low caste men are completely ignorant about this piece of legislation. On the whole, thus, an overwhelming majority of Muslim men also are unaware of this legislation. Awareness of this enactment among men and women can ameliorate the situation of women by shaping the outlook and orientation of Muslim men towards their spouses. It can also give women greater confidence in dealing with their husbands.

TABLE 6: PROFESSION-WISE RESPONSES OF MEN WITH REGARD TO AWARENESS OF THE ACT OF 1942

Profession	Sample size	Response frequency	Percentage
Agriculture	165	2	1.21
Business	55	4	7.27
Professional	145	31	21.37
Low caste	45	-	-
Total	410	37	9.02

Remarriage of divorced women is allowed and practiced. Of course, a divorced woman usually finds it hard to get an unmarried man as husband, but she can always find a divorced man or widower to get married to. Like the widow who remarries, a divorced woman nevertheless faces two distinct disadvantages in case she wants to remarry. First, she may not be able to get an entirely suitable match. If she is looking for a match in her own age group, the chances usually are that he would be quite poor. On the other hand, if she looks for a rich or well-to-do husband, there would usually be a wide disparity between her and her husband's age. Second, even if she has no children from her previous marriage, her husband may have children from an earlier marriage. This can lead to complications, particularly if she has children subsequently. If she has children and remarries, the children are likely to suffer if she takes them with her to the new husband's house where they are likely to be looked upon as step children. Leaving her children from the previous marriage with her parents or husband's parents creates additional problems. At any rate, a divorced woman does not like to part with the custody of her children in favour of her husband or his relations. Consequently, many divorced women prefer not to remarry. This is more generally the case if they have well-to-do parents or brothers with whom they can afford to spend their days in comfort without having to look for a second husband.

Much has been written with regard to the arbitrary powers of Muslim men under the *shar'ia* to pronounce divorce upon their wives, but the present study clearly indicates that in a mainly agricultural-rural society such as that of Jammu and Kashmir, divorce among Muslims is not particularly common or easy. There are so many restraints that a Muslim husband hardly finds it possible to be entirely arbitrary in exercising this power. Even though the unilateral power of divorce guaranteed to Muslim men under the *shar'ia* does not affect women particularly adversely because the incidence of arbitrary divorces is greatly limited, it can hardly be concluded that all is well in this connection. Women continue to be dominated and short-charged in the patriarchal, feudal set up of the state. There are complaints of cruelty and exploitation. The Jammu and Kashmir Dissolution of Muslim Marriages Act, 1942, does enable an oppressed or hapless Muslim woman to seek divorce, but the law is good only in theory. Few economic opportunities are available to women among whom illiteracy is widespread. The almost total economic dependence of women on men has far-reaching implications: the wife has to put up with a lot to preserve her marital and family relationship. Social and economic factors also favour men and not women. Further, as remarriage of divorced women is fraught with inequalities and complications, a divorced Muslim woman ends up becoming dependent upon her parents or brothers who may or may not treat her well. This restrains women from taking recourse to divorce even if they are not well-treated by their husbands. On the other hand, the husband can cast his wife away at will and she has to get out of the matrimonial home if the husband chooses to pronounce divorce on her or otherwise creates conditions for her or her parents to ask for a *khula*. Thus, the women can hardly take recourse to this otherwise progressive legislation.

NOTES

1. This Act is applicable to the whole of India except the state of Jammu and Kashmir.
2. Under the Act, a woman married under Muslim law can obtain divorce on the following grounds: (1) her husband's whereabouts are not known for four years; or failure or neglect by the husband to provide maintenance for seven years; or failure to perform marital obligations for three years; or protracted impotency, insanity, affliction by leprosy, venereal disease and cruelty; (2) the wife's right called in Muslim Law 'option of puberty', if exercised in accordance with the condition laid down in the Act; and (3) any other ground recognized as valid under Muslim Law.
3. This difference is a reflection of a more fundamental difference of opinion among scholars regarding the Qur'anic treatment of women in general. Some writers are of the view that Islam gives equal status to men and women. Amir Ali believes that 'he (the Prophet) placed women on a footing of perfect equality with men in the exercise of legal powers and functions' (1978: 229). Muhammad Qutb is of the opinion that 'as a fundamental principle of its system, Islam holds that woman is a human being and she has a soul similar to that of man. Islam gives her the right to life, to honour and to property like men'(1964: 183). Kapadia has, in this connection, gone to the extent of observing that 'the greatest contribution of Islam to the cause of women was to invest her with property rights. . . . And Islam's contribution lies in recognising her absolute ownership of it' (1966: 211-12). According to those who hold this view, a Muslim husband's arbitrary and unilateral power to inflict divorce on his wife does not accord with Islamic

injunctions. Others are of the opinion that Islam has not given her equal status with men. Levy says, 'It is foolish to claim equality for her in Islam in spheres for which she is not created. Men stand superior to women in that God hath preferred the one over the other' (1957: 183). According to this view, the law of divorce asserted man's domination over his wife in Islam. The contribution of Islam lies in its improvement upon the old Arab conceptions and conventions. One may, therefore, reasonably agree with Justice V.R. Krishna Iyer: ' . . . having regard to the circumstances of pre-Islamic Arabia reeking with sex, promiscuity and social injustice, wives unlimited and divorce at pleasure for men and unbreakable chains for women, this great Messenger of God and revolutionary, had planted restraints on the male and granted cautious rights to the female, and innovated a rational and fair system, astonishingly radical and modern and more than Manu's verdict on women' (1972: 24).

4. Justice Krishna Iyer relies on the verse of the Qur'an which ordains: 'If they obey you, then do not seek a way against them.'
5. According to Sukri, the wife returns the dower and even more to make the husband relinquish his marital right in lieu of this consideration.
6. The Prophet did attempt to check the tendency of the husband to utilize divorce to gain pecuniary advantage from the wife.
7. The word *talaq* is usually rendered as repudiation. It comes from the root *tallaqa* which means to release an animal from a tether; whence to repudiate the wife or free her from the bondage of marriage. In law it signifies the absolute power which the husband possesses of divorcing his wife any time. The pronouncement of *talaq* may be either revocable (*talaq-e-sunna*) or irrevocable (*talaq-e-bidat*). An irrevocable *talaq* dissolves the marriage immediately on its pronouncement, while a revocable one does not dissolve the marriage until the period of *iddat* has elapsed and may at any time be revoked either expressly or impliedly by resuming sexual intercourse. For a good summary of the law, see Wilson (1912: 143-5).
8. A divorce by *khula* (redemption) is a divorce with the consent of the husband and at the instance of the wife, in which she agrees to give a sum to the husband for her release from the marriage tie; in fact, it is a divorce purchased by the wife. It is complete and irrevocable from the moment the husband repudiates the wife. For an account of the law on this point, see *Munshee Buzul-ul-Raheem* vs. *Luttefot-oon Nissa* (8, IA, 1861, 379).
9. *Mubarat* (mutual) divorce proceeds from the mutual consent of both the husband and the wife. As the initiative comes from both sides, no return is required from the wife in this form of divorce. The offer may proceed from either side, and once it is accepted the dissolution is complete and it operates as irrevocable divorce.
10. The grounds for dissolution of marriage under the Jammu and Kashmir Dissolution of Muslim Marriages Act, 1942, are substantially identical with those in the Muslim Dissolution of Marriages Act, 1939.

REFERENCES

Ali, Muhammad (1944), *Manual of Hadith*, Delhi.

Ali, Syed Amir (1978), *The Spirit of Islam*, rpt., Delhi: Idarah-i-Adbiat.

——— (1985), *Muhammadan Law*, vol. 2, rpt., Delhi: Himalayan Books.

Anderson, J.N.D. (1959), *Islamic Law in Modern World*, London: Oxford University Press.

Bhatty, Zarina (1976), 'Status of Muslim Women and Social Change', in B.R. Nanda (ed.), *Indian Women: From Purdah to Modernity*, Delhi: Vikas Publishing House.

Ganjoo, Nila Kanth (1959), *Customary Law of Kashmir*, Srinagar: Fine Art Press.

Husain, Sheikh Abrar (1971), *Marriage Customs among Muslim in India*, New Delhi: Sterling Publishers.

Iyer, V.R. Krishna (1972), 'Reform of Muslim Personal Law', in Tahir Mahmood (ed.), *Islamic Law in Modern India*, Bombay: N.M. Tripathi.

Kapadia, K.M. (1966), *Marriage and Family in India*, Bombay: Popular Prakashan.

Levy, Rueben (1957), *The Social Structure of Islam*, Cambridge: The University Press.

Menon, Indu (1981), *Status of Muslim Women in India*, New Delhi: Uppal.

Qutb, Muhammad (1964), *Islam: The Misunderstood Religion*, Delhi: The Board of Islamic Publications.

Russell, Bertrand (1959), *Marriage and Morals*, New York: Bantam Books.

Shustrey, A.M.A. (1938), *Outlines of Islamic Culture: Philosophical and Technological Aspects*, vol. 2, Bangalore: The Bangalore Press.

Sukri, Ahmed (1917), *Muhammadan Law of Marriage and Divorce*.

Tyabji, Kamila (1972), 'Polygamy, Unilateral Divorce and Mahr in Muslim Law as interpreted in India', in Tahir Mahmood (ed.), *Islamic Law in Modern India*, Bombay: N.M. Tripathi.

Wilson, R.K. (1912), *Anglo-Muhammadan Law*, London: W. Thacker and Co.

12

A Long Way to Go: Divorce Practices among Muslim Families of Hyderabad City

Jameela Nishat

It is well known that the Muslim marriage law discriminates against women as it allows unilateral divorce by the husband. It vests him with the right to pronounce triple divorce upon his wife at one go. In 1984, Shenaz Sheikh, a young woman tortured by her husband and under threat of divorce for three years of her married life, filed a petition in the Supreme Court on the plea that Muslim Personal Law was discriminatory to women and hence violated the fundamental right to equality guaranteed to all citizens under the Constitution. A year later, Shah Bano Begum, a sixty-year old woman won a case for maintenance beyond the *iddat* period after her husband had pronounced triple divorce. In a situation where communal forces were on the rise and getting increasingly polarized, Muslim clergy interpreted the Supreme Court judgement in her case as interference in religious matters and campaigned to end the divorced Muslim woman's legal right to monthly maintenance from her former husband. As a result Muslim women in Hyderabad were provoked to speak out against Shah Bano as they felt that the *shar'ia* was in danger. Muslim women in the Old City of Hyderabad marched in a procession and presented a memorandum to the then Chief Minister demanding no change in Muslim Personal Law, little realizing the wider implications of such a demand by Muslim women.

Our aim in this paper is to focus attention on the issue of triple divorce and to highlight the disparities that exist between the rights guaranteed to women by the Qur'an and the position assigned to them in society. Specifically, our aim is to (1) understand the reasons for the incidence of triple divorce and examine the role of the qazi in such divorces, (2) find the discriminatory provisions in the existing Muslim Personal Law and its practice in Hyderabad, and (3) arrive at a comprehensive understanding of Muslim Personal Law, its significance according to the Qur'an and explore possibilities of reform. The paper is based on materials compiled in the course of working with Muslim women as a social activist and not on any body of data collected through sustained fieldwork. It is hoped that this discussion will contribute towards a more enlightened understanding of the realities of Muslim women's life and will underscore the imperative for suitable intervention to save scores of Muslim women who live under the threat of the sword of triple divorce and have to face innumerable hardships as a result of being thrown out of their matrimonial homes by a simple pronouncement on the part of their husbands who enjoy the unfettered right of such pronouncement under the existing Muslim Personal Law in India.

In Islam marriage is a contract. A good many of the verses of the Qur'an deal with legal aspects and the Hadith (traditions of the Prophet) are also believed to have legal authority. From the very concept of marriage as a contract, it would follow that man and woman are equal in the eyes of God. A contract is possible only between two individuals with equal status. In practice, however, the husband at his mere whim or caprice can break the contract without assigning any reason. According to Muslim laws (Muslim Personal Law) the husband enjoys special privileges and the wife remains at his mercy. For example, he can take more than one wife and has the unilateral right to pronounce divorce on her. This has prompted many scholars to remark that a clear distinction ought to be made between the injunctions laid down in the Qur'an and the Muslim laws. The Qur'anic injunctions are relatively more fair and considerate towards women than the Muslim laws, which were articulated subsequently and reflect the prevailing patriarchal orientations of society. As Anwar Moazzam, an eminent scholar of Islamic studies in Hyderabad with whom I discussed the matter, remarked, 'we are doing many things which are un-Islamic. Sanction accorded to triple divorce under Muslim Personal Law is one example of such un-Islamic practices and puts a Muslim woman in India in an awkward and vulnerable position despite the relative equality accorded to women in the Qur'an.'

Under the Nizam in Hyderabad divorce was not easy to get. The qazi, who was formally charged to deal with questions of marriage and divorce, shouldered the responsibility of issuing a formal decree of divorce and ensuring that the divorce was pronounced in accordance with the principles of the *shar'ia*. He was supposed to preserve records of marriages as well as to act as an arbitrator in settling differences between the husband and wife. The qazi no longer plays this role. There are six qazis in the different areas of Hyderabad, but they are authorized only to maintain records of marriage (more accurately, *nikah*) and *talaq*. This leaves the burden of settling differences between husband and wife either to the elders of their families or to the parties themselves. With the decline in the strength of family ties, a phenomenon almost concomitant with urbanization, the decline of old family values, and considerable rise in geographical mobility precipitated by the possibility of migration to the Gulf countries, the role of family elders has been considerably reduced. The result is that triple divorce can be resorted to by a man without any qualms of conscience as he does not have to account for his action to anyone and his wife is either powerless or too far away to be able to bring any pressure upon him to refrain from exercising his unilateral right of divorce.

At Shah Banda, a predominantly Muslim locality in Hyderabad, we were able to obtain access to the qazi's records. According to these records, the total number of divorces (including applications for divorce) registered between 1 January 1998 and 30 July 1998 was 348. Out of these, 250 were cases of *talaq* pronounced by the husband, 35 where the wife had asked for *khula*, and 63 for dissolution of marriage. Again, between January 1999 and February 1999 as many as 71 cases of divorce were recorded. Out of them, 22 were cases of *talaq* pronounced by the husband and 49 were cases of the wife asking for *khula*. These figures disguise the fact that in many cases where the wife asked for a divorce, the reason might not be that she actually wanted to be free of the marriage bond. She may have been pressurized by her husband to ask for *khula,* as this would enable him to escape legal liabilities he may have towards his wife. It is possible that the husband may have created a situation where the wife or her parents might have agreed to secure her freedom by agreeing to apply for a *khula* at her initiative. The entries in the qazi's records do not, unfortunately, contain enough details to enable us to find out precisely at whose initiate or under what specific circumstances the wife was obliged to move for divorce or if it was at her own initiative.

During our door-to-door survey in two lower class localities (Jhirra and Borabanda), we came across many women separated from their husbands and living with their parents or brothers. They had not even asked their husbands for maintenance. When we enquired about the reason for their strange silence we found that they, like all other Indian women, were waiting for their husbands to come and take them back—some had waited for two years and some for fifteen. The men did not even bother to inflict *talaq* on their wives (free them from the marriage contract) and were, in fact, living comfortably with second wives. The women prefer to live in agony rather than question their husbands or to take them to a court of law probably because their families cannot afford the high cost of litigation or because taking the initiative to move the court would lower them in common estimation. Many women with children fear that asking for divorce would mean parting with their children who are probably their only source of sustenance in the future. Unfortunately, we are not able to go into a detailed discussion of why women prefer to suffer separation and not enforce their right to a matrimonial home or seek divorce through a court of law, but a more thoroughgoing research should be able to go into this aspect in greater detail.

When we moved into the *bastis* like Jhirra and Borabanda, we found that the reason for the pronouncement of *talaq* by the husband or *khula* at the initiative of the wife is not just the other woman. In middle class families, parents of boys take huge sums of money as dowry. It varies from fifty thousand to five lakh rupees, depending on the social status of the boy and his family. Then, after some time the wife is divorced unceremoniously. Let us here give a detailed case study of a girl who was divorced after nine years of married life. She is twenty-five years old and from a well-to-do family. Her parents married her off to a student of medicine thinking that the future of the girl would be very bright. At the time of marriage he was paid one lakh rupees as dowry. After completing his MBBS degree, he was provided with all facilities by his in-laws to do a Master's degree in medicine. After he completed his education his in-laws sent him to the Middle East. His desires had been fulfilled and the girl was happy that her parents could satisfy all her husband's demands. In the Middle East, they lived together for nine years and had one son and two daughters. His in-laws offered the pampered son-in-law many precious gifts during this period. Then one evening the son-in-law put the wife and the children on a flight back home saying that she was too arrogant and non-cooperative. A few days later, he posted a *talaqnama* (declaration of divorce) along with the *mehr* (dower) and broke the marriage. The parents and the girl were heartbroken and in agony for two years, not able to accept her rejection after they had pampered the boy so much. The girl is now working as a schoolteacher, which has enabled her to overcome her trauma to some extent.

The case of another upper middle class graduate girl is equally noteworthy. She was married to an engineer who was settled in the Middle East. After a month of marriage, he went back to his job leaving his wife with his mother and family. The girl insisted on accompanying her husband to the Middle East, but he refused to take her on the plea that he did not have a family visa. Later, the girl felt that she should take up some job rather than sit idle at home. Her in-laws accused her of being too modern and complained that she was not able to serve them as was expected of her. The husband posted a *talaqnama* from the Middle East along with the *mehr*. There is among Muslims in Hyderabad the custom of giving the husband a sum of money as *jodi ki raqm* (money for clothes). According to a woman social activist whom we interviewed this sum of money is much higher than the amount of *mehr*. In this case the *jodi ki raqm* was two lakh rupees and the amount of *mehr* was only fifty-one thousand rupees. The husband quietly kept the two lakh rupees and within two months of married life the girl was divorced.

Another noteworthy case is that of a lower class girl. The father of the girl earned his livelihood as a butcher. He had a house worth one lakh rupees and nothing else. To marry off the daughter, he sold the house for ninety thousand rupees and gave thirty thousand rupees as *jodi ki raqm* and spent the remaining sixty thousand rupees on providing dowry for the girl. The boy is a rickshaw puller. He started expecting more money after three days of marriage. When he found out that his father-in-law was in no position to fulfill his demands, he started beating his wife every evening leading to separation within a week after marriage. The girl came back to her parents. They are too old (the father is 80 and mother is 60) to take care of the girl. The father has become deaf and is bed-ridden. Their source of income has dried up. The girl is living with them in a rented house. Aged 19 years with no education, she is mentally not prepared to go out and work. The boy does not divorce her because he would have to pay the *mehr* and return the dowry. She cannot afford to go to the court because she has no money.

Since our data on the incidence of divorce was drawn mainly from the qazi's records, we had no means of knowing the personal characteristics of the divorced women. The qazi's records contain only the names of the parties. They contain no description of the personal characteristics of the parties in terms of their educational level, social standing or reasons for divorce. In order to get at the personal attributes of the divorced women we collected 27 detailed case studies. Out of these 27 divorced women, 6 were illiterate, 14 had failed in the seventh standard, 2 had failed at the SSC level and 5 were undergraduates. Again, in terms of social class 18 were from the lower class (married to butchers, rickshaw pullers, etc.), 6 were from the middle class (married to petty traders) and 3 were married to government servants. These figures suggest that the incidence of divorce is higher among the poorly educated women of the lower class as compared to the better-educated middle class women. Poor Muslim women are more vulnerable than women from middle class families so far as divorce is concerned.

This is also reflected in the reasons for divorce. Out of the 27 women whose case histories we explored in detail, the reason in 13 cases was want of money. In 7 cases it was the husband's decision to bring in a new wife and in 2 cases divorce occurred because the woman was not able to bear a male child. In 5 cases the reason was frequent personal clash between husband and wife. There are also cases of separation that we have not included. Most of them belong to middle class families. In some cases, the husband goes away to the Middle East after a month or so of marriage and the wife waits for him without knowing his whereabouts. When she does not find any trace of him after three or four years, she appeals for a *khula* in the court. From the register in one qazi's office, we found that from 1 January 1999 to 16 April 1999, there were 58 cases of *talaq* pronounced by the husband, 69 cases of *khula* taken by the wife and in 18 cases the pronouncement of divorce had been posted to the wife from outside India.

A letter enclosing a *talaqnama* sent by post does not require any witnesses. Many times a *talaq* notice is published in a newspaper instead of a *talaqnama* being sent by post. Let me translate a typical *talaq* notice published in *Siasat* dated 16 July 1999. It reads:

Divorce Notice

Md. Sartaj Ahmed
s/o Sheikh Ahmed
Station Courtala

To
Safia Sultana
d/o Abdul Qayum

You are informed that I, Md. Sartaj Ahmed s/o Sheikh Ahmed, in front of two witnesses, pronounce triple *talaq* (*talaq-e-bain*) for your disobedience and personal clashes.

This notice is also sent by Registered post. As a precaution it is announced here in the newspaper.

There are also cases where the husband pronounces triple divorce without giving *mehr*. In such cases the wife is required to file a case for the recovery of the *mehr* from the husband. This is often a difficult course of action. For one thing, there is always the possibility that in order to escape his liability the husband may take the plea that the wife had condoned the *mehr* at the time of marriage and he bears no responsibility for paying it when she had herself voluntarily condoned her right. Even if the facts are to the contrary, the husband's claim can be difficult to contest. Second, the case takes a long time to mature to the decision-stage and there is no guarantee that the wife would be able to recover the amount in the end. Meanwhile, she is required to spend on litigation, which most women are not in a position to afford. Therefore, where the husband refuses to settle the *mehr* the wife accepts it as a *fate accompli* and gives up her claim.

During our survey we came across many cases from middle class families where the husband earned more than two thousand five hundred rupees a month, but pleaded his inability to pay maintenance of five hundred rupees to his wife whom he had discarded. When the wife insisted on getting maintenance and appealed to the court, she was cruelly divorced. The case of a Pathan girl whose marriage was performed in 1981 is worth discussing here. She was just thirteen at the time of her marriage. On the wedding night itself, her husband told her that he was in love with another woman and she should not talk about this to her in-laws. Every night the husband would sneak out of the house and spend the night with his mistress. The husband's parents had known about the affair of their 35 year old son, but had married him to this 13 year old girl in the hope that their son would stop going out to this other woman. This young girl could not understand all this. A few months later the husband went to the Middle East, leaving his young wife pregnant. Soon thereafter, the in-laws started ill-treating her, refusing to give her food and beating her. The reason they gave was that she had not been successful in winning the affection and love of their son. They had thought that their son would leave the other woman after marriage to this young girl. Finally, she left her husband's home, came back to her parents and took *khula* after four months of marriage. Enraged at this, her parents started ill-treating her, calling her an unlucky woman. She was tortured by her own mother for many years and was treated worse than a maidservant. In 1994 she found another man ready to marry her. She was 29 years old. He was 46 years old, the father of six children. He was a government servant and could not take a second wife without the first wife's consent. Thus, their marriage could not be legalized and her *nikah* was not registered. In this marriage the *mehr* was fixed at Rs. 21,000 whereas earlier it was Rs. 25,000.

There are many strange cases of divorce. One case of divorce after twenty years of marriage is worth discussing. With two grown up sons aged 19 and 17, the wife applied for divorce. The reason was that she was being beaten up and tortured every night by her husband. Being a patient and tolerant Indian woman, she had lived with him for twenty years but as the son grew up he could not stand his father's behaviour and stood up against him. When the father saw the young son supporting his mother, he went to the extent of accusing his wife of having incestuous relationship with her son. This resulted in separation and divorce.

Personal tragedies of a grievous nature arise out of divorce in most cases, but they become most pathetic when the divorced has been pronounced in a fit of anger and the husband regrets having pronounced divorce once his temper has cooled down. Gausia Begum, aged 40 years, and Mohammad Yaqoob, aged 52 years, had been living together for twenty-five years. They had a son aged 7. Three other children born to them passed away. The husband and wife had a personal tiff on some petty matter. The husband was very angry. This brought them to the qazi's office where in a fit of anger the husband pronounced *talaq-e-bain* (triple divorce) in the presence of four or five witnesses. Those present in the qazi's office cautioned him that the divorce would be irrevocable, but he could care less. The wife also said that she did not mind the divorce, but as their emotions cooled down they wanted to live together again. This was not possible, because the law lays down a cumbersome procedure for this to be allowed. Under Muslim law, the husband and wife who have been irrevocably divorced cannot be married again until the wife marries and cohabits with another man and obtains a divorce from the second husband. This procedure is called *halala*. *Halala* is not acceptable to the husband. Both he and his wife visit the qazi's office daily to find some solution to their problem but in vain.

Let me at this point quote the eminent lawyer of Hyderabad, Mohammad Abdul Bari, with whom we discussed the issue at some length. He says that the recording of a marriage in Hyderabad is very systematic, but *talaq* (dissolution of marriage) is not very authentically recorded. He condemns triple divorce pronounced in a single sitting. He says that the Qur'an does not approve of it and cites Sura An-Nisa (verse 35) which says: 'If you fear a breach between them appoint an arbitrator from his side and appoint an arbitrator from her side'. This means that if there is a quarrel between the husband and the wife, it is advisable that the problem should be put before the elders and an attempt be made to solve it. The husband cannot and should not pronounce triple divorce. It should be pronounced gradually over a period of three months, so that reconciliation is possible. At the end of these three months a document should be prepared to say that the husband and wife are divorced.

From the records maintained by the qazis, it is clear that cases of *khula* are steadily increasing. This does not really mean that women have become conscious of their rights and are taking divorce from their husbands if the marriage is not satisfactory. On the contrary, what it means is that in many cases husbands are forcing their wives to seek a *khula* for economic reasons. In a *talaq* by the husband a man has to give the *mehr* and return the *jahez*. Where the husband does not want or cannot afford to pay the *mehr* or return the *jahez*, he beats up the wife and forces her to take *khula*. This is happening on a large scale in lower and lower middle class families. When we spoke about *khula* to the scholar of Islamic Studies, Dr. Anwar Moazzam, he narrated the case of a woman who asked the Prophet to grant her divorce for no reason. Divorce was granted to her. These days we cannot be sure that when a woman asks for *khula* whether she really wants divorce or is being forced to take *khula* so that her husband can get rid of her and marry another woman who would again bring *jahez* and *jodi ki raqm*.

Khula requires the husband's willingness. Where a woman is really keen to divorce a man on grounds of incompatibility she is dependent on his mercy. One case we encountered was of a 17 year old girl from Mallepally who was forced to marry a 24 year ruffian. Later, when she wanted to divorce him she was not granted *khula* as the husband was not willing to sign the *khulanama*.

Remarriage of divorced Muslim women is very rare in Hyderabad. There are a few cases where a divorced woman has married an already married man for the sake of security. A woman of 42, a middle class graduate, was married to a man settled in the Middle East who did not call her to live with him. It resulted in divorce. After twenty years the woman got married to a businessman who was 52 years old, had a wife and children. He had accused his first wife of bad character and she thought that he would be suitable for him as she was herself a divorcee. Her assessment was wrong. He went back to his first wife after a few months. After four years he sent her a *talaqnama* and subsequently put in a divorce notice in the newspaper. She believes that his first wife had take him back through black magic and when he comes out of the magical spell he would come back to her.

Superstition and blind faith in sorcery is one of the causes of the ill health of Muslim women. In Hyderabad, especially in the Old City, this belief exists to such an extent that in two separate incidents the husbands and their parents accused their daughters-in-law of black magic and beat them up to death. If we probe into the mind of ordinary Muslim women deeply, we can clearly see that they are conditioned to be tolerant and subordinate. This mental weakness leads them to blind faith in superstition and other such practices. According to Dr. Tauseef, a psychiatrist at Asra Dawakhana whom we interviewed, the fear of rejection prevails among these naïve women and they need psychiatric treatment. There are many cases of hysteria among divorced women and among young women who were married to sheikhs in the Middle East and were later divorced. Living in a new place, new culture and environment, they undergo such trauma that they get hysterical.

Turning the pages of history, we find that a system of registration of marriage and divorce was introduced during the Nizamshahi period in Hyderabad. The Sultan was the ultimate seat of judicial and executive authority, but he generally consulted the Sadar-e-Shar'ia who would be the authority on the Qur'an and commanded great respect in society. The qazi and naib qazis were selected from among the men of learning and scholarship in theology. They were not only given enough land and property, but also enjoyed due regard and respect. The qazi occupied a unique position. Important papers and royal wills were affixed with his seal. The laws of those days were not codified in the modern sense; they were based only on the Qur'an and the Hadith. The *farmans* were the regulations issued by a Sultan in the form of proclamations. Thus, the laws were regulated by the *farmans* promulgated from time to time. The lawyers were either Hindus or Muslims. Hindu lawyers commanded the same position as their Muslim brother lawyers.

Marriages were performed in the presence of the qazi or naib qazi. The chief qazi signed the *nikahnama* and proper registers were maintained. These registers and the *nikahnamas* were kept in the Archives. There was no class discrimination in maintaining the *nikahnama*.

The first *nikahnama* available at the qazi's office is of 1838. If any man would marry in the absence of the qazi, with the help of the qari, he was punished. In the Sadarat Aliah's records every marriage was registered. If the qazi became careless and the registration of the marriage was not submitted within a month, there were methods of checking the lapse. Every *nikahnama* was sealed by the qazi and signed by the Sadar-e-Shar'ia. The *nikahnama* underwent changes as new *farmans* were issued. The Sultan issued a *farman* clearly mentioning which relative a man was allowed to marry and whom he could not marry. This clause got immediately included in the *nikahnama*. Whenever there was a case of corruption, the qazi was dismissed. There was a case of a divorced woman who was married to another man within the *iddat* period and the qazi performed the marriage. The qazi was immediately dismissed and ordered to leave the kingdom. Today the qazi can be bribed to perform the marriage of one girl to three different men within the month and is not answerable to anyone.

Divorce in those days was also registered and *talaqnama* or *khulanama* was issued. They were signed not only by the qazi, but also by the same persons who witnessed the marriage and signed the *nikahnama*. The qazi and the chief qazi then sealed the *talaqnama*. It was not merely a question of affixing signature; they had to certify that the husband and wife were divorced. Divorce in those days was not very easy. Today *talaq* can be communicated by registered post to the girl when she is at her parent's place for delivery or can be published in the newspapers.

When we spoke of the *talaq* issue in the Old City, the women gave us very positive suggestions. They all agreed that the patriarchy within the Muslim society is the root cause of many problems. The consumerist culture and greed for money have made Muslim men take undue advantage of the existing system of *talaq*. The rigidity of the community makes Muslim women feel insecure in private and public life. Muslim women have to be encouraged to stand up against the patriarchal system in the community and raise their voice against the existing denial of their human rights. Girl's education is the key to strengthen women and to develop self-determination in them. Women have to be supported in such a manner that they develop social commitment and progressive social consciousness. For this purpose, we have already started moblizing women in the Old City of Hyderabad. We have a long way to go.

13

Mehr and Divorce among Muslims in Mirzapur District of Eastern Uttar Pradesh

Muniza Rafique Khan

The status of Muslim women, especially divorced women, is a neglected field of study in Indian sociology. Muslims constitute more than 12 per cent of India's population and nearly 50 per cent of them are women. The unhappy fact remains that women in the Muslim community are almost as suppressed as women in general in Indian society. It is only the form and content of exploitation that varies from one religious community to another.

The Qur'an lays down many rules regarding matrimonial relations, the social position of women and their legal and economic rights. It has prescribed certain laws regarding maintenance, *mehr* (dower), inheritance and sharing of property by women in their different roles as daughter, sister, mother and wife. In practice Muslim women are not able to enjoy these rights. The reason is their lack of awareness and feeling of helplessness. This is keeping them backward and suppressed. They are unable to contribute fully to the social, political and economic life of their community.

The present paper is based on an empirical study of 200 Muslim women, including 25 divorcees/separated women, whom we interviewed in Mirzapur district in Uttar Pradesh. Mirzapur district is one of the most backward districts of eastern Uttar Pradesh despite its pre-eminence as the home of a flourishing carpet industry. Leaving aside a small number of well-off families who control the carpet trade, the large majority of the Muslims in the district are either small farmers or labourers depending on carpet manufacturing for survival. The large majority of the Muslim women covered by this study are poor and illiterate without any viable means of sustenance. Our concern in this study was to ascertain women's views on *mehr* and divorce. Case histories of the 25 divorced and separated women are examined here to study the hardships and difficulties faced by Muslim divorcees in Indian society.

MARRIAGE AND *MEHR*

Marriage and *mehr* are important factors in the life of a Muslim woman. The *mehr*, according to Islamic scriptures, is a sum a man must pay to the woman he is going to marry. The amount of *mehr* is determined keeping in view the status of the man. According to Islam, if *mehr* has not been paid by the husband during his lifetime, it has to be paid out of his bequest after his death. Islamic law also lays down that if the husband divorces his wife he must pay her the *mehr* and give her proper maintenance allowance as long as she does not remarry or does not find an alternative means of support. Verse 241 of Surat Al-Baqarah runs as follows: 'For the divorced women maintenance should be provided on a reasonable scale. This is the duty of a righteous husband.' This arrangement seems reasonable if followed according to the spirit of the precept.

MEHR IN ISLAMIC SYSTEM

There are a number of verses in the Qur'an ordaining that a woman's *mehr* belongs to her and not to anybody else whether father or husband.

The Qur'an says: 'And give unto the women (whom ye marry) free gift of their marriage portions; but if they of their own accord remit unto you a part thereof, then ye are welcome to absorb it (in your wealth)' (Surat An-Nissa: 4). The Qur'an encourages a man to give as much as possible to his wife. It says: 'And if ye wish to exchange one wife for another and ye have given unto one of them a sum of money (however great), take nothing from it. Would ye take it by the way of calumny and open wrong?' (Surat An-Nissa: 20). When the second Caliph Hazrat Umar wanted to impose a ceiling on *mehr* a woman stood up and recited this verse and said, 'When Allah wants men to give a heap of gold (by way of *mehr*), who are you to put ceiling on it?' Thus, according to the scripture, a woman can ask as much as a heap of gold by way of *mehr*. The Qur'an also warns men not to take anything away from their wives after gifting it to them. It says: 'And it is not lawful for you to take any part of what you have given them' (Surat Al-Baqarah: 229).

It is usually asserted that *mehr* is a good security against divorce. However, in case the divorce takes place due to her own fault she gets no money. The woman is entitled to *mehr* even after her husband's death and the sons have to pay if it had not been paid during the lifetime of the husband. In case the woman dies, then her father and brothers can demand her *mehr* from the husband. This account paints a very bright picture of a woman's financial position. In reality, however, one finds that very few women actually get this money.

Mehr is categorized into *shar'ai* and non-*shar'ai* depending upon the amount involved. *Shar'ai mehr* is the amount equivalent to the *mehr* Prophet Muhammad fixed for the marriage of his daughter Fatima. It was found in this study that the amount of *mehr* varies widely, ranging between Rs. 21-60,000. In the case of lower caste respondents the amount of *mehr* ranged between Rs. 21 and 1,000. In the case of upper castes respondents the amount of *mehr* ranged between Rs. 500 and 60,000 or one ashrafi (gold coin).

This goes to show that among the lower castes there is little anxiety while fixing *mehr* to use it either to prevent divorce or to provide a reasonable amount of money to the daughter in the event of divorce. This could be either due to lack of awareness or because of hold of tradition or socio-economic conditions. In the higher castes the amount of *mehr* is fixed according to the socio-economic status of the parties concerned.

PAYMENT OF *MEHR*

According to the scriptures *mehr* may be *muajjal* (prompt) or *muwajjal* (deferred). *Mehr muajjal* (prompt dower) is payable immediately after marriage. A wife can refuse to enter conjugal domicile until the payment of the *mehr*. *Mehr muwajjal* (deferred dower) is payable on dissolution of marriage by death or divorce. In India it has been the general practice not to pay *mehr* or pay only a part of it. In our study we found that 172 (86 per cent) women respondents had not received their *mehr*, though 132 (66 per cent) had a strong desire to receive it. The rest did not say directly that they did not want their *mehr*, only admitting that they did not know or could not say so. There is an element of fear here. They think that not claiming the *mehr* is a guarantee of good treatment by the husband. Women who have not freed their husbands from the liability of paying the *mehr* cannot be sure of getting it when they need it.

When we asked the women for their opinion regarding freeing husbands from *mehr*, 138 (69 per cent) said that they did not favour freeing husband from the liability of payment of *mehr*, while 38 (19 per cent) favoured it on the ground that it was according to the *shar'ia*. Another 24 (12 per cent) said it would depend on the husband's economic condition. Also, many maintained that a man completes his worldly duties in order to look forward to a peaceful death. Hence many wives favoured freeing husbands for the liability of paying the *mehr* at the time of their funeral. After the husband's death there was no question of demanding the *mehr* from the sons. In the vast majority of cases the *mehr* is a mere paper transaction. Its fixation is more of a ritual than a realistic assessment of the woman's general requirements in the event of *talaq*. Moreover, if the husband is unable to pay the *mehr* he requests his wife to condone it. The request is a form of emotional blackmail to which the wife invariably succumbs. Thus, the concept of *mehr* which was created to guarantee the economic security of the woman does not serve any useful purpose today.

DIVORCE AND MAINTENANCE

Islam is perhaps the first religion in the world which has expressly recognized the termination of marriage by way of divorce. Islam recognizes every husband's right to divorce his wife with or without reason. But if the wife wishes to leave the husband, she has to persuade him to divorce her. This form of divorce is called *khula*.

The Qur'an does not talk about wives divorcing their husbands. It only talks of husbands divorcing their wives and lays down rules regarding how to pronounce *talaq*, what treatment to mete out after the divorce such as payment of maintenance to the divorced wife and the upbringing and custody of the children, if any, etc. The Prophet is reported to have said, 'with Allah the most detestable of all things permitted is divorce'. The Qur'an ordains '. . . if ye fear a breach between them two (the husband and the wife) appoint an arbiter from his folk and an arbiter from her folk. If they desire amendment, Allah will make them of one mind' (Surat An-Nisaa: 35).

The subject of divorce has proved a great source of misconception and controversy but there can be no question that the Qur'anic verses concerning the treatment of women in the event of divorce show better humanity and regard for justice.

To assess the actual position of divorced Muslim women, case histories of all the 25 divorced/separated women in the sample were compiled. There were 9 divorcees and 16 separated women in the sample, which shows that the number of separation cases is higher than that of those divorced. It was found that almost all the divorces were pronounced at one sitting. It is common among a section of Muslims (lower caste and poor Muslims), where divorce cases are high, to divorce their wives in one sitting, pronouncing the word *talaq* thrice. In some cases men write the word *talaq* three times on an inland letter or a post-card and send it to the wife, who takes it as a written *talaqnama*. The Holy Qur'an prescribed three menstrual periods and during each period divorce is to be pronounced and it can be taken back until it is pronounced the third time during the third menstrual period when it becomes irrevocable. Thus, there is enough time for reconciliation. What is going on in practice is totally different. In our study the respondents were asked about the form of divorce given in Islam. Four options were provided to choose from: (1) It should be more difficult, (2) No change is required, (3) No opinion, and (4) Any other suggestion.

It was found that only 6 respondent (3 per cent) felt that divorce should be made more difficult. One must keep in mind that all these respondents were divorcees. As many as 144 (74 per cent) women respondents did not want any change in the divorce procedure.

When they were asked if they knew how divorce is supposed to be performed in Islam a majority said that 'when the husband says "I divorce you" thrice then divorce takes place.' There was no need of a qazi, witnesses or even a *talaqnama*. A few said that without witnesses *talaq* was not complete. Clearly, therefore, most Muslim women did not even know the correct procedure of divorce which is given in the Qur'an. Only 8 (4 per cent) women respondents said that divorce proceeding should be legal and divorce should be finalized through the court.

CASE HISTORIES

Let me present the case studies and then go on to draw some general conclusions regarding the status of divorced Muslim women in the light of the data collected as part of this study. Since there were remarkable similarities in many cases, we discuss 20 case histories.

Case history 1

Jamila Shamsuddin a 23 years old, illiterate divorcee comes from the lower income group. Her husband, also illiterate, is a carpet weaver. Both are Ansaris and lived in a joint family. She was married at the age of 15. It was an arranged marriage. She has two children, 5 year old Nadim and 4 year old Bablu.

Jamila enjoyed a happy married life for more than a year. After the birth of two children in quick succession tension started growing in the family. Sometimes she was beaten by her husband and sent to her parent's home. The source of tension most of the time was money. Her husband earned Rs. 500 to 600 per month out of which he spent about Rs. 200 on his friends. Jamila told me that it was difficult for her to manage a four member family in Rs. 300. Whenever she asked for more money or told that he take up some additional work, he became angry and started quarreling.

One day, when things were going well, he told his wife that he was going to Mumbai to earn more. His two friends were also accompanying him. Jamila was happy and after a few days he left for Mumbai. Thereafter, she did not receive a single letter from him although he had assured her that he would send his address. One day she received an inland letter telling her that he had divorced her.

After receiving the letter Jamila wrote to her parents telling what had happened. Her father came and after reading the letter took her home. Since 1983 she is staying with her children in her father's home. Nobody from her family went to her husband to enquire about the divorce.

Jamila finds it difficult to reconcile to the reality of her divorce. She did not get her *mehr* even after her husband left her. The behaviour of her family and relatives has also changed. They taunt her and her children. Although she is living in a miserable condition and enjoys no freedom she does not want to marry again because of the bitter experience of her first marriage.

At present Jamila faces no economic problem. In her spare time she splits wool for carpet weaving. For this work she is not paid because she does this to help in her father's work.

Although she is very religious, she is not aware about her rights under the Qur'an and under personal law. She is keen to learn about her rights and she says that there should be laws which could solve the problem of divorcees.

She does not plan for the future. Her children do not go to school or madrasa. They just eat, play and sleep. All of them live as member of a family. She is also not aware of the Shah Bano case. She would like lifelong maintenance to be provided to divorcees.

Case history 2

Shabana Bano, whose husband separated from her, is 27 years old. She is illiterate and comes from a middle-income Ansari family. Her husband was educated up to high school and owns a small shop. Her marriage was an arranged one and she lived in a joint family. She was married at the age of 19 years.

After marriage Shabana went to live at her husband's house. According to custom, the next day she came back to her parent's house. After a few days her husband said to some people, 'She is not good looking and fair, so I will not keep her in my house.' Neither her husband nor anybody from his family came for Shabana's *bidai* (brides return to her husband's house). Therefore, almost since the time of her marriage she has lived with her brother. About divorce she said, 'I never asked for divorce although he has married a second time. He has also not given me *mehr* or any maintenance.'

Shabana has no children and is engaged in income generating activity. She earns Rs. 5 to 6 per day. Although she is not facing any economic problem, she has an inferiority complex. When I asked her about re-marriage she said, 'I have a dark complex and I am also not good looking. So I don't want to marry again. I will live with my parents and brother. In future, if I get another job, I will take it and I will continue to stay with my brother's family.' She has no problem with her brother's family.

Shabana is not aware of the Waqf Board, personal law or the Shah Bano case. But she feels that the government should make a separate law to solve divorce and maintenance problems.

Case history 3

Bilquis Begum, a divorcee aged 30 years, has passed the high school and belongs to a high caste family. Her husband was educated up to the intermediate. He was a shop owner and earned about Rs. 1,500 per month. They had three sons and two daughters. After six years of marriage, her husband started drinking. Bilquis said, 'My husband was very co-operative and a good fellow. After six years of marriage, due to bad company he started taking alcohol. In the beginning he would not drink at home but after a year he started drinking at home also. At first he would create problems at home. Afterwards, he stopped taking any interest in family matters.'

One day after dinner he wanted to drink. Bilquis objected saying that he had five grown up children and that it was not good for him to drink in the presence of the children. He then shouted and took out the bottle. Bilquis tried to argue and snatch the bottle, but he would not give it to her. He started beating her. When the children came to stop him, he said 'I will divorce you. Leave my house with your children as soon as possible.' He gave her verbal divorce at that time. In the morning Bilquis came back to her brother's house who lived in the same city. She still lives there with her children. After a few months he sent her an inland letter informing her that he was giving her irrevocable divorce. She accepted it because she was also fed up of him.

Even after divorce Bilquis' husband has not paid her *mehr* which was fixed at Rs. 11,000, nor any maintenance. She asked her brother to demand the *mehr* but he said, 'There is no need. Under my protection you will not suffer from any problems. Forget about the money and other things.'

Today Bilquis and her children do not face any problem. Her elder son is 18 years old and is now a graduate. All her children go to school. The youngest daughter, aged 10, is studying in class six. None of her children remember their father.

Bilquis is aware of the Shah Bano case and feels that the Muslim Women (Protection of Rights on Divorce) Act, 1986, is not effective enough. In fact, she wants that there should be a more stringent law to tackle the problem of divorce and maintenance.

She is not interested in a second marriage, although her former husband has married for the second time. About the future she says, 'If my future daughter-in-law is nice, then I will stay with her. Otherwise, I will continue in the present place.' She is very fond of her brothers. All six brothers take care of Bilquis and her children. In the beginning, Bilquis was not able to forget the sweet memories of her husband, but now she is busy with her children and thinks only about her children's career and future.

Case history 4

Shabnam is an illiterate low caste Dhuniya woman. She is 27 years old. Her husband was a carpet weaver. She was separated from him after three years of marriage. Her marriage was settled by her parents within the same caste. She has two daughters aged 4 years and 2 years. Soon after marriage her husband started telling her that he would stay with his mother and she should cook her food separately. He gave her only 1 kg flour for one week. After the birth of two daughters his attitude and behaviour further changed. He had already divorced one wife before he married Shabnam. Now he wishes to re-marry his first wife. But his first wife does not want to to remarry him. The first wife is educated and independent. His daughter from the first wife lives with him and he loves and takes care of his daughter.

Shabnam has not received her *mehr* which was fixed at Rs. 101. She is not aware of the laws relating to maintenance. She has no personal opinion regarding solutions for divorce problems.

After separation she is living with her brothers. She does not want to take divorce and marry again as she has been married twice and now has children too. After separation she is facing a financial crisis.

She does not know about the Waqf Board or the Shah Bano case. She works for a *bidi* manufacturer. Regarding her future she says that if her husband asks her to go back to him she would certainly do so.

Case history 5

Rashida, a separated woman, is aged 23 years. She comes from a lower income Ansari family. She was given religious education and her husband passed the high school. He is a weaver and they lived in a joint family.

Rashida was married at the age of 21. Her father had given as much dowry as he could. But her in-laws and husband were greedy. They started demanding more. Rashida was helpless. After the delivery of her daughter, her husband asked her to bring Rs. 2,000 from her father. When Rashida wrote to her father telling her about her husband's demand her brother came to visit her. Rashida's husband sent her with her brother to her parents' house. After a few months, she went back to her husband, but he said to her brother, who had gone to leave her, that if she had Rs. 2,000 then she could live with him, otherwise he would not keep her. Hearing this Rashida took her daughter and came back with her brother. Now she and her father want divorce, but her husband is not interested in giving her a divorce.

Rashida's father is old and does not earn. Her three brothers are *dari* weavers and they have taken over her responsibility. Rashida does not face any problem at present. She splits wool, which is a part of her work at home.

She has some knowledge of her legal rights, and has heard of the Shah Bano case. She does not know how the problem of divorce can be solved. She feels that in her case her husband is at fault.

She is not interested in marrying again, but if her father and brother put pressure on her to marry again, she may. She wants to go to court for divorce and maintenance, but her brothers would not allow her.

She lives with her parents and is keen to know the details of her legal rights. She says that her future is to look after her daughter.

Case history 6

Fatima comes from a middle class Pathan family. She has passed higher secondary school. She was married at the age of 19 and is now 28 years old. Since 1985, she has been living in her parents' house. Her husband has neither divorced her nor taken her to his house. She has two sons and two daughters. Her husband has studied up to Intermediate and has a general merchant's shop. Fatima reported that he earned Rs. 600 per month which was not enough for a family of six. Sometimes tension would develop in the family and they would start shouting at each other. He did not talk too much and would spend most of his time outside the house. One day he said to Fatima that he wanted to marry another girl and if she wanted to live with her she could stay otherwise she could return to her parental home. Fatima returned to her father's house with her children. She has two sons and two daughters. After a few days she heard that he married the other girl. Fatima's brother went to him demanding *talaqnama* but he refused saying that he would not give her divorce or maintenance. 'This is her house also, he said, 'Whenever she wants to come here, she can do so. Nobody will say anything to her.'

Fatima is not very happy in her parental home. She has lots of responsibilities. In a few years she has to marry off her daughter but she has no money. She has been looking for work but has not found any thing yet. Her father and brother are taking care of her, but they are not well. This worries Fatima. She would have liked to remarry, but that is out of the question for the present. She reasons, 'I have four children. Who will marry me? Also my husband has not given me divorce so I cannot marry another person.' She does not think about the future. She has left everything to God's grace and readily accepts her fate.

Case history 7

Nasreen comes from an illiterate, lower caste family. She has seven brothers and sisters. She married Sattar at the age of 21 and at the time of data collection she was 28 years old. Her husband is also illiterate and earns Rs. 1,200 per month as a weaver. After four years of marriage they separated.

Nasreen reported that her husband was fond of delicious food and good clothes and spent a lot of money on those things. He always wanted his lunch and dinner at a fixed time in a quiet and happy atmosphere. He did not like children's cries or shouting. Very early they had two daughters. The younger daughter was very weak and always cried and wept while the elder daughter sometimes shouted and also cried. Once night Nasreen was in the toilet. Their younger daughter was crawling near the bed. She fell down and started crying loudly. Her husband did not bother. When Nasreen came out running from the toilet, she found the baby lying on the floor with blood oozing out of her mouth. This angered Nasreen. She shouted at her husband for being so unfeeling and indifferent as not to even look after the baby when she was bleeding. He then shouted back at her and asked her to live quietly or leave the house. After two hour he returned and again told her to leave his house or he would divorce her. This was not the first time he had behaved this way, but she had always reconciled. After he shouted at her three to four times, she took her things and went to live with her parents. She has been living there for the past three years with her children. Her husband has not come to take them back.

Nasreen is not getting any maintenance from her husband. The responsibility of looking after Nasreen and her children has now fallen on her parents. Neither Nasreen nor her parents want divorce. They feel that it is of no use now. She has never heard of Shah Bano or her case. After being told about the case she said, 'Shah Bano and the Supreme Court are both right.' She felt that there was no need to make stringent laws to teach people a lesson. Although at first Nasreen said that she was not facing any problems, she reported subsequently that sometimes relatives and neighbours taunted her. She felt that if she could find work her economic condition would improve. She does not like the idea of a second marriage. At the same time she says that whatever her parents decide she would have to accept.

Case history 8

Banno, aged 34, is a separated woman. She is illiterate and belongs to an Ansari family. Her husband is an illiterate weaver. Banno comes from a joint family. Her family is traditional and orthodox.

At the time of her marriage she was 16 years old. In the beginning, she says, they were very happy. After a year she delivered a boy, but unfortunately he died of cholera. She became very ill and went to her mother's house for treatment. After two month when she returned things seemed normal. She became pregnant again and this time a stillborn child was born. Her husband was very disappointed and a change came over him. Since the other women in the family were in the business of rolling *bidis*, Banno also joined in. She started earning Rs. 5 per day. At the same time her husband started drinking. Sometimes he would create a fuss over small things like food, washing clothes and other domestic chores. He stopped giving regular money for household expenses to Banno. He also took her money for alcohol. After a few months Banno learnt that he had a gild friend, a divorcee without children. He married her and started living with her in another house. He then stopped coming home. When Banno's father heard this he came and told her, 'What will you do here? Let us go home.' Therefore she returned to her parental home and started making *bidis* there. Now she is earning Rs. 7 to 8 daily. Banno says that she does not want to remember her past life and does not want to return to her husband. A year later he came and told Banno that his second wife had left him and she could return. Banno replied curtly, 'I will not live with you. I am happy here.'

Now Banno and her widowed mother live together. Her mother

is an unskilled labourer. Both are working. Banno has no problem except the lack of a permanent job.

Banno does not know about Shah Bano or any divorce laws. When asked if she wanted divorce she said, 'After four years of marriage I left my husband's house. In the beginning neither did my family demand divorce nor did my husband give me divorce. Now I am 34 years old. What will I do with the *talaqnama*?'

She never thinks about a second marriage.

Case history 9

Marjeena is a 32 years old separated woman. She was married at the age of 19. She is illiterate and comes from a lower caste joint family. Her husband is a weaver and earns about Rs. 1,000 per month. Marjeena's marriage was arranged and initially both husband and wife lived happily.

After two years of marriage Marjeena delivered a stillborn child. Her husband was very disappointed because he wanted children very much. After the delivery Marjeena became very week and sick and could not conceive again. Marjeena's husband started telling her and his family members that he very much wants a child. After three years Marjeena's husband started saying that he wanted a child, and if Marjeena cannot provide him with one, he would marry another girl. One day he married another girl and told Marjeena that if she wanted to live with her she could do so otherwise she could go to her parents' house. She chose to return to her parental home.

Now Marjeena lives with her mother and brothers. Two of her brothers are carpet weavers and one is a motor mechanic.

In the beginning Marjeena's family members asked her husband to divorce her but he said that he would neither divorce her nor give any maintenance. She could if she wanted, live with him. She has received neither her *mehr* nor maintenance. She does not face any economic problem. She earns Rs. 10 to Rs. 12 daily. She is not interested in a second marriage. She neither knows about her legal rights in personal law nor about the Shah Bano case. She maintains that she is happy where she is. She has no suggestions for solving the marriage or divorce problems of Muslims. She never thinks about the future. She is happy with her parental family and feels somewhat better here compared to living with her husband.

Case history 10

Bano, a 27 years old separated woman, belongs to a middle-income family. Both husband and wife are illiterate. She was married into a joint family which had twelve members living together. Her husband worked in a dyeing shop. They had two children, 6 years old Rehman and 4 years old Munni.

Bano was married at the age of 18. In her marital home she found that a separated sister-in-law with her three children was already living in the household. After Bano had her own children, the problems started. Her children and her sister-in-law's children played together and they also frequently quarreled. Her children were younger so they were often beaten up. Following the children's quarrels, sometimes the elders also quarreled. One day Bano's daughter was badly beaten and began to bleed from her head. Bano and her sister-in-law started quarrelling. When her husband sided with his sister Bano quarreled with her husband, who then beat her. After that incident she came back to her parent's home. After a few day her father wrote a letter to her husband. The husband did not reply, but his mother wrote saying there was no need for her to return. When Bano's father visited her husband, he and his family members quarreled and behaved badly with him. Since then Bano is living with her parents. Sometimes she splits wool and earns some money. Her children are not receiving any kind of education. Her father has a shop and earns more than Rs. 1,000 per month. He has to support six members of the family.

Bano is against marriage now. Because she does not want to remarry she has not asked her husband for a divorce.

Bano is not aware of the Shah Bano case or her own legal rights. Even though she recites the Qur'an daily she does not know the meaning of the verses. She says that if she were educated she would have liked to work. About her future she says that it is for her parents to decide and she would do whatever they want.

Case history 11

Noorjahan Begum, a divorcee aged 19, is illiterate and comes from a lower caste Ansari family. Her husband Jabbar studied up to high school and has a small shop in Mumbai. Noorjahan was married at the age of 18 and her marriage was arranged. Both families belonged to the same caste and socio-economic background. She has no children.

Very soon after the marriage her husband left for Mumbai. After sometime she heard that Jabbar already had a girl friend in Mumbai and he wanted to marry her. But since the girl friend came from the Puniya caste the marriage could not take place. After a year, Noorjahan received a letter from Jabbar telling here that he had married another woman and was divorcing her.

After divorce Jabbar did not give Noorjahan her *mehr*, which was fixed at Rs. 51, nor *iddat ka kharch* (maintenance during *iddat*). She does not face any economic problems at the moment. She rolls *bidis* part time and earns Rs. 5 to 6 daily. The behaviour of her family members has not changed; they are very sympathetic and cooperative towards her.

Noorjahan does not know anything about the personal law or legal rights given to a Muslim woman. She has no opinion about the solution of women's or divorcee's problems. She is not interested in a second marriage but her mother maintains that when they are able to find a suitable match for her she will prepare her for a second marriage.

After divorce she is living with her parents. About her future, she says that she would have to do whatever her parents tell her. Her future depends upon them.

Case history 12

Zaibunnisa is aged 29 and comes from a high caste, middle-income group family. She has passed junior high school and her husband who owns a small shop is educated up to high school. They lived in a joint family. She was married at the age of 19 years to a man belonging to the same caste and has no children.

After a year of marriage her husband started taking alcoholic drinks. In the beginning he drank outside the home with his friend.

After some time he started drinking at home too and began quarrelling with her. Sometimes he also beat her. Like this she spent more than four year with him. But one day he drank too much and beat her very badly. He broke her hand and threw her out of the house. For the last five years Zaibunnisa is living with her parents. Here she has no problem. Her parents are interested in getting her a divorce, but her husband is not willing to give divorce, *mehr* fixed at Rs. 501 or maintenance. She is also not aware of her legal rights. But she is very keen to know more about it and says that the government should make a separate law for women that would solve their divorce or maintenance problems.

Right now Zaibunnisa has no future plans. She believes in God and says, 'Allah will help.'

Case history 13

Nigar Anjum, a 30 years old separated woman, comes from a high caste Muslim family. She is educated up to the high school. Her husband has passed the Intermediate and is employed as a clerk in a private office. They come from a middle-class nuclear family. Nigar was married at the age of 21, and now she has an 8 year-old son named Irshad. Irshad is studying in the second standard. Nigar's was an arranged marriage and she left her husband after three years. She is living with her parents for the last six years along with her son.

Nigar said that her husband sent her a letter from Mumbai saying that he had married another woman. He had no objection if Nigar stayed on in his parents' house. After this letter Nigar came to her parents' house. She said, 'My in-laws were very cooperative and well-behaved. They liked me and asked me to not leave as it was my house and I could stay on there.' But Nigar's parents did not agree to this and so she came back. Sometimes her in-laws come to see her and their grand son. But her husband has never visited her nor written to her for the last six years.

Neither party is keen on a divorce. Neither Nigar nor her parents are keen on a second marriage. She has heard about the Shah Bano case and the controversy about it. About the Muslim Women (Protection of Rights on Divorce) Act, 1986, she said that it had not affected the Muslim divorced or separated women. At the same time she has no opinion of her own regarding what the government should do to solve the problems of divorcees and separated women.

Nigar said, 'I have no plans for the future except that I would educate my son as much as I can. The goal of my life is now to educate Irshad.'

Case history 14

Shamim Khan, a divorcee aged 28 years, comes from a high caste, middle-income group family. Both husband and wife are educated. They were living in a joint family. Her husband was a draftsman and earned more than Rs. 1,000 per month. Her marriage was an arranged one. She has two children: Shabana, 12 years old, is studying in the sixth standard, and Shaqeel, 9 years old, is studying in the third standard. She was married at the age of 15 and after four years of marriage she was divorced by her husband who pronounced triple *talaq* in one sitting.

Shamim said, 'My husband lived in Lucknow. When I went to Lucknow last time he refused to recognize me.' So she came back to her in-laws house. She again went to Lucknow with her mother-in-law and brother. He again refused to recognize her. Every one favoured her except her husband. The next day they came back. She says that her husband's family and her parents are related, and so everybody in her marital home is affectionate and sympathetic to her. She is the only daughter of her parents, so she lives with her parents. Her parents-in-law are also her neighbours. She always spends some time with them also. Her husband never visits his own family or hers. Recently, she heard that he had married a poor, illiterate woman, and it was a love marriage.

Shamim said that her husband did not want to marry her because he had promised marriage to another girl. But due to his father's pressure and consideration for his old age he agreed to marry Shamim. His father passed away after four years after the marriage. After that he was free, so he divorced Shamim and after a few years married his earlier lover.

After divorce Shamim has filed a suit in the court for maintenance and she has been fighting the case for seven years. She has not got her *mehr* of Rs. 11,000 or any maintenance order from the court yet.

She is not facing any socio-economic problems. She is interested in a second marriage. She says, 'if she found a suitable man she would marry'. She says that there should be a law to solve the problems of divorcees. For the future she says that if she gets married again there is no problem, otherwise she will stay on in her parents' house where also she has no problem.

Case history 15

Bibbi, a 26 years old separated woman, comes from a high caste. She is educated up to the junior high school. Her husband is also educated and runs a general store. Their marriage was an arranged one and they lived in a joint family. She was married at the age of 19.

When Bibbi went to her husband's house after her wedding, he said, 'You are not the same girl whom I saw before the marriage. So I will not keep you.' Bibbi was shocked and did not know why he had changed all of a sudden. Now she wants a divorce, but her husband is playing tricks and refuses to give her one. He kept promising her brother that he would send her a *talaqnama* (written divorce) within a few days but has not sent one yet.

Bibbi feels that if she had got a divorce in time, she could have married again. But now she is 26 years old and nobody would marry her. So she has given up the idea of asking for a divorce now.

She has heard of the Shah Bano case and feels that the government should make strict laws for divorcees and separated women. She also says that the government should start some income generating schemes for people like her so that they can become self-dependent and do not have to live on the mercy of others. She reports that the behaviour of family members, relatives and neighbours has not changed. They are now more sympathetic and friendly.

She has no plans for the future. She says she will do whatever her parents ask her to do.

Case history 16

Ranno, a separated woman, is 26 years old and comes from a Pathan family. She was educated at home and her husband Rashid has been educated up to the Intermediate. He has a stationary shop and earns near about Rs. 1,000 per month. Their marriage was an arranged one and they lived in a joint family.

Her husband had a very bad temper and would start shouting at small things. He also beat her sometimes. This went on for two years, but Ranno did not tell about this to her parents. Just before Id, her husband asked his mother for Id clothes. Ranno said that she too wanted some at which he began to shout at her and beat her badly. Then Ranno sent a letter to her mother telling her about her problems. Her father went to her marital home and tried to talk to her husband. Rashid did not behave well with her father also. Therefore, Ranno's father said to here, 'Let us go home.' For the last three years she is living with her parents. She has a five year old school-going son. About divorce she says, 'I never asked for one, and actually I don't need it.' She does not know about the Shah Bano case or women's legal rights. She is in favour of a law that can solve the problem of divorced women.

She does not wish to go in for a second marriage. She says that she will not make the same mistake again. She has not received her *mehr* nor is getting maintenance. Her parents have taken the responsibility of providing for her. She say, 'I will educate my child, and I have to live for my child.'

Case history 17

Shahina, aged 29 years, is a separated woman. She comes from a high caste Muslim family. Her husband is a carpet weaver. Both wife and husband are literate. Their marriage was arranged and they lived in a joint family.

Shahina was married at the age of 18 and was thrown out of the matrimonial home by her husband after three years of marriage. Her husband wanted to marry another woman so she told Shahina, 'you are neither good looking nor well behaved so I am going to take another wife. It would be better if you go to your parent's house.' After this Shahina stayed on for a few days, but when the second wife came Shahina felt psychologically hurt so she came back to her parental home. Neither Shahina nor her husband was interested in a divorce. Shahina's father considered it to be a prestige issue. He said, 'why should I ask for a divorce. It is his fault, not my daughter's. And, I know that it is because of the fear of maintenance that he is not giving her a divorce.' Although Shahina has no children, she still faces some economic problems. The economic condition of her parents is not good. Her father has just retired from a teaching job.

Shahina has not heard of the Waqf Board or the Shah Bano case. She is in favour of laws which can solve the problems of women. She is very keen to do some work, to earn some money. But due to the purdah system she cannot go out of the house to work. She wants some job where she works at home.

About the future she says, 'My future is in Allah's hands. I cannot say anything about it.'

Case history 18

Nasim Bano, a 29 year old separated woman, comes from a poor lower caste family. Both the husband and wife are illiterate and roll *bidis*. Nasim earns Rs. 5 to 6 daily by rolling more than a 1,000 *bidis*. She was married at the age of 18. Their marriage was an arranged one and they lived in a joint family.

Tension arose between her and her husband after the birth of the first child. Her husband Salim started telling her that it was not his child and both of them would have to leave his house. He threatened divorce. None of the elders in the family intervened. Indeed, they started looking for another girl and Salim soon married again. This time he got a cycle, radio, sewing machine, van and television, etc., as dowry. Nasim then went back to her parental family.

Whenever Nasim's brother asks Salim or his father for a divorce, they either ignore him or simply say that they would post a *talaqnama*. Nasim does not want to go to court for a divorce or maintenance as she feels that by going to court she would lose her dignity. She would like some maintenance, but cannot do much about it.

Nasim is not in favour of remarriage. She believes that whatever happened to her was because of her bad luck. Her son Rehman never asks about his father. He is an introvert child. The responsibility to look after Nasim and her son has been taken by her parents. Nasim is also earning. She is a religious woman and has a firm belief in God. She has put her future in Allah's hands.

Case history 19

Shabnam Bano, aged 24 years is separated from her husband. She is literate and comes from a low caste joint family. Her husband was a weaver and earned Rs. 600 per month. Shabnam has one child.

She was married in 1985. Sometimes her mother-in-law and sister-in-law would indirectly talk about dowry but her husband never said anything. He was a nice person. Shabnam reported that whenever she visited her parents someone from her husband's house would come to fetch her back. But the last time when no body came for a few months, she went to her in-laws' house with her brother. Her husband was there but did not say anything to her. Her mother-in-law and sister-in-law instead said that her father had not given a TV to their son. If her father and brother want her to live with her husband they must pay Rs. 5,000 or TV otherwise she must return to her parents' house. Shabnam wanted to go to her room, but her in-laws objected and shouted at her. Then her brother forced her to go back with him. Shabnam is now living with her parents.

Shabnam was separated in 1986. Her husband has neither given her *mehr* nor has he divorced her. Her parents are interested in getting a divorce and her *mehr* which was fixed at Rs. 250, but her husband has not responded positively. Shabnam feels that her husband was not a bad person but her mother-in-law and sister-in-law were very greedy and always demanded dowry and money.

Shabnam wants to go to her husband but she is helpless. She is doing what her parents tell her to do. She is working and earns Rs. 5 to 6 daily. She does not know about the Shah Bano case or any law, but she feels that the government should have made stringent laws on these issues.

She would not like to marry again. If her husband asks her, she would be willing to go back to him. She has no ambition and she does not worry about the future.

Case history 20

Nadira, a divorcee aged 25 years, is illiterate and comes from a poor lower caste family. Her husband was an illiterate *dari* weaver. Their marriage was an arranged one and they lived in a joint family. They had two children: 3 years old Irshad, and one year old Noorjahan. At present both are living with their mother in her father's house.

Nadira was married at the age of 21 years. Her husband was very nice to her in the beginning. After the birth of Irshad, he was very happy. He spent a lot of his time with Irshad. Nadira did not keep good health after this delivery. Very soon, she began expecting a second baby, and this time a baby girl was born. Her husband was not happy. Both mother and baby were very sick and became weak. Her mother-in-law and sisters-in-law did not care for Nadira and her children. Sometimes her husband also became irritable and shouted at her. One day he beat her for not helping in the household work. On another occasion, in summer, Irshad was playing in the courtyard when her husband came home and beat up Irshad. He was in a very angry mood and would not stop. He said, 'This is too much, I will divorce you.' When Nadira retorted that this was not such an easy thing to do, he said three times: 'I divorce you.' Like this Nadira's husband divorced her. She has no written *talaqnama*. Even after divorce she has not got her *mehr* fixed at Rs. 51 and maintenance.

Nadira is not aware of her legal rights. She says that she cannot go to court, 'I am not educated.' She feels that the behaviour of her family members and relatives is now more sympathetic and cooperative. Nadira wants to marry again. She is confident that if she marries again, there will be no problem in the future.

At present she is not facing any economic problem. Her parents have taken over her responsibility. She has no ambition. About her future, she says, 'What can I say? Allah knows best.'

CONCLUSION

From the data provided by these case histories a number of conclusions can be arrived at. There is clear indication that the number of separated women is far higher than divorced women.

While this does not enable us to reach a conclusion about the frequency of divorce as such, it does show that in a large number of cases the common response of the husband to marital discord is to severe marital relations with his wife without pronouncing a divorce. Where a marriage breaks down, the husband either asks his wife to go back to her parental family (or simply throws her out of the matrimonial home) or quietly marries someone else which leaves no other option for the wife than to return to her parents.

Evidence provided by these case histories also suggests that where a woman or her parental family is interested to obtain a divorce, the husband quite often evades giving her one. Whether this is done to escape the liability of paying the *mehr* or keep her tied to him is unclear. Even the few women who were initially keen for a divorce eventually became resigned to their fate and did not take any strong action to secure one. Many women are also reluctant to take divorce because this still leaves the door open for an eventual patch up. Some of them clearly said they would readily go back if the husband would be willing to take them back.

Among the divorced women, the tragedy struck them within the first few years of marriage though there were also cases where the divorce took place after several years of marriage. This lends itself to a possible inference that the first few years of a marriage are crucial. If the couple and the in-laws are able to sort out the conflicts, which may arise from any number of causes, the marriage survives and the possibility of divorce recedes into the background. If they fail to resolve the conflict, the marriage usually ends up either in separation or divorce.

It is clear that the role of the in-laws is vital in a large majority of cases. On the one hand, the in-laws themselves sometimes instigate tensions and conflicts by posing a dilemma before the husband to either side with them or with his wife. Where the husband is unable to tide over this predicament, he either ends up separating from his wife or divorces her. The formula of triple divorce comes in handy for simple termination of marriage.

The large majority of women whom we interviewed came from lower caste and poor or deprived family background. They are neither educated nor are in command of special skills to be able to lead a comfortable life on their own. They do not get their *mehr* or maintenance from their husbands. After the divorce, they fall back upon their parents and brothers who, whether grudgingly or ungrudgingly, take the responsibility of providing for them on their shoulders. It is clear that there is a settled pattern that in the event of a divorce the daughter would automatically return to the parental family and would be taken care of as a member of the family.

Even though a divorce is a complex event and isolating the reason why a marriage broke down may not always be easy, there is indication in these case histories that the reasons for separation are fourfold: (1) bigamy or a second marriage, (2) alcoholism leading to frequent quarrels within the family, (3) non-cooperation from the in-laws or hostile attitude of other members of the family, and (4) dowry demands which the wife's family often cannot meet. Whatever the cause, separation or divorce does create social problems for the divorced woman. She loses her status and has to depend on semi-skilled or unskilled work for survival.

14

Muslim Women and the Dowry Prohibition Act, 1961: A Study of Selected Divorce Cases

Mohammad Arif Rasheed

Like other Indian women, Muslim women, too, are today subject to two separate sets of laws. One is the Muslim Personal Law. The other is the set of criminal and civil laws enacted by the state since Independence to mitigate the situation of women in society. These social legislations were enacted to curb certain social customs or to deal with social evils that affected women adversely. For example, the Dowry Prohibition Act was passed to curb the demand for dowry which had, in course of time, assumed an evil form. Section 125 of the Criminal Procedure Code was enacted to curb the evils of vagrancy and destitution. It allowed women the right to claim maintenance from their former husbands if they did not have any other means of subsistence. Again, Section 498A of the Indian Penal Code was enacted to protect women from domestic violence. Even though some of these enactments, such as the Dowry Prohibition Act, 1961 were meant primarily to deal with specific social evils prevalent in Hindu society, their application was not limited to Hindu women. They were enacted as general laws available to all women irrespective of their religious affiliations.

Muslim women traditionally took recourse to courts for settlement of marital disputes under Muslim Personal Law only where substantial property matters were involved. The number of Muslim women landing up in courts was small and restricted to women from propertied families. After the enactment of Section 125 of the Criminal Procedure Code, Muslim women from the lower social strata, who could afford to bear the cost of prolonged litigation, started using this provision when their husbands summarily divorced them under the provision of triple divorce under Muslim Personal Law. Most often, these legal proceedings would be launched with the encouragement and support of women's organizations and social groups which came up to promote the cause of Muslim women. After the enactment of the Muslim Women (Protection of Rights on Divorce) Act, 1986 whose explicit purpose was to bring Muslim women back under the purview of Muslim Personal Law, Muslim women are now required to ask for maintenance under that enactment. However, the option of using the relevant provisions of the Indian Penal Code and the Dowry Prohibition Act, 1961, continue to be available to them and are sometimes invoked in marital conflicts.

There has been growing recognition in recent years that the Dowry Prohibition Act, though a well-intentioned provision, is amenable to gross misuse. Women use these provisions to entangle their husbands and their marital family in legal proceedings to secure a favourable settlement when the circumstances of the case do not warrant resort to them. However, no study on this aspect has been done so far. In this paper I discuss some cases of Muslim women who launched legal proceedings under these provisions against their husbands or their marital family in Bijnor town in western Uttar Pradesh. These cases were located from police and court records and subsequently followed up for detailed interview with the spouses and other close kin to determine the precise nature of the marital dispute as well as the nature of the complaint filed by them with the police authorities. Our aim in collecting both kinds of evidence was to determine the degree of correspondence or otherwise between the nature of the marital dispute and how it had been represented in the legal proceedings launched by them. This should enable us to arrive at some understanding of how the provisions in question are actually used and to what intents and purposes. This kind of thoroughgoing understanding is necessary before any evaluation can be made of the extent of misuse of these provisions.

THE CASE OF SAFANA vs. ZAHID

Safana comes from a Sheikh Siddiqi family in Bijnor. Her mother as well as her maternal grandmother had been through a divorce earlier. Her maternal grandmother's husband married a nurse and brought her home. This annoyed her and she decided to leave her husband and come back to her parental home. She never went back to her husband. Neither did she ask for a divorce. Her brothers supported her and took care of the upbringing and education of her daughter Khushnooda.

Khushnooda was divorced because her husband thought that she had a bad character and was involved with her maternal cousin. Her husband and mother-in-law told her not to have anything to do with her maternal cousin. However, whenever her husband went to Delhi on work, she called him to the house and would be closeted with him for long hours. The mother-in-law resented this and told her son. One day the husband left for Delhi on some work but returned suddenly to find the room locked from inside. When he asked for the door to be opened, he found Khushnooda with her maternal cousin. He promptly pronounced divorce and angrily said that their youngest daughter was not his child. He also returned her dowry.

Khushnooda's maternal uncle was greatly distressed by the divorce. Since Khushnooda had been educated up to the tenth standard only, he encouraged her to study further. She passed the intermediate and BTC and soon found a job as a schoolteacher. Khushnooda never remarried but had friendships with many men. This brought her a bad name. People even gossiped about her relationship with her elder daughter's husband.

As a young girl, Safana had a love affair with a boy. This was in the know of her mother, sisters, brothers-in-law, maternal aunt and neighbours. The boy, however, married some other girl. This rendered Safana's marriage prospects bleak to any one in the town. Whenever a marriage proposal came from a local family, someone or the other would inform them of Safana's past and the proposal would be dropped. Finally, Safana's mother decided to take her to her former husband who lived in Delhi and asked him to find a suitable match for her. One of Safana's father's friends suggested a match and even helped to get the engagement formalities completed.

At the time of the engagement Safana's mother did not invite any of her relatives as she was afraid of exposing Safana's past. She and her elder son-in-law performed the engagement and returned to Bijnor. Sweets were later distributed among her relatives to announce Safana's engagement. This understandably annoyed the relatives.

Soon after the engagement Safana's prospective husband, Zahid, started receiving anonymous phone calls. The caller would give her former boy friend's name while calling. He would say that he was her lover and he would kill her prospective husband. He alone could marry her.

As a result of these calls Zahid's family called Safana's mother to Delhi and broke the engagement. They also returned the gifts they had received at the time of the engagement. Safana's mother pleaded with them, saying that some enemy was doing this out of malice. By thus arousing sympathy in the heart of the boy and his mother she persuaded them to complete the marriage formalities as soon as possible. Zahid's mother refused to bring the marriage party to Bijnor. She insisted on the marriage being performed in Delhi. Safana's mother agreed readily. Zahid lived in Delhi, was the only son of his parents and owned a large bungalow. Safana's mother was apprehensive that if the engagement was broken it would bring a bad name to her family and there would be further difficulties in finding a suitable match for Safana. She agreed to all the conditions and fixed a date for an early marriage.

The marriage was held in a hotel in Delhi and was performed with great pomp and show. Safana was well received in Zahid's house and there was no apparent friction. However, on his wedding night Zahid wanted to know from Safana about her boy friend. Safana pretended ignorance but her husband was not satisfied. Next day he took her to a doctor for a check up and an ultrasound test. He did this because a day earlier he had received an anonymous call and the caller had said that she was carrying his child. Even though the ultrasound was negative, Zahid's suspicion was not assuaged. The following morning he asked Safana to fast and to swear by the Qur'an that she was pure. He was satisfied only after she had done this. Afterwards, he came two or three times to Bijnor with Safana, but the anonymous phone calls kept coming. Whenever such calls came, there would be a quarrel between husband and wife. Safana's mother-in-law and sister-in-law would also taunt her for the calls. Zahid had no trust in Safana. He gave money for household expenses every evening to his mother. He did not give any money to Safana. She was, therefore, always hard pressed for money. When Zahid would be away, her mother-in-law and sister-in-law would sit at a distance and pass rude comments on her work. She had to do all the household work. Her mother-in-law would say that one day her daughter would be married and would go away to her own house so why should she look after this house. Safana should take care of it.

Safana would get tired doing housework all day. Besides, the mother-in-law and sister-in-law found fault with her work. If she received a telephone call, they would pick up the receiver on the extension and quietly listen to her conversation. In the evening Zahid, his mother and sister would sit together and gossip. Zahid would not talk with Safana. Whenever an anonymous call came, Zahid's mother would call up Safana's mother and complain to her. She would tell Safana's mother that her son had been cheated and his life had been ruined.

Whenever Safana's mother went to Delhi her elder son-in-law accompanied her. On one occasion Safana's husband complained about her former lover in the presence of her brother-in-law at which the brother-in-law hit her. Zahid concluded from this incident that Safana's relations with her brother-in-law were not normal, and that relations between Safana's mother and her son-in-law were not normal either. After this incident, Zahid told Safana that her brother-in-law should not accompany her mother to Delhi. Safana conveyed this to her mother and told her not bring him with her to Delhi. However, Safana's mother did not pay any heed and as always took her son-in-law to Delhi with her. This aggravated the situation. When her husband was away, Safana would cling to her brother-in-law and narrate her troubles to him. Zahid's mother would communicate this to Zahid in the evening.

Safana was by this time six months pregnant. Her mother persuaded Zahid and his mother to allow her to take Safana to Bijnor for delivery, as there would be no one to look after her during her confinement. Zahid's mother readily agreed to this suggestion and sent Safana along with her mother.

Safana stayed in Bijnor till her delivery but neither Zahid nor his mother ever asked after her. After Safana delivered a baby girl Zahid, his mother and sister came and brought some gifts for the newborn. When Zahid tried to lift the child to fondle her, his sister objected pleading that the child was too small and might fall out of his hands. They left for Delhi after a few hours.

Two weeks later Safana was sent a *talaqnama* by registered post. She refused to accept the letter. Her brother-in-law consulted many lawyers in Bijnor who advised her to accept the letter. After a month she received a second letter and accepted it. It contained a lawyer's notice of divorce. Let me reproduce parts of the letter. It read:

Madam,
Under instructions from and on behalf of my client . . . I have to serve you with the following notice once again. Last month one notice was serve [*sic*] you dated 20.12.1997, which was refused by you.

1. That my client was married with you according to Muslim rites and ceremonies on 11.11.1996. After marriage both you and my client resided together as husband and wife cohabited with each other. As such the marriage was duly consummated and out of this wedlock one female child was born who is at present in your custody.
2. That after the solemnization of the marriage with my client, you have been harassing, maltreating and torturing my client from time to time to coerce him to accept your illegal and unlawful demands which are/were against the wishes of my client's family.
3. That you left the matrimonial home with the consent of my client and his family members with your mother on 4.12.1996.
4. That you returned back to your matrimonial home on 28.12.1996 and living with my client.
5. That while you were living in matrimonial home you created obscene [*sic*] in the family, which could not be tolerated, and my client requested you time and again not to create any tension in the family.
6. That my client tolerated all these things that best [*sic*] sense will prevail upon you in near future as you were in advance stage of pregnancy at that time but all in vain.
7. That on 10.9.1997 you left the matrimonial home with valuable clothes and gold jewellery weighing 100 gms., i.e. one necklace, one ring, one pair bangles and one pair tops/earrings and one silver set as the marriage was in your relation and you never turned back to your matrimonial home.

8. That you blessed a female child on 21.9.1997 named Atiya Rabbi and no intimation was sent to my client and on telephone my client learnt the same from your parents.
9. That my client was receiving telephonic calls from unknown persons before marriage and my client lodged a complaint to D.C.P. PS. . . on 21.10.1996 as the life of my client and his family members are in danger and after ignoring all these things my client married you with the hope that life partner will help my client in this critical situation but no fruitful result [*sic*].
10. That from the above incidents, my client is sure that he would be murdered or attacked by your hired persons. Therefore, after thinking over the issue, my client has divorced you in the presence of Mohd. Meraj and Zaheer Ahmad as follows:
    (a) I divorced thy [*sic*] Smt. Safana Masood,
    (b) I divorced thy [*sic*] Smt. Safana Masood,
    (c) I divorced thy [*sic*] Smt. Safana Masood.
11. That my client is willing to keep and maintain the daughter Atiya Rabbi born out of this wedlock, who is at present in your custody.

I, hereby call upon you through this notice to accept the divorce and not to claim any right of wife from my client in future, failing which my client shall be free to initiate legal proceedings against you in the court of law, which please note.

After reading the letter Safana called her father in Delhi and told her troubles to him. She tried to persuade him to go and try to talk to Zahid. Though her father had not attended her wedding, on hearing her story he told her not to worry and assured her that he would try to bring about reconciliation. He went to Zahid's house, but Zahid's family pushed him out of the house and shut the door on him. He went a second time along with his lawyer friend who had helped arrange the marriage to persuade Zahid to reconsider his decision. Zahid flatly said that he had divorced her and would not accept her back.

Safana's father came to Bijnor and told her to start legal proceedings against Zahid. 'When they go to jail then they will come round', he said. Thereafter Safana, her mother and brother-in-law consulted a good lawyer in the town. He charged them Rs. 2,100, inflicted some wounds on Safana's body and sent her with his *munshi* to the District Hospital for a medical examination.

Let me reproduce the doctor's report to show how lawyers concoct cases on behalf of their clients. It read:

Examined Smt. Safana age about 28 years wife of Zahid Hassan, resident of . . . in joint District Hospital Bijnor at 1:45 p.m. on 4.1.98. B.B. Ashraf Ilahi son of Karam Ilahi aged about 36 years resident of . . . (paternal cousin). Black mole on back of hand 2 cms. below left wrist joint.

Injuries: (1) Incised wound 11/2 cms. x linear x skin deep bleeding fresh. 2 cms below right wrist joint (distally) on back of right hand.

(2) Red contusion of size 6 cms x 11/2 cms on outer side on middle part of left leg.

(3) Left contusion 5 cms x 11/2 cms on outer side of upper arm 15 cms above elbow joint.

(4) Abraded red contusion of size 2 cms x 1 cm on back of left shoulder.

C/o pain in head and back. Opinion all injuries are fresh, sample no. 1 is by a sharp and rest are by a blunt object.

On the basis of this report Safana's lawyer drafted an FIR in which he concocted an incident of domestic violence and maintained that the wounds he had himself inflicted on Safana's body with a blade were in fact knife wounds Zahid had inflicted. After some middlemen had given Rs. 2,500 as bribe to the police a case under Section 498A, 324 IPC and 3 and 4 of the Dowry Prohibition Act, 1961 was filed against Zahid, his mother and sister. Let me reproduce a part of the FIR:

The applicant was married to Zahid Hassan one year ago. At the time of marriage my parents gave dowry beyond their means, but right after marriage my in-laws used to beat me for not brining enough dowry. They used to turn me out of the house and took me back after my mother gave money. My in-laws turned me out of the house about two and a half months back and said that I should give birth to the child at my mother's place and should not return without a car. On October 21, 1997, my daughter was born at Bijnor. All expenses were borne by my mother. Then my husband and in-laws came to Bijnor and told that I gave birth to a daughter so I should bring a car as part of the dowry. My mother said that she was not in a position to give a car, but she would give the cost of the car in small instalments. My in-laws subsequently conveyed that they would come to Bijnor on 4th January and I should keep the money ready.

Today, i.e. 4th January 1998 my husband Zahid Hassan, son of Tahir Hassan, with my mother-in-law Firdos Jahan, wife of Tahir Hassan, and sister-in-law Farhat Jahan, daughter of Tahir Hassan, resident of . . . came to my house located in . . . around 12 noon. My mother showed due hospitality towards them and told them that they should take Safana with them and she would give Rs. 10,000 for the time being and the rest would be paid later as a lot of expenditure had been incurred in connection with the birth of the child. Thereupon, they hurled dirty abuses and told, 'Can a car be bought for Rs. 10,000? You insult us'. At this, when I held Zahid's feet, all of them attacked me up with sticks, feet and knife and said that until car is given we shall not keep you with us. This was witnessed by Ashraf, Shahana, etc. I have got myself medically examined. In one year's time my in-laws have finished my life. When I was at my in-laws' house my husband had taken my signature on a number of papers and had also taken a statement from me.

After this FIR was filed, the police investigated the matter and a criminal case against Zahid, his mother and sister was instituted. Zahid was arrested from his residence in Delhi and taken to the local Police Post. After his arrest had been entered in the police records, he was taken to Bijnor. He was presented before the Remand Magistrate who ordered his remand and directed that he be housed in judicial lock up. Zahid's maternal uncle went to Bijnor and retained a lawyer who moved for his bail. The Magistrate who heard the bail application recorded on the file:

Accused Zahid Hassan was challaned in case no. 14/98 under Section 498A/324 IPC and Sections 3 and 4 Dowry Prohibition Act, 1961, by the City Police Kotwali. Accused Zahid married complainant Safana Masood with the consent of the co-accused. After the marriage Safana Masood was subjected to cruelty for dowry. Physical injury was caused to her by assaulting her with legs, sticks and knife. Demand for money for purchase of a car was made. The accused is not on bail. His bail application has been opposed.

The Magistrate then passed the following order:

There is no apprehension of the accused absconding. There is no apprehension of the witnesses being pressurized. Committing the incident after coming to Bijnor from Delhi is in accordance with the complainant. Accused has alleged that he has divorced his wife.

In the interest of justice the accused is ordered to be released upon submission of personal bond of Rs. 10,000 and security bond furnished by two land-owning individuals of like amount.

After the bail was granted Safana's mother and brother-in-law brought Zahid and his other relatives who had come from Delhi to secure his bail to her house and fed them. Safana apologized to him and put pressure on him to take Safana with him. After the meal, Zahid and his relatives said that they would work out a solution and left for Delhi.

Safana's brother-in-law was disappointed that Zahid was in the police lock up for just one day. After Zahid and his relatives left, Safana's brother-in-law started consultation with lawyers again. The government pleader in the court of the Chief Judicial Magistrate advised him to move an application for cancellation of bail. He did so, but the Magistrate dismissed the application. As the cancellation of bail was disallowed, Safana, her mother and brother-in-law, apprehending that Zahid might institute a legal case against them, sent an application to the local SHO with a copy to the Police Commissioner, New Delhi, requesting that if Zahid or any other relation or friend of his filed a case against her or her witnesses no action should be taken.

As is clear from the above narrative, this was not a case of demand for dowry. It was a case of routine domestic discord such as taunting by the mother and sister-in-law and suspicion on the part of the husband about the character of his wife. As Safana disclosed in the course of an interview with us,

> my husband was suspicious that I had a relations with my brother-in-law. I told my mother several times not to bring my brother-in-law when she came to visit us but my mother did not pay any heed. My mother wanted that my husband and brother-in-law should act towards each other as brothers. I do not know who made anonymous calls to my husband's house. I do not know which rogue has ruined my life.

Safana maintains that despite the *talaqnama* she is still Zahid's wife. She has not observed *iddat* and has not asked for the return of her dowry and *mehr*. She wants that her husband should take her back and live with her separately. Zahid's mother does not even want to talk about this matter. It is a matter of shame for her family. It is a stigma. Zahid says, 'Safana's grandmother could not lead a family life. Her mother too could not keep her marriage. What else could Safana have done? I was entangled with a shameless and loose woman. Divorce was the only way out left for me and my family.'

As of now the court case is pending adjudication. Safana has in the meantime passed the LTT course and is employed as a schoolteacher. None of her relatives came to her help. They said that the marriage had not been solemnized in consultation with them so why should they get involved. The lawyer who had arranged the marriage went again and again to Zahid and tried to bring about reconciliation, but did not succeed. Safana's divorce became the talk of the town and she was greatly defamed. Most people think that her mother and brother-in-law are really to blame for her divorce. Relatives maintain that if they had been involved, some way could have been found and the marriage could have survived. Her mother and grandmother are bringing up Safana's daughter. Zahid does not even come to see her.

THE CASE OF SHAMA vs. SHARIQ

Shama was married to Shariq about six years ago. Shariq's parents were dead. His widowed sister lived with him along with her son. A few months after the marriage petty quarrels started surfacing, relating mainly to the sharing of household work between Shama and her sister-in-law. Shama's husband was a truck driver and often he would be away for days. When he returned he would get drunk and on the basis of complaints from his sister beat up Shama. He spent his earnings on his widowed sister and her son and kept Shama deprived of money. Shama was also made to do all the household work.

Whenever Shama visited her family, she would complain about life in her husband's house. If Shama's mother tried to tell Shariq to deal kindly with Shama, he would beat her up upon her return. When Shama realized that Shariq's behaviour would not change she decided to return to her parental home on the pretext of going to attend a relative's wedding and refused to go back to her husband.

Shama's brother consulted a lawyer. As usual, he advised him to make an application to the police. Let me reproduce the substantive part of the text of this application:

> The applicant's sister Shama was married on 9 April 1991 to Mohd. Shariq. The applicant gave dowry to his sister beyond his means. Her in-laws were not happy and asked for Rs. 25,000 in cash, a colour television set and jewellery for female relatives. My brother and I pleaded with Mohd. Shariq

several times not to act this way and my sister also told me several times that Mohd. Shariq asked above mentioned items as dowry. Sensing that he will not get any further payments or goods, on 18 March 1996 around 2:30 in the afternoon, he tried to strangulate my sister and his sister and nephew hit her with their legs. On her raising hue and cry the neighbours (named witnesses) came and saved Shama otherwise she would have been killed. Shariq also inflicted injuries on my sister with a knife. It is requested that strong action may be taken against my sister's in-laws and on the basis of her complaint a case under Sections 323, 506, 498A of the IPC and Sections 3 and 4 of the Dowry Prohibition Act, 1961 may be instituted against them.

No action was taken on this application. Shama's brother learned that the Station House Officer had taken a bribe from Shariq to not act on the application. He, then, made another application to the Senior Superintendent of Police. No action was taken on that application either. Finally, he had Shama file an application in the court of ACJM under Section 156 (3) of the CrPC. She also filed an application for maintenance under Section 125 of the CrPC. In both these applications the allegations levelled by her brother in his applications were reiterated. It went on to add further that

> my in-laws kept all my clothes and jewellery. I was medically examined at the Government Hospital. I am staying since then at my mother's house. I am a lowly educate and purdah-observing woman. I am not in a position to maintain myself. My husband owns land, has a transport business and his monthly income is in the neighbourhood of Rs. 40,000. I require at least a sum of Rs. 2,000 for survival in these times of high prices.

Her plea was for the award of maintenance at the rate of Rs. 2,000 from the day she had been turned out of her matrimonial home.

Acting on her application under Section 156 (3) of the CrPC the Magistrate directed the local police station to investigate the matter and, if any truth was found in the allegations, to institute a case against Shariq. The Magistrate also directed that the investigation report be filed in the court in three days time. On receiving the order, the Station House Officer undertook investigations and filed a case under Sections 323, 324, 498A, 506 of the IPC and Sections 3 and 4 of the Dowry Prohibition Act, 1961 against Shariq. Shariq was arrested and sent to police lock up. Shariq engaged a lawyer and got bail. His sister Naseem Jahan was also granted bail.

On one occasion the Magistrate tried to bring about a compromise between the parties. However, Shariq openly declared that his wife was a woman without character. Strangers visited her house. On the pretext of making *bidis* she spent more time at her mother's place. He said that he had already released her from *nikah* and she could stay wherever she wished. After this incident family members and relations on both sides met to work out a solution. Shariq's family said that Shama had already condoned the *mehr*. In addition, Shariq spent roughly Rs. 15,000 on litigation in the case filed by Shama's brother. They wanted that Shama's family should pay Rs. 5,000 to Shariq after deducting *mehr* and maintenance during *iddat*. Shama's family paid Shariq the amount and accepted severance of marital relationship. The court case was withdrawn. Shama observed *iddat*. Later on, it came to light that the sum of Rs. 5,000 was actually paid by Shama's lover who was interested in marrying her after she completed *iddat*. Shama has since married him.

THE CASE OF TAUHEEDA vs. SAJJAN

In this case differences between husband and wife surfaced right on the day of marriage. When Sajjan came to the bride's room he complained to the wife: 'your brother did not even give a fridge and scooter in dowry. I had already announced among my friends and relatives that at least fridge and scooter would be given. Your family owns 60 *bighas* of agricultural land. Your share would be at least 10 to 12 *bighas*. Your brother is sitting tight over it. Your family has put me to great embarrassment.'

After the reception (*dawat-e-walima*) the following day, Tauheeda came to visit her family. She narrated to her mother and brother what Sajjan had said to her the previous night. Her mother told Tauheeda that there would be many occasions to give. She also told Sajjan when he came for the *chauthi* that he would be given a scooter. Sajjan retorted that no one gives anything after the wedding.

As Tauheeda settled down in her matrimonial home, her husband, sisters-in-law and mother-in-law would often taunt her for her dark complexion and for not bringing enough dowry. When Tauheeda started answering them back Sajjan and his mother began thrashing her up. One day Sajjan abused his mother-in-law for not giving a scooter. Later when Tauheeda showed her sullenness and said something against Sajjan her mother-in-law held her hair and slapped her several times for answering back. Tauheeda sat down to say her prayers and read the Qur'an. When Sajjan returned his mother complained that Tauheeda had argued with her and had refused to work. At this Sajjan started beating Tauheeda while she was still reading the Qur'an. She did not reply or resist. Tauheeda and Sajjan stopped talking to one another.

After a few days Tauheeda's brother came to visit her and with him she returned to her mother's house. She narrated the entire episode and told her mother that she would not go back to her husband. No one came from the husband's family either to fetch her. 'Whosoever had taken her should bring her back', the husband said. At this point relatives on both sides intervened and brought about a compromise. They said that nothing would come of quarrelling and that it would be better for the couple to reunite. They decided that Tauheeda should go back and assured Sajjan's family that when the first child would be born Tauheeda's family would give a scooter.

As Tauheeda was going back, her mother gave her two handkerchiefs, one green and the other red, and told her that if Sajjan and his mother beat her she should not react to them. 'I will send your paternal aunt after some weeks. If you are being beaten, return the red handkerchief with her. If you are satisfied and happy, return the green one. This way I will understand your situation,' she said.

As soon as she returned, Sajjan again started beating her for talking against him and his mother and for insulting them in the eyes of relatives. He again demanded the scooter and fridge. Indeed, on one pretext or the other he would beat Tauheeda almost everyday. Therefore, when Tauheeda's paternal aunt came to look her up, as her mother had told her, she sent the red handkerchief to her mother.

After a few days Tauheeda's mother went to Sajjan's house with a few women and brought Tauheeda back. She consulted a lawyer who advised them to file a case of demand for dowry. Accordingly, Tauheeda was made to file an application with the Superintendent of Police where she recounted her experiences at her husband's house and how her husband and mother-in-law were always taunting and beating her up for not bringing a scooter and a fridge as part of the dowry. She also alleged that her husband had turned her out of the matrimonial home without any assets or clothes. She went on to add something that had actually not happened:

> On 5 January 1997, around 8 p.m. Sajjan and his relations [she named some] came to my mother's house. They said that they would take me to their house if the scooter and fridge were given. My brother tried to request them to take me without the scooter and fridge, but they did not agree to his requests. When I asked him to refrain from hurling obscene abuses at my family members, Sajjan started thrashing me with his legs and hands. Hearing my cries and my brother's shrieks, neighbours [she named three in particular] came and saved my life. When they left they threatened that I was saved today but next time they would kill me. I have submitted myself to a medical examination and without going to the police station for fear of being beaten up by my in-laws on the way, I am making this application to you.

A copy of the medical examination report was filed with the application.

No action was taken on her application. Then she went on to file an application to the ACJM under Section 156(3) of the CrPC. On this application the ACJM ordered a case to be instituted against Sajjan, his father and brother. They were arrested and later on released on bail. Tauheeda had also named women relatives in her application but they were not arrested and were granted bail without an arrest.

Tauheeda continued living with her mother and brother. Recently, relatives on both sides have intervened and brought about reconciliation between Sajjan and Tauheeda. Tauheeda was asked to go back and Sajjan's family was paid some money in cash. They are now living together.

THE CASE OF NADIRA vs. MUNEER

This marriage took place six years ago. It was a love marriage. Both Muneer and Nadira lived in the same village and Muneer used to visit her home frequently. They married secretly with the consent of Nadira's parents but Muneer's parents were not informed. After her marriage Nadira continued to live with her parents and Muneer visited her daily.

After five years the first child was born to them. Muneer's parents then came to know that he had secretly entered into *nikah* with Nadira. They then brought Nadira and her child to their house.

Muneer ran a petromax repair shop. Later, he started working as a driver for a Sikh truck owner. After Muneer's family brought Nadira home quarrels began between the daughter-in-law and the mother-in-law, who taunted Nadira for enticing and snatching away her son. She said that Nadira and her mother were without character; that her mother knew everything but did not bother to tell her or take her consent for the marriage. Muneer's mother also taunted her for not bringing any dowry. She would say, 'I would have married my son with great pomp and glory. I would have taken a *barat*. This would have made me happy. Your parents got away rather cheaply.' Soon Nadira also started answering back.

Nadira went to visit her family and told her parents about the taunts of her mother-in-law. They decided that she should make an application complaining that Muneer and his family were troubling her. Accordingly, she submitted an application to the Superintendent of Police. As usual, the report was an exaggeration of what was actually happening. It read,

> my family had given a large dowry, but my in-laws were not happy with it. They wanted a fridge, scooter, Rs. 25,000 in cash and jewellery for women members of their household. They subjected me to mental and physical harassment and deprived me of food and clothing. My family and I entreated them but they did not change their behaviour. When they were convinced that their demand for dowry would not be met, then on 27.5.99 around one o'clock my husband Muneer Ahmad, mother-in-law Rabiya Begum, and my husband's brother Shafeeque Ahmad came to my house and beat me with sticks. My sister-in-law Kamal Parveen hit me with her feet even though I was pregnant. My child and I were sent from the house without any clothes or money and told that until I brought additional dowry with me they would not keep me.

She named a few persons as witnesses to this incident. She also attached a medical report.

The Superintendent of Police directed the local police station to investigate the matter, after which an FIR was filed and Muneer was arrested and sent to judicial custody. Muneer filed a bail application which noted: 'the defence counsel has argued that Muneer had no role in the incident. The medical report is not reliable and there has been delay in filling the FIR. Further, it should be noted that this was a love marriage. Therefore, the plea of demand for dowry is not tenable. The counsel for the complainant has contented that the accused had a major role in the incident.' The AJCM rejected Muneer's bail application. Muneer moved an application for bail in the Sessions Court, which was also rejected. Finally, he moved an application in the High Court. Muneer's father, mother and sister were given bail by the SHO. The case is still pending. Nadira now lives with her parents. She has moved an application for maintenance in the local court.

THE CASE OF SAFINA vs. MASOOD JAVED

Safina comes from a Sheikh Siddiqi family. Members of her family are not highly educated but they are well off. Safina alone studied up to B.A. Safina's father runs a brick-kiln.

Safina was married to Masood Javed in 1996. Masood belonged to a well-educated but middle class family. He was a medical graduate, his sisters and brothers were also graduates and post-graduates. His father held a white-collar job in a government hospital. Thus, there was a great deal of difference in the educational levels, economic standing and the living standards of the two families. Because of its better educational background, Masood's family considered Safina's family to be much below their standard.

Safina's and Masood's mothers are sisters. They were very close to one another as were their fathers. It was for this reason that the marriage between Safina and Masood was arranged. Masood was having an affair with another girl called Rahat so he opposed this marriage. However, his family forced him to marry Safina.

Safina's marriage was an elaborate affair and was reckoned among one of the best in Bijnor. Her parents gave dowry beyond their means. However, on the day after the wedding the father and brother of Rahat passed away within a matter of a few minutes. Masood went to attend their last prayer. Thereafter, he started visiting Rahat's house daily. Since Rahat's mother was observing seclusion (*iddat*) Rahat attended on him whenever he visited. He started paying a great deal of attention to Rahat's family and began neglecting Safina. At the end of Rahat's mother's *iddat*, Masood put forward the proposal of his marriage to Rahat. Rahat's mother and her married sisters were opposed to Rahat's marriage with Masood, but she sensed that her daughter would marry Masood without her consent. Accordingly, she agreed to Rahat's *nikah* to Masood. Masood's friends and Rahat's mother attended the *nikah*. Soon, however, their *nikah* became common knowledge and Safina and her family also came to know about it. Safina threw a tantrum over this development.

Safina's family put pressure on Masood's mother and father to get Masood to divorce Rahat. They also approached other relatives to intervene and bring about a suitable settlement. One day they also went to Rahat's mother with a gun and threatened to kill her and her daughter if she did not ask her daughter to get a divorce from Masood. She was obviously not willing to comply and replied that Rahat was also Masood's wife. Why should Rahat ask for a divorce? If she was destined to die at their hands, so be it. At this Safina's father and brothers created a scene, abused Rahat's mother and left. People in the locality had not, however, taken kindly to Masood's marriage with Rahat. Whenever Masood went out with his wife they would taunt and make fun of him. Therefore, to allow the dust to settle down he decided to go on pilgrimage along with Rahat and her mother.

Masood and his family had been unhappy with Safina's family because they had not given a car as part of the dowry. They now began taking out their resentment by taunting Safina for her background. If Safina styled her hair in a particular way, her sisters-in-law would taunt her for being unfashionable or for applying too much oil. They would taunt her that she dressed like a village woman. Safina's mother had given her a talisman from some holy man so that Masood would be drawn towards her once again. Safina's mother-in-law found the talisman under Safina's pillow and created a ruckus over it. Safina communicated all this to her parents.

Safina's two brothers worked as assistants to lawyers. Her father was on friendly terms with a well-known lawyer of the town. They decided to make a case under 498A and the Dowry Prohibition Act. In all likelihood, at their instigation Safina sent a number of letters to her parents suggesting that her husband and parents-in-law were demanding more dowry. The first letter said:

> Papa, you have married me into a very bad family. They are greedy and dishonest. Soon after the marriage my husband and his family members started troubling me. They would ask, what did your father give in dowry? Not even a car. The scooter that has been given is much below my standard. I have not touched the scooter. Get a Maruti car or two lakh rupees in cash from your father otherwise we will kill you. Papa, please get him a car or pay rupees two lakhs otherwise anything can happen to me.

The second letter followed soon after. It said,

> Papa I sent you a letter earlier in which I had told you about my husband's demand for a car or two lakh rupees but you did not reply. Papa, please for God's sake give them a car or pay rupees two lakhs in cash. Otherwise I am afraid that they will poison me. Everyone from the youngest to the eldest member in the house asks me to do chores for them and I have to do everything single-handed all day. They have threatened to kill me several times. Please come and take me away from here or quietly give them two lakh rupees. Then alone will I be safe.

A third letter said,

> Papa, my in-laws are extremely greedy. They are in the business of selling blood. Everyday people wanting to sell blood come to the house. My husband and father-in-law take blood from them and sell it to doctors and hospitals. Now, they have started taking and selling my blood. They have done so two or three times. If I refuse to give blood, they beat me up and also threaten to kill me. They tell me that unless I get two lakh rupees from my father they will continue to sell my blood. Papa, please pay them the sum they are asking for and save me. You did not reply to my previous letters nor have you arranged for the money. My husband and parents-in-law say that they thought my father was a moneyed man. They had many proposals of marriage but they rejected them all and agreed to marriage with me as they expected me to bring a car as part of the dowry. But their expectations were belied. They also threaten to arrange another marriage for my husband. They have said that they will give another opportunity to me. If you cannot pay the entire sum in a lump sum, they have asked me to tell you to pay in instalments. They also want you to keep this a secret and not tell anyone. If you tell anyone, they will kill me.

Meanwhile, Masood returned with his second wife after performing the pilgrimage. After that Safina's mother-in-law allegedly dowsed her with kerosene. At Safina's wailing and weeping the neighbours forced themselves into the house. One of them called Safina's home. Her father, brothers and other relatives came with sticks. At this, Masood's father also said certain unpleasant things and Masood took out a gun. Finally, Safina's father took her home and had her medically examined. The medical examination report certified 'abrasions on the back of neck, back and middle of right upper arm, multiple linear abrasions on outer and middle left arm, back of right side of chest, on front of the middle chest below superior external notch, scapular region and complaint of pain up to abdomen without visible marks of injury'.

On the basis of this medical report Safina's father filed an FIR under 498A and other sections of the Dowry Prohibition Act. Let us reproduce a part of the text of the FIR to give an idea of how such cases are actually concocted. The FIR alleged:

> I married my daughter Safina Rani in March 1996 to Masood . . . . I had given dowry beyond my means: a colour television set, a three-door fridge, a washing machine, scooter, etc. However, saying that the dowry was inadequate, Mahmoodur Rahman (Masood's father) and other members of the family would trouble Safina Rani. They used to tell Safina Rani to get a Maruti car and two lakh rupees from me. Several times they subjected Sakina Rani to physical torture and beating and sent her away from her matrimonial home. I paid roughly Rs. 50,000 to Masood's family but even this did not satisfy them. Because of constant harassment Safina felt physically and mentally oppressed and fell ill. I spent a lot of money on her treatment. On 29 August 1996, at about 11 o'clock at night I got the news that members of Safina's matrimonial family were beating Safina. As soon as I got the news I (accompanied by close relatives) rushed to Mahmoodur Rahman's house. On seeing us Mahmoodur Rahman took out his gun and threatened to kill me if I advanced any further. He told Masood to finish off Sakina. With the intent to kill Masood dowsed her with kerosene and wanted to set fire to her. On my raising a hue and cry my relations and neighbours saved Safina otherwise Masood would have burnt her alive. Safina has multiple injuries. We have admitted Safina to the Government Hospital, Bijnor. I pray that my FIR may be registered and stern action be taken against the culprits.

Masood, his sisters, father and mother went underground as soon as they came to know about the FIR and succeeded in obtaining a stay against their arrest from the Allahabad High Court. However, they realized that they were badly cornered since Safina's father had filed a complaint under Section 498A, 323, 506, 307 IPC and Sections 3 and 4 of the Dowry Prohibition Act, 1961, Masood's father was afraid that if he was arrested he could well lose his job. Therefore, they decided to compromise with Safina's family. Safina's family laid down certain conditions for a compromise. They demanded that one-half of the agricultural land and the part of the family house to which Masood was entitled be transferred to the name of Safina. Further, they asked Masood's family to open an account in the name of Safina and put two lakh rupees in it. Also, they demanded that Masood divorce Rahat, his second wife, and provide a copy of the *talaqnama* to them. They asked that Masood's ultrasound equipment be kept at the house of their lawyer. Accordingly, Safina's father-in-law transferred the house in the name of Safina, opened an account in Safina's name, deposited two lakh rupees and sent Masood's ultrasound equipment to her lawyer's house. Masood went to Rahat's house accompanied by his maternal cousin and two other witnesses and pronounced divorce thrice. He also gave Rahat a copy of a written *talaqnama* and published it in the local newspaper the next day.

Even after the pronouncement of the divorce Rahat did not observe *iddat*. After a couple of days Masood told Rahat that he had not actually given her divorce. He had gone through the façade of pronouncing divorce under pressure from Safina's parents. He also told her that he would not be able to come to see her but she should meet him at a doctor colleague's house. Rahat then started wearing a *burqa* and went to see Masood at his doctor colleague's house. He only calls her on phone at her house. People of the locality objected to this behaviour but Rahat asked them if they had been a witness to the divorce. As far as she was concerned, she had not been divorced. As a result, some relatives and neighbours do not like interacting with them. Masood and Rahat have a daughter who was born at Rahat's house. She is now two years old but continues to stay with Rahat. Sometimes Rahat sends her to Masood's house with her mother. Rahat talks to her mother-in-law and sisters-in-law on phone and they respond to her rather nicely. However, Rahat has not returned to Masood's house.

Safina's case is still pending in the court. Masood's father is now due for retirement. Fearing that his pension benefits would be put in jeopardy if he were convicted, he is trying to prolong the litigation. No one has a clear idea of when the case will be heard and decided. Meanwhile, Safina continues to live with her parents.

CONCLUSION

Several inferences can be drawn from these case studies. It is clear that the behaviour of the husband's family towards a daughter-in-law after she enters the matrimonial home is remarkably ambivalent. On the one hand, there are great expectations from her. On the other, she is subjected to teasing and taunting by her matrimonial family. Such teasing and taunting may relate to her looks, her way of dressing up, her family background or the dowry that she brought with her. If the daughter-in-law shows patience and forbearance and the teasing and taunting remains within reasonable limits, things eventually improve and the daughter-in-law is able to carve out a place for herself in the family. However, if the teasing and taunting arises from some genuine grievance with respect to dowry, the way the marriage was arranged or the character of the daughter-in-law, it can persist and lead to family discord. Under such circumstances the woman has no other alternative but to share her plight with her mother and other members of the family.

Usually two courses are open to a woman's parental family in such situations. They can involve relatives on both sides to bring about reconciliation or work out a solution acceptable to both families. Our case studies show that this is an effective mechanism available in cases of family discord. Through the intervention of relatives differences are patched up and proper guidelines are laid down for the marital relationship to continue or be terminated. Usually the relatives try to work out a solution so that the marriage continues. Or, they can resort to legal processes to force a compromise or to teach the woman's marital family a lesson or to get even with them for subjecting their daughter to harassment. Where this course is opted for, the provisions of the criminal law and the Dowry Prohibition Act are used. The dispute then assumes an adversarial character between the males of the two sets of families with the woman herself being used merely as a pawn on the chessboard.

Once the litigation process begins her options are foreclosed. She is obliged to wait for a long time for a verdict. Occasionally, as indeed happened in the case of Tauheeda, a compromise is worked out through the intervention of relatives and the case is eventually withdrawn. Or, the husband divorces her after criminal proceedings are launched, rendering the entire process of litigation meaningless. Sometimes, she remarries if a suitable match comes along otherwise she has to reconcile herself to living at her parental home.

Where criminal proceedings are launched against the husband or his family, a case has to be concocted. From these case studies it is clear that an elaborate and well worked out system is in place for the concoction of a case. Lawyers turn and twist incidents and represent them as instances of domestic or dowry related violence, inflict wounds on the body of the girl as proof of violence; invent witnesses and arrange to get a medical examination report from the doctors to show that the wounds were of a sufficiently grievous nature to warrant action under the provisions the lawyers seeks to invoke. Money passes hands freely at every stage of the case. Ultimately, more than the woman and her parental family, it is the lawyers and those whose favour he has to invoke in order to get the case instituted who seem to be the greatest beneficiaries of the litigation process.

15

Muslim Divorce and the Discourse around Muslim Personal Law

Geetanjali Gangoli

In India, personal laws of different communities are construed as markers of identity, more so in the case of the Muslim community. Though a shifting marker, it has generated a set of images, in the perception of the state, in political parties and individuals. Amongst the members of the Muslim community itself, it has helped to generate a set of self-images. In this paper, I explore the contours of the debate on Muslim divorce using legislative discussions, judicial pronouncements and the media as points of entry. I also look at the varied ways in which the discourse has impacted upon the lives of Muslim women. Some moments of historical significance relevant to this study are: the Constituent Assembly debates of the 1950s; the Lok Sabha debates of the 1970s on issues of adoption, maintenance and marriage; the cases filed by Shahnaz Shaikh (1983) and Shah Bano (1985), followed by the law passed by the ruling Congress party, i.e. the Muslim Women (Protection of Rights on Divorce) Act, 1986; the debates on triple *talaq* (1993), and polygamy (1995) and Supreme Court judgements on these issues.

It has been suggested that identity formation takes place at moments of crisis. Even when identity with a group is not strong, it can become intense when there is a perceived or real threat to the interests of the group (for an elaboration of this theme, see Kakar, 1995: esp. Preface: vii-x). Some moments of crisis for the members of the Muslim community in India include the Partition of the country in 1947, frequent communal riots and the demolition of the Babri Masjid in December 1992. I also suggest that personal laws have played a prominent role in shaping the identity of the Muslim and the Hindu communities. However, I try to demonstrate through this paper that identity formation notwithstanding, neither community is monolithic in its responses to the various crises.

The first section takes a look at legislative debates around Muslim Personal Law (henceforth MPL) between 1937-55. Prior to Independence, two major laws were passed that aimed at codifying the *shar'iat*, i.e. the Shariat Act, 1937, and the Dissolution of Muslim Marriages Act, 1939. This section also looks at the debates around the Uniform Civil Code (henceforth UCC) in the years following Independence. The second section examines the legislative debates that took place in 1976 around amendments to the Special Marriage Act, 1955, where mainstream attitudes to Muslim law become apparent. This section also looks at two proposed Bills on adoption introduced in 1972 and in 1980. The third section studies judicial interpretations of various aspects of MPL. The last section examines the initiatives and responses of feminists to these issues, in Mumbai and elsewhere.

LEGISLATIVE INITIATIVES: MUSLIM PERSONAL LAW: 1937-1955

In the 1930s, the process of codifying MPL was initiated at the behest of the members of the community. Two legislations, i.e. the Shariat Act, 1937, and the Dissolution of Muslim Marriages Act, 1939, were passed. The purpose of these Acts was to apply MPL to Muslim men and women who were governed by customary laws. In the eyes of those initiating these laws, it was a progressive move as it gave Muslim women rights denied to them under customary law. Here, it may be relevant to point out that the term 'customary law' has never been defined in the legislature. It is taken as a general reference to conventions observed by people over a long period of time. M.H.M. Abdullah, member of the Legislative Assembly, explained:

> The Bill aims at securing uniformity of law among Muslims in all their social and personal relations. By doing so, it also recognizes and does justice to the claims of women for inheriting family property who, under customary law, are debarred from succeeding to the same (cited in Arif, 1994).

The Shariat Act brought all Indian Muslims under the *shar'ia* in matters related to inheritance, divorce, marriage and guardianship. The 1939 Act extended to all Muslim women rights of divorce that had been restricted until then to Hanafi Muslims (Singh, 1993: 177-97). During this period, the codification of MPL was seen as an example to be emulated by other communities. As Justice Ranade stated: 'If we, [i.e. Hindus], abjure government help under all circumstances, we must perforce fall back, behind Parsees, Mohomeddans and Christians, who have freely availed themselves of such help in recasting their social arrangements' (quoted in Lateef, 1994: 56).

However, the reality of Partition, communal riots and Independence led to a shift so that Muslims were no longer perceived as being pioneers in the area of codification of law. In the decade following Independence, the focus was on reform of Hindu law. The Hindu Code Bill, drafted in the 1940s, faced tremendous opposition both within and outside the Parliament. The Bill was divided into four separate parts, and passed as the Hindu Marriage Act, 1955; the Hindu Minority and Guardianship Act, 1956; the Hindu Adoption and Maintenance Act, 1956 and the Hindu Succession Act, 1955. These laws have long been presented as model laws that initiated progress and enlightenment in Indian society. This is not the place to support or dispute these claims, which has been done elsewhere,[1] but I would like to point out that these sets of laws have created an exclusionist, yet inclusive legal category of a Hindu. It includes in its scope Buddhists, Sikhs and Jains. It includes anyone who is not a Muslim, Parsee, Christian or a Jew. Scholars have suggested that this legal description of a Hindu, as distinct from the four other religious categories, means that these religions become its legal 'other' (Sangari, 1995: 3787-810, esp. 3798-9).

The Hindu Marriage Act, as lawyers have pointed out, offers very limited rights with regard to divorce. It also includes the 'right to conjugal rights', which militates against the rights of women, and legitimizes marital rape. Also, as lawyer Kirti Singh points out:

> Another novel feature of this Act was that it made women equally liable with men as far as payment of maintenance . . . was concerned. Among the Members of Parliament who objected to this clause were: B.K. Ray, Renu Chakravarty and Sucheta Kripalani. They pointed out that the

provision was highly unjust to women since women did not have an equal right to property. . . . Renu Chakravarty . . . declared, 'give us equal laws of inheritance and we shall be prepared to give you that alimony'. (Singh, 1993: 186)

The move to give equal property rights to Hindu women was, however, met with stiff resistance. The Hindu Succession Act, 1956, gave daughters a share in the ancestral property, but did not make them an equal shareholder with their brothers. Even this limited reform was met with opposition. Members argued that it would destroy Hindu society and create discord between brothers and sisters. It was further argued that the government should pass a UCC and until that was done, Hindu laws should not be tampered with (Singh, 1993: 187-8).

Many conservative Hindus used the demand for a UCC as a way to put off reforms in Hindu laws. The Hindu Code Bill was projected as a communal step. It was argued that the Hindu Code Bill was 'absolutely unnecessary' and that it went 'against the principle of having a common civil code' (Thakur Das Bhargava quoted in Kishwar, 1994: 2152). Many members of the Constituent Assembly pushed for a UCC on the grounds that it would facilitate national integration. Others opposed it on the grounds that it would jeopardize the cultural identity of minorities, especially Muslims. This was perhaps a historic moment in that the debate around the UCC became petrified into a debate around individual rights, citizenship and national integration on the one hand, and minority rights and cultural diversity on the other. The following statement by K.T. Shah in 1949 encapsulates this dilemma: 'Rights of minorities are not of the individual, but of the group' (K.T. Shah quoted in Rao, 1967: 39).

The general sense of unease with ideas held paramount up until then is apparent in the following excerpt from a perceptive speech made by Jawaharlal Nehru in 1949:

> Nationalism, of course, is a curious phenomenon, which at a certain stage in a country's history, gives life, growth, strength, a unity but it has the tendency to limit one. . . . Culture, which is essentially good, becomes not only static, but aggressive and something that breeds conflict and hatred when looked at from a wrong point of view. How you are to find a balance, I don't know. (Nehru, 1949: 361)

Nehru here seems to be equally critical of the limitations of nationalism, as of culture. He sees in both these phenomena something that is not immediately apparent. Meanwhile, sections of Muslims who had stayed back in India found it a bewildering experience. In 1950, a member of the Jamiat-ul-Ulema wrote an article in an Urdu newspaper in which he warned Muslims that Hindus were basing 'their' constitution on the laws of Manu (quoted in Karandikar, 1987: 180). Given the rhetoric of some members of the Constituent Assembly, this was perhaps not an entirely unreasonable fear. Yet, to attribute the failure of the Constituent Assembly to implement a UCC to the obstructiveness of Muslim members remains a common, though misguided trend. During the course of the Constituent Assembly debates, R.K. Sidwe exhorted Muslims to give up their 'isolationist outlook on life' for the sake of national integration and unity (R.K. Sidwe quoted in Dhagamwar, 1989: 28).

The UCC was, however, rejected by many non-Muslims as well, for various reasons. One is articulated by K.M. Munshi thus: 'I know there are many among Hindus who do not like a Uniform Civil Code . . . they feel that the personal laws of inheritance, succession, etc., are really a part of their religion' (quoted in Dhagamwar, 1989: 127). Raj Kumari Amrit Kaur, active in these debates, held the view that a UCC could not lead to national integration. As she put it: 'How would a uniform civil code be conducive to national unity when uniform laws for crimes, contracts, torts and constitutional rights could not promote it . . .' (quoted in Bhargava, 1983: 11-13).

Even some of the strong supporters of a UCC stopped short of making this clause legally enforceable. K.M. Munshi and Krishna Swami Aiyyar, who saw a UCC as a means of strengthening nationalism, voted against the inclusion of the clause as a fundamental right. Munshi had claimed that the failure of the state to amend personal laws of different communities would lead to a denial of the rights of women. Yet, he supported the placing of the clause in the section on the Directive Principles of State Policy, a legally non-enforceable section (see Dhagamwar, 1989: 28). Evidently then, it was not just the Muslims who had reason for opposing the UCC. What is interesting is that the debate was conducted mostly in terms of national integration, rather than gender justice.

From the mid-1950s to the mid- 1970s, little or no debate took place on the issue of MPL in the legislature. In the 1960s, when a move was made to reform the MPL, Vice-President Zakir Hussain conveyed a sense of resentment on behalf of the entire community (Karandikar, 1987: 180) and the attempt was promptly dropped. Some possible reasons for the silence on this issue could be the retreat of communal forces during this period, the gender indifference of the Left which seemed in ascendancy at that point, and a greater focus on nation-building in the specific Nehruvian mould.

In 1970, however, the All India Muslim Political Convention resolved, *inter alia*, that: 'a clear announcement be made at an early date by the central government that no attempt would be made to change the personal laws of any community, and especially that of Muslims' (quoted in Karandikar, 1987: 180). The fears of at least one section of the Muslim community will seem puzzling in the absence of any serious or concerted proposal on the part of the legislature to reform or change MPL, or indeed any other personal law. Unless, of course, one locates it in the fear and insecurity that characterized Muslim politics following Partition and widespread communal riots that followed. For many Muslims, personal laws were perhaps already fixed as markers of their identity. The next section examines legislative debates in the period when Hindu communalists were much more in the forefront, that is, the late 1970s and the 1980s.

MUSLIM PERSONAL LAW, COMMUNALIZATION AND LEGISLATIVE DEBATES: 1976-1995

Legislative debates during this period reveal a 'Hinduized' understanding of life and law, within which Islamic tenets are seen at best as aberrant. The language and cultural imagery remained Hinduized, sometimes even when used by non-Hindus, and for subjects that are 'secular'. During a debate on grants to the Ministry of Social and Women's Welfare, Shri E.S.M. Fakir Mohommad said: 'Sir, in India, we worship women as the universal Shakti; the world will not survive without women. We pay homage to our country in the name of Bharat Mata' (Lok Sabha, 1985: 5 May: 239).

Such imagery is recurrent in the lengthy debates in the Lok Sabha in 1976, on the proposed amendments to the Hindu Marriage Act, 1955 (henceforth HMA) and the Special Marriage Act, 1954 (henceforth SMA). The 1976 amendment was meant to bring the HMA 'on a par' with the SMA, but what is disregarded is that the amendment gave to Hindu men their right to ancestral property only if they married a Hindu woman.[2] This amendment to the SMA favouring Hindu men and returning their 'ancestral rights' was passed without any debate or discussion (Lok Sabha, 1976: 20 May: 160-6; 21 May: 8-90; 24 May: 8-38). The clause served the additional purpose of making marriages between Hindu men and non-Hindu women less attractive than marriages between Hindus, as the former would mean a loss of coparcenary rights for Hindu men.

The 1976 debates on the SMA and the HMA were full of allusions to marriage that fitted closely Brahmanical and Hindu perceptions of marriage. What is striking is that the Hindu concept of marriage is passed off as the 'Indian' concept of marriage. The following excerpt indicates this trend: 'According to Indian culture and tradition, marriage is a sacred and eternal bond. When a man and a woman enter into marriage, our culture and civilization tell them that only death can separate the two' (Lok Sabha, 1978: 21 May: 85).

Some MPs quoted from the *Manusmriti*, lamenting the collapse of the romanticized traditions of their mythized histories. We can see a link, by no means tenuous, between these notions of society and marriage, and those expressed a decade later in the Lok Sabha prior to the passing of the infamous Muslim Women (Protection of Rights on Divorce) Act, 1986. In the 1986 debates, several MPs expressed their discomfort with certain tenets of Muslim marriages, so different from 'Hindu' marriages.

> Now, the law of Muslims relating to marriage and divorce is this. . . . Marriage is a matter of contract and is not a sacrament at all. A woman is not married to a man till eternity, as it was with the Hindus and as it was with Catholics in the olden days . . . to the Muslims, divorce was very much known . . . a concept which possibly was revolutionary at that time and might have been considered so. (Lok Sabha, 1986: 5 May: 315: A.K. Sen)

Other MPs put forward a far less carefully worded critique of Muslim law and society: 'a Muslim husband in this country enjoys the privilege of being able to discard his wife at any point of time, whenever he chooses to do so, for reasons good and bad, indeed for no reason at all' (Lok Sabha, 1986: 5 May: 334: H.A. Dora). One MP held it fitting to issue a warning to all Muslims to transform themselves: 'I would like to warn the Muslims also. They have made divorce a very ordinary and easy thing. Recognize the need of the hour and change yourself' (Lok Sabha, 1986: 5 May: 471: Vidyavati Chaturvedi).

On a different level, Geeta Mukherjee put forward her understanding of Muslim divorce, in which she articulated a feminist understanding of the issue. As she pointed out: 'When an Islamic marriage takes place, [the] woman's consent is necessary. But, please remember, at the time of divorce, the divorced woman's consent is not at all necessary' (Lok Sabha, 1986: 5 May: 424: Geeta Mukherjee).

This nuanced understanding was, however not taken up for serious debate, which focused only on simplistic assumptions of Muslim marriages and society. At a general level, the assumption was that sacramental 'Hindu' marriages were superior to 'Muslim' marriages which were contractual.

There was only one recorded protest to the communalization of the debates, a protest that was not acknowledged or responded to: 'The Law Minister talks about Muslim representatives (in the Lok Sabha) . . . no one is a Hindu representative or a Muslim representative in this house. . . . He is communalizing the whole issue' (Lok Sabha, 1986: 5 May : 318: Saifuddin Chaudhry).

Like the issue of marriage and divorce, adoption too has been a somewhat contentious issue. Under existing provisions of personal law, only Hindus can formally adopt children under the Hindu Adoption and Maintenance Act, 1956. The personal laws of all the other religious communities do not allow formal adoption (GOI, 1992: 7-20). In order to redress this, attempts have been made in the Lok Sabha to pass Bills on adoption that would be applicable to all communities, first in 1972 and then in 1980.

Neither of these Bills has been passed because of the strong opposition from members representing different communities and groups: tribes in the north-east, Parsees and Muslims. For different reasons, members of these communities have seen the adoption Bills as being antithetical to their interests. The opposition of some Muslims is based on the fear that the Bill is a way of introducing a UCC—and by extension, Hindu laws—through the backdoor. They also believe that adoption is against the tenets of their religion. Significantly, the second fear is also shared by some members of the Parsee community. The Minority Commission, delegated to look into this question in 1980, reported that many members of the Parsee community feared that if adoption was allowed, economic and religious rights, including the right to use the fire temple, would be jeopardized and therefore demanded their exclusion from the proposed Bill (Minority Commission, 1980). The Minority Commission held that: 'We do not think that we need to go into religious controversy. If there are persons who feel the need to adopt to be greater than any supposed prohibition by their religious texts, they should be allowed to resort to the secular doctrine of adoption' (Minority Commission, 1980).

Significantly, in spite of evidence to the contrary, it has been made out that only Muslims opposed the Bill. According to Vasudha Dhagamwar, a supporter of the Bill and of the UCC, the uneasiness of the Parsees over the adoption issue was 'qualitatively quite different from the stand of unswerving opposition by the Muslim leaders' (1989: 28). I would choose to disagree with this formulation. For, the Parsees interviewed by the Minority Commission held that they desired exclusion from the Bill on the same grounds as Muslims.

In Maharashtra, in 1995, the ruling Shiv Sena-BJP combine introduced a Bill on adoption which was passed without debate by the state assembly and council, but which could not muster the support of the central government. The president of India refused to give ascent to the Bill on the ground that it was too contentious.[3] The 1995 Bill was framed in close consultation with social organizations working on adoption. What was contentious about the Bill was that the desirability of a UCC was a vital part of its rhetoric. The Bill begins with these words:

> Whereas Article 44 enshrined in the Constitution of India, which is one of the Directive Principles of State Policy provides that the state shall

endeavor to secure for the citizens Uniform Civil Code throughout the territory of India;

And Whereas the Uniform Civil Code has become the need of the hour;

And Whereas, the government of Maharashtra feels it necessary to make a beginning for introduction of Uniform Civil Code in the state by introducing enactment of uniform civil law of adoption and for matters concerned therewith, as a first step towards achieving the goal of Uniform Civil Code in the state of Maharashtra. (Legislative Assembly Bill No. XXXI of 1995. A Bill to provide for adoption of child for matters connected therewith)

The adoption Bill states in bald terms the intentions of the state government to introduce a UCC. The timing of the Bill, three years after the anti-Muslim riots led by the Shiv Sena in Maharashtra, and a few months after the election of the Shiv Sena-BJP combine in the state assembly election, gives one cause for concern. It can perhaps be argued that the communalization of the issue of adoption is most apparent in the Maharashtra Bill.

The next section looks at judicial interpretations of issues of civil law.

JUDICIAL INTERPRETATIONS AND MUSLIM PERSONAL LAW

Judges have responded to, and contributed to, public debates on MPL and UCC through various cases on maintenance, divorce, polygamy, guardianship and inheritance.

The issue of the maintenance of divorced Muslim women was politicized in the mid-1980s following a Supreme Court case regarding a divorced Muslim woman's right to maintenance under Section 125 of the CrPC (*Mohommed Ahmad Khan* vs. *Shah Bano Begum and Others*, *AIR* 1985, SC 945).[4] The details of the case are as follows: Shah Bano filed for maintenance in the Court of a Judicial Magistrate after she was thrown out of her house after thirty years of marriage. Following this, she was divorced by her husband who maintained that he had paid her *mehr* (dower) and was not entitled to pay her any more maintenance under MPL. The magistrate awarded maintenance to the effect of Rs. 25 a month and this sum was enhanced to Rs. 179.20 on an appeal to the High

Court. The husband appealed to the Supreme Court, stating that he was not obliged to pay her maintenance following the provision of divorce under MPL.

The Supreme Court judgement on the surface took a valid legal stand, that Section 125 of the CrPC was a part of the criminal law of the country, hence was applicable to all Indians. What were contentious were the statements on Islamic law made during the judgement. Sir William Lane was cited as saying that the fatal point in Islam was its degradation of women. The statement made in 1843 was held relevant in the mid-1980s. The judge went on to say: 'It is a matter of regret that article 44 of our constitution has remained a dead letter . . . a common civil code will help the cause of national integration by removing disparate loyalties to laws that have conflicting ideologies' (*AIR* 1985, SC 945).

The judgement raised a furor at various levels. As a sociologist pointed out: 'The (Shah Bano) case . . . raised the entire question of the relationship between, on the one hand, secular law as promulgated and implemented by the institutions of the state, and on the other, the rights of minorities and the rights of women' (Das, 1995: 93).

What is relevant is the political context within which the controversy grew. This was certainly not the first judgement which held that Muslim divorcees had the right to maintenance under Section 125 of the CrPC. Another Supreme Court judgement in 1979 had raised precisely the same point, but had not, like the Shah Bano case, commented on the limitations of MPL (*Bai Tahira* vs. *Ali Hussein Fissalli Chothia and Another*, *AIR* 1979, SC 362). Among possible reasons for the furor could be the communalized ambiance of the mid-1980s, and the statements of the judges on MPL.

The judgement itself became an arena of conflict with Hindu fundamentalist leaders hailing it as a positive step and Muslims leaders opposing it. Shah Bano, unable to bear the pressures exerted on her from within the community, recanted in an open letter to Muslims. The letter, poignant in its helplessness, stated:

> Maulana Mohommad Habib Yar Khan, Haji Abdul Gaffar Sahib and other respectable gentlemen of Indore came to me and explained the commands concerning *nikah*, divorce, dower and maintenance in the light of the Qur'an and the hadith. . . . Now, the Supreme Court of India

has given the judgement on 3 April 1985 concerning maintenance of the divorced woman, which apparently is in my favour. But since the judgement is contrary to the Qur'an and the *hadith* and is an open interference in Muslim Personal Law, I, Shah Bano, being a Muslim, reject it and disassociate myself from every judgement that is contrary to the *Shar'iat* (*Inquilab*, 13 November 1985).

The Rajiv Gandhi government gave in to the pressure exerted by the more orthodox in the community, passing the Muslim Women (Protection of Rights on Marriage) Act, 1986. The Act removed divorced Muslim women from the ambit of Section 125 of the CrPC, choosing to focus on one-time relief to divorced women. What is significant is that the voices of those members of the community who had taken a different stand on the judgement were ignored. A memorandum was submitted to the prime minister on 26 February 1986, signed by several members of the community, including teachers and advocates, bemoaning the threat to the 'secular fabric' of the country posed by the controversy. The signatories distanced themselves from those members of the community who opposed the judgement and stated:

We believe that Muslim women have the right to maintenance—a right that they enjoy in several Muslim countries, through the rational and progressive interpretation of Islamic principles, as in Morocco, Iraq, Egypt, Turkey, Libya, Tunisia, Syria and Algeria. . . . We emphasize the necessity of safeguarding the interests of all sections of the minorities. That is why the demand to exclude Muslim women from the purview of section 125 CrPC . . . would adversely affect both the rights and interests of Muslim women (Memorandum by Committee for Protection of Rights of Muslim Women, reprinted in Engineer, 1987: 217-21).

Following the enactment of the Muslim Women (Protection of Rights on Divorce) Act, 1986, Daniel Latifi and Sona Khan, Delhi-based lawyers, filed a writ petition in the Supreme Court. The petition stated that the Act was discriminatory 'and calculated to disrupt and divide the most exploited and vulnerable section of our people'. It also stated that the Family Courts Act, 1984, excluded Muslim women and aggravated this 'situation of apartheid whereby the weakest section, namely the women of the minority community, would per se be prejudiced'. The petition submitted that the Act be struck down on various grounds, including that it violated the right to equality before law and equal protection of the law guaranteed under the Constitution; that it would encourage divorce and female infanticide, thus militating against 'two of the causes to which the Holy Prophet of Islam dedicated a great part of his life' (Writ Petition No. 868 of 1986).

The petition is remarkable in that it combined religious and secular arguments to oppose the law that had been passed.

Muslim Women's Act was opposed at different levels. As an elderly school teacher pointed out, the contention that the 1986 Act enjoyed majority support of the community was erroneous. 'When they say this, they simply ignore the views of countless Muslim women whose voices are muffled by their fathers, husbands and the mullahs' (Sabiha Rahman quoted in Hensmen, 1987: 217-21).

The BJP, however, chose to read the debate in a different way. The party, responsible for violence against women in riots, chose to oppose the 1986 Act on the ground that it violated women's rights. In an official statement made in 1986, that Act was called 'retrograde, anti-women and a surrender to obscurantism and bigotry' (statement by the BJP National Executive in a meeting in Chandigarh, 1986).

The BJP's 'politically correct' stand was offset by some virulent statements made by its ally, the Shiv Sena, in Maharashtra. Bal Thackeray, in a statement in 1985 had this to say: 'Communal minded Muslims have no place in this country. . . . Those who do not accept our constitution and our laws, should quit the country and go to Karachi or Lahore' (quoted in *Loksatta*, 12 December 1985).

It might be useful to look at the interpretations of the 1986 Act and to see the impact that this law has had on women. Some of the judgements based on this Act have tried to interpret it as liberally as possible, in order to provide a fair settlement for divorced Muslim women. Under Section 125 of the CrPC, as we have seen, the maintenance awarded was most often measly, in fact there was a ceiling of Rs. 500 (see, for instance, *Shahzadi Begum* vs. *Mohommad Abdul Gaffar*, 1981. *Cri L J* 1532, where a maintenance order of Rs. 75 was awarded under Section 125 CrPC). In 1995, Justice T.V. Ramakrishnan of the Kerala High Court dismissed the petition of K. Haji who pleaded that the maintenance amount of Rs. 30,000 as one-time settlement after divorce granted to Amina, his ex-wife, by the Sessions Court was illegal under the 1986 Act which granted 'reasonable and fair provision' and maintenance during the period of *iddat*. Justice Ramakrishnan ruled that:

> We are of the view that the Legislature has deliberately used the two provisions 'provisions' and 'maintenance' with the intention of expressing two different things or ideas . . . Following the Shah Bano case, the revolt from a section of the Muslims was only against the continued liability (post-iddat) declared by the Supreme Court. There was no dispute regarding iddat maintenance. From the statement of objects and reasons, it is evident that the Parliament has enacted the new legislation partly to contain the revolt . . . and to protect the rights of divorced women who may not have the necessary means of livelihood after the period of iddat. It is difficult to think that Parliament has, by enacting the Act, completely taken away the right of Muslim divorced women under Section 125 CrPC . . . without making any provisions as a compensatory measure . . . (*K. Haji* vs. *Amina*, II [1995] *DMC* 260).

In an earlier case, the Gujarat High Court ruled that the 1986 Act provided for a fair settlement according to the financial status of the husband. Justice M.B. Shah ruled that:

> . . . Under S 125 CrPC, the maximum amount which a divorced woman would get is only Rs. 500, even though her former husband is a rich person. Therefore to give her full protection or benefit, this Act was enacted and her rights are specified. . . . It has not only provided for free and fair provision and maintenance to the divorced woman and her minor children, but it has also specifically provided that she is entitled to get mehr or dower amount from her former husband (*Arab Ahemadhia Abdulla* vs. *Arab Bail Mohmuna Saiyadbhai*, *AIR* 1988, Gujarat 141).

Given the understanding of lawyers, activists and litigants that a one-time settlement is better than monthly payments, the 1986 Act does benefit Muslim women, but only if interpreted by a pro-woman judge. In its conception, however, it remains discriminatory as it denies a section of women access to a secular law on the grounds of religion.

Other judgements bring out the anomalies of the Act more clearly. While MPL allows for the mother to be the natural guardian of her children—a right denied to women of other communities—

the Act does not spell out the responsibilities of the father in providing child support following divorce. In a 1991 Calcutta High Court judgement, the judge criticized the Act saying:

The Act of 1986 is remarkably silent as to the futures of the minor children who have crossed the age of two years. . . . As no provision is made subsequent to that age in the Act of 1986, the mother as natural guardian of such unfortunate minor children shall have to fall back upon the all-embracing and beneficial provisions of Section 125 CrPC (*Mohommad Murtaza* vs. *Kauser Parveen*, 1991 *Cri L J* 3202).

Thus, the judge found a way to circumvent the 1986 Act, and restore to the destitute woman her right to Section 125 of the CrPC, but only in her role as mother:

We are not concerned with the divorced wife, as she has rightly and justifiably not claimed any maintenance for herself in view of the provisions of the Act of 1986. But we are concerned with the fate of minor children. Here, it is pleaded that the minor children are unable to maintain themselves, and not only that, the divorced wife is also unable to maintain them without any maintenance amount from her former husband (*Mohommad Murtaza* vs. *Kauser Parveen*, 1991 *Cri L J* 3202).

If the mid-1980s were taken over by legal debates on maintenance and divorce, the legal issues that came up for debate in the 1990s were those of divorce under Muslim law, and polygamy. The issue of *talaq-e-bidat*, known more popularly as triple *talaq*, has been seen as the marker of Muslim identity by Hindu fundamentalists.[5] In 1993, Justice Tilhari of the Uttar Pradesh High Court struck down *talaq-e-bidat* as invalid, but only after holding forth on the joys of marriage, the sorrows of divorce and the 'plight' of a Muslim divorced woman:

The plight of a divorced woman can be realized . . . marriage is a status which creates vested rights and interest of cohabitation, succession and maintenance. It brings a bloom to the life. Divorce brings a plight of vagaries . . . and upheaval in the life of a woman. . . . The Hindu Marriage Act introduced divorce and a divorced woman has been declared to be 'entitled to claim maintenance from her husband'. Under Muslim law, the plight of a woman divorced by her husband is more pathetic. It is the husband who has the free hand to divorce his wife . . . even orally, by declaring *talaq* thrice . . . the poor Muslim woman has been held to be entitled to maintenance for a limited period of three months and then left to the vagaries of fate (*Rahmatullah* vs. *State of UP*; *Khatoonisa* vs. *State of UP*, Judgement dated 4 April 1993).

The judge then went on to declare triple *talaq* as unconstitutional, sinful under Islam, under the mandate of the Holy Qur'an. Justice Tilhari seems to share the commonly-held perception that triple *talaq* is a common practice in Islam. The term of the discourse within which the learned judge operates is to reiterate the 'superiority' of Hindu laws and cultural practices and the centrality of marriage as an institution. As a political commentator pointed out soon after the judgement, Justice Tilhari's sympathies with the right were abundantly clear when he passed a judgement allowing 'darshan' (the right to worship) to Hindu pilgrims at the spot of the demolished Babri Masjid in 1992, where a make-shift temple had been erected. He went on to state:

> While supporting the Tilhari judgement, the left and feminist groups should take care to expose the pseudo campaigners of Muslim women's rights, who remain silent about the plight of Hindu women. Is the judgement and the support thereof based on women's rights, or on communal arguments of Muslim obduracy and backwardness? (Navlakha, 1994: 1264).

Justice Kuldip Singh's judgement in 1995, in a case on bigamy, raised similar issues. The case was about a Hindu man who converted to Islam in order to solemnize a second marriage. The Supreme Court judgement compared MPL unfavorably with Hindu law and Justice Singh advised the Parliament to enact a UCC so as to prevent further such cases. He ruled that:

> The personal law of the Hindus, such as relating to marriage, succession and the like have a sacramental origin, in the same manner as in the case of the Muslims or the Christians. The Hindus, along with Sikhs, Buddhists and Jains have forsaken their sentiments in the cause of national unity and integration, some other communities would not, though the constitution enjoins the establishment of a common civil code for the whole of India (*Sarla Mudgal and Others* vs. *the Union of India and Others*, II 1995, *DMC* 351 SC).

Justice Singh held that a common civil code would prevent errant men from converting to Islam in order to escape the provisions of their personal laws, which penalized them for bigamy. The stated purpose of the proposed common laws was, therefore, to 'save' Hindu marriages, not to empower Muslim women from the ill effects of polygamy. At another level, the judgement reflects the patriarchal agenda of preserving and glorifying marriage at all costs:

> Marriage is the very foundation of a civilized society. Marriage is an institution in the maintenance of which the public at large is deeply interested. It is the foundation of the family, and in turn of the society without which no society can exist (*Sarla Mudgal and Others* vs. *the Union of India and Others*, II 1995, *DMC* 351 SC).

It can be argued that the Hindu Marriage Act, 1955, meant to discourage polygamous marriages, has not been very effective in actually doing so. Judges have recognized as valid only a marriage ceremony that includes the *saptapadi*, leaving out a range of other customary practices. Hindu men have used this clause with impunity to deny their wives—first or second—the rights due to them. In a 1994 case, the marriage between Gulab Singh and Surjit Kaur, performed through local rites, was invalidated by the Supreme Court. Surjit Kaur had been married before, which was held against her by the learned judge, who held,

> merely because there was distribution of sugar or *gur*, that would not constitute a valid marriage. Surjit Kaur was in the habit of changing husbands frequently . . . the bare fact that the man and the woman (have been) living together as husband and wife does not, at any rate give them the status of husband and wife, even though they may hold themselves out before the society and the society treats them as such (*Sarla Mudgal and Others* vs. *the Union of India and Others*, II 1995, *DMC* 351 SC).

Such judgements have prompted feminist lawyers to argue that the loopholes in the HMA allow Hindu men 'to escape the criminal consequences of a bigamous marriage, and from the economic responsibility towards the second wife' (Agnes, 1995: 3238). What is significant is that under the HMA, 1955, the second wife, because she is denied legal status, is not entitled to maintenance while under MPL this is not the case.

Not surprisingly, these aspects have not been taken up in the

1995 judgement on bigamy. Even less surprising is that this judgement, like the Shah Bano and the Tilhari judgements before it, have been appropriated by Hindu communal forces. A Bill initiated by the Shiv Sena-BJP combine in Maharashtra in 1995, to prevent bigamous marriages quotes approvingly from it in its statement of objects and reasons (Legislative Assembly Bill Number XXXII of 1995, Maharashtra Legislative Secretariat. A Bill to provide for the prevention of bigamous marriages in the state of Maharashtra). While moderate rightist forces may want to prevent Muslim men from marrying more than once, the more extreme right displays an envy for the Muslim man's legal right to marry more than once. Swami Muktanand Saraswati, a member of the VHP, held that there 'are no (equal) laws regarding marriage. Today, a Hindu man can marry only one woman, while a Muslim man can have five wives. If a man wants to have 25 wives, let him' (quoted in *Frontline*, 6 January 1993).

It might be relevant to point out that the limits of legal and judicial discourse on UCC become apparent when one recognizes that there is hardly ever any discussion or debate on those areas of MPL that might be considered progressive such as the proviso on inheritance. A Muslim woman has the right to parental property. A married woman inherits her husband's property in its entirety in the absence of children, otherwise she shares it with her children. Unlike in Hindu Succession law, there is no concept of coparcenary rights, nor can Muslim women be cut off from the property completely through the provision of a will (GOI, 1992).

The judgements and debates that have focused on MPL, however, look mostly at the anomalies within it. The focus remains on the 'obscurantism' of MPL. Debates on a UCC are initiated with a view to 'proving' that the Muslim community is stagnant and resistant to reform. The more militant believe that a UCC should be forced on a reluctant population and they cite the cause of 'nationalism' in support of this view. Chief Justice Lodha, in a public meeting stated: 'More fantastic is the belief that a common civil code should not be forced upon the Muslims, that they should agree to it voluntarily. As if the imams will let them' (quoted in Aiyyar, 1995: 15-18).

At a more 'moderate' level, it has been argued by Hindu communalists that the fear of the minorities that a UCC would mean the implementation of a Hindu code was unfounded. A statement by L.K. Advani, the BJP president, in 1995 was meant to allay the fears of the minorities:

> When the BJP talks of a Uniform Civil Code, it does not contemplate imposing the Hindu Law on the country. Our party manifesto has clearly stated that the BJP would ask the Law Commission to examine the Hindu Law, the Muslim Law, the Christian Law, and the Parsee Law and cull out the modern, progressive, equitable ingredients of these laws and on that basis, draw up a Common Civil Code. If some of the laws relating to the Hindus today have to go on that account, they have to go. For example, the Hindu Undivided Family may have to go. Whatever has to be done has to be done for all (L.K. Advani quoted in Deolekar, 1995).

The next section will focus specifically on the responses of the women's movement to articulations such as these and comment more generally on the entire issue of the communalization of Muslim Personal Law.

WITHIN THE WOMEN'S MOVEMENT: MUSLIM PERSONAL LAW AND COMMUNAL POLITICS: 1975-1995

The role of women legislators and the All India Women's Conference in the debates in the 1950s around personal laws has been well documented (Singh, 1993: 177-97). The feminist movement since the 1970s has been sporadically, though meaningfully, engaged in the debates around personal laws. In 1974, *Towards Equality Report on the Status of Women* studied, among other things, the range of personal laws applicable to women. Regarding MPL, the report recognizes that while Muslim women have the right to divorce under some provisions, Muslim men clearly enjoy more power as they have the right to unilateral divorce. The report simultaneously recognizes the limitations of legal reform, and the need for legal change: 'Legislation alone cannot eliminate rigid traditionalism, with its desire to preserve the status quo. . . . [However] legislation is the only instrument which can bring the Muslim divorce law into line with not only the needs of society, but with the prevailing laws in other Muslim countries' (GOI, 1974: 121-2).

The report recommended that the unilateral right of divorce for Muslim men be done away with and the right to maintenance be made available to Muslim women. It recognized the superiority of MPL over the personal laws of other communities in the area of inheritance rights for women: 'Muslim law makes no distinction between movable and immovable property, and the rights of a female heir, unlike a widow or daughter, have always been recognized, and they have inherited absolutely (unlike the old Hindu law)' (GOI, 1974: 140).

The authors of the report conclude that there is an urgent need to implement a UCC. What is noteworthy is that they, too, base this demand primarily on grounds of national integration, rather than gender parity. The report reads:

> The absence of a Uniform Civil Code is an incongruity that cannot be justified with all the emphasis that is placed on secularism, science and modernization. The continuance of various personal laws which accept discrimination between men and women violates the fundamental rights and the Preamble . . . and is against the spirit of national integration and secularism (GOI, 1974: 140).

By the early 1980s, Muslim law ceased to be, in itself, a topic for debate. A bulletin brought out by a civil liberties group in 1982 notes that there were few seminars and discussions on reforms in MPL. The issue was no longer popular; the explanation proffered being that there was a feeling that this was not the right time to raise it (Tyabji, 1982: 25).

In October 1983 the issue of MPL was raised legally by Shahnaz Shaikh, a 24 year old Muslim woman who was actively involved in the women's movement in Mumbai and was a member of the Women's Centre and Forum Against Oppression of Women. Shahnaz Shaikh had been married to Abdul Rab Ravish in 1981. Abdul Rab Ravish was 17 years older than her and had displayed great mental and physical cruelty to her during the course of their marriage. He divorced her orally in September 1983 and threw her out of the house without giving her the *mehr* fixed at Rs. 12,000 at the time of marriage. In her petition, filed against the Union of India and Abdul Rab Ravish as the second respondent, Shahnaz stated that she was not claiming any relief from her ex-husband. The petition stated: 'The Petitioner says that she does not blame the Respondent No. 2 for whatever has happened to the Petitioner as the Petitioner feels that the Respondent No. 2 behaved in the manner he has done only because the existing personal law is so much loaded in his favour' (*Shahnaz Shaikh* vs. *the Union of India and Adbul Rab Ravish*, Civil Writ Petition No. 32 of 1983: 3).

Shahnaz laid the responsibility for her oppression on the state. She pointed out in her petition that although there were enough provisions in the Constitution, the Union of India had not enacted fair laws for Muslim women. The petition stated:

> Respondent No. 1 has not deemed it proper or necessary to make any laws to ensure social justice for Muslim women and have restricted themselves to law making only for Hindus, Christians and for Scheduled Castes and Tribes. The Petitioner says that the Respondent No. 1 is fully aware that Muslim women constitute over 4 crores in number and are a weaker section of the Indian society. A careful and unbiased research into the various provisions of law affecting Muslim women would easily reveal the need for social reform and balancing legislation. (*Shahnaz Shaikh* vs. *the Union of India and Adbul Rab Ravish*, Civil Writ Petition No. 32 of 1983: 4)

Shahnaz went on to dismiss the excuse put forward by political leaders that they had left it to the leaders of the Muslim community to initiate reform from within the community. As the petition pointed out: 'The Petitioner says that by their default in this regard, Respondent No. 1 has allowed the beneficiaries of a socially unbalanced law to continue superiority over Muslim women at their option' (*Shahnaz Shaikh* vs. *the Union of India and Adbul Rab Ravish*, Civil Writ Petition No. 32 of 1983: 4).

The petition felt that the Islamic faith and legal provisions needed to be separated as one could be a believer and yet not believe in the validity of MPL. Due to practices like triple *talaq* and polygamy, Islam, instead of being revered as one of the greatest religions of the world, was being subjected to derision and abuse. The petition went on to submit that as a Muslim woman she had been discriminated against by the state by a dereliction of its duty to make laws applicable to all Indians. She pleaded that practices such as purdah, polygamy, and unilateral *talaq* were unconstitutional, and 'not essential for the practice of Islam' and hence prayed that the court rule that these practices be struck down as 'unconstitutional, null and void, inoperative and of no effect' (*Shahnaz Shaikh* vs. *the Union of India and Adbul Rab Ravish*, Civil Writ Petition No. 32 of 1983: 6-10).

Shahnaz's petition made her famous and she was attacked and targeted by Muslim fundamentalists, forcing her to go into hiding. In addition, she found to her dismay that her lawyer was a member of the RSS, and wanted to use her case for Hindu communal purposes. The Shah Bano controversy that followed further revealed the polarization on the issue of reforms. Shahnaz's sharp and valid criticism of the Indian state was completely taken over by communal forces. Meanwhile, she also found herself isolated within the women's movement: 'We debated the UCC a lot, but even within the women's movement, I felt my minority status, felt that this is Hindu feminism. They were all very nice people, but they were not trying to understand me' (see Shahnaz Shaikh's interview in Menon, 1994: 174).

Shahnaz's isolation within the movement and her community led her to withdraw her petition. In a shift in perception, she felt that changes in MPL should come from within the community, as appeals to the state vitiated the debate. In 1987, she started a collective meant primarily for Muslim women, called Awaaz-e-Niswaan (The Voice of Women). Articulating the question of strategy, she said: 'On the UCC, we felt that we should frame it differently, call it women's code and that's what we have been calling it from day one in Awaaz-e-Niswaan . . . that's how we avoid the religious framework' (see Menon, 1994: 174).

However, her conviction that work needs to be done within the community did not detract from her belief that Islam has its limitations as far as women's rights are concerned: 'When I started reading the Qur'an for my petition, I became interested in some of the very progressive things it was saying for women. . . . I liked those, but then in the same Qur'an, there are other things that are oppressive' (Menon, 1994: 186).

Asghar Ali Engineer, a Mumbai-based Bohra reformer, however, looks at Islam in a very different, perhaps less nuanced way. His perception is that the Qur'an provides almost unlimited scope for reform and that Qur'anic injunction that 'women have rights similar to those of men' is unambiguous. Any anomalies that have crept into the law are the result of misrepresentation (1996). This view has informed the efforts of a Mumbai-based group made up of Muslim women who identify themselves with the women's movement and call themselves the Nikahnama Group. The group has worked out a model *nikahnama*, a marriage contract, on the basis of which women can claim rights to matrimonial property and some safeguards from unilateral divorce and polygamy. The *nikahnama* states that maintenance at divorce be given to women according to the financial status of the man and that if unilateral divorce does take place, the woman is entitled to an enhanced *mehr*. It also states that the permission of the first wife be taken if the man wants to contract a second marriage and in the case of subsequent marriages, the permission of all the wives be taken.[6]

At one level, this prism does have its positive aspects as it could potentially enable women to evolve a feminist understanding of practices and laws, without alienating the men in the community. The flip side is that the terms of the debate become restricted to the ones set by the community and the texts prescribed by it. To elaborate, the model *nikahnama* has no provisions for women who do not enter into marriage. Besides, the provisions for 'regulated' polygamy, which the *nikahnama* sets out, are inadequate and unjust from a feminist viewpoint. Feminists argue that women in oppressive marriages have no choice but to accept various indignities at the hands of their husband, and 'regulated polygamy' will not ensure the rights of women. 'The responsibility to prevent polygamous marriages cannot be placed at the doors of women, who are already vulnerable. As a conception, regulated polygamy is unfair unless it is accompanied by regulated polyandry' (Hensmen, 1987). Another factor that emerges out of the experience of the group is that even these limited reforms, clearly unacceptable to many feminists, are not taken seriously by religious leaders (see note 8).

It has been argued that customs like polygamy and triple *talaq* are not very common among Muslims, hence they do not pose a major threat to women within the community. The implication is that these are issues blown out of proportion by political parties. However, this has been questioned by empirical studies based on the experiences of women. Mumbai-based Women's Research and Action Group, the Indian chapter of the international network Women Living Under Muslim Laws, has conducted studies in different parts of India to research the conditions within which Muslim women live and their attitudes to Muslim laws. A part of the study in Vadodara questions the generalized feeling that Muslim women are impervious to change. The report states that, while polygamy is not really common among Muslims, it does acquire threatening dimensions for women situated within the community. As the report states:

> Most of the 388 women seemed to say, 'we do not want it, whether it is common or not'. 81.7% were unambiguous and clear that they wanted abolition of polygamy, an indication that they felt threatened by it. Polygamy makes their position within marriage insecure, for they do not really think their husbands can treat two or more women on a par, nor are women willing to be put in competition with another woman for their husband's affections (Srinivasan, 1994: 31).

Within the women's movement, there has been some criticism of the 'reform from within' position. One of the more sophisticated articulations of this point of view is that this form of legal pluralism is based on the primordial identity of community, and is thus antithetical to feminism.

> I believe that a feminism which is based on a critique of biologism and on the sexual division of labour rests, definitionally, on the right to choose political affiliations and privileges social identities . . . above birth bound ones, it cannot flirt uncritically with primordialism. Primordial claims cannot be a feminist principle, because they are a principle of irrevocable distention, and will divide women by region, caste, religion and race (Sangari, 1995: 3289).

The argument glosses over the context within which women live their lives, suggesting that an allegiance to feminism, defined in rather rigid, monolithic terms, means an automatic break with all that is defined as 'primordial', that is, region, caste, religion and race. We have seen that women within minority situations, in this case Muslim women, try to balance their feminist politics with their religious identity. There is an attempt, apparent in efforts like those of the Nikahnama Group, to change both. Nor do women like

Shahnaz Shaikh 'flirt uncritically' with community ties. Besides, as the Women's Research and Action Group study reveals, attachment to religious identity does not necessarily preclude a feminist orientation.

There are, therefore, within the women's movement, multiple perceptions to the issue of reform. On the one hand are the efforts of groups like Awaaz-e-Niswaan and the Nikahnama Group who work towards internal reform. Then there are perceptions that the debate should be articulated only in terms of women's rights, a view shared by Sangari and the Mumbai-based Forum Against Oppression of Women: 'We believe that religion-wise categorization (of personal laws) tends to become inward-looking and leads to the logic of internal reforms. It also detracts from the inadequacies and discrimination that all women face and share in common' (Gandhi and Shah, 1992: 229).

The All India Democratic Women's Association (AIDWA), attached to the CPI-M, takes a somewhat different position on the issue. In a convention held in December 1995, it suggested that the debate on a UCC and personal law reform be taken out of the realm of communal propaganda. This can be done by separating religion from politics. The convention demanded a legal ban on the use of religion for electoral purposes. Regarding the question of law, the convention took the following position:

> The convention asserts a step by step approach to strengthen the common legal ground for women of all communities by bringing in legislations in specific spheres with immediate effect. This will provide benefit to all Indian women, as well as strengthen their unity. At the same time, the existing personal laws of all communities need drastic reform to make them more equal.[7]

AIDWA resolved to push for changes in areas that affected all women, that is, the issues of matrimonial property, registration of marriages and domestic violence. Simultaneously, they supported the push for reforms within different communities.

A Delhi-based group, Working Group for Women's Rights (WGWR), in 1995 worked out a position that is conceptually different from that of the ways in which family laws have been perceived so far. They suggested a comprehensive package of legislation that would embody gender justice, including equal family laws, as well as equal laws in employment. This package would be available to all men and women in the country, yet they could choose allegiance to personal laws in moments of legal dispute, or at any other point. The suggestion is:

> All those who are born as or become citizens of India would come under the purview of this framework of common laws. . . . All citizens would also have the right to choose at any point in their lives to be governed by personal laws if they so desire. The choice to be governed by personal law has to be a conscious decision by an individual citizen. If such a choice is not made, the new gender just legislation would be applied. In keeping with our conceptual framework of gender just laws as the rights of citizen, we believe that citizens, who have chosen personal laws should be able to revoke their choice and move back to the common laws at a moment of legal conflict (WGWR, 1996: 90-1).

The suggestions made by the two women's organizations do mark a conceptual shift in the ways that internal reform and common laws have been looked at. While the AIDWA position aims at careful reform in which reform of 'non-controversial' areas be accompanied by reforms of personal laws, the WGWR position stakes a more direct claim to women's rights by aiming at a comprehensive package of gender just laws. A concession is made to the pressures that women may face by allowing the option to choose personal laws at any point. WGWR's efforts are not unlike those made by Shahnaz Shaikh in 1983, that is, to make an unresponsive state aware of the oppression of women as citizens of the country—except that here, women (and men) are given the option of choosing personal law if they so desire. The effort is to make available to women a set of laws that are non-communalized; in other words, to take the debate away from communal forces. What is significant is that in both these efforts the focus is not only on personal laws but on other areas of law—criminal law, employment and labour law—that are perhaps as misogynist and unequal as personal law.

An issue not always explored in the discourse around MPL is that of another kind of denial of rights. In family courts set up in the mid-1980s at the behest of the IWM to expedite civil matters pertaining to family laws, Muslim women were kept out of the purview of the court.[8] In other words, for matters such as economic settlements, Muslim women have to go to the High Court, involving a process that is longer and more cumbersome than approaching the Family Courts. This is an issue that the women's movement has not taken up. The focus on law within the movement has often left out the problems inherent in the implementation of some of these laws leading to the denial of justice. As we have seen, this is apparent in the practice of several laws—civil and criminal.

NOTES

1. Madhu Kishwar (1994: 2145-61) gives a detailed analysis of the debates during the drafting and the development of the Hindu Code Bill.
2. This right had been denied to them under the Act in 1954, when it had been ruled that any person marrying under this Act would be governed by the Indian Succession Act, 1925.
3. Adoption, being a topic on the concurrent list, needs presidential assent before it can be amended by any state.
4. Section 125 CrPC is a part of criminal law, the purpose of the section being that to prevent destitution. Under this section, the 'destitute' person was entitled to relief to the maximum amount of Rs. 500.
5. *Talaq-e-bidat* essentially means a form of divorce where a husband can divorce his wife by uttering *talaq* (divorce) thrice in a single sitting.
6. Oral presentation by Vahida Nainar and Nahida Sheikh at Seminar on Reforms in Law organized by Women's Centre, Mumbai, March 1996.
7. Resolution passed at the All India Democratic Women's Association National Convention on Equal Rights, Equal Laws held at New Delhi on 9 and 10 December 1995.
8. I owe this point to Flavia Agnes. The Family Courts Act, 1984 was followed by The Maharashtra Family Courts Rules, 1987.

REFERENCES

Agnes, Flavia (1995), 'Hindu Men, Monogamy and Uniform Civil Code', *Economic and Political Weekly*, 16 December, pp. 3238-42.

Arif, Kamran (1994), 'The Evolution of Muslim Family Law in India', unpublished paper.

Aiyyar, Mani Shankar (1995), 'Uniform Civil Code: A Primer for the Village Idiot', *Sunday*, 20 August.

Bhargava, G.S. (1983), 'Towards a Common Civil Code', *Mainstream*, 6 March, pp. 11-13.

Das, Veena (1995), *Critical Events*, New Delhi: Oxford University Press.

Deolekar, Madhu (1995), *India Needs a Common Civil Code*, Mumbai: Vivek Vyaspeeth.

Dhagamwar, Vasudha (1989), *Towards a Uniform Civil Code*, New Delhi: Indian Law Institute.

Engineer, Asghar Ali (ed.) (1987), *The Shah Bano Controversy*, Hyderabad: Orient Longman.

——— (1996), 'Women and Muslim Law', Presentation at Consultation on Gender Just Laws, organised by Forum Against Oppression of Women, Lawyers' Collective and Human Rights Law Network, Mumbai, 5-8 June.

Frontline, (1993), 'Saffron Brigade', 5 January.

Gandhi, Nandita and Nandita Shah, *The Issues at Stake: Theory and Practice in the Contemporary Women's Movement in India*, New Delhi: Kali for Women.

Government of India (1974), *Towards Equality: Report on the Status of Women*, New Delhi: Government of India.

Government of India, Ministry of Human Resource Development, Multiple Action Research Group and Women and Child Development (1992), *Humare Kanoon*, vol. IV, New Delhi: Publications Department.

Hensmen, Rohini (1987), *Oppression Within Oppression: The Dilemma of Muslim Women in India*, Working Paper No.1, Paris: Women Living Under Muslim Laws.

Kakar, Sudhir (1995), *The Colours of Violence*, New Delhi: Viking.

Karandikar, M.A. (1987), *Islam in India's Transition to Modernity*, New Delhi: Orient Longman.

Kishwar, Madhu (1994), 'Codified Hindu Law: Myth and Reality', *Economic and Political Weekly*, 13 August, pp. 2145-61.

Lateef, Shahida (1994), *Muslim Women in India: Political and Private Realities*, New Delhi: Kali for Women.

Lok Sabha (1985), *Lok Sabha Debates*, New Delhi: Lok Sabha Secretariat.

Loksatta (1985), 12 December.

Menon, Ritu (1994), 'The Personal and the Political', in Kamala Bhasin, Ritu Menon and Nighat Saead Khan (eds.), *Against All Odds*, New Delhi: South Asian Women's Forum, Kali for Women and ISIS.

Minorities Commission (1980), *Recommendations of the Minority Commission on the demand from a section of the Parsees for exclusion of the Parsee community from the purview of the Adoption Bill, 1980*, New Delhi: Minorities Commission, Government of India.

Navlakha, Gautam (1994), 'Triple *Talaq*: Posturing at Women's Expense', *Economic and Political Weekly*, 21 May, p. 1264.

Nehru, Jawaharlal (1949), *Speeches: 1949-53*, vol. II, New Delhi: Publication Department, Government of India.

Rao, B. Shiva (1967), *Framing of the Indian Constitution: Select Documents*, vol. II, New Delhi: Indian Institute of Public Administration.

Sangari, Kumkum (1995), 'Politics of Diversity: Religious Communities and Multiple Patriarchies', *Economic and Political Weekly*, 23 December, pp. 3787-810.

Shah Bano (1985), 'Open Letter to Muslims', *Inquilab*, 13 November (translated from Urdu).

Singh, Kirti (1993), 'Women's Rights and the Reform of Personal Laws', in Gyanendra Pandey (ed.), *Hindus and Others: The Question of Identity in India Today*, New Delhi: Viking.

Srinivasan, Bina (1994), *A Cry For Change: A Report on Muslim Personal Law and their Implications for Women in Baroda*, Mumbai: Women's Research and Action Group.

Tyabji, Kamala (1982), 'Muslim Women and the Uniform Civil Code', *PUCL Bulletin*, September.

Working Group for Women's Rights (1996), 'Statement in Uniform Civil Code: A Debate', *Alternatives/Vikalp*, vol. V, no. 3.

16

Muslim Law of Divorce in India: A Legal Reflection

Seema Durrany

Indian society has been living under a dual system of laws: laws based on the Indian Constitution and personal laws based on religion and tradition. Equality before law or equal protection under the laws and the prohibition of discrimination on grounds of religion, race, caste, sex or place of origin is the responsibility of the state (Articles 14 and 15) and the judiciary is obliged to implement them. For this we have civil and criminal procedure codes and a host of other laws for all citizens. However, personal laws relating to marriage, maintenance, inheritance and divorce differ from one community to another and discriminate against women on the simple ground that they are women and men and women cannot be equal. In this sphere there is a constant struggle on the part of women to achieve equality with men.

In this paper I propose to focus on the law of divorce in India, as it has become a very contentious subject. In some religious communities divorce was not allowed at all while in some others it was allowed conditionally. Though Indian society has accepted secularism as a principle in all fields of life, religious prejudices persist in personal laws. India is the favoured home of a variety of personal laws which had been observed as traditional customs till we experienced Western impact.

It was in the nineteenth century that the customary practices began to be codified. The first systematic central law enacted was the Indian Divorce Act (Act 4 of 1867). This law was enacted to amend the law relating to divorce and matrimonial causes applicable to the Indian Christian community. The Parsi Law of Marriage and

Divorce (Act 3 of 1936) was also amended and codified. In this Act Sections 30 to 48 provide in detail suits for nullity, dissolution and divorce, judicial separation, conjugal rights, etc. Chapter VI of the Special Marriage Act provides for the nullity of marriage and divorce. This Act is applicable to all citizens of India irrespective of their religious affiliations. The Hindu law of divorce is contained in the Hindu Marriage Act (Act 25 of 1955) which is an Act to amend and codify the customary practices relating to marriage and divorce among Hindus. The subject of the nullity of marriage and divorce is dealt with under Sections 11 to 18.

Indian tribal communities practice divorce in different ways. The Bodo community of Assam allows divorce by mutual consent of the wife and the husband. Both are given an opportunity to explain their grievances before the village panchayat. If the village panchayat is satisfied with the grounds put forward, divorce is allowed. Unilateral and unjustified grounds of divorce carry a fine, but if the complainant is a woman she has to pay a higher fine. In the Kharia tribe of Orissa if the husband wants to divorce his wife he may announce his intention before his wife, his parents and relatives. When the wife decides to dissolve the marriage, she has to desert the man by eloping with another man, or her lover, or stay with her parents and relatives and away from her husband. She can refuse to return to her husband. And this is treated as dissolution of marriage. Among the Juangs, also of Orissa, divorce is rarely practiced in spite of the provision available for it.

In the above-mentioned communities the husband has no arbitrary power to divorce his wife. He has to explain his grounds for separation or divorce before some authority. It is this judicial authority that has to take into consideration all aspects of marital life and the consequences thereof and thereafter. Therefore, the said laws of divorce have some provision for the maintenance of a divorced woman including alimony *pendente lite* and permanent alimony if the woman is without reasonable means of livelihood.

MUSLIM LAW OF DIVORCE

The Muslim law of divorce differs substantially not only from the above-mentioned laws of divorce, but it also provides different yardsticks for women and men. For men the divorce may be an extra-judicial act while for women it has to be through the intervention of some judicial authority. The Muslim law of divorce has been defined by the courts as follows: 'If the words of divorce used by the husband are express, the divorce is valid even if pronounced under compulsion or in a state of intoxication or to satisfy his father or someone else' (*Rashid Ahmad* vs. *Anisa Khatoon*, *AIR* 1932).

A Muslim man can repudiate his marriage unilaterally and arbitrarily without assigning any reason. Although this act may not be sustainable in the eyes of law, it cannot be challenged before the court of law. Section 2 of the Shariat Act, 1937, enumerates different kinds of divorce such as *talaq*, *ila*, *ziha*, *khula*, and *mubarat*. Except for the provision of *khula* none of the others are codified. Hence, no Muslim woman can challenge the provision of divorce in the courts. The Dissolution of Muslim Marriages Act (Act 8 of 1939) intended to consolidate and clarify the provisions of Muslim law relating to suits for dissolution of marriage by a woman married under Muslim Law. Section 2 of the Act mentions several grounds with explanatory clauses on which a Muslim woman can seek divorce from the courts. This Act, to be implemented through the Civil Procedure Code, makes it difficult for a Muslim woman to prove her grounds for seeking divorce. As to consequential relief to divorced Muslim women, there is no provision for alimony *pendente lite* and permanent alimony in Muslim Personal Law. Section 5 of this Act protects only *mehr* (dower). The articles of gift and maintenance during the *iddat* period have also been protected under the Muslim Women (Protection of Rights on Divorce) Act (Act 25 of 1986).

The provisions of Muslim law of divorce are scattered through religious texts and their interpretation is beyond the reach of our judicial system. No advocate can convincingly argue a case in favour of a wrongfully divorced Muslim woman. Ultimately, the woman has to suffer for the wrongful act of her husband. It is the rule of law. If the aggrieved party cannot establish the fault or guilt of the other party, then the court is helpless in granting relief how-soever it may be satisfied that the aggrieved party needs remedy.

The Shah Bano verdict is now living history. It shows that the legal battle of Muslim women begins with their right to maintenance and ends with cruel divorce. These two issues are interlinked and cannot be dealt with in isolation. The legal fights of Shah Bano and Jaitunbi make the point tellingly.

THE ROLE OF JUDICIARY

The Constitution (42nd Amendment) Act, 1976, has revolutionized our judicial system. It has made the state socialist and secular and in the Directive Principles of State Policy it has provided for equal justice and free legal aid on the basis of equal opportunity for women and other weaker sections of society. And, among his fundamental duties every citizen has to renounce practices derogatory to the dignity of women (Act 51A[e]) and 'to develop the scientific temper, humanism and the spirit of enquiry and reforms'. Thereafter, many developments have taken place for the welfare of women. In this scenario our judiciary has become more responsive towards elevating the status of divorced Muslim women who lose everything in the event of sudden and arbitrary divorce by their husbands. In the *Bai Tahira* vs. *Ali Hussain* case the Supreme Court held that 'the payment of illusory amounts by way of customary or personal law requirement will be considered in the deduction of maintenance rate but cannot annihilate the rate unless it is a reasonable substitute' (1979 *Supreme Court Reporter*, p. 75).

In the Shah Bano case (*Mohd. Ahmad Khan* vs. *Shah Bano Begum*, *AIR* 1985, SC 945) the Supreme Court held that it would be incorrect and unjust to interpret the principle of Muslim law to mean that a Muslim husband is liable to provide maintenance to his divorced wife only for the period of *iddat*. The apex court concluded that if the divorced wife is able to maintain herself, the husband's liability ceases with the expiration of the period of *iddat*, but if she is unable to maintain herself after the period of *iddat* she is entitled to have recourse to Section 125 of the Criminal Procedure Code. This was a reform of Muslim Personal Law in favour of helpless divorced Muslim women, but it was not acceptable to the Muslim clergy and politicians. Therefore, this judgement led to the enactment of the Muslim Women (Protection of Rights on Divorce) Act, 1986, which served an immediate but limited purpose under Section 3 and opened the door for the judicial interpretation of clause (a), that is, 'a reasonable and fair provision and maintenance to be paid and made to her within the *iddat* period by her former husband'. 'A reasonable and fair provision' was made equivalent to the benefits granted under Section 125 of the Criminal Procedure Code.

A recent Bombay High Court judgement by Justices Mr. A.V. Savant and Mr. T.K. Chandrashekhar in the case of *Jaitunbi Mubarak Sheikh* vs. *Mubarak Fakhruddin Seikh* (May 1999) has interpreted the aforesaid clause in the light of the Shah Bano judgement. The judgement has observed that reasonable and fair provision should be made in such a way that it should cover the expenses of food, clothing, shelter, health, etc., for the future life of the divorced woman and be paid during the *iddat* period. The court has suggested that, if the parties to the dispute so desire, they may file, in the alternative, their affidavits to the effect that they may be governed by the provisions of Sections 125 to 128 of the Criminal Procedure Code before the court of the Magistrate while finally deciding the case. Earlier, in 1997, a judgement of the Punjab and Haryana High Court had instructed a Muslim husband to maintain his wife even after the *iddat* period.

Muslim Personal Law as applied in India recognizes arbitrary and unilateral triple *talaq* by the husband. The Muslim wife can seek divorce, as pointed out earlier, on any one of the grounds enumerated under Section 2 of the Dissolution of Muslim Marriages Act, 1939, of which ground (VIII) says: 'that if husband treats her with cruelty, that is to say—(a) habitually assaults her or makes her life miserable by cruelty of conduct even if such conduct does not amount to ill-treatment', etc. In the *Itwari* vs. *Asghari* case (*AIR* 1960, All. 684) the Allahabad High Court expressed its view on cruelty in the following words: 'Indian law does not recognize various types of cruelty such as "Muslim cruelty", "Christian cruelty", "Jewish cruelty" and so on and that the test of cruelty is based on universal and humanitarian standards, that is to say, conduct of the husband which would cause bodily or mental pain as to endanger the wife's safety and health. . . .' In the same case a second marriage by the husband during the subsistence of his first marriage was considered to be a source of cruelty to the wife and withdrawal from the society of the husband was considered to be just. The suit of the husband for restitution of conjugal right was dismissed. Delivering the judgement Justice Dhavan said:

In deciding what constitutes cruelty the courts have always taken into consideration the prevailing social conditions. The onus today would be on the husband who takes a second wife to explain his action and prove that his taking a second wife involves no insult or cruelty to the first. But in the absence of a cogent explanation the court will presume under modern conditions that the action of the husband in taking a second wife involved cruelty to the first.

In a subsequent judgement in *Shakila Bano* vs. *Ghulam Mustafa* (*AIR* 1971, Bombay 167) the court held that any treatment falling short of actual violence but such as to jeopardize the health or sanity of the wife is also held to be cruelty. In *Husain Begum* vs. *Mohd. Rustam Khan* (1906, 20, All. 322) it was held that throwing insults on the wife amounted to cruelty.

For such criminal behaviour, as pointed out in various judgements there is no punishment for the husband, but the wife has the right to seek divorce on this ground alone. But cruelty of this kind by the husband or relatives of the husband has been made a cognizable offence under Section 498A of the Indian Penal Code since 1983 with Criminal Law (2nd Amendment) Act. This section defines cruelty as 'any wilful conduct which is of such a nature as is likely to drive the woman to commit suicide or cause grave injury or danger to life, or health (whether mental or physical) of the woman; or harassment of the woman where such harassment is with a view to coercing her or any person related to her to meet any unlawful demand for any property or valuable security. The punishment for cruelty against a wife is imprisonment for a term that may extend to three years and shall also be liable to fine. Besides, Section 498A of the Indian Penal Code, Sections 3 and 4 of the Dowry Prohibition Act, 1961, and Section 406 of the Indian Penal Code for criminal breach of trust are also made applicable to marital dispute where cruelty is involved.

One may see in the application of these provisions in Muslim marital dispute the nature of Muslim Personal law. Let us demonstrate this point by giving an example from Criminal Misc. (Main) 2100/95 and Criminal Misc. (Main) 1080/96 at Delhi High Court which were filed by a husband against Section 498A of the Indian Penal Code. Under this law the husband has no choice except to face trial where he can get three years' imprisonment and also has to pay fine or to reach a compromise with an ill-treated wife. The outcome of the dispute was that the husband made a compromise to the satisfaction of his wife by offering her permanent maintenance for life, a residence and damages caused to her by keeping her away from the matrimonial home. This relief became possible in favour of the wife in the dispute in spite of the fact that her husband had sought a *fatwa* (decree under Muslim Personal Law) that he had divorced his wife. The High Court order dated 15 November 1996 is still in operation and may continue till her death or second marriage. This is what judicial activism has achieved where parliament has failed.

REFORM AND CODIFICATION

There is an urgent need to reform the Muslim Personal Law on divorce. The law allowing arbitrary and unilateral divorce has been reformed all over the Muslim world. Men and women have similar rights in matters of divorce. The Turkish spouse can seek divorce on any grounds specified under Articles 129-38 of the Turkish Civil Code. In Iran, under the Family Protection Law, 1967, all traditional forms of divorce are recognized, but they do not come into effect without the due process of the court. This allows for all possible means of conciliation between wife and husband. When conciliation fails, a certificate is issued to that effect and then the parties are free to divorce each other. The Family Law Ordinance of Pakistan may also be cited as an example for the reform and codification of Muslim Personal Law in India.

In Lebanon, Egypt, Jordan, Syria, Morocco and Sudan a divorce outside the court is possible, but it has no validity when uttered by a man who is intoxicated or under duress, anger or provocation. On the contrary in India such a divorce is recognized and given legal effect. Under the Indonesian Family Regulation Act of 1955 a man desiring to divorce his wife must move the local marriage council whose officials will do their best to discourage him and to reconcile the parties. These examples show that what has been gradually abandoned in these countries as wrong and obsolete interpretations of customary laws is still followed by Indian Muslims without any reason.

The reform and codification of personal laws is not unknown to us. The various enactments referred to in this paper are examples of codification of personal laws. These codified laws are a result of constant struggles. When the draft of the Hindu Code Bill was introduced in the Constituent Assembly many members (the so-called no changers) came out openly to oppose the passage of the Hindu Code Bill. Eloquent speeches were made on both sides. They saw the Bill as an attempt to demolish the entire fabric and structure of Hindu society. Even Dr. Rajendra Prasad, the then President of India, urged Prime Minister Jawaharal Nehru to withdraw the Bill on the ground that a vast majority of Hindus were opposed to its adoption. Dr. Syama Prasad Mookerjee and Pandit Govind Malviya asserted that 'Hindus would accept monogamy only when Muslims did, that divorce could not take place in Ram Rajya and that they were against a daughter's share in her father's property since that would be imitating Muslims.' In spite of such opposition, the Hindu Code Bill came into force in 1954-6 as a series of Acts relating to intestate succession, marriage and divorce, minority and guardianship and adoption and maintenance.

This codification of Hindu Personal Law was an important step in recognizing Hindu women as legal entities. This is not to say that further modifications are not required. Though the Hindu Succession Act, 1956, reformed the Hindu Law of succession by making a daughter a simultaneous and equal heir along with the son and by abolishing the limited estate of Hindu woman, it did not abolish the *mitakshara* coparcenary system. The Act gave a share to a daughter in the coparcenary (joint property) held by her father but did not make her an equal shareholder with her brother who from birth inherited a share equal to that of his father. By virtue of Section 4(2) of the Act, laws providing for the prevention of fragmentation of agricultural holdings, or for the fixation of ceilings, or for the devolution of tenancy rights in respect of such holdings were left out from the application of this Act. This has allowed women to be discriminated against in inheriting tenancy rights under which a great deal of land is held and controlled in rural India. Under the Hindu Adoption and Maintenance Act, a Hindu male can adopt a child without the consent of his wife. A married woman cannot adopt a child without the consent of the husband. This Act, however, allowed the adoption of a girl child for the first time in Hindu law.

The Hindu marriage law is based on the doctrine of matrimonial offence. This calls for reforms. The Hindu Marriage Act, 1955, does not provide any remedy for broken marriages. In *Mohinder Pal Singh* vs. *Kulwant Kaur* the court did not grant the relief prayed for by the husband, as the husband could not establish the guilt of his wife. The judges observed, 'There is a touch of sadness in this case. It appears to me that the husband and wife are not for each other. There is no give and take. And that is the stuff of which marriage is made. There is no play in the joints. Peaceful coexistence of husband and wife is now outside the realm of possibility' (*AIR* 1976, Delhi 141). The court observed that the case called for reform in the existing law.

Christian women raised their voice for further reforms in their law of divorce under the banner of the Joint Women's Programme (JWP) in Delhi. The Christian clergy, too, have realized the need to do away with discrimination and formed an Ecumenical committee for changes in Christian Personal Law. The government has been requested to present a bill in parliament to this effect and it is pending at the official level since 1995.

With regard to Muslim law also there are instances where parliament has debated matters falling under Muslim Personal Law. If we take a historical perspective we find that during the regime of Lord Cornwallis (1785-93) the legal system in India was drastically changed. He introduced the concept of administration according to law. He passed forty-eight regulations in 1793 known collectively as the Cornwallis Code. He introduced reforms both in civil and criminal administration of justice. On the line of the Cornwallis Code further reforms were made. Earlier, religious heads and rulers/dynasties had enacted a variety of criminal laws and many different criteria for punishment of criminals were used. There was no uniformity in the criminal laws. The First Indian Law Commission presided over by Lord Macaulay was appointed to draft a code based on English law which was passed on 6 October 1860. This Indian Penal Code, 1860, suspended all previous rules, regulations and provisions of criminal law in India and provided a uniform criminal law for all Indians. The Muslims resisted this move but failed. Section 376 of this Code provides punishment for rape different from the *shar'iat* law which requires the testimony of four male witnesses to prove that rape has indeed taken place. The Evidence Act was passed in 1872 to frame rules on evidence. According to this Act, all women are treated equally while the *shar'iat* law of evidence treats a woman's testimony as worth half that of a man. In 1929 the Child Marriage Restraint Act (Sarda Act) came into force with the purpose of restraining the solemnization of child marriages. This Act applies to all citizens of India. A number of influential Muslim members presented a petition to the Viceroy against the proposal asking that Muslims be exempted from the purview of the Sarda Act, but did not succeed. In 1937 the Shar'iat Act was passed by the central legislature. The objective of the Act was to secure a uniformity of laws for all Muslims in British India.

In 1932 the state of Baroda passed a Divorce Act and many urged that a similar Act be passed for British India and the right to divorce conceded by Islamic law to Muslim women be recognized in British courts. Then came the Dissolution of Muslim Marriages Act, 1939. The Special Marriages Act, 1954, allows two Indians to marry without renouncing their religion. It provoked strong opposition from Hindu and Muslim members of parliament, but to no avail.

The central and state legislatures have passed a number of Acts for the better administration and supervision of waqfs. The Waqf Act, 1954, was passed by parliament and has been amended four times subsequently. The need for further amendment was felt and a consolidated Waqf Bill, 1995, was introduced in parliament for better administration of *waqfs* and for matters connected therewith. The Waqf Bill was passed and came on the statute books as Waqf Act, 1995 (Act 43 of 1995).

The aforesaid examples show that the state has legislated on issues of personal law despite opposition. It is ironical that only on the issue of the maintenance of divorced women, divorce, polygamy and inheritance do our law-makers show their inability to legislate and bow down to the clergy and fundamentalists. This is simply because most politicians need the support of fundamentalists to further their electoral gains. The Indian state must repeal their reservations to favour just and human laws for women. The state must honour its commitment to the Convention on the Elimination of All Forms of Discrimination, International Covenant on Economic, Social and Cultural Rights and other international human rights standards as well as its own constitutional provisions to safeguard the interest of women citizens.

The Muslim clergy argue that those seeking change and reform in Muslim Personal Law are irreligious. The *shar'iat* is a divine law that cannot be questioned and that it makes women as equal as they should be. The reality is that there is no one Islamic law. The difference in Islamic jurisprudence in various schools of law—Hanafi, Shafei, Maliki, Hanbali, Jafariya and Ahl-e-Hadis—show that Muslim law is not *per se* divinely ordained. The Holy Qur'an is considered to be divine revelation, but not its interpretation. The differences in Islamic jurisprudence are because of differences in interpretation by the imams of these schools of law. This is contrary to the claim of the fundamentalists and the clergy that there is only one Islamic tradition which can never be changed.

CONCLUSION

In conclusion we may say that the codification of Muslim law on divorce will not contravene any Islamic principles. If all schools of law are taken into consideration a very good Muslim personal law of divorce can be codified. For instance, women are entitled to judicial divorce under Maliki law while Hanafi law allows women to stipulate conditions in their marriage contracts, and *talaq* under Shia law has to be pronounced orally in the presence of two competent witnesses.

Those Muslim countries where Muslim personal laws have been reformed or codified have realized that the moral precepts of a religion no longer command much respect. They have, therefore, turned some of them into binding laws. In India moral precepts and legal provisions are confused. Those who can twist them in their favour conveniently use them. We should understand that Muslim Personal Law is not a law exclusively for Indian Muslims. The same legal system is followed by millions of Muslims all over the world. We should not brush the progress made in the Muslim world aside. If we have to change the *status quo* we shall need a Muslim women's movement to mobilize public opinion on the basis of facts and knowledge of law in our modern context.

17

Divorce and Remarriage among Indian Muslims: A Sociological Reflection

Abdul Waheed

In an article published in 1983 Lucy Carrol observed: 'The ongoing debates concerning *the status of Muslim women*, reform of Muslim Personal Law and India's Constitutional commitment to a uniform civil code . . . have infused the atmosphere with partisan argument, and polemics too often take the place of scholarship. The responsibilities of both legalists and social scientists in these circumstances are greatly enhanced' (1983: 207; emphasis added). So also Imtiaz Ahmad wrote: 'Unfortunately, this debate has become so highly emotional and politicized that an academic discussion is ruled out for the present' (1976: xviii).

Both these statements, one by an authority on Muslim law and another by a social scientist widely known for his studies on Indian Muslims, point to the fact that 'emotions' and 'polemics' rather than neutral and objective scholarship have dominated the debates on the reform of Muslim Personal Law. Indeed, it is because of such politically motivated and emotionally charged debates as well as media hype on the issue that Muslim Personal Law has virtually become the symbol of Muslim identity as well as a prejudice against them.

Among the innumerable provisions of Muslim law concerning marriage and divorce, the ones relating to divorce, that is 'triple divorce'[1] and a Muslim man's right to marry four women at a time are widely projected as examples of the inhuman treatment meted out to Muslim women. One can find repeated claims both in the media and in the writings of scholars that divorce among Muslims is effected by the husband saying to his wife three times 'I divorce you'. This gives the impression that divorce is very frequent amongst Muslims, and that a Muslim man is a malevolent patriarch who does not merely divorce his wife on a whim but also marries another woman/women whenever and wherever he likes. On the other hand a Muslim woman is projected as a helpless person who always lives under the fear of being arbitrarily and unilaterally abandoned by her husband. She is a mere chattel. Thus, a sociologist writes:

> A Muslim man can have up to four wives at a time with no legal protection to the woman against the exercise of the privilege. The law does not admit polygamy as a cause for seeking divorce by a Muslim woman. Of course, the corresponding right of a woman to have more than one husband in any circumstance is inconceivable, much less granted under law. . . . A man can divorce at will just by uttering the word 'I divorce you' three times, anywhere, any time without any witnesses. He is also not required by law to give any maintenance to the wife beyond the period of *iddat*, which is three months and a few days. If a man divorces his wife, he is obliged to pay *mehr*, a sum of money agreed upon at the time of marriage. This provision is also taken as security for Muslim women against easy divorce. But as long as the right to have four wives continues to be enjoyed by a man, he need not divorce his wife, if he does not wish to pay *mehr*, he can simply discard her or ill-treat her, while still taking another wife . . . so at every stage Muslim Law is fettered with inequities, with the women in every case being less equal (Bhatty, 1976: 102-4).

Commenting on this statement from a legal perspective, Lucy Carrol says: 'This is not scholarship, it is polemic. It is also factually incorrect as far as Muslim women in India are concerned' (1983: 208).[2] Imtiaz Ahmad taking a sociological perspective notes: 'she shows little awareness of the possibility that the dismal picture she draws of Muslim women may not conform to existing reality and the inequities she draws attention to may not be so severe in practice' (1976: xix).

The aim of this paper is not to discuss Muslim law relating to marriage and divorce. Rather, our aim is to understand divorce and remarriage among Indian Muslims from a sociological perspective. Sociology views divorce as a social fact and thus, seeks to explore its causes and consequences in society. No social phenomenon occurs in a vacuum. It emerges out of the interplay of the various socio-economic forces in a given society. Social elements or institutions like family, marriage, kinship, economy, education, etc., must also be taken into consideration while analysing a social phenomenon like divorce. Any attempt to explain marital dissolution solely in terms of law would be reductionist as it would undermine the significance of the social context in which it occurs. This is not to deny the reality and importance of law. What is being suggested is merely that law should be seen in a social context. It is also not always the case that the social action of divorce always corresponds to law. There may be contradictions between what the law says and what really happens in society. Therefore, it seems proper that we try to understand the empirical reality of divorce and remarriage among Indian Muslims.

SOCIETY AND DIVORCE

Divorce is the product of a long process of marital discord which may be engineered either by adverse socio-economic conditions or by personal reasons such as disloyalty to a marital alliance, physical handicaps, psychological disturbances, etc. Even though all societies try to evolve mechanisms to combat marital conflicts and maintain a stable family system, yet conjugal conflicts exist everywhere and sometimes they result in marital dissolution. Therefore, divorce exists universally in one form or another as a mechanism to save an individual from being forced to live with an undesirable spouse. William Goode writes:

> Of course divorce is one of the major solutions for an intense degree of marital disharmony and is to be found in most societies and nations. Yet I know of no contemporary society, primitive or industralized, in which divorce is actually valued. Divorce has its consequences for the society, the kin networks and the individual. And the consequences are tedious when not awkward, and burdensome when not destructive (1970: 139).

Because of the adverse consequences which divorce, especially excessive rates of divorce, create, every society evolves certain impediments or barriers to minimize both the propensity to and the act of divorce. These barriers are generally related to 'the emotional, religious and moral commitment that a partner feels towards his marriage or towards his children, the external pressure of kin and community, of law, the church and other associational membership' (Levinger, 1970: 108). However, the effectiveness of these social barriers is neither uniform nor static. It varies from one period of time to another, from society to society and within a society from group to group. It is observed that the pressure of social barriers is strong in a society which is in a 'state of equilibrium', i.e. where individuals are sufficiently integrated with their groups. In such a society the divorce rate can be kept in check. Likewise, social barriers are generally strong in those classes or groups of people who occupy a high socio-economic position in the social hierarchy, but tend to be less effective among those who are at the lowest echelon of the social stratification system.

However, many people believe that ideological tolerance of divorce by a society or a group leads to a higher divorce rate though this assumption is belied by empirical facts. For example, the upper strata seem to be more tolerant of divorce than the lower strata in the United States. Even so, available evidence shows that the divorce rate is higher in the lower social strata. Indeed, there is an inverse relationship between class and the divorce rate (Goode, 1970: 142). A variant on the above can also be observed in India.

India is a segmentary as well as a stratified society. There are various cultural zones in which different communities live. Each community or group within the social setting of a particular cultural zone follows different customs and traditions. Each exhibits different moral and ethical values. There are differences in the nature of marriage and the practice of divorce among the various groups. In each cultural zone, people are also arranged in a hierarchical order either on the basis of caste or class. Caste generally corresponded to class in traditional Indian society, but dissonance between the caste status and class position has begun to emerge in modern Indian society. Family organization, marriage and divorce practices not only differ from region to region but also from one caste to another within a region. Thus, not only is the regional variation very important in India but the stratification system also should be taken into consideration while analysing a social phenomenon like divorce.

Generally speaking, Hindus of the higher castes/classes did not allow divorce nor encourage remarriage in the past. They viewed marriage as a sacrament or as indissoluble. On the other hand, 'a large section of Hindus among lower castes have traditionally practiced divorce. These customary forms of divorce were recognized both socially and judicially. The usual customary forms are: (a) by mutual consent, (b) unilaterally at the pleasure of the husband or by the abandonment of the wife, and (c) by deed of divorce' (GOI, 1974: 17).

Why did high caste Hindus shun divorce and remarriage? And why did lower caste Hindus practice them? At a very simple level the answer could be that higher caste Hindus were Sanskritized. They followed the Hindu Great traditions which did not admit dissolution of marriage whereas lower caste Hindus did not follow the Hindu Great traditions and were not Sanskritized. This argument may appeal to those who like to analyse social phenomena solely in terms of ideology or religion, but it would certainly not convince sociologists who analyse social phenomena in a social context. Explaining the pattern and causes of divorce in a stratified society, Goode observes:

> Where there is a well developed stratification system, it would seem likely that the lower class (or caste) does not count on the stability of marriage, that the marriage itself costs less, less is invested in it than in the upper strata, the kin ties are less important and therefore the ambiguity created by divorce would not be taken so seriously as in the upper strata (1970: 113).

Contemporary India is in the process of rapid social change. The displacement of people and differentiation between caste status and class position is growing day by day. An increasing rate of industrialization and globalization, the urban way of life and hedonistic and individualistic values have brought about tremendous changes in family organizations and attitudes towards marriage and divorce. Many people have started believing that marriage is more an alliance of social convenience than a perpetual bond made in Heaven. As a result, the practice of divorce is increasing in urban areas. Lower and middle class people, who mostly come from the higher castes, are exhibiting more proneness to divorce. Madhu Jain reports: 'Divorce has now, in fact, gone democratic, fashionable, mundane. Even school teachers, receptionists, petty traders, government servants, insurance agents and of course, housewives fill the courts' (1986: 86).

DIVORCE AMONG INDIAN MUSLIMS

Like the other Indian communities, Muslims too are heterogeneous and stratified. They display an enormous variety of customs and traditions, beliefs and social organizations which vary from region to region and within a region from one social group to another. Imtiaz Ahmad writes:

> In terms of the structure of family and kinship groupings, the Muslims in India are not necessarily distinguishable from their non-Muslim neighbours. They seem to be a part of a wider cultural complex shared equally by all those who reside in the region as a whole. The imprint of the regional cultural environment on Muslim kinship and marriage patterns is not restricted to family norms and role relationships alone. It extends to marriage customs and practices as well of to the distribution of inheritance (1976: xxiv-xxv).

Socio-cultural diversity among Indian Muslims also has a deep imprint on the practice of divorce and remarriage. Indeed, these practices are neither uniform nor absolutely in accordance with the *shar'iat.* Though Islam permits dissolution of marital alliance, it is allowed only in extreme circumstances where husband and wife, defying every reconciliatory effort, no longer want to live together. 'Divorce in Islam', writes Esposito, 'serves as a safety valve in cases where the spouses can no longer live in harmony and so the very purpose of marriage would be defeated' (1982: 29). Islam does not merely allow divorce but also encourages remarriage after divorce and the marriage of widows. Marriage with a widow is considered to be one of the highest virtues as the Prophet himself first married a widow.

Contrary to Islamic principles, Indian Muslims display different attitudes towards divorce, remarriage after divorce and the marriage of widows. Traditionally, Muslims of the higher social strata who looked upon divorce as social stigma encouraged neither divorce nor remarriage. Among Muslims of the lower social strata divorce was widely practiced and remarriage was commonly encouraged. Bhatty, who frequently attributes divorce to the single factor of law, herself observed in a village of eastern UP: 'Divorce permitted by Islam carries a strong stigma among the Ashraf, but to much less degree among the non-Ashraf. In Kasauli I found that divorce, remarriage after divorce and marriage of widows were more frequent among the non-Ashraf than among the Ashraf' (Bhatty, 1980: 203-4). Similar observations were also made by Vreede-de-Steurs in her study of family among the Ashraf of western UP. She writes, 'However, there is legal and religious difference between upper caste Hindus and Ashraf Muslims, but their common past has nevertheless so conditioned the general mentality that Ashraf Muslim women, like upper caste Hindu women, hardly ever divorce or remarry' (1968: 16).

In many folk and tribal Muslim communities divorce is effected through un-Islamic means. Among the Gujjar Bakarwals of Jammu and Kashmir, divorce is generally disapproved and the normal expectations are that marriage should remain intact. Men rarely divorce their wives. Even if divorce takes place it is mostly at the initiative of women and assumes the form of elopement. When a married woman elopes with another man, which usually creates a feud, attempts are made to bring her back. However, if persuasion fails, the husband is pressurized by his parents to divorce his wife (Khatana, 1976: 101-2). Partap C. Aggarwal reports a similar practice among the Meos of Rajasthan. Meo men rarely divorce their wives and Meo women cannot divorce their husbands. Yet, a 'common way of leaving a husband is by eloping. If a woman abandons her husband and wishes to marry another man, the first husband must be paid *jhagra* (compensation) by the man who wants to marry her. Unless the amount of *jhagra* is amicably settled, elopement can lead to serious feuds which sometimes last for generations' (1976: 76).

These divorce and remarriage practices seem to be more or less similar to those prevailing among non-Muslims. Despite this similarity, Muslims are generally represented as 'unique' in respect of marriage and divorce practices. They are thought to be more prone to divorce. This is assumed to be the case simply because Muslim law allows a man to divorce his wife unilaterally. But can the provisions of law be made the basis to suggest that the divorce rate, family instability and the vulnerability of women is higher among Muslims as compared to other Indian communities? Available empirical evidence seems to suggest otherwise.

Any attempt to understand a social phenomenon among Indian Muslims in a scientific manner is impeded by the dearth of empirical evidence. As Indian Muslims have been neglected by both sociologists and social anthropologists, neither are a sufficient number of empirical studies available on the social structure of Indian Muslims nor does the Indian census provide community-wise data that can be used to gauge their social conditions. Indeed, it is this paucity of empirical data that has given wide currency to the many stereotypes about them, including the notion that divorce is frequent among them and women are mistreated. Contrary to stereotypes which are generally based on emotions and speculations, our effort in this paper is to discuss divorce and remarriage among Indian Muslims on the basis of empirical evidence. We culled these from the Indian census of 1931, the survey of some villages by the Indian census in 1961 as well as some empirical studies on Indian Muslims. These data may seem somewhat disparate, but still indicate broad patterns of divorce and remarriage among Indian Muslims *vis-à-vis* other Indian communities.

The Census of India, 1931, the last census to provide community-wise data, compiled statistics on 'widowed persons' which included divorced persons who had not remarried. The percentage of such persons was less among Indian Muslims as compared to the percentage for other major communities and All-India percentage. Table 1 sets out the percentage, according to marital status, for India as well as for the different communities. The table shows that

TABLE 1: COMMUNITY-WISE BREAK UP OF POPULATION BY RELIGION AND MARITAL STATUS

Unit	Sex	Unmarried	Married	Widowed
India excluding Burma	Males	47.6	47.0	5.4
	Females	33.8	50.5	15.7
Hindus	Males	46.3	48.0	5.7
	Females	32.4	50.7	16.9
Jains	Males	50.3	41.5	8.2
	Females	33.7	44.2	2.1
Sikhs	Males	55.0	37.0	8.0
	Females	41.1	47.5	11.4
Muslims	Males	50.0	45.6	4.4
	Females	35.8	51.3	12.9
Others	Males	53.6	42.6	3.8
	Females	45.2	43.9	10.9

Source: Hutton, 1933: 222.

in India, widowed males comprised 5.4 per cent whereas widowed females comprised 15.7 per cent. Compared with the All-India percentage, widowed males and females were 4.4 per cent and 12.9 per cent respectively among Muslims. If we compare the Muslims with the Hindus the difference widens further as there were 5.7 per cent male and 16.9 per cent females widowed among Hindus. One can object that the data merely shows marital status and not the rate of divorce. This is true. But why should one be interested in knowing the rate of divorce except to understand the state of the institution of the family and the status of women. Even if we assume a higher rate of divorce among Muslims, we have to recognize that Muslims were managing divorce and widowhood more effectively than the others. That is the reason why the percentage of widowed persons is less among them. Again, since unmarried widows and divorced women in our society are generally more susceptible to social atrocities than those widows and divorced women who have remarried, the data suggests that there were fewer women among Muslims as compared to other major communities who would be susceptible to social atrocities.

The Census of India discontinued the practice of publishing community-wise data after Independence because of the state policy of not showing the differential development patterns of the various segments of Indian society, except Scheduled Castes and Scheduled Tribes. However, in 1961 a survey was undertaken by the Census of India in 587 selected villages with a sample of 1,33,775 families covering a period of 50 years on the incidence of marriage with consanguineous and affinal relations in different parts of the country. This survey also provides data on the incidence of divorce among different religious communities. The survey indicates wide acceptance of divorce in the villages with some variations of incidence among different communities. Incidence of divorce was highest among Muslims (6.06 per cent), followed by Hindus (3.21 per cent), Buddhists (3.07 per cent), Jains (1.68 per cent), Sikhs (0.91 per cent) and Christians (0.47 per cent). The causes for divorce show that adultery, barrenness and extreme poverty were common grounds for divorce in most of the villages (Basu, 1985: 33).

As the causes of divorce are social, so the pattern of divorce is conditioned by social forces. The survey says:

There has not been persistent trend in the incidence of divorce in all religions during more than fifty years. There has been, however, persistent rise in divorce upto twenty years before the survey. After this there has been marked decline in the incidence of divorce. The sharp rise in the incidence of divorce during 21-30 years prior to the survey is particularly noticeable. These were the periods of war, partition and other conditions of instability in the country. These events had an impact on the marriage institution as well (1973: 4).

Among the various destabilizing events, the Partition of the country had a more catastrophic impact on Indian Muslims than other communities. It did not merely tear their social fabric it also tarnished their image. The unprecedented migration of Muslims to Pakistan, which continued till about 1960, resulted in broken families, dispersed kin and dissolved marital alliances. Most of the middle class, traders, government servants, etc., migrated to Pakistan. Those who stayed behind in India constituted mostly lower strata of Muslims (see Imam, 1975: 71-103). Though the impact of Partition was felt more in urban areas than rural India, yet rural Muslims, especially those belonging to areas adjoining the then East and West Pakistan, could not be saved from the brunt of Partition. Indeed, Partition created fluid and anomic conditions for Muslims. Also, for centuries Muslims have been highly urbanized. The prosperous sections have always migrated to cities, leaving the poor in the villages. So we can assume that most of the Muslim villagers would be poor. And among the poor in an anomic condition a higher rate of divorce is not unimaginable.

DIVORCE AMONG URBAN MUSLIMS

Though many of the customary practices and a higher rate of divorce persist among Muslims of the rural areas since most of them are poor and uneducated, much has changed among urban Muslims since 1961. Overcoming the fluid situation created by Partition, many occupational and artisan groups like the Ansaris (weavers), Qureshis (butchers), Saifis (blacksmith), Idrisis (tailors), Sulaimanis (barbers), etc., have prospered from businesses in arts and handicrafts, hide and skin and other articles in which Muslims have been traditionally engaged. Most of them are self-employed.

One can also see among them an increasing trend towards education and reform. This is not to argue that all is well with Muslims in urban areas. Large numbers continue to be poor, uneducated and slum dwellers. We can expect a higher rate of divorce among them as they occupy the lower and lower middle class position in urban society and economy. But contrary to our expectations, as the following data will show, divorce rate among them is not higher than the national average.[3]

In his study of fertility behaviour among Muslims of Kanpur city, M.E. Khan found only three cases of divorce among 330 couple respondents. The data was collected from dominant Muslim wards and included all classes and sections of Muslims. He writes:

> Though divorce can be easily obtained, its frquency is very low among all sections of Muslims. People view divorce with disapproval and social pressure forbids individuals to go in for such an extreme action. In our sample three cases, less than 1 per cent, of divorce were reported. A widow or divorcee can remarry after completing her period of *iddat*. Widow remarriage is quite prevalent and encouraged by all sections of Muslims (1979: 33).

Similar findings were also reported by Shibani Roy in her study of Ashraf middle class families in Delhi and Lucknow. The investigation was conducted in the most populous Muslim areas and was based on a sample of 300 families, 150 each from Delhi and Lucknow. The respondents had white-collar jobs, their income ranging between Rs. 400 and 1,000 per month. She found only three cases of divorce in the entire sample. The causes were social and varied. She explains:

> In the first case the woman was divorced the very next day of her *nikah* due to her physical deformity. In the second case, the husband was not of a balanced mind and could not provide for his wife and children regularly. The woman after having two children realised that her husband was incapable of looking after the family. Moreover, the man used to keep away from the family for months together. The girl's parents were sympathetic towards her and they brought their daughter back to their home. Later the woman signed the divorce paper and succeeded in getting her husband's consent. But to get the possession of her children, she had to forego *mehr*. In these two cases the women were educated upto middle school. The last case is of a graduate girl who had to divorce her husband due to his infidelity. In this case the woman demanded her *mehr* worth Rs. 75000/.

The divorce case went from the lower court and ultimately she won her case, the court granted her one-third of *mehr* money. This woman being educated could face the situation with courage and determination (1979: 90).

Moving from Delhi to Rajasthan Sushila Jain, in the city of Jaipur, surprisingly also finds only three cases of divorce in a sample of 375 respondents. As many as 86.7 per cent, that is about 350 of the respondents were married, 10.7 per cent were unmarried and 2.6 per cent were widowers. If we calculate the divorce rate among married respondents, it would work out to less than 1 per cent. It is not only the rate of divorce which is similar to the other two findings. But more interestingly and surprisingly, the causes were also of the same nature. Using surprisingly similar language Jain writes:

In the first case the reason was reported to be infidelity on the part of the woman. In the second case, the husband was not of a balanced mind and could not provide for his wife and children. Moreover, the man used to keep away from the family for months together. The girl's parents were sympathetic towards her and they brought their daughter back to home. Later the woman signed the divorce paper and succeeded in getting her husband's consent. But to get the possession of her children, she had to forego her *mehr*. The last case is of a couple where the husband had divorced his wife due to the prolonged incurable disease of the wife (1986: 88).

The data provided by these three studies of Muslims in four major cities of India—Kanpur, Lucknow, Delhi and Jaipur—is significant for three reasons. One, the data may be said to be comparative as it shows trends of divorce among Muslims in four different urban settings. Two, the data is unprejudiced as none of the studies was concerned primarily with the study of divorce among Muslims so one cannot say that the data is 'cooked'. Three, the data is from those cities where Muslims have been living for centuries and their cultural imprint is visible.

A close scrutiny of the data leads us to say that divorce is not as frequent among urban Muslims as is generally assumed. Indeed, only 9 cases of divorce are reported out of about 980 marriages. Thus, a divorce rate of less than 1 per cent is reported among urban Muslims. Secondly, there is a distinct trend in the three studies as each reports only 3 cases of divorce. Thirdly, contrary to the popular impression that Muslim men divorce their wives as and when it suits them, the data shows that divorce is also sought by women. In fact, out of 6 cases in two studies, 3 women themselves sought divorce. And divorce is neither given by husbands nor sought by wives on flimsy grounds. Rather, the grounds of divorce are well-defined: infidelity of the man or the woman, inability of the husband to support his family, or physical deformity, etc. Fourthly, Muslim women are not as helpless as it is presumed. They are well supported by their parents in times of crises. Thus, in two cases out of six, it was the parents of the women who brought them back home when they found their daughters in miserable conditions. Later on they forced the men to consent to the divorce. Fifthly, if women are educated, they can face the situation boldly and fight for their rights. This is symbolized by the case of the graduate girl who fought for her divorce as well as for *mehr*.

CONCLUSION

We started this discussion by stating that divorce is a social phenomenon and its pattern is controlled more by structural conditions than by law or ideology. Our data supports this assumption by showing irregular trends of divorce in different times and places among Indian Muslims. If the incidence of divorce was highest among rural Muslims in 1961, its rate as reported by three empirical studies of Muslims conducted during the 1980s in four major cities of India is less than 1 per cent. Had religion or law been the sole cause of divorce, we would have found a uniform rate of divorce both among rural and urban Muslims at all times.

Secondly, Indian Muslims seem to have a more positive outlook towards widow marriage or marriage after divorce. As a result, a lower percentage of unmarried, widowed or divorced women were found among them in 1931. This could be either due to a low rate of death and divorce or due to a high rate of widow marriage and marriage after divorce, if we assume a higher rate of death and divorce among them. In either case, Muslims have proved to be more stable than the other major communities in the areas of family and marriage. There are no reasons to believe that remarriage trends among them would be drastically different in free India. If we have all India figures of marital status among the different communities, we would still find a lower percentage of unmarried, widowed and divorced women among Indian Muslims. Unfortunately, this kind of information is not available as the Indian census no longer provides us with community-wise data.

By arguing for the primacy of society over law or religion in analysing a social phenomenon like divorce or by showing a strong tendency towards remarriage among Indian Muslims, we do not intend to underrate the significance of law. We cannot deny the harshness of the 'triple divorce' provision in Muslim law which legally enables a Muslim man to divorce his wife and it suits him. But to assume that this provision is extensively misused for exploiting and discarding women would be wrong. Moreover, to assume that the unilateral discarding of women is confined only to Muslims and does not exist among non-Muslims would also not be right. Unilateral breaking up of marital alliances also exists among non-Muslims. Generally, separation and desertion as means of evading marital obligations are widely used by those who cannot legally break marital alliances unilaterally. In cases of triple divorce and separation or desertion, the consequences are the same for women. It is for this reason that the Indian census clubbed divorce and separation together. As Rukmani Basu observes:

> In our country, separated couples are far greater in number than divorced ones for the simple reason that divorce is difficult to obtain. . . . Among the lower class in both rural and urban areas desertion by the husband has reached alarming proportions since it is still the easiest way of evading martial obligations (1986: 33).

Thus no law, howsoever stringent, can control divorce or family disorganization in adverse social circumstances. Only the cohesiveness of individuals with the family and society can prevent the breaking down of marital ties.

NOTES

1. Divorce, as recognized by Muslim law in India, can be initiated either by the husband or the wife or can take place by mutual consent. 'Triple divorce' is one of the forms of *talaq* or repudiation by the husband. It is

known as *talaq-e-bidat* (innovative divorce, which means that it was not prevalent during the time of the Prophet). The other two forms of *talaq* are *hasan* and *ahsan*. Among the various differences between *talaq-e-bidat* and *talaq-e-hasan* and *talaq-e-ahsan*, one is to be noted. In the former kind of *talaq*, irrevocable divorce takes place instantly. In the latter two forms of *talaq*, the husband is enjoined to complete the process over a period of about three months. There are provisions to revoke *talaq* within this period (see Fayzee, 1987, for details). Among the four schools of Muslim Law—Hanafi (Sunni), Shafai (Sunni), Ithna Ashari (Shia) and lsmaili (Shia) represented in India, only the Hanafi school recognizes triple divorce to be a legally valid form of divorce.

2. Lucy Carroll explains in detail the provisions of Muslim law whereby a man can be restrained from going polygamous as well as women obtain divorce and maintenance. She writes: (a) 'Muslim law recognizes the validity of stipulations in Muslim marriage contracts; a common stipulation (at least in terms of marriage contracts upon which there has been litigation and the reported decision) is one restraining the husband from taking another wife, sanctioned either by allowing the wife to dissolve her own marriage by pronouncement of *talaq* on behalf of her husband (*talaq-i-tafwid*) should the stipulation be violated, or by allowing her to live apart from her husband and still be maintained by him, or by incorporating both sanctions into the contract, thereby giving the wife the option of choosing which remedy she may prefer in the actual circumstances. The Courts of South Asia have upheld contracts of this nature for more than a century, (b) A woman may also contract for a large *mehr* as prompt dower (rather than, or in addition to, differed dower). The prompt dower is payable 'on demand', and there is at least one reported case where the wife demanded payment of her prompt dower when her husband began to contemplate a second marriage. He refused to pay; she sued and won—and as nobody would wish to marry a man on the verge of bankruptcy, it may be assumed that the second marriage did not materialize' (1983: 208). The Dissolution of Muslim Marriage Act, 1939, allows a woman to seek judicial divorce on the following grounds: (i) that the whereabouts of the husband have not been known for a period of four years, (ii) that the husband has neglected or has failed to provide for her maintenance for a period of two years, . . . (iv) that the husband has failed to perform without reasonable cause his marital obligations for a period of three years, . . . (viii) that the husband treats her with cruelty, that is to say, (a) habitually assaults her or makes her life miserable by cruelty of conduct even if such conduct does not amount to physical ill-treatment, or (f) if he has more wives than one, does not treat her equitably in accordance with injunctions of the Qur'an . . . (section 2). Carroll adds: 'It should be noted further that the fact that a woman has recourse to the Dissolution of Muslim Marriages Act to secure a divorce does not affect her right to receive the *mehr* due to her' (1983: 210).

3. According to the Census of India, 1971, the total number of divorced or separated women in the country was estimated to be 8,70,700 of which 7,45,220 were in rural areas and 1,27,500 in urban areas. In the country as a whole the divorce rate was placed at 1 per cent (Basu, 1985: 33).

REFERENCES

Ahmad, Imtiaz (1976), 'Introduction', in Imtiaz Ahmad (ed.), *Family, Kinship and Marriage among Muslims in India*, Delhi: Manohar.

Aggarwal, Pratap C. (1976), 'Kinship and Marriage among the Meos of Rajasthan', in Imtiaz Ahmad (ed.), *Family, Kinship and Marriage among Muslims in India*, Delhi: Manohar.

Basu, Rukmani (1985), 'Divorce in India: Position in Law', *Mainstream*, vol. 23, no. 27.

Bhatty, Zarina (1976), 'Status of Muslim Women and Social Change', in B.R. Nanda (ed.), *Indian Women: From Purdah to Modernity*, Delhi: Vikas Publishing House.

______ (1980), 'Muslim Women in Uttar Pradesh', in Alfred de Souza (ed.), *Women in Contemporary India and South Asia*, Delhi: Manohar.

Carrol, Lucy (1983), 'The Muslim Family in India: Law, Custom and Empirical Research', *Contributions to Indian Sociology* (new series), vol. 17, no. 2, pp. 205-22.

Esposito, John L. (1982), *Women in Muslim Family Law*, New York.

Fayzee, A.A.A. (1987), *Outlines of Mohammedan Law*, Delhi: Oxford University Press (6th impression).

Goode, S. William (1970), 'Marital Satisfaction and Instability: A Cross-cultural Class Analysis of Divorce', in Paul Glasser and Lois N. Glasser (eds.), *Families in Crisis*, New York: Harper and Row.

Hutton, J.H. (1933), *Report of Census of India, 1931*, part I, vol. I, Delhi: Manager of Publications.

Imam, Zafar (1975), 'Some Aspects of the Social structure of the Muslim community in India', in Zafar Imam (ed.) *Muslims in India*, New Delhi: Orient Longman.

India, Government of (1973), *Position of Divorce in India*, New Delhi: Office of the Registrar General, Ministry of Home Affairs.

_______ (1974), *Toward Equality: Report of the National Committee on the Status of Women in India*, Delhi: Government of India.

Jain, Madhu (1986), 'Divorce Getting Common', *India Today*, 31 December.

Jain, Susheela (1979), *Muslims and Modernisation: A Study of their Changing Role Structure and Norms in an Urban Setting*, Jaipur: Rawat.

Khan, M.E. (1979), *Family Planning among Muslims in India: A Study of the Reproductive Behaviour of Muslims in an Urban Setting*, Delhi: Manohar.

Khatana, R.P. (1976), 'Marriage and Kinship among the Gujjar Bakarwals of Jammu and Kashmir', in Imtiaz Ahmad (ed.), *Family, Kinship and Marriage among Muslims in India*, Delhi: Manohar.

Levinger, George (1970), 'Marital Cohesiveness and Dissolution: An Integrated Review', in Paul Glasser and Lois N. Glasser (eds.), *Families in Crisis*, New York: Harper and Row.

Roy, Shibani (1979), *Status of Muslim Women in North India*, Delhi: B.R. Publishing Corporation.

Vreede-de-Steurs, Cora (1968), *Parda: A Study of Muslim Women's Lives in North India*, Essen: Von Gorkum Co.

Contributors

IMTIAZ AHMAD is former Professor of Sociology at Jawaharlal Nehru University, New Delhi, India.

SABEEHA BANO is an independent researcher based at New Delhi, India.

ANINDITA DASGUPTA is Lecturer in Sociology at Cotton College, Guwahati, India.

SEEMA DURRANY is a practicing lawyer based at Delhi, India.

NISAR AHMAD GANAI is Professor of Law at Jammu University, Jammu, India.

GEETANJALI GANGOLI teaches at St. Xavier's College, Mumbai, India.

SABIHA HUSSAIN is Fellow at the Centre for Women's Development Studies, New Delhi, India.

PATRICIA JEFFERY is Professor of Sociology at University of Edinburgh, UK.

MUNIZA RAFIQUE KHAN is Lecturer at Gandhian Institute of Studies, Varanasi, India.

MALIKA MISTRY is Lecturer at Poona College of Arts, Science and Commerce, Pune, India.

SYED ABDUL HAFIZ MOINUDDIN is Senior Lecturer at Vidyasagar University, Midnapore, India.

JAMEELA NISHAT is a social activist associated with Asmita at Hyderabad, India.

ZAKIYA RAFAT is Reader in Sociology at RBD Post-Graduate Girl's College, Bijnor, India.

MOHAMMAD ARIF RASHEED is a practicing lawyer based at Bijnor in Uttar Pradesh, India.

SHAIKH ABDUL AZEEZ SAHEB is Senior Antropologist, Southern Regional Centre, Mysore, India.

MOHAMMAD TALIB is Professor of Sociology at Jamia Millia Islamia, New Delhi, India.

SYLVIA VATUK is former Professor of Anthropology at University of Illinois at Chicago, USA.

ABDUL WAHEED is Lecturer in Sociology at Aligarh Muslim University, Aligarh, India.

Index